McDaniel (*at far right*) enjoys a laugh at a 1941 gathering in Singapore with Sir Shenton Thomas, governor of the Straits Settlements (*at far left*). Standing at McDaniel's immediate right is Carl Mydans of *Life* magazine. Harold Guard of United Press is closest to Thomas, while the woman is Shelley Mydans, Carl's wife, who wrote for *Life*. *American Geographical Society Library, University of Wisconsin-Milwaukee Libraries*

McDaniel snapped this photograph of Singapore burning just before he left on the small rescue ship *Kung Wo* in February 1942. *AP photo*

McDaniel, wearing a dark sports shirt, listens as Australian general Gordon Bennett briefs correspondents on the Malayan campaign in early 1942. Bennett was a good source for reporters such as McDaniel. *Australian War Memorial photo, public domain*

Binoculars in hand, McDaniel and AP photographer Frank Noel scan the sky from the balcony of Yates's apartment in the Cathay Building in Singapore, shortly after the outbreak of the Pacific war in late 1941. Noel won the Pulitzer Prize in 1943. *AP photo*

# THE
# LAST ONE
# OUT

Yates McDaniel:
World War II's Most
Daring Reporter

## JACK TORRY

SCHIFFER █ MILITARY

4880 Lower Valley Road █ Atglen, PA 19310

Library of Congress Control Number: 2020952569

Cover design by Brenda McCallum
Type set in Mailstamp/Minion

ISBN: 978-0-7643-6268-2

Printed in Serbia

Published by Schiffer Publishing, Ltd.
4880 Lower Valley Road
Atglen, PA 19310
Phone: (610) 593-1777; Fax: (610) 593-2002
E-mail: Info@schifferbooks.com
Web: www.schifferbooks.com

For our complete selection of fine books on this and related subjects, please visit our website at www.schifferbooks.com. You may also write for a free catalog.

Schiffer Publishing's titles are available at special discounts for bulk purchases for sales promotions or premiums. Special editions, including personalized covers, corporate imprints, and excerpts, can be created in large quantities for special needs. For more information, contact the publisher.

We are always looking for people to write books on new and related subjects. If you have an idea for a book, please contact us at proposals@schifferbooks.com.

For Saundra

# CONTENTS

# PREFACE

When C. Yates McDaniel died in Florida in 1983, few outside his family paid much attention. At age seventy-six, he seemed like just another white-haired retiree whose final years passed with little notice amid so many other senior citizens in Florida. The only hint of his fame came in a brief obituary buried on the inside pages of the *New York Times.*

The obit suggested danger and bravery and a past far more exciting than almost anyone knew. Even those who had worked at desks alongside him in the 1960s at the Associated Press were startled to learn what McDaniel had seen, what he had survived, what he had done when he was a young man and the world was at war.

That anonymity, that reluctance to write his memoirs or tell spellbinding stories, is why he was forgotten by 1983, why his name is rarely mentioned in the pantheon of war correspondents, giants such as Edward R. Murrow and William L. Shirer of CBS, and Ernie Pyle of Scripps Howard.

This story is about the life of that remarkable reporter who followed the Pacific theater from its beginnings in the early 1930s in China to the savage struggle in 1945 to regain Manila. Yates McDaniel covered the Japanese attack on Shanghai in 1932, the fall of Tientsin and Nanking in 1937, and the collapse of Singapore in 1942. He landed with the 1st Marine Division on the shores of New Britain in 1943 and was among a handful of correspondents in the landing craft with Gen. Douglas MacArthur when the Allies landed in Luzon in 1945. He saw so much combat that one newspaper wrote that "probably no other man has been more closely and constantly in touch with our land operations against Japan" than McDaniel. The late Chinese American journalist Iris Chang considered him "perhaps the most daring" of the Western reporters who covered the pitiless Japanese massacre in Nanking.

Colleagues described him as stoic, scholarly, and a total pro. "Before anything else, Yates McDaniel was a journalist," Australian press officer Athole Stewart wrote in 1943 after he and McDaniel escaped from Singapore. "It was his hobby and his profession. His stories have always been a jump ahead of his colleagues. His messages are simple statements of facts, and his deductions are uncannily accurate."

He was an old-fashioned reporter who strove for accuracy. "Today we've got to tell the truth, the whole truth," he would say. He understood the need for military censorship during wartime, but in his dispassionate style he fought the unreasonable restrictions imposed by British and American censors, once appealing directly to Gen. MacArthur about US Army limits on covering the burning of Manila in 1945.

He had one soft spot: he hated covering news without his wife, Natalie, close by. "I do love you so much, you may not realize how deeply I love you, and how utterly lost I am without you," he wrote her. They formed what today would be considered a modern marriage of equal partners. They escaped from the Japanese in Tientsin in the summer of 1937, enduring a miserable eighteen-hour drive in an ambulance to their home in Nanking, the ride's monotony broken by Japanese bombs. She took messages, typed stories, helped him report, and—because she was fluent in Japanese—monitored Japanese-language radio news and interrogated Japanese prisoners. When Hankow, now part of Wuhan, fell to the Japanese in 1938, she stayed with Yates until the end, before they joined a handful of other Western reporters on a flight to the relative safety of Japanese-occupied Shanghai.

McDaniel covered Asia at a time when people largely learned about the world through newspapers. Although radio and newsreels were cutting into the newspaper and magazine monopolies, the *Chicago Daily News*, *New York Daily News*, *Chicago Times*, *Life*, *Time*, *Saturday Evening Post*, and *Collier's* sent reporters abroad. F. Tillman Durdin, Martha Gellhorn, Arch Steele, Peggy Durdin, Hallett Abend, and Freda Utley were among those covering the fierce fighting in China in the 1930s. The Associated Press and United Press were intense competitors in the battle to get a story first. "New York was most pleased that we beat United Press by four minutes" on a bulletin announcing an American landing in New Britain in 1943, Yates wrote Natalie.

The era stood in sharp contrast to today, when only a few newspapers maintain foreign bureaus. We are a poorer nation because of that.

This book covers an ugly chapter in Japanese history. Today's Japan is a staunch US ally and a vibrant democracy and has nothing in common with the Japan of the 1930s. McDaniel and his colleagues covered in riveting detail the Japanese massacre in Nanking. By actually being in Nanking, McDaniel, Steele of the *Chicago Daily News*, Durdin of the *New York Times*, and Leslie Smith of Reuters offered readers around the world a vivid description of the savagery of Japan's invasion of China.

When the war ended, McDaniel's life as a foreign correspondent ended as well. For the next quarter of a century, he labored at desks in Detroit and Washington, producing relatively few of the impact stories he wrote from China, Singapore, and the Philippines.

I have tried to tell this story from McDaniel's vantage point. A good example is the sinking of the battleship *Prince of Wales* and battle cruiser *Repulse* on December 10, 1941. McDaniel, to his regret, turned down a chance to sail from Singapore with the *Repulse*, a move that prevented him from writing a first-person account of the battle cruiser's destruction. Instead, I focused on McDaniel reaching Singapore's naval base as survivors from the two great ships arrived in a driving rainstorm. The dramatic story of the sinking of the two ships has been told in detail by Colin Smith, Cecil Brown, O'Dowd Gallagher, Martin Middlebrook, and John Toland. I could not improve on what they have written.

In an effort for clarity, I decided to use the names of places in Asia as they would have appeared in newspapers in the 1930s and 1940s. To do otherwise would create endless confusion. Thus, I used Nanking instead of Nanjing, as it is known today; Tientsin as opposed to Tianjin, Batavia instead of Jakarta, Peking rather than Beijing, and French Indochina instead of Vietnam.

# FOREWORD

Looking out a window of Singapore's tallest building, Yates McDaniel of the Associated Press had a panoramic view of the city and what would be the final moments of a century of British rule. McDaniel watched swarms of Japanese planes dive on the city, challenged only by a handful of obsolete British biplanes left over from another era. The British were on the verge of surrendering their prized colonial possession to Japanese troops, who had marched and bicycled their way down the Malay Peninsula and crossed the Straits of Johore into Singapore itself.

All the other Western correspondents were gone. Just the day before, Ian Morrison of the *Times* of London had boarded a Dutch cargo ship bound for Java. Correspondents for Reuters, United Press, and International News Service had departed, while Tillman Durdin of the *New York Times* left a few days earlier for Batavia. Fortunately for the *Times*, the newspaper had access to all the AP stories and could publish McDaniel's latest dispatches from Singapore.

McDaniel too was getting ready to leave, but not quite yet. The night before, he burned a pile of his papers, notes, and a thousand negatives of photographs he had taken years earlier as a correspondent in China, keeping only his passport and British War Office credentials. He had one more story to file before he boarded a rickety Yangtze River steamer whose captain hoped to weave its way past the Japanese navy to Java.

It was 10:30 in the morning of February 11, 1942. McDaniel pecked away at the portable typewriter in his room, crafting a dispatch that he was not sure would ever make it out of the besieged city. Capt. O. K. Fearon, a British censor, sat next to him, eating a breakfast of biscuits and sipping brandy while Capt. Henry Steel, a British press officer, was exhorting McDaniel to finish his story before the Japanese seized the city.

Outwardly, the slender thirty-five-year-old reporter, whose brown hair already was turning gray, appeared "calm and unemotional," a perfect trait for a wire-service reporter under constant pressure. A colleague once joked that "Mac was the sort of guy who could sit in a building during an earthquake and write a story." But now as bomb explosions rattled his typewriter, McDaniel noticed that his hands were sopping from nervous perspiration.

Besides grace under pressure, his trademark was to be the last reporter to leave the scene of a story. He had done that in Nanking in 1937 as Japanese troops stormed through the city and murdered tens of thousands of Chinese. Whatever the risk,

McDaniel always was willing to take it. He even joked about his luck, once telling his wife, Natalie, in a letter that "I had one of my narrow" escapes when Japanese shells barely missed his transport ship off the Philippines. He regretted the few times in his life when he played it safe. In December 1941, he turned down a chance to sail on the British battle cruiser *Repulse* as it searched for a Japanese convoy in the South China Sea. When Japanese planes sank the *Repulse*, Cecil Brown of CBS and O'Dowd Gallagher of the *London Daily Express* survived to write gripping first-person stories, prompting McDaniel to say that Brown "came back a hero."

On this morning, McDaniel began to type: "The sky over Singapore is black with the smoke of a dozen huge fires . . . as I write my last message from this once beautiful, prosperous and peaceful city."

Just nine weeks earlier, McDaniel could not have imagined such a scene. Nobody could. Singapore was impregnable, or so it was claimed. British officials assured McDaniel that their defenses in the Malay Peninsula and Singapore were so strong the Japanese would need "nearly 500,000 men and more than 1,000 planes all in action at once to give Tokyo any hope of gaining an invasion foothold." Japanese transports carrying troops to Malaya "would be subjected to constant submarine and air attack once [they] entered the China Sea." In October 1941, Durdin reported that "authorities here are confident that a Japanese attack could be repulsed." The arrival that December of the battleship *Prince of Wales* and battle cruiser *Repulse* "left everyone moved and overexcited," noted Lady Diana Duff Cooper, whose husband was Prime Minister Winston Churchill's resident minister in Singapore.

Yet, everyone had been so wrong. After the Japanese bombed Pearl Harbor on December 7, 1941, Japanese troops quickly seized Hong Kong and large swaths of the Philippines and captured the US garrisons at Guam and Wake Island. It was much the same in Singapore. The Japanese seized command of the sea three days after the attack on Pearl Harbor, when torpedo bombers sank the *Prince of Wales* and *Repulse*. Japan's modern aircraft ruled the sky by brushing away the antiquated British planes. Thirty thousand Japanese troops made their way down the peninsula, undeterred by its thick jungles, deep ravines, swamps, and swollen rivers. By the middle of January, it was clear that the 100,000 British, Australian, and Indian soldiers in Singapore could not last long. Alarmed at the swift Japanese advance, Yates persuaded Natalie to sail to Java. Then he packed the last of his personal belongings in a trunk and shipped them to the United States.

Now on this Wednesday morning in February, the black and gray smoke from Japanese bombs and oil storage tanks torched by the British swirled about the city and obscured the sun. Sailors aboard a British cruiser making its way to Java could see the columns of smoke 50 miles away. It was so dark from the smoke that McDaniel turned on the lights in his room so he could see well enough to type. He saw anti-aircraft guns "peppering smoke into the sky," but they were barely a threat to "relay after relay of Japanese planes circling and then going into murderous dives upon our soldiers." A single Japanese observation balloon hovered over the western side of the island to direct artillery fire.

An explosion rocked the building. McDaniel typed a wry joke: "Please overlook the break in continuity, but a packet of bombs just landed so close I had to duck behind a wall, which I hoped—and did—screen the blast."

Except for McDaniel, everyone was getting desperate to leave. A Chinese official showed McDaniel three well-known Chinese paintings he planned to take to the rescue ship. The director of the Malaya Broadcasting Corporation, who also was in the room, telephoned for permission to destroy the broadcasting equipment. Permission was denied, yet another example of what McDaniel thought was the mindless optimism of Singapore's officials. They switched on the radio, and as an MBC announcer urged the people of the city to "stand firm," the broadcast suddenly "went dead."

Capt. Steel said time was up. Calling himself the "first-to-arrive and last-to-leave" foreign correspondent, McDaniel typed a grim prediction: he and his colleagues had "less than a fifty percent chance of getting clear of this beleaguered fortress . . . So, goodbye from Singapore."

Then he added these parting words: "Don't expect to hear from me for many days, but please inform Mrs. McDaniel, Hotel Praenger [*sic*], Bandoeng, Java, that I have left this land of the living and the dying."

# SOOCHOW

ates McDaniel liked to tell the story of seeing America for the first time when he was nearly three years old. As the new German ocean liner *George Washington* glided into New York harbor on June 20, 1909, Yates's parents held him up to the rail for a view of the Statue of Liberty. Boats scattered throughout the harbor blasted their sirens. From the top of the new forty-one-story Singer Building at Liberty and Broadway, the League of Peace saluted the great ship by raising its flag. Tugs then moved the steamer to the North German Lloyd docks in Hoboken, New Jersey.[1]

Yates would regale friends with the story. Yet, except for recalling his first look at the Statue of Liberty, Yates was too young to remember what he thought of the country he knew about only from listening to his parents, Charles and Nannie McDaniel, who were Americans and ran a Baptist missionary in China.

Yates's first glimpse of America came when his parents took a four-month break from their school in Soochow. On the final lap of their long trip from Shanghai, they boarded the *George Washington* in Southampton, England, for her maiden voyage to New York City. At 25,000 tons, she was the world's third-largest passenger liner, and Yates's father marveled that she was "the finest vessel" he had ever been on.[2]

Although Yates was an American, throughout his life he was a more comfortable fit in Asia. He was schooled in Soochow and Shanghai. He spoke fluent Chinese. He was so comfortable speaking Chinese, years later after he retired in Florida, that he and his sister Helen eschewed English and instead conversed in the Wu dialect common in Shanghai. After graduating from the American school in Shanghai, he went to America to study at Richmond College in Virginia. He made his mark as an undergraduate with an essay about a young Chinese man studying to take the imperial examinations in Peking. As a graduate student at the University of North Carolina, he wrote a play about Eurasians in China. As soon as he earned a master's degree in arts in 1929, Yates—alone among his brothers and sisters—returned to China, where he taught, wrote for newspapers, and "roamed" throughout the country. His best and most descriptive stories were written in Asia—not the United States.

Even his name had a Chinese origin. His father named him Charles Yates after two Westerners equally at home in China—Matthew Tyson Yates and Gen. Charles Gordon. Matthew Tyson Yates, no relation to Charles McDaniel, was a scholarly American missionary in China, while Charles Gordon was a glory-seeking British soldier and adventurer who organized a small army in Shanghai in the 1860s.

Matthew Yates had been among the earliest Southern Baptist missionaries in China, arriving in Shanghai in 1847 and spending much of the next three decades trying to convert the Chinese to Christianity. He undertook the exhausting task of translating the New Testament into a Chinese dialect widely used in Shanghai. When he died in 1888, he was buried in Shanghai, and a boys academy in nearby Soochow was named after him. Years later, Yates McDaniel's father would be tapped to run that very same Yates Academy.

Gen. Gordon was a different sort altogether. As much as Matthew Yates loved books and learning, Gordon thrived on action and risk. Although Gordon is best remembered for his heroic death at Khartoum in 1885, he served in China as a captain in the British army during the Second Opium War between Britain and the Qing dynasty. He trained a force of 3,500 men in Shanghai in 1862 and helped suppress a rebellion in China. He ritually accepted risks in battle that other men would have shunned. When he returned to Great Britain in 1865 as a national hero, he was publicly proclaimed "Chinese" Gordon.

It is almost certain that Matthew Yates and Gen. Gordon knew each other. Both were in Shanghai during the Taiping rebellion, and each would have been difficult to miss. Matthew Yates was a giant of a man at 6 feet 2 and 240 pounds, while the flamboyant Gordon would have stood out with his rugged good looks and handsome mustache. Yates's father admired Gordon because he was also a fervent Christian, an advocate for the poor, and an ardent opponent of slavery. So, Charles McDaniel named his second son Charles Yates after both men. And Yates grew up with a blend of Gordon's and Matthew Yates's qualities.

Years later, Yates McDaniel acknowledged that being named after Gen. Gordon, a towering figure of the British Empire, "had a great effect on me." It may explain why, unlike many of his colleagues who held a dim view of the British Empire, Yates saw Great Britain as a bulwark of stability and progress in Asia.[3]

Like Gen. Gordon, Yates relished taking risks. At age seventeen, Yates leaped into a lake to rescue a drowning young boy and his nurse.[4] "It seemed inevitable that I would be involved in war," he once said.[5] He jeopardized his life on countless occasions, such as the time he and Arch Steele of the *Chicago Daily News* trailed a patrol of Chinese soldiers in Nanking. Japanese planes pummeled the patrol with bombs, forcing McDaniel and Steele to jump into a dugout for cover. A bomb exploded less than 200 yards away. McDaniel lifted his head. The street was filled with injured and dead Chinese soldiers.

But Yates also had a love of scholarship like his missionary namesake Matthew Yates. "Since my early childhood I have done nothing but study the classics," Yates wrote in a college essay in 1925. Although the essay was a work of fiction, it was in many ways autobiographical. The leading character in the essay often expressed Yates's emotions. "Musty old books have been my toys and near-sighted scholars my companions," he wrote. As a young man, Yates studied poetry from the Han dynasty dating back to 220 CE and American works from the nineteenth century. Washington Irving—author of *Rip Van Winkle* and *The Legend of Sleepy*

*Hollow*—became a particular favorite. One of his Chinese boyhood friends called him a "scholar of great attainment and virtue."[6]

Yates could not have been any more different from his father. The Reverend Charles Gilbert McDaniel was strict and so single-minded about running the Yates Academy that years later, when asked what clubs or patriotic organizations he and his wife joined, he tersely replied, "We have never joined any clubs." Charles did not dance, drink alcohol, or smoke. Every day he required his children to read from the Bible. During evening meals, he preached to them as opposed to engaging in freewheeling conversation. He was not outwardly lovable and was regarded as "one of those Baptist ministers way out in his own world."[7]

Born in a rural area in central Virginia, Charles showed interest in religion as a teenager, in part because his mother was a devout Christian who regularly attended church and insisted the family say grace before all meals. In the spring of 1900, Charles graduated from the Rochester Theological Seminary in western New York State and was named pastor of a Baptist church in Newport News, Virginia. There he met his future wife, Nannie Bartlett. They were ideally suited for each other. Born in Warwick County in southeastern Virginia, Nannie attended a small women's college founded by a Baptist minister.[8]

At the end of 1901, Charles earned an appointment to head the Yates Academy in Soochow. Charles and Nannie married on April 9, 1902, and that same day sailed for China. American missionaries like Charles and Nannie had long flocked to China. While the US government joined European powers in meddling in China, American missionaries saw themselves with exalted motives. They believed "they had a special role" and considered themselves "somehow different from the imperialist powers of the Old World." Pearl S. Buck, whose 1931 novel, *The Good Earth*, won the Pulitzer Prize and became an epic MGM film, was the daughter of American Presbyterian missionaries, as was Henry Luce, the founder of *Time* magazine.[9]

Charles admired the Chinese, although he was convinced they needed a nudge in the right religious direction. They "have ability," and when "vitalized by the Holy Spirit, they can do some things more efficiently than we missionaries."[10] But scholars later pointed out "there was a fundamental misconception at the heart of much of the American thinking about China . . . a widely held belief that the Chinese aspired to be like Americans, and that it was the job of the Americans to train them to achieve that goal." Much as Americans learned in the late twentieth century, the Chinese had their own way of doing things.[11]

Charles's rigid commitment to religion, which one family member called "overkill," did not resonate with the children. Each of Charles's children rebelled in his or her own way. Given their stark differences in temperament, a clash between Yates and his father was inevitable. Yates puffed on Camel cigarettes, sipped German Rhine white wine, enjoyed the theater, and loved playing tennis and running track.

Yates was religious, but not in his father's demonstrable way. Years later, while covering the Allied campaign in the Philippines, he wrote his wife, Natalie, that

"God is watching over us both. I thank Him for that every night, for he has been good to me, good in protecting me, and so much better in giving me you."[12]

Yates was one of six children—three boys and three girls. The eldest son was Paul, who Charles hoped would become a physician, followed by Yates and Gordon. The three sisters were Virginia Moring—named after Matthew Yates's wife, Eliza Emmeline Moring—Nancy Russell, and Helen Grace.

Yates was the most active of the children and seemed to grow up faster. Born on August 28, 1906, by the age of one Yates was standing "alone for a minute," could say a few words, and seemed "interested" in just about everything. His mother described him as "by far the most active child" in the family. By his second birthday, he was speaking words in English and Chinese and could recite two Bible verses. During the evening, Nannie would read to Yates, with Longfellow's *The Song of Hiawatha* being one of his favorites.[13]

The family lived in a two-story home. The house did not have electricity until the early 1920s, so kerosene lanterns provided light at night. They cooked on wood-burning stoves, which also heated the home. A Chinese houseboy kept the house immaculate. Because they lacked a refrigerator, a Chinese cook went to the market every day to buy vegetables and chickens. A Chinese tailor fashioned clothes for the kids, but they also ordered outfits from a Montgomery Ward catalog. Schoolwork consumed much of their time, but the kids loved it when acrobats, theater performers, and musicians regularly stopped by the academy.[14]

Soochow was known for producing scholars, and young Yates fit right in. Soochow is only 60 miles from Shanghai and was lined with so many canals that it was dubbed the "Venice of the Far East." The city's skyline was dominated by eight towering pagodas. When newspaper editor Carl Crow climbed to the top of a 250-foot-tall pagoda, he marveled at the breathtaking scenery of the "small hills and lakes, the latter connected with each other by innumerable small canals."[15]

But not all was idyllic in this beautiful land. Yates grew up at a time when malaria, dysentery, pneumonia, and measles swept through the cities and villages of China. Dysentery, in particular, posed the worst threat. In the muggy August heat of 1912, four-year-old Gordon contracted dysentery. Within four days, he was dead. Paul and Nancy caught the same disease, forcing Charles and Nannie to "shut in our grief" for Gordon and "nurse our sick." Nannie spent agonizing days caring for Paul and Nancy until they recovered. Gordon's death devastated both parents, although they maintained a fatalistic front. Charles wrote, "Our hearts are full of grief over the death of our dear little boy. God in his goodness gave him to us and for our good, we believe, took him from us unto himself."[16]

In a separate letter, Nannie wrote, "We are so thankful that" Paul and Nancy "have been spared. Our children have always been so healthy; that is the first break in our family circle and of course it is hard. We know that trouble enters every home at some time, and we could not always expect to be spared. We feel the Lord definitely directs all lives, and some of the choices he takes to himself early in life. The cooler weather is doing much to stamp out cholera and the other prevailing intestinal trouble."[17]

Yates did not come down with dysentery, a sign of his robust health. But the death of a brother or sister often spurs surviving siblings to work harder to make up for the loss to their parents. Yates had always been earnest and serious, but after Gordon's death, Yates intensified his studies, particularly as a teenager, when he attended the American School in Shanghai. The school was in the French Concession of Shanghai, an area founded by the French and whose residents included Russians, Chinese, and Americans. Yates stayed in a boardinghouse with the other students, most of whom were the children of missionaries, Western diplomats, or business executives. Every night he was at study hall. He also set aside time to become an accomplished tennis player, excellent golfer, and outstanding bowler, and to compete in the shot put and the 75-yard dash. He thrived so much on being active that he often had trouble sleeping. Years later, while covering the Allied attack in the Philippines, he complained to Natalie, "I don't sleep well, but that is nothing new."[18]

In the summer of 1920, Yates and his family planned to visit Yates's older brother Paul, who was in his second year of school at Richmond College, a Baptist school. They sailed from Shanghai on the 16,000-ton Canadian passenger ship *Empress of Asia*, a three-funneled, coal-fired vessel that served as a British auxiliary cruiser during World War I and helped search the Indian Ocean for the daring German raider *Emden*. Now, with Yates and his family aboard, the *Empress of Asia* cruised across the Yellow Sea to Yokohama on Japan's east coast. The liner crossed the Pacific Ocean at a comfortable 19 knots before docking in Vancouver on August 16. The family boarded a train for the trip across country to Richmond, where they lived for the next year.

When Yates and the family returned to China in August 1921, Paul and Virginia remained in the United States, with Virginia enrolling at Intermont College, the same school Nannie graduated from years earlier, when it was known as Southwest Virginia Institute. The family traveled by train to the West Coast, where they received an enthusiastic reception by the China Club of Seattle. As they departed the train station, newspaper cameramen snapped photos, which delighted Charles.

The next morning, Charles, Nannie, Yates, Nancy, and Helen joined a handful of missionaries and boarded the 22,000-ton steamer *Hawkeye State* for the return to Shanghai. Except for two small storms, which caused sea sickness among some of the missionaries, the Pacific Ocean was "fairly smooth." Passengers loved playing deck sports such as shuffleboard. On the night before the *Hawkeye State* docked in Yokohama, the ship's captain invited the McDaniels and the other missionaries to dinner. The dining room was "beautifully decorated" and they enjoyed a sumptuous meal, with Charles writing that "everybody was in fine spirits," although he couldn't help but point out "without any flowing of wine."[19]

The *Hawkeye State* arrived in Shanghai on September 14 as a driving rainstorm drenched everyone. The Chinese greeted the ship's docking with "one of the greatest receptions that we have ever received in our lives," Charles wrote, adding the firecrackers were so noisy he thought for a moment that World War I had broken out again.[20]

Two years later, in 1923, when Yates graduated from the American School, it was his turn to attend Richmond College. The day before Yates sailed to America aboard the British liner *Empress of Russia*, he won a men's tennis tournament in the elite retreat of Mokanshan, a three-hour train ride from Shanghai.[21]

College was the first extended time he spent free from his father's grip. He won the college's men's singles tennis championship in 1924, which earned him a silver cup.[22] He ran varsity track and in 1925 was named captain of the soccer team. He joined the dramatic club, where he played the role of Lorenzo in the school's production of the *Merchant of Venice*.[23]

He also sang in the glee club and joined Kappa Sigma fraternity, where friends dubbed him "Mac." One classmate joked Yates was "one of those versatile geniuses who never lets his studies interfere with his education."[24] An avid reader, Yates discovered he enjoyed writing. Years later, Yates joked that while "in school he stubbornly defied his destiny by avoiding all contact with academic journalism." That was only partly true, since he served as an assistant editor for the *Messenger*, the college's literary magazine, and helped pick stories and essays for the publication.[25]

In June 1925, the *Messenger* published an eight-page essay by Yates, which simultaneously showed his fascination with China and his gift for descriptive writing. It was the story of a young man named Wu leaving his father's house to take the imperial examinations in Peking. Wu traveled by houseboat to Peking to the house owned by Ming, a friend of his father's. Yates then offered an example of what would become his greatest strength as a reporter—his ability to paint a vivid portrait of events happening thousands of miles from the reader, while making readers feel as if they were right there.

In the essay, Wu was "graciously" received by Ming, who welcomed him with a "bountiful" feast before escorting him to his apartment. Wu "pored over" his studies, but the more the young man studied, the more exhausted and discouraged he became. Ming suggested a rest in "my summer home in the hills outside of the city. There you will be unbothered and at your leisure, and to be entirely at leisure for one day is to be for one day an immortal." Wu did as he was told and the next day wandered about the home's gardens. Yates wrote:

Like all such gardens, this one was surrounded on all sides by high walls. I had by this time reached the lower end of the park and was on the point of turning around to retrace my steps when I caught sight of a bit of color at a small oval window high up in the wall in front of me. I soon realized that the color was that of a silk sleeve. . . . The sleeve kept moving slowly back and forth, so I concluded the owner of the sleeve was working at an embroidery frame. . . . A face appeared at the window and what a face! The beautiful pattern of the sleeve was forgotten. . . . I had never beheld such a vision of beauty.

Wu wanted to say something to the young woman, "but each time my reason came to mind to remind me that a true gentlewoman could not, would not speak to a strange man. Then the face disappeared from my view and the window was shut."

The next day, Wu readily answered all the questions on the exam until the very last one, which required him to write an original poem on a topic called *Silver Bells*. Wu had no idea what *Silver Bells* even meant. But seizing his pen, he began writing of "my love" for the woman in the window "much in the same manner that a certain poet of the Han dynasty had written of a lady he had seen but once and loved." Wu was certain he would fail the exam, but the delighted chief examiner told him:

> It almost seemed to me that the author must have seen or known my daughter, who bears the name of Silver Bells. But that would be impossible, as my daughter has, for the last month, been staying with her aunt at their summer home in the hills outside the city.

The chief examiner decided "to give the young poet a chance to compare his written description with the actual person of his dream. Then, perhaps, he will change his poem of tragic sadness to one of joy and gladness."[26]

Yates excelled at Richmond but pushed himself to exhaustion. The year he graduated from Richmond in 1927, Yates was hospitalized for what one of his sisters described as a "nervous breakdown." She provided no other details on what Yates suffered from, although it is possible that he simply was worn out from his typical grueling pace. One Australian press officer in Singapore said he "scarcely ever saw [McDaniel] relax." Years later, family and friends could not help but notice that Yates's hands shook on a regular basis, although it may have been the result of malaria at a young age.[27]

As Yates studied in the United States, China erupted into violent conflict between the Communists and the Nationalists, the latter headed by Chiang Kai-shek. It culminated in the brutal repression of the Communists in Shanghai on April 12, 1927, when Chiang's troops killed as many as 5,000 people. "Soochow is still quiet, in spite of the rumor in Shanghai that a battle is raging here," Yates's father, Charles, wrote on March 16. As the violence continued, Helen and Nancy remained at their boarding school in Shanghai, although authorities had to protect the school. "Despite the sound of heavy gun fights and cannons, we continued our lessons," Nancy later said. She and her sister went months without talking to Charles or Nannie. The US consulate in Shanghai ordered Charles, Nannie, and all other American missionaries to leave Soochow for Shanghai. Charles arranged to send Nannie to the United States but decided if he left China, "it would be for other causes than the present upheaval in this land." Charles had no use for the Communists, nor did he sympathize with what he called the right-wing elements of the Nationalists, although he was convinced "that out of all this chaos a new China is going to emerge."[28]

By the summer, Soochow was in the hands of the Communists, and Shanghai once again plunged into turmoil. Charles booked passage for Helen and Nancy on a passenger ship sailing from Shanghai to Seattle. During the seventeen-day voyage, Helen was the "belle of the ship" as she was accompanied by two young men who loved dancing with her. When the sisters arrived in Seattle, they were without money or train tickets to Virginia because an absentminded Charles forgot to give them cash. Nancy sat on a trunk at customs and cried. But the two men smitten with Helen found a place for them to stay. They took in the sights of Seattle and waited for Nannie to wire money for train tickets to Richmond. A year later, Charles arrived from Shanghai and preached in a church in Richmond to earn enough money for Yates to attend graduate school.

After graduating from Richmond College, Yates moved to Florida in 1928, where "destiny caught up with him."[29] He joined the *Sarasota Morning Herald*, splitting time as a general assignment reporter and a sportswriter. By the fall of 1928, he enrolled as a graduate student at the University of North Carolina and, always yearning to remain busy, joined the staff of the nearby *Durham Herald* to cover courts and police. He also wrote a play about the "tragedy of the Eurasian problem in China," one of five plays read aloud at the campus theater in December 1928.[30]

At age twenty-two, Yates stood just a shade under 6 feet and weighed 137 pounds. He had brown eyes, a high forehead, and a full crop of dark-brown hair. He spoke in a soft but clear voice with a slight Virginia accent. His friends described him as serious, while others thought of him as "calm, unemotional."[31] He "always listened rather than spoke out himself." Like the character Wu in his essay, Yates had the word "gentleman stamped all over him and he couldn't hide it" even if he tried.[32]

At North Carolina, Yates studied for a master's degree in English. He soaked up the writings of Washington Irving, burrowing through scores of books about the writer. Yates's years in America moved him closer to a break with his father, and that deepening separation seeped into Yates's graduate thesis on Irving. Irving was rebellious and wanted to strike out on his own, yearning to travel abroad, spend time at the theater, and write.

Yates plunged into research on Irving's life with the maniacal intensity that would become a trademark of his later reporting style. Disappointed that the biographies of Irving by Charles Dudley Warner in 1881 and Henry W. Boynton in 1901 did not offer any real insight into Irving's interest in theater and drama, Yates delved into that void with a vengeance and found what he was looking for by rummaging through Irving's notebooks. He discovered letters that Irving wrote to actor and playwright John Howard Payne—published in 1910 by *Scribner's Magazine*—and letters between Irving and his close friend Henry Brevoort Jr., an adventurer who took part in Lewis and Clark's expedition to the Northwest.

There were remarkable parallels between Yates's and Irving's upbringings. McDaniel grew up with a strict Baptist preacher, while Irving had been "reared in the household of a strict Scotch Presbyterian," which meant, according to Yates, the "pleasure of the theatre was in his youth a forbidden sweet." Irving said his father was "somehow over-strict in his discipline," and "as a child I was led to think that somehow or other, everything that was pleasant was wicked."

Yates wrote that when Irving turned thirteen, he first defied his father as he "slipped away from the home" in New York City and "violated his father's interdict against the theatre" to watch the five-act comedy *Speculation*. Irving was soon addicted to the stage, and Yates approved of his rebellion against his father, writing that he "visited the playhouse as often as he was able to escape the vigilant eye of his unbending father. After the evening meal, young Irving often slipped of out his window into the back and went from thence to the theatre in Johns Street where he remained until near the time for the evening worship. Then, leaving the theatre, he would enter his home in the same manner he had left it and be back in his room when called for the family prayers. The devotions over, Washington Irving would return to his room, again slip out of the window and be back in his seat at the theatre in time for the afterpiece."[33]

Yates also was enthralled with Irving's love of travel. Most of the first fifty pages of Yates's thesis describe in detail Irving's restless travel between Europe and United States. In 1804, Irving sailed to France, where he stayed for six weeks. Then he was off to Italy, then back to Paris and across the English Channel to London, devoting his time to the theater. Irving seemed more at home at the theaters in Madrid, London, Paris, and Dresden than in his native America. When Irving returned to the United States in 1832 after a twenty-eight-year absence, Yates wrote that "the country was almost new to him."[34]

Yates's professor enthusiastically approved the thesis in August 1929. Yates had demonstrated a scholar's determination to sift through volumes of information, while displaying a descriptive writing style teeming with remarkable details. As a reporter, he was at his best when he adopted the same approach, vividly describing the Japanese massacre of Nanking in 1937, his escape from Singapore in 1942, and the destruction of Manila in 1945.

Like his brothers and sisters, he could have stayed in the United States. But like Irving, he was a stranger to America. In August, Yates joined Charles and Nannie to sail from Vancouver to Shanghai. Yates wanted to live in China.[35]

# SHANGHAI

ates's return to China delighted his father. "How fine it is to have Yates with us," Charles wrote a friend. For Charles and Nannie, the timing was perfect since they were finalizing holiday plans. They invited the teachers and their families for a Thanksgiving dinner, and while they could not get a turkey, they bought a "fat goose" and "a nice roast of beef." Charles enjoyed having Yates at home, but with a twinge of sorrow he and Nannie had to content themselves with only occasional "good news from the rest of the children in America from time to time."[1]

For his first year in China, McDaniel lived at home and taught English at the Yates Academy. But like Gen. Charles Gordon and Washington Irving, McDaniel was too restless to be confined to a classroom. So he "roamed the country" for a year. Everywhere he traveled, McDaniel struck up easy conservations with just about everybody. He spoke the Wu dialect, which was common in Shanghai. He also spoke Mandarin "reasonably" well and had "a working knowledge of Cantonese."[2]

The China that McDaniel roamed was one of astounding contrasts—pockets of prosperity and unspeakable poverty. Nearly 80 percent of China's 400 million people labored in agriculture and produced more than 60 percent of the nation's gross domestic product. Farmers in Chinese villages lived despairing lives, with a "year of sickness or poor weather plunging them over the edge of subsistence." They contended with drought or, even worse, catastrophic flooding such as the Yangtze floods of 1931, when a staggering two million people died.[3] China's death rate was "the highest in the world" and "two and one-half times" the rate in the United States.[4] But the China that McDaniel saw firsthand was gradually modernizing. From 1931 through 1936, industrial output expanded at a healthy 6.7 percent a year, while between 1928 and 1937, electrical output doubled, production of cotton soared, and bank deposits increased by 16 percent.[5] Thousands of miles of roads and railroad tracks were constructed.[6] The Nationalists held a tenuous grasp on the country and fought brutal civil wars with the Communists and warlords that killed tens of thousands of people. But Chiang Kai-shek, the Nationalists' strong man, always emerged as the winner of these battles.

By the late summer of 1930, McDaniel settled in Shanghai with an eye on becoming a reporter. With newspaper jobs plentiful, McDaniel worked as a police reporter while covering politics and finance for the *Shanghai Times*, one of the city's English-language dailies. He got a major break in 1931, when he landed a reporting job at the *Shanghai Evening Post* and *Mercury*.

The *Evening Post* was an American-style broadsheet and was among four English-language dailies competing for the roughly 10,000 American expatriates in Shanghai. Rarely has one newspaper attracted such a wealth of young reporting talent—ambitious young Americans who saw the *Evening Post* as a rare opportunity to make names for themselves. The newspaper had been founded in 1928 by Cornelius V. Starr, who made a fortune in life insurance in China. By 1930, Starr had merged the paper with the British-owned *Shanghai Mercury*, and he hired the finest reporters and editors. There was Carl Crow, a reporter and author who later turned advertising man. Crow, like many American reporters who gravitated toward China in the first third of the twentieth century, was part of a group dubbed the "Missouri Mafia," all alums of the University of Missouri journalism school. Crow moved to Shanghai in 1911 to work as an associate editor for the English-language *China Press*, which offered a one-year subscription for only $28. He reported on diplomatic affairs and grew close to Sun Yat-sen, the first president of the Chinese Republic, whom Crow saw as the promising leader of a democratic and prosperous China.[7]

Others followed, including Ted Thackrey as managing editor of the *Evening Post*. Years later, Thackrey edited the *New York Post* and married the paper's publisher, Dorothy Schiff. He was succeeded in 1932 as editor by Randall Gould, who had made a name for himself as a reporter at United Press in Peking. Many of the reporters were like McDaniel—restless, eager to work long hours, and addicted to risks. Tillman Durdin, a graduate of Texas Christian University, found himself bored working for a newspaper in Texas, so he hopped aboard a ship for Shanghai, where the *Evening Post* hired him. Harold Isaacs, who graduated from Columbia in 1929, made his way to China in 1930 and joined the *Evening Post*, as did Jack Belden, who, after graduating from Colgate in 1931, reached Shanghai and made money gambling before becoming a full-time reporter. Unlike McDaniel—who did not seem to have any deep ideological beliefs—Belden, Thackrey, Isaacs, and Gould veered left in politics.[8]

The newspaper offices were on Edward VII Avenue in the International Settlement, an area founded by the British and Americans and adjoining the equally upscale French Concession. Edward VII Avenue ran from a racecourse to the Bund, a broad avenue that ran along the Whangpoo River and was the center of opulence in what was then the world's fifth-largest city. Western-style art deco structures rose from the Bund, none more magnificent than the Cathay Hotel, opened in 1929 by Sir Victor Sassoon. The hotel's doors opened on both the Bund and Nanking Road. A few blocks down Nanking Road, the fashionable Park Hotel was set to open in 1934, while to the north stood the Astor House, the place to stay before the Cathay opened.

For a young reporter like McDaniel who thrived on adventure, Shanghai was the ideal setting. The city competed with New York, Paris, and Berlin to attract the rich and famous who loved nightclubs, dancing, and the city's very available vices of gambling, opium, and drinking. Opium was plentiful, and Westerners, such as writer Emily Hahn, were among those addicted to the drug. US Army colonel Joe Stilwell thought Shanghai "would ruin anybody in no time."[9] Yet, the city remained a celebrity magnet. Noel Coward wrote an early draft of *Private Lives* while staying at the Cathay. Charles Chaplin, Douglas Fairbanks, Paulette Goddard, Will Rogers, and Aldous Huxley flocked to Shanghai. When they checked into the Cathay Hotel, they were handed a sheet of paper that introduced them to pidgin English for tourists. To order tea, they would tell the Chinese waiters, "Catchee tea chop chop." The word "savvy" meant "Do you understand?," and "No can cuttee?" meant "Is that the lowest price?"[10] Westerners showed up despite temperatures climbing to 97 degrees in the summer, prompting British writer Harold Acton to write, "Shanghai was hot, humid, and crawling with people."[11]

In one way, Shanghai was a microcosm of China's poverty and prosperity. Bill Dunn of CBS once called the city of 3.5 million an "amalgam of opulence and abject poverty."[12] It was China's most important port, and for ambitious people with the right connections, it was prosperous. But for the unlucky majority, life was sheer misery. In the International Settlement alone, 20,000 beggars worked the streets, while, to the dismay of missionaries, the city included 150,000 prostitutes. The foreign-owned factories treated their Chinese workers abominably, forcing them to work seven days a week for only $15 a month. A Chinese man or woman was lucky to live beyond the age of thirty, and every day dozens of Chinese simply died in the streets.

Although covering the darker side of Shanghai consumed his time, McDaniel dabbled in sports and the theater. In October 1931, McDaniel bowled 274 in a major tournament in Shanghai.[13] That same month, he portrayed the young millionaire G. Clifton Blackburn in the American play *Is Zat So?* The Americans and British performed the play at the newly opened Lyceum Theatre, built with the help of Sir Victor Sassoon. The play is about a boxer in New York City who through Blackburn's help becomes a sophisticated butler. It premiered on Broadway in January 1925 and ran for 618 performances with Robert Armstrong, who later starred in the 1933 epic film *King Kong*, playing the lead. In 1927, Fox Films brought it to the silent screen with a young Douglas Fairbanks Jr., playing Blackburn. The play premiered in Shanghai on October 5, 1931, and while the *North China Herald* made no mention of McDaniel's performance, the paper enthusiastically approved of the play.

As much as McDaniel loved his second career as an amateur actor, this part of his life was about to end. A couple of weeks before he walked on stage at the Lyceum, Japanese troops armed with rifles and artillery attacked Chinese forces in the Manchurian city of Mukden. It was the opening act of what would become World War II, and the opening act in McDaniel's life as a war correspondent. More than seventy Chinese soldiers were killed, and Japanese soldiers marched triumphantly through the city's massive west gate. Although the government in Tokyo insisted the Japanese troops attacked Manchuria without orders, the assault prompted nearly four months of fighting before Japan assumed ownership of the vast Chinese province of thirty million people that bordered the Soviet Union and Korea. Manchuria's 360,000 square miles, roughly the combined size of Germany and France, were rich in deposits of coal, limestone, and iron, while its farms produced soybeans, barley, wheat, oats, and rice. It was a strategic asset that China regarded as its "first line of defense" against the Soviet Union and Japan.

Western officials had brushed off earlier signs that Japan might seize the wealthy province. Nelson T. Johnson, the minister at the US embassy in Peking, who eventually would become ambassador to China, ignored warnings from both Hallett Abend of the *New York Times* and John C. Ferguson, the founder of Nanking University and an adviser to Chiang Kai-shek.

Abend and Ferguson turned out to be right. On September 18, the people of Mukden heard the crash of Japanese artillery. Because the Japanese had engaged in night maneuvers for much of the previous week, few took it seriously until the next day, when they discovered Japanese forces controlled the city.

Johnson eventually apologized to Abend. "I'm sorry, but I simply thought you were talking through your hat."[14]

For the world powers, the Japanese seizure of Manchuria was the first real test of the League of Nations. Both Japan and China had signed the 1928 Kellogg-Briand Pact, which outlawed war. Now Japan had violated both the spirit and terms of the treaty. The league sent a five-member commission headed by Lord Victor Bulwer-Lytton of Great Britain to China and Manchuria, to determine the aggressor and deliver a report to the league.

Most officials assumed Japan provoked the conflict if for no other reason than the Japanese army was far superior to China's forces. Although *Time* magazine publisher Henry Luce during a 1932 visit detected "a new spirit in and among the Chinese soldiers" and noted they "were more natty in appearance" than before, Maj. Gen. Frank McCoy, a US advisor to the Lytton Commission, bluntly told Luce, "No one should make a mistake about the Japanese Army. The Japanese Army was a magnificent war machine."[15]

Tensions mounted between the Japanese and Chinese in Shanghai. On January 18, 1932, five Japanese Buddhist monks sang the Japanese national anthem as they walked through the Chapei district in Shanghai. They were badly beaten by Chinese crowds, and one was killed. Two nights later, a crowd of 12,000 Japanese civilians held a demonstration in front of the Japanese consulate. Then they marched through the streets, smashed windows of Chinese shops, and beat up Chinese civilians. Japan dispatched 7,000 troops, the large aircraft carrier *Kaga*, four cruisers, and seventeen destroyers to Shanghai, where they anchored on the Whangpoo River.[16]

Late in the afternoon of January 28, Adm. Koichi Shiozawa, who commanded the Japanese naval forces in the harbor, told Hallett Abend that at 11:00 that night, he would send Japanese marines into Chapei "to preserve order." Abend returned to Shanghai on the admiral's barge, cabled a story to New York, and tipped off Edwin Cunningham, the US consul general in Shanghai. Then Abend went to his sixth-floor apartment, with its view of the Bund, and waited. Rain fell. At precisely 11:05, Abend heard two shots. Then the sound of machine guns. Not far away in the Astor Hotel, Bill Donald, a former Australian reporter who advised Shanghai mayor Wu

Tiecheng, heard the same shots. He telephoned the mayor and held his phone out the window so the mayor could hear the chattering of shots as well.[17]

The next morning, seventeen Japanese planes hovered above the city, dropping bombs on Chapei. The earth "seemed to jar and shake," followed by "the blast of sound." Except for the relatively ineffective zeppelin bombing of London in World War I, it was the first time a modern military used airpower to target civilians. When American journalist Edgar Snow ventured into Chapei, he was stunned to find the bodies of Chinese men and women stacked "four-deep" inside a rice shop that had been hastily converted into a crematorium. Japanese troops advanced into Shanghai and shot out streetlights to cast the city into darkness. Shots were fired in the International Settlement. The Odeon Theatre, one of Shanghai's premier movie houses, was torched by the Japanese and "entirely gutted to the ground." Newspapers reported meat supplies were down to three days.[18]

The *Evening Post* assigned McDaniel to cover the Japanese troops. It was the first time McDaniel ever reported on a war. The Japanese swarmed through the city and set up pickets at key posts. Japanese soldiers shot anyone suspected of being a sniper, killing a Chinese chauffeur who made the mistake of parking his car and trying to flee on foot. An alarmed Capt. Parker Tenney, assistant US military attaché in Peking, cabled Washington that the "Japanese General Staff is now war mad and . . . would not hesitate at hostilities with the United States if their course is blocked." To protect American civilians in the International Settlement, President Herbert Hoover ordered the heavy cruiser *Houston*, six destroyers, and 1,400 US troops from Manila to Shanghai. The move sparked an angry debate in Congress, where Democratic congressman Thomas Blanton of Texas complained that Hoover's move was risky, warning that "we are going to get into it as sure as we live if we don't stay away from there."[19]

The Japanese gave McDaniel and the world a brutal preview of what was to come in the next decade. Ted Thackrey and one of his *Evening Post* reporters—he did not say if it was McDaniel—snuck into the Kiangwan International Race Club in Shanghai, where Japanese soldiers lined up Chinese men and women dressed in peasant clothing. A Japanese officer forced them to face the sun and then killed two men with a sword. In a front-page story in the *Evening Post*, Thackrey wrote that the dead included women and children, some of the children repeatedly shot.[20] The *Philadelphia Inquirer* denounced the slaughter as "butchery."[21] A Japanese major called Thackrey's accusations "much exaggerated and in some portions untrue. Of course, it has been impossible to avoid some unfortunate incidents. In some cases, the women themselves were caught shooting at us." As the major spoke to reporters, gunfire could be heard. The major was informed Japanese soldiers had been fired upon by Chinese soldiers in a nearby house. The Japanese retaliated by burning the house.

"You see," the major continued. "This is unfortunate."[22]

Western reporters found the Japanese claims ludicrous and witnessed some of the atrocities. Morris Harris of the AP saw Japanese soldiers approach an older

Chinese woman who was weeping. One soldier aimed his rifle and fired. He missed. The soldier "leisurely aimed and fired again." The woman died.[23]

On March 14, members of the Lytton Commission reached Shanghai and attempted to negotiate a settlement. McDaniel used the opportunity to develop sources among senior Japanese officials, including Adm. Kichisaburō Nomura, who commanded the Japanese forces in Shanghai. In a telephone call to British foreign secretary Sir John Simon, US secretary of state Henry Stimson called Nomura "one of the most liberal minded men" in the Japanese navy, and "US naval and diplomatic officials were confident he would offer a very restraining . . . influence."[24]

Tensions remained high as Japanese forces secured the city. On the morning of April 29, senior Japanese officers and civilian officials gathered at Hongkew Park to celebrate the thirty-first birthday of Emperor Hirohito and honor the memory of the more than 500 Japanese soldiers killed in Manchuria and Shanghai. Four motorcars carrying Gen. Yoshinori Shirakawa, Adm. Nomura, Japanese ambassador Mamoru Shigemitsu, and other officials entered the park under heavy guard. Ten thousand Japanese soldiers conducted a military parade. After the Japanese crowd sang the national anthem at 11:30 in the morning, Shirakawa, looking resplendent in dress military uniform and white gloves, approached the microphone at the reviewing stand. McDaniel stood only 30 feet away.[25]

A Korean nationalist in the crowd heaved a homemade bomb that he had hidden inside a tin can of cigarettes. The explosion shattered the wooden reviewing stand and mortally wounded Shirakawa. Nomura, who was standing behind him, lost his left eye, while Shigemitsu lost his right leg. Those in the crowd seized the assassin while Japanese troops fanned out throughout the park.[26]

The *Evening Post*'s comprehensive stories on the bombing did not include bylines. But McDaniel clearly contributed to the stories. McDaniel's editors, impressed with his coverage of the Japanese campaign, promoted him to managing editor of the English and Chinese editions of the *Evening Post*, where he wrote a regular column. The promotion took place as the Lytton Commission delivered its final 146-page report to the League of Nations. In a stinging rebuke to the Japanese, the commission concluded, "The military operations of the Japanese troops" during the attack on Mukden "cannot be regarded as measures of legitimate self-defense." The report said, "It is a fact that, without a declaration of war, a large area of what was indisputably the Chinese territory, has been forcibly seized and occupied by the armed forces of Japan." Yet, the report concluded that returning Manchuria to the status quo before the outbreak of the war was no real solution. On February 24, 1933, the League of Nations accepted the report's conclusions. The Japanese were enraged. Two days later, Japanese delegate Yosuke Matsuoka walked out of the league. The best hopes of collective security and preventing another world war were coming to an end.[27]

McDaniel took the view that any attempt by China to recover Manchuria was hopeless. In an *Evening Post* column, he wrote, "If peace and security are maintained and the economic stabilization of the country assured, the great majority of the people will come to take less and less active interest in supporting or opposing whoever happens to be holding the reins of power in Hsinking," a reference to Manchuria's capital. McDaniel had yet to figure out Japan's real aims in Asia.[28]

In the fall of 1933, the *Evening Post* transferred McDaniel to Nanking, the capital of the Nationalist government. For McDaniel, it turned out to be a major opportunity. Shanghai, not Nanking, had been considered the "news capital" of China, where the "correspondents of leading foreign newspapers were based." But now, the senior officials of the Nationalist government were in Nanking, and for two years, no other foreign correspondent had worked there.[29]

McDaniel had access to Chiang Kai-shek; his wife, Soong Mei-ling; and her brother, T. V. Soong, a Harvard graduate and the government's finance minister. The move also provided him entrée to scores of foreign diplomats stationed in Nanking, such as Willys R. Peck, the counselor of legation at the US consulate, and Yakichiro Suma, first secretary of the Japanese embassy.[30]

Perched on the Yangtze River and in the shadow of the Purple Mountain, Nanking was ringed by massive ornamental walls that had taken more than twenty years to build in the fourteenth century. Constructed with roughly 350 million bricks, the wall ranged between 46 and 67 feet high and originally included eighteen large gates. The heavily forested Purple Mountain east of Nanking was also home to a mammoth mausoleum where Sun Yat-sen was interred in 1929. Since making Nanking its capital in 1928, in what became known as the Nanking decade, the Nationalists had worked feverishly to build a modern city, prompting Tillman Durdin of the *New York Times* to write that Nanking "assumed an appearance worthy of the capital of a great nation."[31] Unlike most Chinese cities, which grew in a haphazard fashion over centuries, Nanking was carefully planned with Western-style zoning measures. The 21-square-mile city featured a wide boulevard named after Sun Yat-sen. The new Centre Hotel, a favorite of Americans and British because it offered an elaborate Western menu, opened onto the boulevard. A one-million-dollar power plant supplied the city with electricity, and scores of trees were planted by the government along major roads. The Nationalist government was headquartered in an imposing building featuring three enormous arches and six columns.[32] At the city's center was the University of Nanking, founded by John Ferguson, who in 1931 tried in vain to warn Nelson Johnson that Japan would seize Manchuria. Pearl S. Buck was on the university's faculty during the 1920s.

Near the tomb of the first Ming emperor, a $100,000 mansion for the chief executive of China was nearing completion. The *Times* described it as a "blend of decorative motifs of the old China and more modern Chinese Renaissance." A paved road led to the mansion with its blue-glazed tile roof, yellow-brick walls, and airy verandas.[33]

McDaniel arrived in Nanking as Chiang Kai-shek was simultaneously dealing with a deeply divided cabinet, trying to deflect Japanese advances in North China, and hoping to cripple a Communist insurgency. An intense quarrel erupted between

Chiang and T. V. Soong, who had overhauled the country's tax system and founded China's stock and bond markets in Shanghai. Soong urged an alliance with the United States and Great Britain to deter Japan, a move opposed by Chiang, who was convinced he could accommodate the Japanese and free his army to crush the Communists. In October 1933, Chiang sided with Premier Wang Ching-wei, the leader of the pro-Japanese faction. Soong stepped down as finance minister. McDaniel wrote that "differences of opinion between" Chiang and Soong "have occurred with increasing frequency since the beginning of 1932" over issues such as military spending.[34]

Chiang tapped H. H. Kung to replace Soong as finance minister. Like Soong, Kung was educated at elite American schools, earning a degree at Oberlin College in Ohio and a master's at Yale University. He also had the requisite family connections, having married Soong Ai-ling, the eldest sister of Madame Chiang Kai-shek. McDaniel quickly scored a scoop when he reported a week later that Gen. Huang Fu, chairman of the Peking political council, would not assume the key post of foreign minister as had been widely expected. Instead, Premier Wang remained acting foreign minister.[35]

In late November, McDaniel produced another major scoop when he drove 15 miles from Nanking to a Buddhist monastery to interview Chao Kung, a Buddhist monk and one of the truly remarkable con artists of the twentieth century. He was a Hungarian, originally named Ignatius Timothy Trebitsch-Lincoln. He was born to a Jewish family but converted to Christianity and lived in Great Britain, where he won a seat in Parliament. He seemed to have a talent for associating with the seediest characters. One was Wolfgang Kapp, who in 1920 organized the first of many right-wing coups against the German Weimar Republic. In the aftermath of the failed Kapp coup, Austria deported Trebitsch-Lincoln. From there, he made his way to China, converted to Buddhism, proclaimed himself an abbot, and changed his name to Chao Kung. Now he was angry with the British and wanted the world to know about it.

McDaniel and Chao Kung chatted informally as they drank what Yates described as excellent coffee made by the abbot himself. "I welcome the opportunity of being able to address a few serious words to the whole world and quite particularly to the British government," Chao Kung began. "I have been persecuted, libeled, calumnied, and treacherously denounced during eighteen long years by agents of successive British governments," he told McDaniel. He complained that when he visited Europe in 1932, the British prevented him from going to Sweden and arranged to have him expelled from Belgium.

"I want it to be clearly understood that I demand a clear apology from the British government for all the lies that they have manufactured and disseminated against me, and if this apology and rectification is not forthcoming, then they shall have to accept the consequences," Chao Kung said. If not, he warned, he would force all Western missionaries in China "to get their luggage ready and go home."

The *Evening Post* played McDaniel's story on the front page. Chao Kung's threats were nothing more than bluster. Within a few years, he was backing the Japanese invaders and ultimately worked for the Nazis in Tibet. But McDaniel's story drew attention from all the right newspapers in the world, including the *New York Times*, which published the interview in December 1933.[36]

Just a few days before the Chinese New Year in February 1932, Yates's father came down with a severe case of flu. Despite fighting a high temperature, Charles insisted on completing the financial accounts of the academies on schedule. Only then did he rest in bed. But "the mischief had been done," and he developed a cataract in his right eye. For the first time in his life he needed glasses to read, and it became apparent he needed eye surgery, necessitating a return to the United States. He made a point of not telling his children, writing to one friend in America he did "not care for this to be generally known yet."[37]

Charles and Nannie sprinkled their letters with updates about all their children except Yates. When Charles went to the United States for a few months in 1934 for eye surgery, he wrote he would be staying with Paul in New York.[38] In 1936, when Nannie traveled to the United States, she wrote excitedly about spending a few days with Paul, Virginia, and Helen in New York City, before visiting Nancy in Washington, DC. Later that year, when Charles returned to New York for surgery on his left eye, he wrote that "Paul and his wife have shown the love and sympathy worthy of a son and daughter-in-law."[39]

But except for a reference to Yates by Nannie in 1934, Yates's name cannot be found in any of her other letters and is notably missing from Charles's letters. There was a reason. Yates had met a woman in Shanghai who as far as Charles was concerned was the wrong choice in every possible way. Natalie Eills was Catholic, flamboyant, and worldly. Charles wanted Yates to have nothing to do with her.

When Yates met Natalie in 1933, she was the private secretary for Edwin Cunningham, the US consul general in Shanghai. Natalie spoke such fluent Japanese that she often joked she did her multiplication tables better in Japanese than English. She was, in many ways, the opposite of Yates. While Yates was scholarly and displayed a calm exterior, Natalie was a "fireball" with "a lot of personality." She was stylish and "had a closet full of clothes." At the evening cocktail hour, she ritually delivered a toast: "First of the day and badly needed." In photos, Yates often appeared serious, while Natalie always wore an infectious smile.[40]

As a child, Olga Natalie Eills—whose last name often was incorrectly spelled "Ellis"—was at the center of what was called New England's "most sensational kidnapping." People across the United States and Japan were riveted by the story of the "fair-haired and dimpled" five-year-old girl who had been taken from her mother by her father. The nation's newspapers followed the story of the blue-eyed girl while film theaters in California ran her photo and included the plea "Children, I am lost. Won't you help send me home to my mother?" The story featured lurid details—a messy divorce, a father who placed his wife in an institution, and court battles over Natalie in Massachusetts and Japan.[41]

Natalie was the daughter of John Eills and Harriet Cox, who lived in a number of small towns in Massachusetts before settling in Revere, just north of Boston. John was scholarly, earning bachelor degrees from Harvard and Tufts College and a master's degree at Tufts. He married Harriet in 1904, and Natalie was born in 1907. By all accounts, the marriage was miserable, although nobody seemed quite sure whom to blame. Eills tried his hand at a number of livelihoods. He was a private secretary, taught French, worked as a telegraph operator and stockbroker, and became a Unitarian clergyman. In 1912, Eills briefly committed Harriet to an institution in Northampton, but after having her examined by physicians, Massachusetts governor Eugene Foss ordered her released. In April of that year, a court granted Harriet custody of Natalie and ordered John to pay $34 a month for her support.

But in February 1913, a judge in Boston permitted John to have custody of Natalie two days a week. The court ruling gave John his chance to execute an elaborate scheme to take control of his daughter. On a Friday morning, Eills went to the home in Revere and picked up Natalie. It was the beginning of an odyssey that would take them halfway around the world. Everyone seemed to be on the lookout for Natalie. Newspapers couldn't get enough of the story. In May, the *Detroit Free Press* reported that a man and a little girl "answering the description" of Eills and Natalie were seen "in the vicinity of Detroit only a few days ago and are believed to be now in Canada." The paper's scoop was wrong because by then, John and Natalie had left the United States.[42]

What actually happened was that John reached San Francisco in March, where he rented a hotel room. On April 9, he booked passage on the 13,000-ton liner *Wilhelmina*, which was sailing to Honolulu and Yokohama. "Heart-Broken Mother Seeks News of Child," screamed a headline in the *Honolulu Star-Bulletin*, while the *Oakland Tribune* ran the headline "Nation Appealed to by Mrs. Eills to find Olga."[43] When Eills and Natalie were discovered in Tokyo in October, the *Boston Globe* ran a page 1 story headlined "Eills Arrested in Tokyo, Japan," with the subhead "Worldwide Search of Mother in Revere is Rewarded."[44]

President Woodrow Wilson called on the Japanese government to extradite Eills, a request rejected by Tokyo. Eills took a job as an English teacher in the Higher Commercial School in Tokyo. Unwilling to give up, Harriet traveled to Japan to launch what became an arduous series of court battles. But in 1917, Harriet lost when the Supreme Court in Japan ruled that Natalie should remain in the custody of her father.[45]

By then, Natalie was ten and a comfortable fit in her new country. She wore native Japanese dresses to grammar school and conversed easily with Japanese friends. She attended the Convent of the Sacred Heart in Tokyo, was a superb typist, and learned to take excellent dictation. As a young woman, she taught English in a school in Nagasaki before moving to China, where in 1929 she joined Cunningham's staff.

Yates was enchanted the moment he met this fashionably dressed woman who smoked, drank, and was at home in diplomatic and journalistic circles. When John Eills visited Shanghai in 1933, Yates asked, "Mr. Eills, may I marry Natalie?"

Knowing his daughter's independent mind, John answered, "If she wants to marry you, it won't make much difference what I say." John liked the earnest young man and added, "You have my blessing."[46]

By contrast, Yates's father in Soochow was appalled. "She is not welcome in this house," Charles told his son.

Yates did not back down. "Then neither am I."[47]

Neither Charles nor Nannie attended the wedding in Yokohama in April 1934. It was a private ceremony held at the apartment of the US vice consul. John Eills gave away the bride, while a friend of Yates's from Shanghai served as best man. Yates wore a traditional cutaway suit, and twenty-six-year-old Natalie dazzled everyone in a pale-blue gown with a ruffled net cape and a blue straw hat. She wore the diamond-and-platinum wristwatch Yates gave her as an engagement present.

After the wedding, Yates, Natalie, and a small group of guests were honored with a wedding breakfast in the dining room of the Hotel New Grand. That night, Yates and Natalie boarded the liner *President Hoover* to sail to Shanghai. Then it was off to Nanking and their home.[48]

# TIENTSIN

ates and Natalie settled into a home on the outskirts of Nanking, where his career began to take off. Nanking put him at the epicenter of two major stories—the brutal civil war between the Nationalists and the Communists and Japan's efforts to subjugate northern China. In the next few years, Yates wrote of death and destruction on a scale unimaginable to Americans. He took so many risks that one colleague joked that "Japanese bombers seemed to follow Yates wherever he traveled in China."[1]

For the first time in his career, McDaniel's stories were regularly appearing in the United States. He was selling freelance stories to top publications, including United Press and the *New York Times*. Because he was the only Western correspondent in Nanking, abundant freelance work provided him with an average of $700 a month. Natalie was thrilled when one month he earned $1,200. They did not have to pay taxes, and Yates loved the freedom, but Natalie described freelancing as "feast or famine." She helped by taking messages, typing stories, and monitoring Japanese-language radio news.[2]

As an up-and-coming correspondent, McDaniel needed a home that was "suitable as an office," and "impressive enough" to host cocktail parties and dinners for scores of officials from the Nationalist government, ambassadors and diplomats from the city's embassies, and Western business executives. The house was tastefully furnished, with a grand piano as the prized possession, and the yard was large enough for their beloved Scotties—Lassie and Sandy—to run about. They dug up enough money to buy a car, a necessity for McDaniel to drive to the telegraph office to file his stories. McDaniel kept up his golf game by joining a club on a nearby hill with a nine-hole course and locker room to store his clubs.[3]

Like all foreign correspondents, McDaniel found that he was a general assignment reporter as much as anything. Most of McDaniel's stories for United Press and the *New York Times* were breaking news, such as the mysterious disappearance of a Japanese diplomat in the summer of 1934. Hideakai Kuramoto, a vice consul in the Japanese embassy in Nanking, vanished after attending a diplomatic party in Nanking's suburbs. Convinced that China was responsible for his disappearance, the Japanese sent two cruisers and a destroyer up the Yangtze to menace the Chinese government in Nanking. An armed clash seemed imminent before a Chinese coolie discovered Kuramoto alive in a cave on Purple Mountain. Japanese officials said Kuramoto had fasted and contemplated suicide, although when McDaniel interviewed him at a Nanking police station, the diplomat insisted he never planned to kill himself.[4]

McDaniel also found time to write enterprise pieces, stories he found and developed on his own. He crafted a scholarly article on Buddhism for *Asia* magazine, an American publication whose writers included Pearl S. Buck. To McDaniel, Buddhists in China had come to accept the idea of a modern state emerging in which material progress was key. "Not only has Buddhism made its peace with the new order in China, but it is also endeavoring to make itself an integral part of this new order," McDaniel wrote.[5]

A month later, McDaniel produced a major feature on a $1 million memorial outside Nanking to honor Chinese soldiers killed in battle. McDaniel reported that a few years earlier, Chiang Kai-shek, Madame Chiang, and an American architect walked about a five-century-old monastery on Purple Mountain and conceived the first war memorial. Within months of Chiang's visit, the area's tranquility was shattered by the roar of trucks hauling cement and crushed rock up the hillside to begin construction of a nine-story pagoda. A tree-lined road led the way to the memorial, which McDaniel wrote was a "brick and concrete symbol of a complete change in China's attitude toward the common soldier," calling it China's "first gesture of honor" to the Chinese soldiers who died. "Like it or not, a humiliated China is being forcibly convinced that in militarism lies its only salvation."[6]

The smoldering civil war between Chiang and Communist leader Mao Tse-tung erupted in full fury in 1934, when 700,000 Nationalist troops launched a series of attacks against the Communists and their 160,000 soldiers. By November 14, the Nationalists captured the city of Ruijin, where in 1931 Mao had declared the establishment of the Chinese Soviet Republic. But Mao and his troops had already left the city, beginning what became known as the Long March. The Communists ended their journey more than 5,600 miles away.

Chiang claimed to Western reporters that the Communists had killed more than one million people in only one province. Chiang said that "the people are responding enthusiastically to the government's program of recovery and reconstruction and are now very hopeful."[7]

But Chiang showed no inclination to chase the Communists throughout China. As McDaniel wrote: "It became clear that he considered the suppression of the Communist bandits a minor issue compared to the carrying out of his scheme for the utilization of the Red threat as an excuse for the extension of his personal authority and that of the central government."[8]

In April 1935, McDaniel flew to Nanchang, where the Nationalists had established headquarters for their campaign against the Communists. There, Italian military advisers were helping build a modern air base for Chiang Kai-shek. Twenty Italian pilots were teaching 100 Chinese cadets how to fly up-to-date aircraft. McDaniel wrote that the Italians were taking advantage of "Washington's disinclination" to help China develop an air force of its own. The Chinese needed the planes, not so much for use against the Communists but to deal with the ever-increasing menace from Japan.[9]

The mounting carnage in China prompted the Associated Press in the fall of 1935 to offer McDaniel the opportunity to be their Nanking bureau chief. He eagerly accepted. It meant trading the "uncertainty" of freelancing for a "more settled salary." The drawback? McDaniel was now on call for the Associated Press twenty-four hours a day. Typical was the night when the AP was desperate for a story on the selection of a new Dalai Lama in Tibet. There was a shrieking buzz of the house phone, and a Chinese operator asked, "Is this Da Fong Hsiang one-eight-two-two? Shanghai is calling you. One moment please." For the next few minutes Yates waited. He lit a cigarette. Sandy and Lassie barked, so Natalie let them outside.

"New York wants 1,000 words on the crowning of the Dalai Lama and rush pictures," the AP bureau chief told Yates.

"I'll do the best I can," Yates replied.

Tibet was 1,700 miles from Nanking, which meant Yates had no chance of getting there anytime soon. So, he did the next best thing. He pulled out files from past coronations, translated an article from a Chinese newspaper, and wrote a story. Toward dawn, Yates drove to the telegraph office and filed.

Natalie was irritated with the AP. Why didn't the Shanghai office look up the same files and write a story "without passing the buck" to Yates?[10]

Barely a month after joining the Associated Press, McDaniel covered a meeting of the senior Nationalist government leaders in Nanking. It was the largest gathering of military leaders in years, and Japan's continued advances in North China dominated the discussion. Japan had just presented the Nationalists with a list of demands that would have transformed China into a vassal state. The Japanese insisted China renounce all claims to Manchuria, withdraw from the League of Nations, abolish Chiang's office, abandon help from the United States and Great Britain, and join Japan in fighting the Chinese Communists. Premier Wang Ching-wei led the Chinese government faction favoring an accommodation with Japan, a stand that made him a mortal enemy of those who wanted a tougher approach. Wang's critics saw the meeting as a chance "to modify the policy of conciliation" toward Japan.[11]

Following the morning session, Chiang, Wang and the others walked outside the Central Party Headquarters to allow news photographers to snap photos. McDaniel was among the 150 people gathered outside. Suddenly, McDaniel saw a young Chinese man only 35 feet from Wang raise a pistol and fire. Three bullets struck Wang, who crumpled to the ground with wounds to his left cheek, left arm, and left lung. McDaniel saw Chiang and some of his bodyguards return fire. In a scene of the "wildest confusion" punctuated by the "sharp rattle" of as many as twenty shots, scores of people raced for cover. Wang was rushed to a hospital, and although he was seriously wounded, hospital attendants said he was "resting easily." Chiang himself was not struck. The assassin was among those killed.[12]

McDaniel filed a straight news story. He reported the assassin was Sun-Ming-hsun from Canton. "Speculation was rife in political circles that the attempt on the premier's life was possibly the first blow of proponents of Chinese resistance against Japan," McDaniel wrote. Then he filed a dramatic first-person account of the shooting, writing that "the rattle of pistol fire" would "live in [my] memory."[13]

On the morning of December 7, McDaniel covered the Chinese government's central committee assembly in Nanking as officials approved broad powers for Chiang, making him "a virtual" dictator. McDaniel wrote that stopping the Japanese was now solely up to Chiang.[14] The decision reflected growing anger in China against the Japanese. Hundreds of students from Tsinghua and Yenching Universities in Peking demonstrated against the Japanese. The student protest spread to Shanghai. Chiang sent the students a telegram saying he understood "their patriotic motives," which he sympathized with, but "urged them to return to their schools."[15]

Chiang also invited students and heads of the universities to Nanking to meet with him. The students presented Chiang with a series of demands, including punishing traitors, resisting Japanese demands that Chinese textbooks be revised to "meet Japanese wishes," and restoring press freedom. Raising their voices, some students asked when "the limit of endurance would be reached and resistance to Japanese aggression would begin."

Chiang took the floor at three in the afternoon. War, he told them, was "only a question of time, and when it comes the whole nation will be mobilized and responsibility will not rest on the students alone." But Chiang warned that Japan's army was superior to China's and that "war cannot be declared recklessly."[16]

"The entire nation," Chiang told them, "should be reassured that I will never surrender to Japan or sign any agreement injuring the state," adding he did not "fear death for the cause."

Reporters were prohibited from publishing Chiang's speech to the students. McDaniel found a clever way around the ban by producing a positive feature on Chiang that included a handful of comments from the meeting itself. He wrote that "after twelve years of ups and downs in the political and military arenas of China," Chiang had "forsaken his 'power-behind-the-throne' role" to become the nation's dictator. He traced Chiang's rise from the death in 1925 of Sun Yat-sen, which "thrust" China into utter chaos as warlords battled one another. Chiang, he wrote, emerged "out of the confusion of resulting factionalism in 1927" to defeat the war lords and establish a central government in Nanking.

Having praised Chiang, McDaniel got to the inside story of the meeting, writing if Chiang "surrenders to" Japan's territorial and commercial demands, "his own people may rise against him." At the end of the story, McDaniel reported that when the students shouted in anger that the government had to resist Japan, Chiang flung them a challenge: "If you want to fight, join the army!"[17]

Despite such tough rhetoric, Chiang often had to adopt a passive approach to Japan because, as Nanking officials privately told McDaniel, war with Japan "would be suicidal."[18]

Like most foreign correspondents at the time, McDaniel engaged in a time-honored practice of sharing as much information with his US sources as they shared with him. Much of what he learned from Japanese or Chinese diplomats would be provided to the US embassy in Nanking.

Throughout December 1935, McDaniel badgered the Chinese Foreign Office about possible talks with Japan. On the evening of December 30, Chinese officials gave him and other correspondents a statement declaring that a "proposal for the fundamental readjustment of Sino-Japanese relations through proper diplomatic channels has been put forward by the Chinese Government to the Japanese Government which is said to have expressed agreement in principle." He drove to the US embassy the next morning and handed the statement to US consul general Willys Peck, who cabled it to Secretary of State Cordell Hull.[19]

During the first week of February, McDaniel met with Jabin Hsu, director of general affairs at the Chinese Finance Ministry. Jabin Hsu told him that Yakichiro Suma, first secretary of the Japanese embassy in Nanking, had warned British officials that "in view of the imminent rapprochement between Japan and China, it would not be fitting for any other nation to offer advice or otherwise intervene in China's currency or fiscal matters." It was a blunt reminder that Japan considered China its area of influence and for the West to stay out. McDaniel passed on the warning to US diplomats.[20]

In April, McDaniel secured an interview with Suma, who insisted the session be on background, which meant that McDaniel could not directly quote the Japanese official. Suma's message was harsh. While he doubted the Japanese military would "take any decisive steps in the near future," Suma revealed he was telling Chinese officials in "a friendly way" that if Chinese intransigence continued, there was a growing possibility of "a grave disaster to China." Suma said it was his "personal belief" that "Japan will have to use force against China before China will consent to accept Japan as their friend and guide."

Suma told McDaniel that Japan was irritated by China's purchase of modern weapons from abroad, weapons he implied could be used only against Japan. McDaniel gave details to Peck, who cabled them to Washington. It was a sure sign Japan was preparing for war in North China.[21]

McDaniel also picked up worries from Chiang and his advisers that war between Japan and the Soviet Union could erupt. McDaniel wrote that if war between Japan and the Soviet Union broke out, China "would gain little and possibly lose more than she has" since Japan's seizure of Manchuria in 1931. Citing "mature Chinese official opinion," McDaniel wrote that officials feared any move toward Moscow by Chiang would provoke Japan.

"We are resting precariously on the horns of a dilemma," McDaniel quoted one senior Chinese official. "Whatever we do will be wrong."[22]

In the fall of 1936, McDaniel produced a major piece on Chiang. It was a positive portrait of the Nationalist leader, with McDaniel pointing out that a decade earlier, Chiang was "just another Chinese general." Now he was the dictator of the country's only political party, and in those ten years he had "accomplished the work of 10—of even 100 ordinary men." He had won four civil wars, "reduced the once powerful Communist armies to scattered bandit bands," was developing a modern air force, and was training "the largest potential army in the world." The miles of modern highways had increased dramatically, air lines were providing service to all major cities, and thousands of miles of railroad tracks had been added. "Even if he wanted to, Chiang Kai-shek cannot retire," McDaniel wrote. "The government and the nation are too dependent upon him."[23]

McDaniel's apparent enthusiasm for Chiang was not shared by others. In a private memo to *New York Times* publisher Arthur Hays Sulzberger, the *Times'* reporter Hallett Abend wrote that Chiang "is not popular with the public, and even his military and political supporters have little personal enthusiasm of him."[24] US Army colonel Joe Stilwell, who was attached to the US consulate in Peking, grumbled that "we are allied to an ignorant, illiterate, superstitious peasant son of a bitch,"[25] while Col. Frank Dorn, an aide to Stilwell, thought that "like all low people in high places, Chiang could only see the floor and lower walls; never the high ceiling nor the stars above."[26]

Two months after McDaniel's profile of Chiang, the generalissimo was in the city of Sian. At four in the morning on December 12, Chiang awoke to the sound of gunfire. Four trucks with 120 Chinese soldiers surrounded Chiang's home and seized him. They were under the command of Marshal Chang Hsiao Ling, who had commanded Chinese troops in Manchuria in 1931. Marshall Chang, known as the Young Marshall, was not the ideal symbol of rebellion. He had been addicted to opium, and Abend referred to him as a "young crackpot." But the Young Marshall commanded 120,000 soldiers, making him a force.[27]

It was a major international story, but McDaniel was in bed suffering from a painful middle-ear infection. When Yates insisted that he had to write, Natalie firmly told him no. "After much brow-beating and argument," Natalie persuaded him to stay in bed while she pursued the story. Natalie telephoned Yates's sources and learned that Chiang's Australian adviser, Bill Donald, was trying his best to win Chiang's freedom. After listening to Natalie's report, Yates sat up in bed and dictated a story. When she finished typing, Natalie drove to the telegraph office and cabled the story to New York and Tokyo.

Natalie returned home, and to make sure she was not missing any details, she telephoned Yates's sources again. She learned that Donald and Madame Chiang Kai-shek had flown to Sian to persuade the Young Marshall to free Chiang. Once again, Natalie took dictation from Yates and cabled his story. Then she flopped into bed. At four in the morning, she heard a loud knock at the front door. Their houseboy walked upstairs with a sternly worded telegram from the Associated Press:

Opposition claims Donald and Madame Chiang alighted from plane amid waving banners and torch lights parading in snow up to their knee boots, etc. Why did you not elucidate similarly?

Yates and Natalie had reported the major news—the rebellion had collapsed. The *New York Times* added details McDaniel did not have: so many celebratory firecrackers were set off in Shanghai that for a "short time the whole immense city sounded as though under intense machine gun fire. In Chinese areas, impromptu parades formed, and makeshift bands were recruited."[28] A story without Yates's byline reported that Chiang, "smiling and triumphant," swiftly "assumed firm control of the Nationalist government."[29]

Natalie was "fit to be tied" at the AP's nasty telegram. Her husband had dictated the story from his sickbed. She vowed she would "never again attempt to back-stop my husband."[30]

When McDaniel recovered, he resumed his hectic schedule. The US embassy in Nanking in the spring of 1937 finished an expansion from one to six buildings. To celebrate the "new and spacious quarters," US ambassador Nelson Johnson hosted a glittering party. Yates and Natalie attended the Saturday evening affair, whose guest list included George Atcheson, the embassy's second secretary, and his wife, who just returned from a four-month vacation in the United States. Other guests were Wu Sung-kao of the Chinese foreign ministry and his wife, and Harold Bixby, a representative of Pan American Airways.[31]

McDaniel snagged an interview with Madame Chiang Kai-shek and produced a feature story. He pointed out that she graduated from Wellesley College, could write and speak fluent English, enthusiastically advocated for women's rights, and overcame years of air sickness to learn how to occasionally "take over the controls of her huge" airplane. "Few evenings go by that Madame Chiang does not read" to General Chiang "from Chinese classics, the Bible or current periodicals."[32]

Yates planned to stay in Nanking while Natalie decided to summer with her father at the picturesque Kanko Hotel near the Unzen hot springs in Japan. Neither was happy to spend the summer apart, but it gave Natalie a chance to escape Nanking's miserable summer heat.

Yates's parents had yet to reconcile with their son or his wife. That same summer, both Charles and Nannie were scheduled to return to the United States; Nannie on a furlough and Charles for cataract surgery. The original plan had been for them to sail together to the United States, but Charles opted to stay a few more weeks at the school until Henry McMillian, another Southern Baptist missionary, could reach Soochow and manage the academies. On July 14, Nannie sailed from Shanghai to the United States and took a "comfortable" train trip to New York City to spend a few days with Paul, Helen, and Nancy, who had recently taken a job with the city library. Nannie then planned a trip to Richmond to visit her daughter Virginia.[33]

In November, Charles arrived at Paul's house in Katonah in Westchester County. His cataract operation was a success. He was doing so well that on December 11 he dictated a letter to Nannie: "The doctor says I am making splendid progress. He will probably let me out of the hospital before you can answer this letter."[34] Later that day, Charles was released. He and Nannie rented a room in New York City so his doctor could check on him. Charles was looking forward to spending Christmas in Katonah with "as many members of our family that can get there." He did not mention Yates.[35]

After resting for a few months, Charles and Nannie boarded a train to Seattle on the evening of July 26, 1937. With reports that Japan was launching new strikes in China, Charles trusted "the Japanese attacks will not develop into real war. How foolish and wicked such a war would be." On July 31, they sailed from Seattle on the liner *President McKinley*, scheduled to reach China on August 17.[36]

By the time they docked in Shanghai, the war Charles feared so much had broken out. Japanese and Chinese soldiers exchanged gunfire at a historic bridge in Peking. At the time, it was referred to simply as the "Marco Polo Bridge Incident." But Natalie McDaniel knew better. She called it "the real beginning of World War II as far as the Pacific was concerned."[37]

Constructed of stone and granite, the Marco Polo Bridge is just 10 miles west of Peking and spans the Wudung River. Columns of white marble rise at each end of the bridge. In the thirteenth century the bridge won effusive praise from Marco Polo, who wrote that "it has very few equals in the world." On the evening of July 7, the area was so quiet that Nelson Johnson invited Col. Joseph Stilwell and a handful of guests on a leisurely barge ride on the nearby Pei Hai Lake.[38]

During military exercises near the bridge that night, a Japanese soldier was reported missing. He was later found unharmed, but that did not prevent Japanese and Chinese soldiers from shooting at each other that night.

For years, the Japanese army had been looking for an excuse to attack Peking and seize most of North China. As early as 1931, Gen. Shigeru Honjō, commander of the Japanese forces in Manchuria, told Hallett Abend of the *New York Times* that "Japan could not rest without control" of Peking, Tientsin, and their surrounding areas.[39] In April 1934, the Japanese announced they would regard China the same way the United States used the Monroe Doctrine to prevent European meddling in South America. The Japanese government proclaimed that Japan "has been standing like a watchdog in East Asia. We have fought several times for that. Other powers have an interest in China, but ours is more vital. The Chinese question to us is a matter of life or death." Chiang's Australian adviser, Bill Donald, warned that it "was now or never" for Japan to attack China. China was growing stronger economically, its army was improving, and the Nationalists were working to develop an alliance with the Soviet Union.[40]

Japan portrayed itself as a savior who would liberate ordinary Chinese from the grips of brutal warlords and Western imperialists. Writing for *Asia* magazine in 1935, Hirosi Saito, Japan's ambassador to the United States, argued the "poverty-stricken Chinese people" had been "looted to provide food for" the warlords' armies. He argued that Japan had "liberated thirty million" people in Manchuria "who were oppressed outrageously by a group of warlords who had risen from actual banditry to government authority":[41]

We too have given medicine and instruction to the Chinese. We have probably educated more thousands of them than any western country, and our hospitals in Manchuria and elsewhere have relieved thousands of physical distress. We have also done more; we have given law and order in Manchuria.

Saito insisted "what Japan wants is peace." But Western correspondents in China saw through his claims. In the summer of 1937, Abend told Nelson Johnson he had seen Japanese troop trains heading from Korea to Harbin in Manchuria. After Johnson acknowledged how wrong he himself had been about Manchuria in 1931, he once again dismissed Abend's new warnings as "utterly and ridiculously wrong. Why in Heaven's name would the Japanese want North China?" Johnson argued the Japanese needed to colonize Manchuria before taking on a new adventure. He said North China was overpopulated and marked by poverty. It would, Johnson insisted, be the "height of folly" for Japan to launch an attack.

Abend was stunned. How, he wondered, could an American diplomat "delude himself into believing that the Japanese were satisfied with what they had" in Manchuria? Why would Japan permit China additional time to upgrade its own military forces?[42]

In Shanghai, the AP bureau chief Morris Harris also was convinced that the incident at the Marco Polo Bridge was the beginning of a major war. He assigned McDaniel to Tientsin, a city of almost one million people less than 90 miles from Peking. Because Natalie was still in Japan, McDaniel asked friends in Nanking to look after Lassie and Sandy, boarded a train to Tientsin, and took a room at the fashionable Astor House Hotel in the British Concession. Its rooftop terrace offered a panoramic view of Nankai University, which had a $500,000 science hall financed by the Rockefeller Foundation. The university's graduates included Chou En-lai, who later would become premier of Communist China.[43]

Tientsin was a major trading center. Goods from Peking were shipped by rail to the Hai-Ho River in Tientsin, and finally to the sea. An American missionary once sarcastically described Tientsin as little more than a "stepping-stone to higher things," a reference to Peking. But it was much more. Like Shanghai, Tientsin attracted foreigners from Germany, Britain, Italy, France, and Japan who built and lived in their own concessions. The French and British Concessions were side by side on the banks of the Hai-Ho River. The Imperial Hotel, one of Tientsin's better addresses, was in the French Concession and, as early as 1908, boasted it had "every modern comfort," including electric lights, steam heating, and attached bathrooms.[44]

Next to Victoria Park was Gordon Hall, a gray Gothic structure with two massive towers at each end. Like McDaniel himself, the hall was named after Gen. Charles Gordon, and it was home to the British administration. Its library claimed to have more than 8,000 volumes. When King George VI was coronated in London in May 1937, British officials in Tientsin celebrated by switching on every light in Gordon Hall, offering a dazzling illumination of the towers. British and Americans flocked to Kiessling's Café, which was famous for its rich pastries. The café was a favorite for Scotland's Eric Liddell, a missionary born in Tientsin and who won a gold medal for Great Britain at the 1924 Olympics. The US 15th Infantry Regiment, which had been stationed in Tientsin since the Boxer Rebellion, guarded the US consulate in the British Concession as well as the roughly 750 Americans living in the city. In the city's center stood the three-story Drum Tower, whose balcony offered "the best possible bird's-eye view" of Tientsin. Mosquito curtains were a must during Tientsin's brutal summers, when temperatures reached 105 degrees in June, although daily temperatures dropped into the 80s by August. Winters were bone chilling, although just about everyone seemed to love the "beautiful succession of bright shiny days of winter."[45]

Shortly after his arrival, McDaniel met with Kenneth Yearns, the assistant consul in the US consulate in Tientsin; his wife, Ruth; and Wilfred Pennell, the editor of the *Peking and Tientsin Times*. Ruth said that she and Ken had stopped at McDaniels' home in Nanking and the dogs were doing just fine. The Yearnses invited McDaniel to have dinner at their house later that day. But McDaniel reluctantly turned it down because he had scheduled an interview with Japanese officials the next day.

In addition to McDaniel in Tientsin and Harris in Shanghai, the Associated Press had James White in Peking, while James Mills reported from Tokyo. To McDaniel's annoyance, Harris sent Joy Lacks, a twenty-three-year-old freelance photographer, to Tientsin, who seemed "to be able to take pictures" but did not speak Japanese or Chinese and seemed to know little about politics. McDaniel grumbled about playing "nurse maid" to her and vowed to send her as soon as possible to Peking "for White to look after." McDaniel was being unfair. Lacks was born in Shanghai, and the photographs she took that year in China were riveting, particularly one of a Chinese woman who lost her leg in a bombing.[46]

The AP reporters in China and Japan, including McDaniel, filed more than 62,000 words of copy during the first three weeks of August. They cabled their stories to either Manila or San Francisco, which in turn transmitted them to New York. There, John Evans, executive assistant in charge of the AP foreign service, supervised thirteen editors and rewrite men who reworked the copy. The AP boasted that McDaniel and other reporters in China "have lived there for years and speak Chinese and Japanese so fluently they get their eyewitness stories direct. They handle cameras as skillfully as typewriters."[47]

Japanese and Chinese troops engaged in skirmishes near the walled city of Wanping, only 10 miles southwest of Peking. By July 11, Nelson Johnson reported that eighteen Japanese soldiers had been killed and another forty wounded in the Wanping fighting. Japan, he reported to Washington, demanded all Chinese troops withdraw from the Marco Polo Bridge, and those responsible for "the incidents" be punished. The Japanese embassy in Peking advised Johnson "an agreement is near," but five days later Johnson cabled Washington that he and the French ambassador were convinced Japan "is determined to take all steps necessary" to seize Peking.[48]

Japanese troops were pouring into Tientsin. On July 18, Japanese soldiers occupied the railway stations and the post offices and imposed rigorous mail censorship.
By July 20, more than 6,000 Japanese troops with two dozen 75 mm artillery guns
had tramped through Tientsin, with half of them marching on to Peking.[49]

That same day, McDaniel and Joy Lacks took a train to Peking. Although Harris
in Shanghai was convinced a "first-class" war was about to erupt, McDaniel thought
the chances were "about one in five" of a major war between China and Japan. It
was wishful thinking on his part. McDaniel's aversion to the misery of war clouded
his judgment on Japan's aggressiveness.

When they arrived at the Japanese headquarters not far from Peking, McDaniel
spent hours trying to obtain the permits needed to visit the headquarters. By the
time he finished, it was seven in the evening. Instead of spending the night "pacing
the platform" at "some dinky railroad junction," McDaniel and Lacks made the short
trip to Peking. They found time to clown around by having a photographer snap a
photo of a grinning McDaniel helping Lacks board the train.[50] They looked up the
AP's James White and his wife, Jennifer, who offered dinner and bedrooms to sleep.
McDaniel and a Reuters correspondent shared one room, while Lacks slept in a
separate room.

The next morning, McDaniel and Lacks reached the front lines. McDaniel wore
a summer white business suit, but because Lacks had packed only one dress, she
borrowed a pair of shorts from a British soldier and a shirt supplied by an American
Marine.[51] By afternoon, it was a brutally hot. They saw more than 14,000 Japanese
soldiers wearing steel helmets that were camouflaged with tree leaves. The Japanese
manned machine guns in trenches protected by barbed wire, while behind them
were menacing howitzers.[52] McDaniel acknowledged that Lacks took "good pictures,"
and he sent a first-person story to Shanghai, which Harris loved. Unfortunately,
Harris's wire congratulating McDaniel arrived at the Astor House at 3:45 in the
morning, prompting Yates to joke he was "getting quite used to being waked at
intervals throughout the night."

Yates was frustrated that his letters were not reaching Natalie in Japan. So, he
tried again. On the afternoon of July 22, he sat in his hotel room and typed a letter
on Astor House stationery:

This is the longest I have ever gone without hearing from you, and, for that matter,
without even knowing where you were. I don't like it a bit. It's bad enough being
separated from you this long . . . There is censorship on mails to and from Tientsin
right now, but that would not have accounted for the non-receipt of private letters.
I do love you so much, you may not realize how deeply I love you, and how utterly
lost I am without you. I am not going around moping or wearing my heart on
my sleeve, but that does not mean you are not the one and only girl I love and
want, and always will.

Tientsin remained relatively quiet. That would soon end. On July 28, Japanese planes dropped leaflets on the city, warning that any Chinese soldiers resisting would be annihilated. A Japanese army spokesman said, "We will easily wipe them out. They are very stupid people."[53] The next day, Japanese planes swarmed over the city, armed this time with bombs instead of leaflets. Western reporters gathered on the roof of the Astor House to watch. McDaniel saw Chinese soldiers on the ground shooting back with rifles and machine guns. He quoted Chinese officials as claiming that "thousands of non-combatant men, women and children were killed or wounded."[54]

To McDaniel, the attacks were "the most destructive and longest aerial bombardment ever undertaken" by the Japanese. Nankai University was reduced to "smoldering ruins." Japanese planes struck freight yards and warehouses. The Japanese bombers avoided the British and French Concessions, but many of the 750 Americans in Tientsin were so frightened they "huddled" in cellars. At dusk, McDaniel walked about the "unscathed" concessions. They were "ringed" by thick smoke from the Chinese areas. By midnight, Japanese and Chinese troops shot at each other near the freight yards, their presence illuminated by the "flickering light" of fires. US and British soldiers formed a protective screen around the British Concession. McDaniel checked in throughout the evening with John Caldwell, the US consul general who cabled Washington that while no Americans had been injured, an Italian sentry and French soldier were killed inside the foreign concessions.[55]

McDaniel's vivid accounts were published throughout the United States. For years, American correspondents in China found their stories buried deep inside their newspapers. No more. Yet, reading was one thing, acting another. Despite the carnage, there was no appetite on the part of Congress or President Franklin Roosevelt to intervene.

Chinese resistance crumbled. On July 30, the Japanese bombs and artillery shells destroyed what remained of Nankai University and wrecked the Nankai middle school and girls school. The next day, the city was once again quiet. Japanese troops occupied the Chinese sections of Tientsin, sparing the foreign concessions. When the shooting stopped, Westerners flocked to the theaters, dance halls, and rooftop gardens of the international concessions. The scene was in marked contrast to the rest of Tientsin, where Western correspondents reported that "bombs and flame had destroyed whole blocks of Chinese shops and homes.[56]

The Japanese army seized control of the judiciary and police in Tientsin. McDaniel saw Japanese soldiers paste posters throughout the city proclaiming that Chiang Kai-shek would "never fight Japan and is now only deceiving the Northern Chinese."[57]

As the Japanese tightened their hold on Tientsin, Gen. Kiyoshi Katsuki, commander of Japan's forces in North China, met with McDaniel and other Western reporters. For the meeting, Katsuki chose the imposing Tientsin official residence, which McDaniel described as "luxuriously furnished." The general bluntly told the correspondents "the Japanese Army must go on against the Chinese until anti-Japanese instigation from Nanking or anywhere else ceases." He set no limits on how much Chinese territory the Japanese would occupy.[58]

In Japan, Natalie had no idea where Yates was. Because she spoke fluent Japanese and her husband was a war correspondent, Japanese officials assumed she was a spy. The letters she wrote Yates were "scrupulously scanned and held-up" for weeks at a time. Even more alarming, she heard that Japan might suspend shipping to China. Then she got lucky. An American tourist traveling to Japan showed her a newspaper with Yates's byline and the dateline of Tientsin. She went to the local shipping company and, acting "real dumb and innocent-like," persuaded a clerk to sell her a ticket to Tientsin. She sailed to China and miraculously caught up with Yates.[59]

It was getting more difficult for McDaniel to file his stories. On August 24, McDaniel radioed a story from Tientsin about Japanese attacks north of Peking.[60] At the end of August, the Japanese army announced new limitations on how reporters could cover the war. In written orders, the Japanese prohibited reporters from making their way to the front except under "the direct supervision" of Japanese officers, "who must be obeyed." The Japanese officers held the sole power of censorship. McDaniel wrote that the new orders "closed with the reassuring statement that the Japanese Army does not guarantee the lives of the foreign correspondents."[61]

Given the new restrictions and the difficulty in filing stories, Yates and Natalie made the decision to return to their Nanking home. It was a rule he followed the rest of his career: Stay in a war zone until it was impossible to transmit a story.

Normally it was a direct train ride to their home, but Japanese soldiers had cut the rail link between Tientsin and Nanking. That forced Yates and Natalie to book passage to Shanghai on a British coastal ship.

Getting to Shanghai was easy. But finding a way from Shanghai to Nanking meant passing through a war zone filled with Japanese and Chinese soldiers. They heard that an automobile dealer was delivering a new ambulance to the Chinese government in Nanking, and Yates and Natalie persuaded the dealer to let them hitch a ride.

The ambulance lacked seats, so Yates and Natalie plopped down on stretchers in the back for what would be an eighteen-hour trip. They left at dawn and crossed through what Natalie called "No Man's Land" between the Chinese and Japanese armies. The drive was routine until they reached a wide river. The only way to cross was by ferry. Halfway across, twenty-seven Japanese planes roared above and dropped their bombs. Huge geysers of muddy water erupted around the ferry. The ambulance was spared and continued its journey.

To avoid more Japanese bombers, the ambulance drove at night with headlights off. As the ambulance wildly bounced about on a cobblestone road, Natalie was overcome with car sickness. The ambulance stopped until she recovered. They resumed the drive, and once again the "rolling and pitching" of the ambulance prompted a second bout of nausea for Natalie. The driver suggested she might be more comfortable up front on an improvised seat of 10-gallon gasoline cans covered by a blanket.

Exhausted, they reached their Nanking home, where Lassie and Sandy were waiting. It was midnight. They flopped into what Natalie described as "Chinese-made imitation Simmons beds." The news was bleak. With Japanese troops moving on Nanking, most American families—on orders from Ambassador Johnson—had left the capital. But Natalie planned to stay with Yates. In a few moments, both were fast asleep.[62]

# NANKING

ith bombs falling nearby and an ominous ultimatum set to expire the next day, Yates had a long talk with Natalie in their Nanking home. Since August 15, the Japanese had conducted periodic bombing raids on Nanking, but there were signs the raids were only a prelude. In late August, the British military attaché in Nanking notified an American diplomat that the Japanese would "blow the whole place off the map with high explosive, incendiary, and gas bombs."[1]

The Japanese had warned that as of noon on September 21, they would intensify their bombing campaign and could not guarantee the safety of any foreigners who remained. American and Chinese friends pleaded with Yates and Natalie to leave Nanking, warning that the Japanese would not show mercy to anyone.

Yates and Natalie reached two decisions that day: they would leave their home for the relative safety of the US embassy and remain in Nanking as long as he could transmit his stories to New York. Along with a handful of Western reporters from the United States, Great Britain, and Italy, McDaniel stayed where the story was—as he wrote—"to help inform the outside world of the heightening crisis here."[2]

Natalie arranged to ship their furniture, drapes, rugs, linen, and wedding presents to a fireproof American warehouse near Nanking. At least their belongings would be safe for a time. Their fate was less certain. Then it was off to the embassy with eighteen other Americans—twelve men and six women. The only diplomat to remain was J. Hall Paxton, the vice consul, who like McDaniel was the son of American missionaries in China. The new embassy residents discovered they were temporarily without servants. But there was some good news. A quick search uncovered enough food to last three months.[3]

US ambassador Nelson Johnson and his senior staff had already taken refuge on the *Luzon*, one of a handful of US gunboats patrolling the nearby Yangtze River. Although Johnson told one American reporter that he hated the thought of leaving, his decision sparked a major controversy with American reporters, missionaries, and Chinese officials.[4] McDaniel pointedly noted in a dispatch that while he and Natalie were in the embassy, Johnson and his senior staff "were safe aboard" the gunboat *Luzon*. A "disagreement on policy was believed to have risen between Ambassador Johnson and Admiral Harry Yarnell, commander-in-chief of the United States Asiatic Fleet," McDaniel wrote. "Yarnell was known to be strongly against any yielding to the Japanese threat and was thought to have opposed Johnson's evacuation of the embassy." An American physician at Nanking University Hospital wrote that the decision by US diplomats to leave the embassy "brought down on them the ridicule of all the Chinese." Clark Lee, the AP bureau chief in Honolulu, delivered a shot of his own against Johnson when he wrote that while Johnson left the embassy, Natalie "moved in with her husband . . . and remained there throughout the bombardment by Japanese planes. . . . No AP man has left his post in China."[5]

Johnson, a longtime American diplomat in China whose photo later graced the cover of *Time* in 1939, was infuriated by the criticism. A heavyset man with a ready smile, Johnson was known for common sense, an affinity for reading, and playing guitar at dinner parties. He had a clever sense of humor: during one negotiation over Japan's occupation of Manchuria, a French diplomat said Western governments were confronting an illegitimate child in the region and had to somehow legitimize it, prompting Johnson to reply, "It was getting somewhat dangerous when a Frenchman began to be concerned about an illegitimate child." Johnson was readily accessible to reporters and editors, having hosted visits to China by Henry Luce of *Time* and Roy Howard, the powerful president of Scripps Howard and United Press. He frequently talked privately with correspondents stationed in China, such as Hallett Abend of the *New York Times*.[6]

Following the critical news reports by McDaniel and Tillman Durdin in the *Times*, Johnson fired off a telegram to Secretary of State Hull, complaining that the "Associated Press statement is incorrect in saying I was going on board the *Luzon* under orders of the department. I did say that I was unhappy as it was the first time I had left my office in thirty years of service. I said that under the circumstances I did not feel I could remain at my post on premises and subject my [staff] to possible danger and that for this reason I was taking them with me and expected to maintain offices afloat at Nanking and contact with Government. I tried to make it clear that I was not leaving Nanking."[7]

The Japanese noon deadline passed. Not a single Japanese plane appeared. McDaniel wrote that Nanking seemed like a "great city waiting for death."[8]

The next morning, air raid sirens "screamed out their dreadful warning." City residents took cover in shelters, while thirteen Chinese pilots flying American-built fighters raced across the sky. Moments later, forty Japanese planes swarmed above Nanking. On their flight leader's signal, they dropped their incendiaries and high-explosive bombs. McDaniel counted four Japanese bombers erupting in smoke and fire before crashing. A second group of Japanese bombers swarmed overhead. Their bombs ignited huge fires in a slum district near the Yangtze River. "The straw huts burned like match boxes," McDaniel wrote. Even though he had covered civil wars in China, nothing prepared him for the carnage: "Women, children, and old men already burned to death or beyond aid."[9]

The Americans in the embassy were relatively safe. The only real danger came from Chinese antiaircraft guns firing away. One Chinese shell smacked into the gatehouse of the embassy compound. Aboard the *Luzon*, Johnson watched the Japanese bombing, and when the all-clear siren sounded, he and his staff returned to the embassy. "Johnson indicated he is ready to remain at the capital, notwithstanding today's air raids," McDaniel wrote, adding that "Americans here assumed the ambassador had received instructions from Washington to return." McDaniel seemed unaware of a cable to Johnson from Hull: "Putting an end to confused reports, unfounded inferences and speculation, you return to the embassy premises as soon as in your opinion this can be done consistently with the principle of avoiding imminent danger."[10]

A few days later, Japanese planes pulverized Nanking for seven hours, destroying the city's one-million-dollar electric power plant. McDaniel joined Johnson and his staff to watch the air raids from the embassy's rooftop terrace as two Japanese planes crashed "like comets with tails of smoke and fire." Japanese bombs destroyed "three blocks of the city's best shops" in the heart of Nanking, while smashing the glass windows in the operating rooms of Central Hospital. The next day, thick clouds and heavy rains made it impossible for the Japanese to launch new air attacks, prompting an announcer on Nanking radio to say, "We are living in a strange world. Foul weather brings us peace, fair weather brings us hell."[11]

As Yates risked his life to cover the bombing of Nanking, his father returned from America and reached Soochow. With his vision restored, Charles planned to open the Yates and Wei Ling academies for the fall session. Worried about his own wife's safety, Charles arranged for Nannie to stay with a family friend in Macao, not far from Hong Kong. She sailed on a steamer from Hong Kong on August 26 to Macao, where there was a Baptist mission. Macao "is considered a safe retreat from the Japanese invaders because it belongs to Portugal."[12]

The day before Charles hoped to reopen his schools, Japanese planes bombed Soochow, "which so frightened the people that many of them left the city." Undaunted, Charles set a new date for reopening, and once again Japanese planes scared people away. The Japanese flew low and directly over the schools, dropping their bombs about a mile away. Because it was virtually impossible to open the academies, Charles arranged to have a boat carry the first load of teachers and students across Lake Tai to a school in Huchow about 100 miles away.[13] But when most of the students and teachers refused to board the boat, Charles abandoned the plan. "Practically all of our Soochow teachers have moved their wives and children to other places of safety—and who can blame them when murderous bombs are raining almost daily upon this city," Charles wrote.[14]

That left Charles and colleague Henry McMillian to deal with the increasing number of homeless in Soochow: "We feel that our duty to our Christians and to humanity demands that we stay here—of course—at our risk."[15] Charles converted the auditorium at the Yates Academy into a hospital, while utilizing the basement of the Wei Ling dormitory as a shelter. The servants dug a large hole in the ground for additional protection, and whenever the city's alarms sounded a series of "quick, jerky sounds," Charles and the servants took cover in the dugout shelter. But some were too frightened even to seek safety. Charles and McMillian saw a woman plopped against a wall "trembling like a wild animal." They pleaded with her to take cover at Wei Ling, "but she was too scared to speak or move."[16] They desperately tried to save another woman who had given premature birth. But she was suffering from cholera; she and her baby died, leaving a despairing Charles to write, "The day of reckoning [for the Japanese] has not yet come, but come it will."[17]

On a Sunday morning in October, the Japanese unleashed their most "frightful air raid" yet in Soochow. Japanese planes roared over the academies and dropped seventeen bombs on the nearby railway station. The explosions were so loud that at first, Charles thought they hit Wei Ling. The Japanese planes appeared with such frequency during the day that Charles decided it was too dangerous to venture upstairs in his home to take a nap.[18]

Every day, more wounded arrived. Japanese planes machine-gunned and bombed small boats trying to escape from Kunshan. A fourteen-year-old girl, whose parents had been killed in the attack, was wounded in the chest and arms. Charles was sickened because the Japanese had attacked "just plain boat people who did not even know how to shoot a gun."

The Japanese attacks were horrifying. "Oh God, how long will these invading barbarians be allowed to frighten and slaughter these innocents and helpless people," Charles wrote. He ran a line through the word "barbarians" and changed "invading" to invaders. "I often have to call upon David to express my feelings against these Nipponese," he wrote in a reference to the Old Testament. "This is the first time in my life that I have been able to appreciate some of his expressions against his own enemies and the enemies of God."[19] To him, the Japanese were "vultures" for bombing civilians: "These Japanese are the enemies of God and man." He predicted a Japanese victory in China would lead to "moral and spiritual degradation."[20]

Charles retained hope that the Western powers eventually would intervene: "Surely the democratic nations, when New Testament principles prevail, will not allow Japan to enjoy the fruits of her savage victory." But there was no mood in those days for the United States to intervene and become entangled in an Asian war.[21]

On November 12, Japanese airplanes dropped leaflets warning the next day their aircraft would bomb Soochow "indiscriminately."[22] Three days later, Japanese planes "severely bombed" Soochow, forcing Charles and McMillian to move first to the nearby city of Kwangfu and then to Shanghai.[23]

Nannie was in Shanghai as well, having taken a train from Macao. But unlike her husband, Nannie was softening toward her daughter-in-law. She planned to see Natalie in Shanghai.

In Nanking, Yates was urging Natalie to seek safety in Shanghai. The Japanese had pounded areas of Shanghai, leaving Jim Marshall of *Collier's* to write that "whole blocks have been blasted into heaps of rubble." But Shanghai still was safer than Nanking. As always, Natalie was hesitant to leave Yates. For her, it was "easier to experience the close calls myself than to worry about Yates' safety." But when Yates insisted, she decided not to "be in Yates' way" if he had to make a quick escape.[24]

British officials welcomed her aboard a river steamer heading down the Yangtze to Shanghai, but limited her to 40 pounds of luggage. That presented quite a challenge: suitcases or her beloved Scotties—Lassie and Sandy. Ever resourceful, Natalie scooped up the dogs, donned four suits and two topcoats, stuffed her jewelry into her pockets, and boarded the steamer.[25]

With Japanese planes soaring above, the trip downriver was harrowing. To make it difficult for the Japanese to navigate the Yangtze, the Chinese sank river junks and old steamers to create two barriers, one just below Nanking and the other near Shanghai. When the British steamer reached the first barrier, Natalie and her Scotties embarked on a small barge that squeezed its way down the narrow canals and beyond the blockade. She and other passengers sat on uncomfortable wooden benches while she kept one dog in her lap and the other wrapped around her neck life a scarf. The barge lacked heat, and it was bitterly cold. The only light in the night sky came from the flashes of Japanese artillery.

At eight in the morning, they passed the blockade and boarded a British steamer carrying a load of pigs. Joining pigs on a steamer was far superior to the barge. At least it was warmer. When the steamer docked in Shanghai, Natalie rented an apartment at the exclusive Cathay Mansions in the French Concession, just across the street from the Lyceum Theatre, where years earlier Yates performed in *Is Zat So?* Like the Cathay Hotel, the Cathay Mansions were built by Sir Victor Sassoon and offered luxurious apartments for rent by the month. Natalie's mother-in-law joined her there. It was their first real effort to bridge their differences. Together, they waited for word from Yates.[26]

In Nanking, officials of the Nationalist government were starting to evacuate. By the third week of November, homes and offices were emptied and windows were shuttered. One night, the sky was illuminated by huge fires as government officials burned records and documents. A steady mist created "ribbons of mud" on the roads leading to Hankow and safety. The docks on the Yangtze were crowded with thousands of women and children waiting for boats to fetch them to safety. A thick mist covered the docks.[27]

Tillman Durdin of the *New York Times* watched thousands of men and women from nearby villages push their oxcarts through the main streets. One Chinese man told him, "We are leaving ninety percent of our things." As a Chinese official packed his records and office furniture, he told Durdin, "What's the use? We have tried hard to pull our country up to the standards of others so we could look at other nations with a feeling of equality and rightly demand mutual respect. It now appears that all those efforts are coming to naught."[28] Chinese officials pleaded for help from the West. McDaniel quoted one of them: "In this dark hour, some assurance from the foreign powers would immeasurably bolster China's spirit." Western officials meeting in Brussels answered with soothing words, but no action.[29]

Except for the British consul, most foreign diplomats followed the Chinese government 300 miles up the Yangtze River to Hankow. On November 22, Johnson and most of his senior staff departed for Hankow. Only four senior embassy staff officials, a handful of missionaries, and McDaniel and four other Western reporters stayed in Nanking.[30]

With Natalie gone, Yates was on the go from "morning until night." Because most of his diplomatic contacts were gone, McDaniel wandered about the city to personally view the latest developments. New barriers popped up everywhere as Chinese soldiers dug trenches and strung up barbed wire. The city's main gates were left open just enough for a single car to pass through at a time. Japanese air raids grew heavier. There was so much smoke hovering above Nanking that "the city looks more like Pittsburgh than our Nanking."[31] From the US embassy, McDaniel watched the bombs fall and then dashed off to inspect the damage. Because the telegraph office no longer sent cables to Shanghai and telephone service was out, McDaniel devised a creative alternative, using the radio aboard the US gunboat *Panay*, which was just offshore. Lt. Cmdr. James Hughes, the *Panay*'s captain, promised McDaniel a private cabin when it came time to evacuate Nanking.[32]

Yates typed a two-page letter to Natalie, although he had little hope it would be delivered. He wrote he was "terribly lonesome. In my imagination I take you around with me everywhere I go, and actually find myself talking out loud to you when driving through the streets."[33]

He arranged passage on a small boat for his male servant, the man's wife, and their children. Then he decided to "find the war" outside the city and, on December 5, drove his car 30 miles east of Nanking. A Japanese shell exploded 200 yards ahead of his car. From a nearby ridge, he heard the chattering of machine guns and realized they were being fired by Chinese soldiers. "We are from Canton," a Chinese officer told McDaniel. "We are cold and know nothing about what is taking place over that ridge. But Generalissimo Chiang Kai-shek told us to hold this road. And we will hold it until we are all killed."[34]

McDaniel drove back to Nanking. He could have boarded the *Panay*, but like the other Western correspondents in the city, he was there to report, not hide. Instead of seeking safety, he again drove his car 15 miles from Nanking, passing burning villages, apparently set afire by the fleeing Chinese army. When a Japanese plane roared ominously overhead, McDaniel steered his car behind a farmhouse for shelter before continuing his journey. He passed the hot springs at Tangshan only to realize he was in "no man's land" between Japanese and Chinese artillery fire. He saw a menacing Japanese battery about 300 yards ahead, so he turned his car around and returned to Nanking.[35]

The city was under intense assault from Japanese forces. McDaniel and Arch Steele of the *Chicago Daily News* saw Chinese troops manning Nanking's southeastern gate and firing at the advancing Japanese about a half mile away. Japanese planes soared overhead and dropped their bombs. The two reporters took shelter in a dugout. One bomb exploded just 200 yards away. After the explosions stopped, McDaniel cautiously lifted his head. Not far away were dead or injured Chinese soldiers. The two reporters quickly left.[36]

About 6 miles to the north and west, the Yangtze riverfront was in chaos. Paxton, the remaining US embassy officials, and Colin McDonald of the *Times* of London had boarded the *Panay* on December 9. Two days later, McDaniel wrote that "hugging the farther shore," the *Panay* "steamed up the Yangtze amid loud explosions as [Japanese] shells continued to burst in the river ahead of the quivering gunboat." Seeking safety from the Japanese artillery, the *Panay* sailed 27 miles up the river and out of McDaniel's sight. The city gates to Nanking closed, and large fires were burning out of control on both sides of the Yangtze. Chinese troops detonated the bridges in Nanking's eastern suburbs. Japanese planes strafed the city and dropped bombs on the waterfront, which was largely deserted.[37]

The afternoon of December 12 was sunny and warm. Paxton of the US embassy worked in a small office belowdecks on the *Panay*. He heard a shout: "Planes overhead." Paxton ignored the warning until he heard a "tremendous crash." As Japanese bombs fell, filing cabinets, desks, chairs, and a steel safe were tossed about, and a Navy enlisted man broke his leg. Paxton and his aides helped the sailor to the upper deck. Water was already up to their ankles as they gently buckled a life belt around the sailor. For the next forty minutes, six planes continued to dive on the mortally wounded gunboat, dropping thirty bombs and hitting the *Panay* at least seven times.

Paxton was sure he would not live through the attack. For some reason that thought kept him calm. He was so preoccupied with applying a tourniquet to a chief petty officer that he did not notice his left arm had been hit by five bomb splinters. When the bombing stopped, Lt. Cmdr. Hughes ordered the crew to abandon the gunboat. Motorboats carried them safely to the nearby shore. The 470-ton gunboat sank just offshore. The Japanese government apologized and claimed the bombing was an accident, but Americans in the United States were furious. The attack was the first step toward war between Japan and the United States.[38]

Nanking no longer functioned that second week of December. Food shops and banks had closed, while water, heat, and lights no longer worked. With plumbing in tatters, the stench of human waste filled the air. An American surgeon at the University of Nanking hospital performed eleven operations in one day, lamenting that they could not release patients because "they have no place to go."[39] Heavy smoke rising from nearby burning villages blanketed the city. Thousands of terrified Chinese were fleeing. Some jumped on the running board of McDaniel's car, forcing him to push them away. The cracking sounds of bullets whizzed by his car. Once again, he took cover. He watched as the ministry of communications erupted in flames, although he was not certain whether the explosion was caused by Japanese bombs or the Chinese themselves.

Unaware the *Panay* had been sunk, McDaniel drove to one of the city's walls, where Japanese soldiers poured through a breach. A Japanese soldier menacingly lifted his rifle. McDaniel opened his car door and held up his hands. To McDaniel's surprise, the soldier permitted him to continue. Dead Chinese littered the streets. He saw the head of a decapitated Chinese man plopped on top of a barricade, with a biscuit stuffed in his mouth. Some Japanese soldier's macabre sense of humor, McDaniel thought.

Accompanied by Arthur Menken, a newsreel photographer for *Paramount*, McDaniel saw Japanese soldiers engage in uncontrollable looting, with one soldier using his bayonet to persuade a civilian to hand over cash. Dead horses and humans were strewn about one city wall, and when a Japanese army car raced through a gate, the driver nonchalantly rolled right over the bodies.[40]

The mounting horror transformed the reporters from "neutral observers" of the war into "full-fledged participants."[41] McDaniel and the other Westerners urged the Chinese soldiers to get into civilian clothes, abandon their weapons, and head for a safety zone in Nanking set up by international diplomats and clergy. McDaniel loaded his car with machine guns, grenades, pistols, and rifles left behind by the Chinese. Then he tossed them into the nearest pond he could find.[42]

Believing they had saved the Chinese soldiers from execution, McDaniel and the other four Western reporters—Menken, Durdin of the *New York Times*, Steele of the *Chicago Daily News*, and Leslie Smith of Reuters—had to figure out a way to send their stories. Durdin commandeered a car to drive to Shanghai, but after driving 60 miles, Japanese soldiers forced him to go back to Nanking. On December 14, the Western correspondents made their way to the wharf on the Yangtze River. They asked a youthful Japanese navy officer to radio the *Panay* to rescue them.

The Japanese lieutenant apologized. The *Panay*, he explained, had been sunk. Stunned, McDaniel and Menken asked the officer whether he was certain. It was one of Nanking's bizarre moments: as Japanese army soldiers murdered tens of thousands of Chinese men and women, some Japanese navy officers tried to be helpful to Western reporters.[43]

The next day, Durdin, Steele, Menken, and Smith reached two Western gunboats anchored on the Yangtze's left bank. Durdin watched in horror as the Japanese lined up 200 Chinese men against a wall, shot them, and then walked about the bodies and fired pistol shots into anyone who still appeared alive. Shortly after the massacre, Durdin, Steele, and Menken boarded the US gunboat *Oahu* while Smith, a British reporter for Reuters, grabbed a spot on the British gunboat *Ladybird*. Before Steele boarded, Dr. Robert O. Wilson, an American physician from the University of Nanking Hospital, handed him an envelope filled with pages of his typed description of the massacre.[44]

Amid the chaos, McDaniel chose to stay one more day. It was foolhardy or courageous—or perhaps both. He returned to the embassy, and when Japanese soldiers attempted to enter the building, McDaniel firmly told them no. Amazingly, the Japanese soldiers left. He persuaded a Chinese guard at the embassy to give up his pistol and stay inside the building, a move the *New York Times* said "probably saved" the Chinese guard's life. McDaniel volunteered to help a servant from the embassy find her mother, and "found her body in a ditch."[45]

There was no water in the embassy for the Chinese staff, so McDaniel filled buckets from a street well. He saw several hundred of the Chinese soldiers he had helped disarm. Japanese soldiers forced them from the safety zone and out of McDaniel's sight. "None returns," he wrote in despair. They had been executed. It was a scene repeated throughout the safety zone.

The next afternoon, McDaniel returned to the wharf and boarded the Japanese destroyer *Tsuga*. He carried a letter from George Fitch, an American missionary who headed the Nanking YMCA and had documented the carnage.[46] McDaniel left behind the prized grand piano in his home, his car, and a set of golf clubs that had been destroyed by a Japanese shell, prompting him to ruefully admit years later, "That's how I happened to give up the sport."[47]

McDaniel's decision to stay an extra day gave Steele the opportunity to scoop him because Yates no longer had any way to send a story. Just after boarding the *Oahu*, Steele persuaded the US Navy radio operator to break regulations and send his story. "I think he slipped him a $50 bill or something," Durdin joked years later. That very night, Steele's story of the massacre appeared in the *Chicago Daily News*.[48]

"Streets throughout the city were littered with the bodies of civilians and abandoned equipment and uniforms," Steele wrote. He reported watching as "a band of 300 Chinese [were] being methodically executed before the wall near the waterfront where already corpses were piled knee deep." Two days later, Steele wrote in a second dispatch that he saw "the Japanese beating and jabbing helpless civilians. I saw the dead scattered along every street, including some old men who could not possibly have harmed anyone; also mounds of executed men."

Durdin's story—radioed by the *Oahu* to New York on December 17—appeared on the front page of the *New York Times* on December 18 under the headline "Butchery marked capture of Nanking." Durdin wrote, "Wholesale looting, the violation of women, the murder of civilians, the eviction of Chinese from their homes, mass executions of war prisoners and the impressing of able-bodied men turned Nanking into a city of terror. The killing of civilians was widespread. Foreigners who traveled widely through the city Wednesday found civilians dead on every street. Some of the victims were aged men, women, and children. Policemen and firemen were special objects of attack. Many victims were bayoneted and some of the wounds were barbarously cruel."

Durdin reported that Japanese soldiers seized money and watches from the staff of the American Mission Hospital. "I witnessed three mass executions of prisoners within a few hours Wednesday," he wrote. "In one slaughter a tank gun was turned on a group of more than 100 soldiers at a bomb shelter near the Ministry of Communications. A favorite method of execution was to herd groups of a dozen men at entrances of dugouts and to shoot them, so the bodies toppled inside. Dirt then was shoveled in and the men buried."[49]

Menken radioed his own story from the *Oahu* on December 16. The day before, he and McDaniel together had watched the unspeakable horror, with Menken writing, "The once-proud capital of ancient China was strewn today with the blood-splotched corpses of its soldier defenders and civilians killed in the bombing, shelling and fierce fighting." A photo of McDaniel accompanied Menken's story, which noted Yates was the last Western correspondent in Nanking.

With the Japanese having cleared a path through the booms, the *Tsuga* raced down the Yangtze to Shanghai. McDaniel provided horrifying descriptions of

Nanking's death throes. "Throughout the night I heard wild cries of Chinese, rifle fire, and deafening explosions," McDaniel wrote in a story that appeared in American newspapers on December 17.[50]

In their apartment at the Cathay Mansions, Natalie and her mother-in-law waited for word about Yates. On December 12, Colin McDonald of the *Times* of London left a telephone message: "Yates is well. Prefers to see it through." Three days later, the US Navy sent a vague report that Yates and the other reporters had left Nanking. But nothing from Yates himself. It was agony for a worried wife and mother waiting to see whether Yates was alive.

Finally, on the seventeenth, the telephone rang. It was Yates. The *Tsuga* had just docked in Shanghai.

"I'm down here at the office and have to write my story before I can leave," Yates said in his stoic, matter-of-fact style. "It will probably take two or three hours. They want about 5,000 words or so. But I've got the first sandwiches, beer and cigarettes I've had in five days here in front of me, so it won't be difficult."[51]

Natalie started to cry in relief. Nannie took the receiver and chatted with her son. After she hung up, this stern Baptist missionary stepped out of character and said quietly, "My dear, I think you should have a small sip of spirits—for medicinal purposes, you know—to brace you up. I think this is one instance where it will do one good."

Natalie ordered a highball while Nannie sipped a shandy—beer mixed with lemonade. Natalie then persuaded her mother-in-law to put on one of her dinner frocks. When Yates reached the apartment at nine in the evening, they all walked across the street to the French Club. They ordered steaks. Yates and Natalie shared a bottle of wine.

Yates's story appeared the next day in scores of newspapers in the United States. It was a grim diary of Nanking's final days. He wrote that he "saw many more bodies in the streets. Passed a long line of Chinese, hands tied. One broke away, ran and dropped on his knees in front of me, beseeching me to save him from death. I could do nothing. My last remembrance of Nanking: Dead Chinese, dead Chinese, dead Chinese."[52]

# HANKOW

**T**wo days after McDaniel arrived in Shanghai, the AP ordered him to "proceed immediately" to southern China, prompting Natalie to grumble that despite the approach of Christmas Eve, he had no choice but to pack a few belongings and leave his wife and mother.[1]

McDaniel's destination was Hong Kong, the British Crown colony and one of the world's most prosperous ports. From there, he would be only 75 miles south of Canton, a city of one million located on the 1,200-mile Pearl River, the third longest in China after the Yangtze and the Yellow Rivers. Like Shanghai, Canton was a prosperous trading center and a key shipping link for goods en route from South China to Hong Kong's harbor, where cargo ships were waiting to sail into the South China Sea and markets around the world. During a brief visit in the summer of 1938, English writer Freda Utley wrote that "with its many wide streets and large concrete buildings, Canton was the concrete symbol of the New China which Japan is determined to destroy."[2]

With the fall of Nanking, Japan had two choices: a strike up the Yangtze River to seize Hankow, or a drive south to capture Canton. Both offered strategic advantages. Attacking Hankow would force the Nationalist government to once again shift its capital farther inland to Chungking. An assault on Canton, which could be a joint operation between Japan's army and its modern navy, would pose a mortal threat to Hong Kong.

The AP had moved James Mills from Japan to Hong Kong in 1937. But with McDaniel arriving in Hong Kong, he would cover any attacks on Hong Kong and Canton while Mills moved to Hankow. Because McDaniel spoke Cantonese, he was a perfect choice to cover that city.

Since the end of August 1937, Japanese planes based in Formosa combined with naval planes launched by the carriers *Kaga*, *Hōshō*, and *Ryūjō* to pound Canton. On January 1, 1938, United Press reported that forty Japanese planes had bombed Canton, which was "believed to herald the long-threatened Japanese offensive in the south." Although Japan had not yet officially declared war against China, the Japanese government severed relations with the Nationalist government.[3]

The Japanese bombing of Canton was the most intense so far in the war. In a letter to a friend in the United States, an American schoolteacher wrote of the raids at night when Japanese planes dropped their bombs at a height of 20,000 feet for the "simple purpose of terrorizing the people." The daylight raids were easier to cope with because "they are carried out at a much lower level and the bombs are dropped at a particular target." Meanwhile, Canton had to contend with another unrelenting enemy. Cholera swept through the city, killing as many as 1,000 people every day.[4]

Before he left, James Mills reported that British officials in Hong Kong were spending $40 million to upgrade the city's harbor and defenses. He wrote that Hong Kong was being "fortified to such an extent that" it might soon be compared to Singapore and Gibraltar as well-defended British possessions.[5] Two weeks later, McDaniel wrote that rumors were circulating throughout Hong Kong that the Japanese were plotting a coup to depose the Canton government, adding "reliable sources reported that an attempt was made" on February 3 "to assassinate" the mayor of Canton.[6] In Canton, Chinese officials declared martial law and arrested as many as 100 suspected Japanese agents.[7]

McDaniel also discovered that Madame Chiang had arrived in Hong Kong, which prompted fears that the Nationalists were worried their government in Hankow could collapse. Deepening those fears was a report by McDaniel that Gen. Han Fu-chu, despite commanding 150,000 soldiers, had abandoned Shantung Province, prompting Chiang Kai-shek to rush to the front "to stiffen [the] morale of troops." But citing sources "closest" to Madame Chiang, McDaniel wrote that her visit to Hong Kong was "chiefly for a physical rest and had no political significance." Writing that Madame Chiang had been injured a few days earlier when her automobile "plunged" into a ditch near Shanghai, McDaniel quoted the same sources as saying she would return to Hankow in a few days.[8]

In March 1938, the AP transferred McDaniel to Hankow, where he replaced James Mills, who had been assigned to India. Like many of McDaniel's assignments before and after, Hankow would soon be a war zone. The Japanese were expected to continue their march up the Yangtze to seize Hankow.

Hankow was a blend of Chinese, Americans, French, British, and White Russians, the latter of whom fled their country after the 1917 revolution and established restaurants, bars, and clothing stores. While certainly not as glamorous as Shanghai, Hankow attracted an eclectic mix of diplomats, reporters, poets, and philosophers. American and British drugstores provided Westerners with the latest pharmaceuticals. Theaters offered English-speaking feature films. Just outside Hankow, the largest studio in China produced feature films, with some suggesting China was winning a great victory over the Japanese.

US ambassador Nelson Johnson and most international diplomats had moved their embassies to Hankow, where Chiang Kai-shek had established his new capital. Gen. Alexander von Falkenhausen, a German officer who had the challenging task of trying to develop an effective Chinese army, was there along with Bill Donald, the former Australian journalist advising Chiang. Chou En-lai, one of Mao Tse-tung's top allies who later became premier of Communist China, frequently held court with international reporters, who were impressed with his charm.

Many of the reporters, novelists, and poets in Hankow were adventurers who followed wars wherever they erupted. Novelist Christopher Isherwood and poet

W. H. Auden sailed to Asia on the same ship as *Life* magazine photographer Robert Capa, already legendary for his photographs from the Spanish Civil War. Agnes Smedley, a left-wing American journalist whose lovers included Richard Sorge, a Soviet spy who served in Shanghai and Tokyo, arrived in January. Peter Fleming, a correspondent for the *Times* of London, was there with his wife, film actress Celia Johnson. Edgar Snow, who had interviewed Mao and Chou a few years earlier, was in Hankow, while Freda Utley, a bestselling author, arrived in July.

Reporters such as McDaniel, Fleming, Steele, Durdin, George Hogg of United Press, Rex Warren of the *Melbourne Herald*, and R. Graham-Barrow of Reuters flocked to Hankow. They all arrived in February and March just as frigid winds swept down from Russia and snow and slush covered the streets. Some reporters took rooms at the posh Hôtel Terminus in the French Concession, while others— trying to save money—stayed at the Lutheran Mission, where United Press kept its office.[9] McDaniel was the only newspaper reporter whose wife accompanied him. The rest of the reporters along with British and American embassy officials left their wives behind, prompting Utley to quip, "It seems to be a fixed Anglo-Saxon prejudice that men should at once get rid of their wives if the remotest danger offers sufficient excuse." But Yates and Natalie were so much in love they refused to be separated for long. They had a marriage that was ahead of its time, not only as lovers and companions but as a team on Yates's career.[10]

Every afternoon at five, the reporters gathered in a crowded conference room in the offices of Hollington Tong, a former editor of the *China Press* and a graduate of the University of Missouri. The conference room was stuffy and featured a long table on which Chinese officials placed cigarettes, chocolate, and tea. Tong had been handpicked by Chiang to place China in the most favorable light for Western reporters.[11] The correspondents liked and respected Tong, whom they called "Holly." Described by one reporter as "genial," Tong set up interviews with Chiang Kai-shek or senior members of his government and "tried in every way I could to help the correspondents visit the front and secure eyewitness stories."[12] The official briefing bulletin was read by T. T. Li, a spokesman for the Nationalists, although it quickly became apparent that accuracy was not his prime objective. Li once proclaimed, "Of seven planes brought down by Chinese ground forces, fifteen were destroyed by infantry."[13] When air raid sirens screeched, reporters climbed to the roof of the Lutheran Mission where they had a sweeping view of the attacks. As they waited for the inevitable arrival of Japanese bombers, the reporters quietly talked to each other. Finally, they could see the Japanese planes evading Chinese antiaircraft fire, their bombs falling on "the miserable shacks of the working-class population" near the Yangtze.[14]

McDaniel and the other regular Western correspondents took pride in the many years they had spent trying to understand China. "They had seen the war from the beginning and had been in danger many times, but they rarely spoke of their personal experiences," Utley wrote. "The sufferings and the constant danger to which the Chinese were exposed loomed too large for any of the foreign correspondents to feel that the moments in which they themselves had been close to death were any-thing to 'crash into headlines about' unless one's ego had obscured all sense of proportion."

Some of the correspondents were already famous internationally. In 1938, MGM released the film *Too Hot to Handle*, in which Clark Gable and Walter Pidgeon portray newsreel cameramen in China. During one scene, Gable aims his camera at a Japanese plane that strafes and bombs a ravaged area of a Chinese city. MGM clearly modeled Gable's character after Capa.

These hardy and knowledgeable reporters did not warmly embrace journalists who made a quick stop in Hankow and "thought they could go home and tell the world all about China after a few interviews with prominent Chinese in Hankow," Utley wrote.[15] Theodore White referred to them as the "trained seals, the swooping stars of big American and British newspapers" who would write glowing stories of heroic Chinese resistance.[16] When Isherwood and Auden attended their first press conference, they quickly noticed "the old hands viewed us with inquisitively hostile eyes."

"These young fellows are desperate to go to the front at once," one correspondent said of Isherwood and Auden, prompting another reporter to say sarcastically, "Why isn't that just fine."[17]

Hankow offered good food, clean sheets, and running water. These seemed like luxuries to the reporters who made their way to the front lines. They traveled in the back of trucks, on mules, and by foot. The presence of malaria-carrying mosquitoes was as much of a threat as Japanese shells, forcing reporters to scrounge up mosquito nets when they slept, often on the ground. Swiss photographer Walter Bosshard snapped a shot of Utley sleeping under a mosquito net as a group of pigs gathered around her. Bathing was virtually impossible, although correspondents used wet sponges and towels dipped in bowls of water to do their best to stay clean. Traveling through similar Chinese villages in 1941, Martha Gellhorn discovered "the unfair fact that a female cannot modestly relieve herself . . . in a landscape of bare rice paddies, a sea of mud."[18] When Japanese planes soared above, reporters scrambled for cover in nearby ditches. By the time reporters returned to Hankow, their clothes were filthy and grimy, although for some curious reason Tillman Durdin of the *Times* astonished his colleagues by always looking so "elegant" in slacks and a light-weight hat.[19]

Hankow was one of three cities within sight of another and separated by two rivers. Across the Han River to the south was the smaller municipality of Hanyang, while directly across the Yangtze was Wuchang, where Chiang and Madame Chiang Kai-shek lived in an army headquarters building. Today, the three have been merged into the metropolis of Wuhan, but in 1938 McDaniel and other Westerners would have referred to each city by its separate name.

Nobody seemed quite certain whether the Chinese could hold the three cities and their 1.5 million people. In a private letter to President Roosevelt, Chiang argued that Hankow would serve as the bastion of democracy, although there was nothing terribly democratic about Chiang's government. Falkenhausen assured reporters that China had more than enough troops to defend the city, while a Chinese official boasted that "an iron cordon of crack divisions will be ready when the occasion arises to fight advancing Japanese to the last ditch."[20] A British diplomat sharply reprimanded Utley when she said, "when Hankow falls," telling her she should use the word "if" instead.[21] Johnson cabled Secretary of State Hull that "at considerable expense of lives, material and treasure" the Japanese could seize Hankow and control the railway to Peking. But at what cost? Johnson thought that "Japan must soon come to a realization that up to the present time all that her efforts have netted her has been hostility abroad and expense in China. Japan can hardly expect to recoup this expense from Chinese trade in another 20 or 30 years." Once again, Johnson's reliance on logic led him to misread Japan's aims. To Westerners, Japan's continued attacks in China would only drain the Japanese resources, because China was too vast to be conquered. But the Japanese were not thinking in those terms. They wanted to dominate the economy of Asia, no matter the cost.[22]

In early April, Chinese forces repelled a Japanese advance at Taierchuang, northeast of Hankow. More than 20,000 Japanese soldiers were reportedly killed in China's first victory over Japan. Holly Tong later insisted that "morale was never higher throughout the eight years of the war than it was in April 1938."[23] The *New York Times* proclaimed in a major headline that the Japanese defeat provoked a cabinet crisis in Tokyo.

McDaniel tried to track down the exact number of Japanese prisoners taken, which seemed a moving target. The Chinese initially claimed 1,000 Japanese soldiers had been captured at Taierchuang, but McDaniel was skeptical because he knew Japanese soldiers rarely surrendered. The Chinese kept lowering the number, first to 700, then 600, while independent observers told McDaniel the number was actually 100. When McDaniel and other reporters insisted on talking to the Japanese prisoners, Chinese authorities made only nine available. With her fluent Japanese, Natalie served as interpreter. Yates reported that the prisoners were held in "clean and comfortable" quarters. Some of the Japanese told McDaniel they were resigned to their fate—either the Chinese would execute them, or they would be shot by their own soldiers if they escaped and reached Japanese lines.[24]

The battle of Taierchuang sparked a sense of optimism among the Chinese. Even though China had suffered more than a half-million military casualties during the first year of the war, McDaniel reported twenty new divisions had been trained and equipped and would soon be deployed against Japanese forces. Japan was spending far too much time pacifying areas of North China it already had conquered, and the "long-threatened Japanese push southward from the Yellow River toward Hankow has not materialized." The Japanese forces were at least 225 miles from Hankow, and as he moved about the tri-city region, McDaniel discovered that the Chinese were intent on proving to the world that they could defeat the Japanese. The Nationalists postponed plans to move their government and military offices from Hankow.[25]

McDaniel's own optimistic reporting was buttressed by Johnson's upbeat reports. Johnson cabled Hull that "conditions here at Hankow have changed from an atmosphere of pessimism to one of dogged optimism," based more "upon the hope of wearing out the Japanese than any expectation of being able by force to drive out Japanese forces now on Chinese soil." Johnson also could "find no evidence of a desire for a peace by compromise among Chinese" and doubted "whether the government could persuade its army or its people to accept such a peace. The spirit of resistance is slowly spreading among the people, who are awakening to a feeling that this is their war. Japanese air raids in the interior and atrocities by Japanese soldiers upon civilian population are responsible for this stiffening of the people."[26]

McDaniel reported the Soviets were becoming increasingly involved on behalf of China, particularly in the air. Although the Soviets would not permit McDaniel to see their planes "at too close a range," he counted about 100 of them, including a handful of four-engine bombers—all bearing Chinese insignias. The Russian pilots lived and ate in Russian mess halls in Hankow.[27] To McDaniel, they were well trained, and every day they strafed Japanese troops and ships heading toward Hankow on the Yangtze River. A Chinese nurse told him about a wounded Russian pilot in a Hankow hospital. The dying pilot said his parents in the Soviet Union would very shortly receive a terse note saying their son "died at work." That prompted McDaniel to write that the Soviet pilots "receive no praise in the Chinese press for success; they remain anonymous in failure."[28]

Despite limited training, Chinese fighter pilots were doing their best to ward off Japanese air attacks. On a sunny April 29, the birthday of Emperor Hirohito, air sirens shrieked. Within moments, more than forty Japanese planes swarmed above the Hanyang arsenal, an industrial sector on the banks of the Han River. Chinese fighter planes roared off to intercept, and for a few minutes it looked like a World War I film. Planes chased one another. Some erupted in explosions. Pilots bailed out. As one US Navy sailor aboard the gunboat *Guam* watched, a fighter plane machine-gunned to death a pilot parachuting to the ground. The exuberant Chinese claimed to have shot down more than twenty Japanese planes, although at a cost of a dozen of their own fighters. Nearly 1,000 people died on the ground.[29]

The optimism was fleeting. In June, Japanese officials bluntly informed US admiral Yarnell that they would capture Hankow before the end of the year. They made clear that if China did not consent to peace talks, Japan would step up its offensive. A year earlier they had given China a chance to recover after the fall of Nanking, and they would not make that mistake again.[30]

In a desperate effort to halt the Japanese advance, Chiang Kai-shek turned as merciless as his enemies, even if it meant killing his own people. In June, he ordered his troops to blow up the dikes along the Yellow River north of Hankow. Combined with heavy rains, the shattered dikes spread water over 500 square miles, killing 130,000 Chinese civilians and destroying vast areas of farmland. The Chinese tried to blame Japan's forces for the destruction. Western news organizations wrote that the dikes collapsed because of heavy rains, which was only partially true. Within a month, US officials concluded the Chinese themselves had caused the catastrophe.

The Chinese remained desperately short of modern aircraft. The French agreed to sell sixty airplanes on generous credit terms. But when the planes arrived, many of the parts were missing. To McDaniel it made little difference because the Chinese pilots were so "pathetically uninstructed they posed little threat to the well-trained Japanese airmen." A year earlier, in 1937, McDaniel estimated 100 Chinese planes crashed either landing or taking off. The United States had supplied China with six bombers, but five were lost within a month. The US also provided China with scores of modern P-36 Hawk fighters, but thirty crashed because the Chinese misused them as bombers.[31]

The Japanese advanced with a relentless combination of speed, brutality, and superior equipment and training. "Widespread and ruthless destruction of towns and villages and considerable killing and wounding of Chinese civilians by Japanese military" in the provinces of Shansi, Shantung, and Hopei, reported one US diplomat on July 13.[32]

Yates's parents, Charles and Nannie, were trying to get out of Shanghai. Charles wanted to return to his academies in Soochow but complained the Japanese would not permit him to take the trip. By the time Yates moved to Hankow, the Japanese had agreed to let Charles return to Soochow. But his bitterness toward the Japanese deepened. "I am sorry if what I have said offends any Japanese Christian, but for the sake of humanity the Japanese Army must be condemned," Charles wrote. "They are here to conquer China," whose "conquest would mean a death blow to mission work."[33] A few months later, Nannie wrote that it appeared Japan "will accomplish her wicked purpose in China without any interference on the part of other nations."[34]

Nannie and Miss Ling, one of the school's teachers, carried on missionary work as best they could. They discovered hundreds of refugees gathered at an abandoned theater in Shanghai. The interior was "dark, unclean and most unsanitary." Brooms, mops, soap, and lights were desperately needed. Refugees had to make do without beds, tables, or chairs. She saw a seventy-year-old woman with a "sweet face" living in an area the size of Nannie's bed. Yet, despite the hellish conditions, the woman had "the tidiest spot in this place of refuge." One woman was fighting a fever, while a very sick older man whom Nannie said was a Christian folded his hands in prayer. As Nannie and Miss Ling left, a young man called out, "God bless you."[35]

In late July, McDaniel made his way to Kiangsi, a picturesque province of mountains and rivers 225 miles southeast of Hankow. He knew the area well. Three years earlier he had written a story for the *New York Times* about a Chinese air base in the nearby province of Nanchang, financed by the Italian government at a cost of one million dollars. More than 20,000 workers constructed the 10-square-mile base, which included four large concrete hangars and repair shops. Japan hoped to seize the airfield before turning its full force on Hankow.[36]

McDaniel saw Japanese planes drop bombs that did not explode. When he examined the duds, the markings showed they had been manufactured in 1918. Chinese soldiers told McDaniel that at least 20 percent of all Japanese artillery shells did not explode. He filed a story from Nanchang that the Japanese might be running short of ammunition.[37]

Despite the unexploded bombs, the Japanese continued their relentless march toward Hankow. When McDaniel returned to Hankow, he encountered deepening despair: except for the Americans, French, and British, all other foreigners evacuated the city. It was becoming clear that Chiang's hope of holding Hankow was wishful thinking. The French maintained a small garrison of 350 troops, while tiny American and British gunboats plied the Yangtze River. McDaniel reported 150 American missionaries remained in the tri-city area to protect Chinese civilians, schools, and hospitals. US oil companies placed American flags near their oil rigs, hoping the Japanese would spare them.

Japanese aircraft were regularly pounding Hankow. On July 20, the Japanese bombers struck their targets without a single Chinese fighter challenging them, prompting one American sailor to grumble, "We don't see the Chinese Air Force anymore and don't know where it is."[38] Ever-confident Japanese fighter pilots strafed the Chinese airfields and destroyed what few planes were left. The heavy attacks forced much of the Nationalist government to move to Chungking, nearly 600 miles up the Yangtze. The Chinese foreign minister told Johnson that China would make Japan's capture of Hankow as "expensive as possible," leading Johnson to believe that if Hankow fell, the war would continue. On August 1, Johnson and his advisers followed the Nationalists and established a temporary embassy in the old Standard Oil building in Chungking.[39]

McDaniel and the other reporters opted to remain in the doomed city, calling themselves the "Hankow Last Ditchers." The reporters made a point of including Col. Joseph Stilwell, who was still serving as a military attaché, as well as Capt. Evans Carlson, a Marine assigned to China. They kept each other company with lunches at the US Navy YMCA, which offered hotcakes for breakfast and ice cream at an American-style soda fountain. Then in the evening it was drinks at Rosie's Tea Room, renowned for the rare luxury of air-conditioning, as well as being a gathering place for reporters, diplomats, and American, British, and French naval officers.[40] On some evenings, the correspondents went to the movie theaters, although they were baffled when one theater aired the wildly inappropriate *Last Days of Pompeii*, a 1935 film featuring Preston Foster, Basil Rathbone, and Louis Calhern.[41]

Agnes Smedley once persuaded the reporters to go to a hospital and sing American songs to the wounded Chinese soldiers, who were astonished by the gesture.[42] When Utley and Carlson decided to leave Hankow on October 1, the correspondents held a "mock trial," charging both with "desertion." Arch Steele presided as the judge, wearing a damp towel as a wig. They sang songs written by

Smedley, danced, and drank. But all were miserable about the inevitable fall of Hankow. They particularly sympathized with Carlson, who had resigned his commission after repeatedly warning that Washington's failure to firmly oppose Japan's expansion in China would eventually lead to war between Japan and the United States. It was a message nobody wanted to hear in Washington.[43]

As Utley and Carlson were leaving, the main Japanese column was less than 60 miles from Hankow. McDaniel reported the Japanese were only 25 miles away from the rail line linking Hankow to Peking.[44] Four days later, the Japanese bombed the railway yards and huge flames erupted. McDaniel watched as Japanese fighter planes machine-gunned and shelled the main highways. Thousands of Chinese civilians dropped their belongings into rickshaws and "stole away in the night," leaving "a city virtually without transportation."[45] Chinese junks loaded as many civilians as possible and sailed up the Yangtze toward safety, but 400,000 Chinese civilians and at least 1,000 foreigners remained in the city. Despite Japanese warnings, the US gunboats *Luzon* and *Guam* remained at their anchorages near the tri-city.

The weather turned cold and snow fell as the Chinese fought back in a desperate effort to stop the Japanese. Chinese soldiers went about setting up demolition charges at Japanese-owned buildings. McDaniel saw a Chinese officer directing workers to drill holes in the foundation of the Yokohama Bank building before planting explosives. The Chinese declared martial law.[46]

The night of October 25, Chiang Kai-shek flew out of Hankow. He left a defiant statement for his chief spokesman, Hollington Tong, to give to reporters. Tong scheduled a news conference for the next morning, but the breakdown in communications made it difficult to notify the correspondents. Tong solved the dilemma by asking Tillman Durdin to drive about Hankow in his 1925 Ford, collect as many correspondents as possible, and bring them to the YMCA for the news conference. Durdin's ancient Ford repeatedly broke down, but by 10:30 in the morning it reached the YMCA. Tong handed the reporters Chiang's statement:

> The shifting of our armed forces on this occasion marks a turning point in our struggle from the defensive to the offensive. It also marks a beginning of a change in the tide of the war. For the key to victorious conclusion of our war of resistance lies not in what happens in Wuhan, but in the conservation of our strength for continuous resistance. Ours is a nation of vast territory, huge population, and large resources. The wider the sphere of hostilities extends, the stronger will become our active position.[47]

As the Chinese soldiers demolished key structures, McDaniel felt the shudder of explosions throughout the city. The Chinese destroyed the Japanese consulate, along with Japanese navy headquarters and a large ironworks. McDaniel reported the Americans, British, French, and Italians landed a handful of sailors and marines to protect the lives of Westerners. The *Luzon* deployed thirty American sailors. The British and American gunboats hugged the waterfront even as low-flying Japanese planes roared over them. But unlike a year earlier at Nanking, when the Japanese sank the *Panay*, this time the Japanese guns were silent. "Ravaged by fire and explosions and virtually bereft of defenders, Hankow was an easy objective for the Japanese armies massing at her gates," McDaniel wrote. He telegraphed the story to the United States, but for some reason it was delayed, and by the time it appeared in newspapers, a Japanese column had entered the northern outskirts of the city.[48]

A four-year-old Chinese girl was among the first to meet the advancing Japanese. McDaniel watched as Japanese soldiers searched the girl before shooing her away. A Catholic priest met the Japanese and explained that the international community had established a safety zone to protect the lives of Westerners. Those boundaries would soon be ignored by the Japanese.[49]

Pandemonium erupted in parts of the city. Japanese soldiers broke into shops just south of Hankow, leaving Chungshan Road littered with debris.[50] At one point, McDaniel found himself surrounded by hundreds of refugees seeking to be protected by Western troops. The sidewalks were so clogged that McDaniel could not find room to walk. Japanese planes bombed Chinese soldiers retreating from the battered city. McDaniel saw Japanese destroyers and gunboats pass one of the Italian gunboats, which dipped its colors in a courtesy salute. By the evening of October 27, US embassy officials counted thirty-five Japanese warships and transports offshore.[51]

Although the Japanese had promised to honor the international zone, in a matter of days they scrambled throughout the area looking for Chinese soldiers. Within sight of the *Luzon*, the Japanese shot at least twenty Chinese soldiers. In Wuchang, Japanese soldiers swept into homes and buildings. They seized jewelry and money, and loaded trucks with stolen furniture.[52]

For three consecutive days, while the Japanese plundered homes and offices, heavy rains drenched the city. There was no escape from misery. Gathering news was becoming impossible. Nationalist officials were gone, and the Japanese military spokesmen "maintained silence," forcing correspondents to glean the latest news by monitoring radio reports from Shanghai, Manila, and Hong Kong.[53] It was time to go. On the afternoon of November 4, Yates and Natalie joined a dozen other correspondents heading to the airfield, where a Japanese military plane awaited. The reporters brought so many suitcases that a Japanese naval officer objected, warning their luggage would overload the plane. Natalie quickly took charge. Speaking Japanese, she persuaded the officer to allow the baggage on the plane. The reporters, who included Yates, Arch Steele, Jack Belden, Victor Keen of the *New York Herald Tribune*, George Hogg of United Press, and Colin McDonald of the *Times* of London, boarded the aircraft. When they landed in Shanghai, reporters from the English-language papers descended upon them. McDaniel and his colleagues said more than 100,000 people were left in a city that once was home to 1.5 million. The rest had fled, leaving the city "quiet, but deserted."

Most of the reporters had left Hankow, but United Press asked Doris Rubens, an American who arrived in Hankow just a few weeks earlier, if she wanted to remain. She "jumped at what" she "thought would be a real chance at last to help the Chinese people by reporting the truth." Graham Barrow of Reuters also stayed. Unlike in Nanking, this time McDaniel was not the last to leave.[54]

McDaniel finished the year with a trip to Nanking. He had persuaded Japanese officials to allow him to check on the furniture and other belongings Natalie had sent from their house to a warehouse. He arrived to find Japanese soldiers had pried open the warehouse's skylights and looted everything in the building. Japanese soldiers had bayoneted their overstuffed chairs, mattresses, and wooden furniture. The ruined remnants had been left to rot under the open skylights. Everything else was gone, including Yates and Natalie's wedding presents, drapes, and silver. Yates learned a Japanese officer had seized his car.

Yates and Natalie filed a series of claims against the Japanese government, but they knew it was futile. For the next three years, Yates and Natalie "lived out of our suitcases" while on assignment to Hong Kong, Bangkok, and Haiphong. Natalie joked they would not even buy an ashtray for fear the Japanese eventually would get their hands on it.[55]

# HONG KONG

hortly after New Year's Day in 1939, McDaniel won an assignment that any foreign correspondent would covet. The AP transferred him from Shanghai back to Hong Kong, where McDaniel had been briefly stationed in 1937. From Hong Kong, McDaniel not only could cover Japan's aggressive moves in China and French Indochina but also would be in the right spot if Japan opted to seize Hong Kong from the British, who were distracted by Germany's efforts to gobble up Czechoslovakia.[1]

Whether by design or improvisation, Japan's ultimate goal was to control the major ports of Shanghai, Hong Kong, and Haiphong in Indochina, which would allow Tokyo to dominate the economy of Asia, including most exports to the West. It also would achieve the dreams of Japanese nationalists to emerge as the preeminent Asian power and protector of the Asians against the Westerners, whom Japan blamed for plundering the Far East.

The British were just as determined to hang on to Hong Kong. Precisely how was another matter, but they talked tough. The British mined the entrances to the harbor, installed artillery on the coast, and set up barbed wire and machine guns on the beaches. Maj. Gen. Arthur Grasett, a Canadian-born officer who commanded all British forces in China, said it "is our intention to defend the colony to the end."[2]

But the British faced many challenges, and not just from Japan. Hong Kong's very location made it vulnerable. Much of its food and water came from mainland China, which made it easy for a determined invader to starve the population into submission. Filing a story just before he vanished trying to reach the United States in a daring voyage on a Chinese junk, travel writer Richard Halliburton wrote, "The Japanese can take the place at their own convenience." One British soldier concluded, "Hong Kong was an isolated, unprepared military death trap."[3]

Once again, the Japanese would follow Yates and Natalie.

Known as 香港, the name "Hong Kong" is a phonetic translation of Cantonese, meaning "fragrant harbor." To Westerners, Hong Kong's capital, Victoria, was "one of the world's most beautiful and picturesque cities."[4] Madame Chiang's older sister Soong Ai-ling kept a large home there, and Madame Chiang often visited to escape Chungking's miserable weather.[5] Located just off the coast of China, Hong Kong was also one of the world's most important harbors. In a typical year, more than 50,000 ships arrived or departed from Hong Kong carrying cotton, silk, tin, wool, leather, and sugar.[6] By 1938, Hong Kong's exports to the United States had doubled from three years earlier. [7]

When the British seized Hong Kong in 1841 in the aftermath of the Opium War, the island was a hilly fishing village and home to a handful of pirates. The British quickly crushed the pirates and set about building an English-style city, which they named Victoria. They constructed elegant new homes and even went so far as to ship tons of English topsoil to build lavish gardens, prompting British residents to refer to Hong Kong as a "little bit of England." By 1938, Hong Kong's population had grown to more than 1.3 million, most of them Chinese who had moved from the mainland. Just 23,000 Westerners lived on the island, but they held the most-important government posts.[8] The police force was composed of British, Indian, and Chinese officers but always was led by a British official. Rickshaws carried Westerners to exquisite hotels such as the Repulse Bay Hotel, with its stunning view of the beaches. Glamorous young Chinese women wore "printed silk dresses slit up the side in the traditional manner" and adopted Western styles with "their black hair cut short."[9]

There was another, less opulent side to Hong Kong. The city was two completely different worlds occupying a single island. Near the harbor were crowded streets "like a bustling colorful country fair," where you rarely heard a word of English. "On the Peak above the city there are big comfortable homes, cool breezes, and that air of peaceful stuffiness which is the hallmark of British colonial existence."[10] Peak Tramways Limited advertised that its cable cars could scoop people up near the harbor for a "thrilling, romantic," and "scenic" ride to the top of the Peak—day or night.[11] Martha Gellhorn, with her "usual way of looking at a society from the bottom rather than from the top," discovered brothels, opium dens that looked like "sad little rooms," and a "dank ill-lit basement factory" where children carved out ivory balls to sell to tourists.[12] She wrote that "to newcomers, Hong Kong seems like a combination of Times Square on New Year's Eve, the subway at five-thirty in the afternoon, a three-alarm fire, a public auction and a country fair. Bursting out of the mountains or outlined against the sky, are the vast white palaces of the rich. The Peak dwellers can see all the beauty of their harbor and their terraced city, but they can neither hear it nor smell it." Gellhorn wrote that far too many of the Chinese lived "eight-to-ten in one room. The city smells of people. It smells also of Chinese cooking and old sweaty clothes, of dust and refuse in gutters, and of dirty water in drainless houses."[13]

Hong Kong was humid, but the wealthy found relief because of the "cool breezes" in their homes on the Peak.[14] Nobody, however, could be completely safe from typhoons, which swept through the island. In the fall of 1937, 125-mile-per-hour winds killed more than 500, littering streets "with the debris of shattered windows, collapsed walls, blown-down signs, and the wrecks of automobiles."[15]

McDaniel knew the Japanese were preparing to expand their empire, either in French Indochina or Hainan, a huge Chinese island less than 300 miles from Hong Kong. In 1937, just before the Marco Polo Bridge incident, McDaniel had written about the endless economic possibilities Hainan offered China, particularly the right soil and temperature to produce rubber. The Nationalists recognized the "strategic possibilities" of Hainan, which McDaniel pointed out was close to Hong Kong, where the British were building "an impregnable fortress. A thousand miles due south is Britain's great naval base of Singapore. Midway between is Cam Ranh Bay, which France is fortifying to protect its Indochina coastline."[16] More than two million people lived on Hainan, only 15 miles off the Chinese mainland and only 750 miles from the American-occupied Philippines. Madame Chiang's father was born on the island and moved to the United States in 1878. Joseph Grew, the US ambassador to Tokyo, warned Secretary of State Hull that if Japan transformed Hainan "into a well-equipped naval and air base, this island will dominate the whole coast of the mainland between Hong Kong and the southern tip of the Indo-China peninsula. Its holders can check all traffic into and out of Hanoi if a blockade were desired and possession of it by the Japanese would have a great effect on the matter of control of the South China Sea between the mainland and the Island of Luzon." In addition, US officials worried about the fate of American missionaries on the island.[17]

By attacking Hainan, Japan risked a confrontation with France and Great Britain because Tokyo had pledged not to occupy the island. But after Nanking and Hankow, Japan's leaders were convinced neither Western power would do anything more than launch verbal protests. As early as 1937, Freda Utley warned that "Japan considers herself strong enough, or England and the USA weak enough, for her to strike out on her own." In February 1939, Japanese naval forces landed troops on Hainan and swiftly occupied the entire island, McDaniel wrote from Hong Kong.[18]

Unlike his reporting from Nanking and Hankow, where he was at the center of the conflict, McDaniel was forced to write about an invasion 293 miles away. He needed a lucky break to offer the personal brand of reporting that was his specialty. And in a few days, he got one. US officials sent the old four-stack destroyer *John D. Edwards* to Hainan to evacuate American missionaries. When the *Edwards* arrived in Hong Kong, McDaniel was waiting. He met Luella R. Tappan, whose husband, the Rev. David Tappan, founded the Hainan Christian Middle School. McDaniel persuaded her to write a first-person account of the Japanese occupation of Hainan.

Mrs. Tappan wrote that on the morning of February 10, they were jarred awake by "the sound of bombs exploding, planes whirring and machine guns rattling." They quickly hid behind "stoutest" walls for protection: "All was noise and confusion until noon, when our radio picked up Hong Kong broadcasting an announcement that the Japanese were landing on Hainan. The tumult finally gave way to the rumbling of tanks and the tramp of completely equipped Japanese soldiers."

She was impressed with the efficiency of the Japanese troops and contrasted them to the Chinese soldiers defending the island, who "evaporated into thin air."

That afternoon, a Japanese officer made his way to the mission gates. He scribbled Chinese characters in the road's dust, asking the location of an unused airfield. The Japanese then carried equipment ranging from tents to wind vanes and occupied the huge field that Chinese farmers had been using to plant sweet potatoes. The Japanese leveled the crop and, Mrs. Tappan reported, within twenty-four hours planes were taking off and landing. She wrote that "there was a minimum of fighting and bloodshed," but she saw a bus filled with Chinese civilians accidentally drive into an area manned by Japanese troops, who opened fire with machine guns. She then watched Japanese soldiers loot Chinese civilians of furniture and pigs. But the Japanese soldiers tried to keep her mission safe by posting "keep out" notices.[19]

As Yates and Natalie settled in Hong Kong, Yates's parents were more than 750 miles away in Shanghai. Charles was trying his best to keep the academies open in Soochow, but he was writing fewer letters to America, a sure sign of the strain he was under. During the winter of 1939, Nannie's hostility toward the Japanese intensified. She was also growing impatient with Americans who did not believe that the Far East war would eventually involve the United States.

In January 1939, Nannie sent a friend in the United States an article from the *New York Times* written by an American businessman in Shanghai, with the headline "Japan's attack on America in the Far East." Nannie wrote that "contrary to Japanese propaganda, the war is not all but over in China. The fighting strength of the Chinese Army has been preserved intact, and the Chinese national spirit to drive the invader from the land was never stronger."

Nannie wrote that "Americans here feel the maintenance of America's position in the Far East is vitally important, not just because of the values of our China trade, business investments in China . . . but because America's whole future as a Pacific power . . . is involved." She said, "It is our firm belief that it is still not too late to stop Japan's mad military leaders in their wild career in defiance of humanity and all treaty obligations." Then she added a stern warning: "Americans should remember that the China 'Incident' is only one step towards war with America in the avowed plans of these same Japanese leaders."[20]

Nannie's belief that Japan was willing to go to war with the United States stood in stark contrast to Yates's views. Her son was still convinced that Japan wanted to avoid a conflict with America at all costs.

In the winter of 1940, Yates and Natalie traveled to the United States, his first real vacation in eleven years. They sailed from Shanghai on the 22,000-ton liner *President Coolidge*, which could carry as many as 1,000 passengers and steamed at 20 knots. Its real attraction was its art deco interior and air-conditioned first-class staterooms. The *President Coolidge* featured a barber shop, beauty salon, indoor movie theater, gymnasium, soda fountain, telephones, and two outdoor swimming pools.

Among those making the voyage was Sir Victor Sassoon, who was visiting the Hollywood studios in Los Angeles. When the liner docked in San Francisco on February 1, reporters and photographers swarmed about Yates, Natalie, and Sir Victor. McDaniel, whose reporting from Nanking had made him something of a celebrity, told the reporters it would be difficult for Japan to conquer all of China: "It's a matter of sheer space and population that they cannot lick. They have found they can win battles and campaigns with limited objectives, but it seems they have little intention or prospect of driving through to the western border of China and throwing the Chinese forces out bodily." McDaniel's description of Japan's objectives in China was spot on, but his insistence that Japan wanted the United States as "their friendly neighbor" was a fundamental misreading of Tokyo's plans.[21]

Yates and Natalie rested for a few days in San Francisco before boarding a train that eventually would take them to Boston to visit Natalie's relatives. But the Associated Press expected its bureau chiefs to deliver speeches, and planned an itinerary that would culminate at a gathering of newspaper publishers in New York City, where Yates would speak.[22]

Yates and Natalie reached Des Moines on February 9 as the temperature plunged to 5 degrees above zero in the early-morning hours. A light ground fog mixed with smog limited visibility to a few blocks downtown. William Wesley Waymack, winner of the 1938 Pulitzer Prize and editor of the *Des Moines Register*, greeted McDaniel at the *Register*'s offices. Once again, McDaniel assured everyone that Japan did not want war with the United States: "The middle-of-the-road class in Japan wants to do everything possible to avoid any further weakening in the relations of the United States and Japan." He added, "The United States is the one nation Japan fears."

"At present, there is no reason to fear a direct attack, nor do I think there will be as long as the international situation remains as it is," McDaniel said. The slaughter he had seen in China convinced him of the utter waste of warfare. He hoped the United States would avoid any moves "that might take this country into the futile destruction of armed conflict."[23]

Yates and Natalie arrived in New York in April, where he was among the featured speakers at the annual meeting of the Associated Press and American Newspaper Publishers Association at the Waldorf-Astoria in midtown Manhattan. Just about everyone who was anyone in American journalism attended the luncheon in the hotel's grand ballroom—Col. Robert McCormick, publisher of the isolationist *Chicago Tribune*; Frank Knox, publisher of the *Chicago Daily News*, who was soon to join the Roosevelt administration as secretary of the Navy; Robert McLean, publisher of the *Philadelphia Bulletin* and president of the Associated Press; Frank Noyes, president of the *Washington Star*; and Kent Cooper, the AP's general manager.

After a toast to the president of the United States, McLean said he wanted the audience to hear from four Associated Press reporters covering the war in Europe and Asia. McLean called it "staff day" and introduced the panelists—McDaniel, London bureau chief J. C. Clark, Wade Werner, who covered the Soviet invasion of Finland, and Lloyd Lehrbas, who reported on the German invasion of Poland in 1939.[24]

Cooper then stood and reminded the audience of the dangers these correspondents faced. "The wholesale devastation of fortified and unfortified regions has left no place of reasonable safety for the war correspondent," he said. "The war correspondent of yesterday has disappeared. In his place is the modern, active news reporter in the field."

McDaniel was the third reporter to speak. He said the war in the Far East "hasn't really begun yet," a clear warning Japan and China would be fighting for years. "Japan still has a million men or more on the Asian mainland who are quite capable of doing a lot of damage," McDaniel told the audience. "China has several million soldiers and more armament than she started the war with. These immense forces are now sparring, their generals waiting for the right moment to deliver their blows."[25]

The McDaniels enjoyed themselves for the next two months in New York. Yates worked on the cable desk in the New York bureau and dined with colleagues, including one evening with DeWitt Mackenzie, the AP's *Wide World's* war analyst, who described McDaniel as "a grand young fellow."[26]

In early June, Yates and Natalie embarked on the long trip back to Hong Kong. They went by train to San Francisco, where on June 8 they once again boarded the *President Coolidge*, which sailed first to Honolulu, followed by scheduled stops in Yokohama, Shanghai, and Hong Kong. The passengers included a host of people McDaniel would have known, such as Hugh Grant, the new US ambassador to Thailand; Ray Scott, a *Life* magazine newsreel photographer heading for Chungking; Violet Haven, who had worked in Japan as a newspaperwoman; and Charles Cooper, the American vice consul in Chungking.[27]

The *President Coolidge* docked at the end of June in Hong Kong, where McDaniel immediately found himself in the middle of a clash between Japan and Great Britain. The Japanese were applying intense pressure on the British to shut down the 755-mile-long Burma Road, a vital supply line that linked southern China to the port of Rangoon—where it was so hot and sweaty "you felt you could cut the heat and hold it like chunks of wet blotting paper," as Martha Gellhorn described. A railway ran from Rangoon to Lashio, where goods were transferred to the Burma Road, which wound its way through the mountains to southern China.[28]

With tensions rising between the Japanese and British, McDaniel reported that the *President Coolidge*, which had just left Hong Kong for Manila, had been recalled "on orders from Washington" to evacuate Americans from the British colony. According to McDaniel, 1,500 wives and children of British service members were scheduled to depart for Manila. British warships would escort the liner. The evacuation, he wrote, was "a precaution against possible Japanese enforcement of a land and sea blockade of the colony to underscore demands for the closing of the Burma route to China for war supplies."[29]

Japan was relying on the chaos in Europe—where the French and Dutch had surrendered to Germany, and Great Britain was fighting alone against Adolf Hitler—to force French, Dutch, and British concessions in Indochina. From Tokyo, US ambassador Grew cabled Hull that "the Japanese are well aware that Great Britain is now impotent in the Far East."[30] The British had fewer than 2,000 troops to defend all of Burma. They relied largely on rifles, and when one American showed them a Thompson submachine gun, a British soldier told a reporter in astonishment, "Oh, so that's a Tommy gun."[31]

In the middle of July, against the wishes of Secretary of State Hull and Chiang Kai-shek, Britain closed the Burma Road for three months. While the move averted an immediate armed clash with Japan, a spokesman for Chiang tartly declared, "The British authorities have in this hour of China's gravest need taken a decision which will be long remembered and deeply resented by all patriotic Chinese."[32]

Japan's more immediate target was the feeble Vichy French government in the Indochina capital of Hanoi, which lacked the soldiers and equipment to repel a Japanese attack on France's Indochina Empire. Japan was pulled in competing directions. The Japanese government hoped to avoid an armed conflict with the pro-German Vichy government, but the Japanese military wanted to seize bases throughout Indochina. In the summer of 1940, the Japanese sent Gen. Issaku Nishihara, a French-speaking former military attaché in Paris, to negotiate with the French government in Hanoi.

In early September, McDaniel reported the French and Japanese had reached a "preliminary" agreement to permit the Japanese to send troops to Haiphong, a vital port on the South China Sea. If the agreement were finalized, McDaniel wrote, it "would open up for Japan a great new avenue of attack on the forces" of Chiang Kai-shek in southern China.[33]

But negotiations stalled when Japanese airplanes flew over a French military garrison at Lang Son at the northern tip of Indochina. With the possibility of war breaking out between Japan and France, Yates and Natalie flew to Hanoi to be at the center of the action. They joined up with Arch Steele of the *Chicago Daily News* and Mel Jacoby, a young reporter for United Press. Their favorite gathering place was the bar at the Metropole Hotel, a structure of French colonial design built in 1901. Although Alice-Leone Moats of *Collier's* thought it was a "grimy place with lumpy beds," it was the best Hanoi offered, and its past visitors included Somerset Maugham, Charles Chaplin, and Paulette Goddard. Jacoby often spent six hours a day in the hotel lobby, buying "drink after drink" in an effort to "pick up news tips."[34]

Befuddled French officials did not seem to know what to do with the American reporters. The French had created a confusing system in which censors held up stories for anywhere from ten to forty hours before allowing the cable office to send them out. But French officials soon adapted. They assigned an English-speaking aide to Adm. Jean Decoux, the French governor general of Indochina, to conduct regular news briefings for McDaniel, Steele, and Jacoby. Each day at eleven in the morning and six in the evening, the reporters gathered at the elegant residence of the governor general, an imposing yellow structure built by the French at the turn of the century. The three reporters peppered the French aide with questions, largely based on tips they had picked up. He tried to be helpful, although Jacoby joked at times that he denied events the reporters had seen themselves. As soon as the briefing concluded, the reporters wrote their dispatches "right in the government building" and sent them to censors.[35]

The reporters developed other sources as well. On September 16, McDaniel cited unnamed sources saying the Japanese army might send troops into Indochina without "any resistance by the French." The French were in such a weakened state,

McDaniel wrote, the "feeling is widespread that only the United States might deter Japan, but authoritative sources said the fear of arousing Japanese feelings has kept Indochina authorities from making any appeal to Washington." McDaniel believed that the French officials were frustrated because they could not stand up to the Japanese. Adm. Decoux, in particular, was "very bitter." The whole French head-quarters was enveloped with a "defeatist, gloomy attitude."[36]

French officials in Hanoi told McDaniel that "Japan's real purpose is to secure a foothold in Indochina as the first major move of her long-heralded southward expansion." Japan could then employ long-range aircraft to cut the Burma Road. They also would move closer to the tin, rubber, and oil of the Dutch East Indies and Malaya, all badly needed by the Japanese army and navy. Speaking to reporters during a short visit to Los Angeles, Arch Steele said that Japan "still covets" the Dutch East Indies, and that the "biggest deterrent" to the Japanese "is the United States."[37]

Adm. Thomas Hart, commander of the US Asiatic Fleet in Manila, warned Adm. Harold Stark, chief of US naval operations, that "a Japanese attack on British or Dutch possessions, or both, is a most likely development, unless the Japs are fairly certain that we will intervene." Hart cautioned that Japan would either attack the Dutch East Indies or the British "either wholly water-borne direct against Singapore or step by step—Indochina, Thailand, Burma and Malaya to Singapore."[38]

This echoed an earlier message to Stark from RAdm. Walter Anderson, chief of US naval intelligence, that clearly was based on intercepts of Japanese diplomatic communications. Anderson wrote that Kensuke Horinouchi, the Japanese ambassador to the United States, told Tokyo that "the United States is incapable of taking action at the present time to prevent Japanese seizure of the Dutch possessions in the Far East and that no time should be lost in effecting such a seizure. The Japanese Consul General at Batavia has on two recent occasions urged the early seizure of the Dutch possessions by Japan, and this advice is echoed by the diplomatic head of the Japanese Economic Mission that is now in the East Indies. Within the last few days the Japanese Ambassador at London has added his advice to those urging early action to seize the Dutch East Indies."[39]

The possibility of US intervention was zero. If Americans were unwilling to enter the war as an ally of Great Britain in 1940, they had even less appetite to become entangled with Japanese forces in Indochina. The US had only a few thousand troops in the Philippines and fewer than 200 aircraft at Clark, Nielson, and Nichols airfields. Many were obsolete P-35 and P-26 fighters. The US Asiatic Fleet, under Hart, consisted of thirteen four-stack destroyers from World War I, and twenty-seven submarines armed with torpedoes that often failed to explode. The heavy cruiser *Houston* was scheduled to arrive in Manila on November 19, but she would be hopelessly outgunned by Japan's battle fleet of ten battleships, ten aircraft carriers, eighteen heavy cruisers, and 113 destroyers.

Brushing off worries of American intervention, the Japanese intensified their demands on Vichy French authorities, who were doing their best to stall Japan. On

September 19, Charles Reed, the American consul in Hanoi, cabled Hull that Gen. Nishihara demanded that French officials allow the Japanese to occupy Hanoi with 20,000 troops and Haiphong with 5,000 troops, and to deploy additional forces to seize five airports: "Unless the demand is accepted, Japanese armed forces will invade Indochina Sunday night September 22, 10 p.m."

The next day, at a news conference attended by McDaniel, Nishihara said he was taking a special train from Hanoi to Haiphong, where he would board a ship to Japan. "When I leave French territory, you may say a crisis has been reached," Nishihara said. The general insisted that Japan was not threatening the territorial integrity of the French colony, although none of the Western reporters believed him. Given the military realities, Vichy French officials capitulated, allowing the Japanese to occupy three air bases and station 6,000 troops near the Gulf of Tonkin.[40]

Reed cabled Hull that French officials warned "the Japanese would endeavor eventually to push towards the south, thus endangering Singapore and the Philippines."[41]

Japanese troops—"in full war kit," according to McDaniel—launched separate attacks against French troops in Lang Son, 80 miles northwest of Hanoi. McDaniel reported that twelve Japanese planes flew above Hanoi and Tonkin, although French antiaircraft guns held their fire. The planes flew off without dropping bombs.[42]

McDaniel followed Nishihara to Haiphong. The agreement between the Japanese and the French allowed Japan to land troops on September 26 at the mouth of the Red River, which opened up to the Gulf of Tonkin. In an effort to soothe tensions, the French made barracks available for the Japanese troops. But before they even landed, three Japanese planes appeared ominously above Haiphong and bombed a railroad crossing, killing fifteen Vietnamese civilians and forcing others to scramble for shelter under nearby trees. At noon, McDaniel watched 2,000 Japanese troops land. Behind a formation of light tanks, the Japanese tramped to the barracks, occasionally exchanging "curt" salutes with French officials. The Japanese commander apologized for the bombing, insisting it had been a mistake.[43]

McDaniel was back in Hanoi on October 1 as French survivors from Lang Son arrived by train, trucks, and planes. The Japanese had captured the commanding French general, his staff, and more than 2,000 French and colonial troops and were feeding them one bowl of rice every day. One French officer told McDaniel his post had only a handful of machine guns and mortars to repel Japanese tanks. Another officer said he was forced to blow up his heavy 155 mm guns after the Japanese attacked from the rear. A third officer said his machine guns killed scores of Japanese trying to cross a bridge, but the Japanese continued to attack by leaping over the pile of bodies.[44]

A few days later, McDaniel reported 2,100 French prisoners were returned to Hanoi.[45] That same day, Reed cabled Hull, "It appears fairly certain that the release was predicated on new concessions to the Japanese as regards Hanoi." He also notified Washington that 200 Japanese soldiers were already in Hanoi.[46]

The Japanese amphibious landing in Haiphong and the speed of the Japanese advance in Indochina left its mark on McDaniel. On his own initiative, he drafted a report on the Japanese tactics. When he finished, he decided he would give it to the British army at the first opportunity.[47]

The British and Americans watched the Japanese moves in Indochina with mounting alarm. While trying to avoid war with Japan, Roosevelt struck back economically. On September 24, the US government said it would loan an additional $25 million to China. Two days later, Roosevelt announced an embargo beginning October 16 of all exports of scrap iron and steel to Japan. The British then said they would reopen the Burma Road on October 18, with one official in London privately acknowledging that closing the road had been a mistake, and that appeasement would not work with the Japanese. The British also announced that US warships were welcome to use the naval base in Singapore.[48]

The Japanese were furious. The day before the Burma Road was reopened, McDaniel interviewed Maj. Gen. Raishiro Sumita, chief of the Japanese military mission in Indochina, who warned that Japan "is resolutely determined to prevent war materials supplied by the United States or any third power from reaching Chiang Kai-shek's armies." Sumita vowed Japanese aircraft based in Indochina would "make the utmost effort to strike a fatal blow" against China's supply lines, although he insisted the attacks on the Burma Road would take place in China and not Burma. Sumita said, "If both the United States and Japan spent the same huge sums they now are devoting to preparations for a possible future conflict on promoting trade between the two countries, there would be no conceivable question of war. If only the United States would understand Japan's position." It was standard Japanese fare—the United States and Great Britain simply did not understand Japan and its need for natural resources.[49]

On November 17, McDaniel flew to Bangkok, although he hated to leave Natalie that Sunday morning. He took a room at the Oriental Hotel, Bangkok's oldest and most luxurious. He planned on boarding a flight the next morning to Lashio in Burma. But before he left, he took time to write Natalie:

> Believe me, I miss you badly, though I know this sort of a trip would be difficult in the extreme for you. So far I haven't seen any mosquitoes here, though my net is set up and my quinine bottle is out and ready to be dipped into. . . . Good night my darling and remember that I love you too dearly to stay away a day longer than is absolutely necessary.[50]

The next day, McDaniel reached Lashio, where freight was unloaded from trains and placed on trucks for the arduous 700-mile trip to the Chinese border. The Chinese considered the road vital to their survival, although Hallett Abend of the *New York Times* insisted the road was "greatly overrated for its military importance," adding it was of "less importance as a military supply line to the Chinese than was the Indo-Chinese railway."[51] Once again, McDaniel was about to take a major risk. Driving on the road was terrifying because it often was only one lane, and trucks had to navigate their way on the edge of huge cliffs. Traveling on the road in 1939, Carl Crow was horrified to see one truck topple into a deep ravine, never to be seen again.[52]

McDaniel reported that an average of 200 trucks left Lashio every day. Japanese planes attacked a number of the 500 bridges along the road, bombed some refueling stations, and strafed trucks. Yet, despite the attacks, a stream of military supplies were reaching China. The next day, McDaniel hitched a ride in a truck to the Chinese border, where the Japanese had bombed an aircraft production facility operated by the Americans: "Here the Americans erected a model American community for themselves and their Chinese workers in a place so remote that few Chinese have penetrated or been welcomed."[53]

Although Sumita had pledged that Japan would bomb only the Chinese section of the road, on November 23 an American diplomat in London reported to Hull that some bombs had fallen in Burma itself, adding, "The British are trying to put the best face they can on it and to act as though nothing had taken place."

The Japanese also launched efforts to intimidate the Western reporters trying to cover Indochina. On November 21, the Japanese arrested United Press correspondent Mel Jacoby and Robert Rinden, the US vice consul in Hanoi. Jacoby had photographed Japanese soldiers in Haiphong relaxing at a warehouse with an American flag nearby. As Jacoby and Rinden drove away, Japanese soldiers chased after them, forced the two out of their car, seized Jacoby's camera, and prevented them from entering a hotel near the center of Haiphong. After a few hours, the Japanese released them. But even as late as December 13, Reed reported to Hull that "the Japanese were bringing great pressure to force Jacoby to leave the country."[54]

Even as McDaniel was reporting from Hanoi, his bosses in New York pressed him to move to Singapore. "New York apparently had it in its head that Singapore would be a hot spot," McDaniel said years later. The AP had only a few stringers in Singapore, and its editors wanted a full-time bureau chief. Reuters had a bureau in Singapore, and United Press planned to transfer Harold Guard from Hong Kong to open one as well. For months, McDaniel stalled, arguing that Indochina remained a big story. Finally, in November 1940, the AP sent him a direct order: Proceed to Singapore as quickly as possible.[55]

# SINGAPORE, 1941

O n December 1, 1940, Yates and Natalie boarded a train in Bangkok for the two-day trip down the Malay Peninsula to Singapore. The train chugged through the western edge of Malaya, past Penang and Kuala Lumpur, before crossing the narrow Straits of Johore into Singapore.

With his arrival, McDaniel became the first US reporter to work full time in Singapore. He quickly called on Gen. Lionel Bond at his office at Fort Canning. He found Bond, who commanded all British ground forces in Singapore and Malaya, to be "refreshingly different" from other British commanders, who tended to be on the stuffy side. Bond ordered his staff to cooperate with Yates. The general and his staff, while acknowledging that London was "preoccupied" with Nazi Germany as opposed to Singapore, believed that the United States could help "prevent the Japanese from pushing down" from Indochina to threaten Singapore. They even expressed the hope that Japan would "hit the Russians instead" in the Soviet Union.

They also chatted about the Japanese amphibious landing in Haiphong that McDaniel covered earlier in the fall. McDaniel handed Bond a copy of the ten-page report he had drafted. Bond promised to turn it over to British intelligence.[1]

For more than a century, Singapore had been an exotic symbol of the British Empire. Joseph Conrad and Rudyard Kipling were drawn to the city. Somerset Maugham's years in Singapore inspired to him write *The Letter*, a short story in which the wife of a Malayan planter shoots her lover because he left her for a Chinese woman. Maugham turned it into a play, and Jeanne Eagels and Bette Davis played the title role of the wife, Leslie Crosbie, in films produced in 1929 and 1940. Charles Chaplin visited Singapore twice, the second time in 1936, when he was accompanied by his glamorous fiancé, Paulette Goddard. They arrived just a month before Chaplin's *Modern Times* was shown at Singapore's Capitol Theatre.

The city of 750,000 had a harbor that opened to passageways to India, China, and Australia, allowing the British to export tin and rubber. The Strait of Malacca, which separated Singapore from Sumatra, led into the Indian Ocean toward the British colony of India. To the east was a shipping lane into the South China Sea to ports in China, the Philippines, and Japan. And to the southwest was a lane through the Java Sea that led to Australia.

The British were a distinct minority. Singapore was home to 600,000 Chinese as well as thousands of Malayans and Indians. But the British held the key posts in the government, military, and the police and managed the rubber plantations.

Martha Gellhorn nailed the city's singular allure. "Every luxury is on sale, from perfume to champagne," adding with approval that the city "is one of the few places left in the world where you can still eat fresh caviar." In the summer of 1941, Gellhorn wrote in *Collier's* that "Singapore is like a movie about itself. It has everything: The deadly heat, rickshaws and Rolls-Royces, the native kampongs, Chinatown, low dance halls, the country club for white gentry, beautiful houses, Indian officers with beards and bright turbans, Australian troops in rough-rider hats, English officers like actors impersonating English officers, Chinese taxi-dancers, elegant milky-skinned ladies, planes roaring overhead, Malayan royalty, orchids for five cents a bunch, Pahits, gin slings, gossip, intrigue, parties, and a possible war." The poorer sections where the Chinese lived were another matter. Chaplin's brother Syd thought the sanitation in those areas so bad, he quipped that the city should be called "Stinkapore."

No matter the season, the temperature hovered around a sticky 90 degrees. Although George Weller of the *Chicago Daily News* insisted that the temperature was "never so insufferable" as New York City in midsummer, Arch Steele disagreed, writing that the British "surrendered to the heat and the ennui by drowning their care in whiskey and gin."[2]

For reporters such as McDaniel, Singapore was a journalistic paradise. For the latest information, McDaniel stopped by the Adelphi Hotel, at the corner of Coleman Street and North Bridge Road. Chaplin and Goddard stayed on the top floor of the Adelphi in 1936, with the fashionably dressed Goddard attracting scores of photographers and ordinary citizens as she was whisked about the city in a rickshaw.[3] The Adelphi's popular grill offered "excellent food and courteous service," a famous roof garden, and influential residents, including O'Dowd Gallagher of the *London Daily Express*, Tillman Durdin of the *New York Times*, and his wife, Peggy—a foreign correspondent for *Time*. The hotel had a well-deserved reputation as a center of intrigue with its blend of Japanese spies, British agents, and French Resistance members who had fled Indochina. As a member of the French Resistance in 1941, Pierre Boulle, who later wrote the novel *The Bridge on the River Kwai*, rendezvoused with another Resistance member at the Adelphi to hatch a plan to train soldiers in Indochina.[4]

Another handy gathering place was the Long Bar and café at the Raffles Hotel, which first opened in 1887 and now billed itself as "Malaya's Premier Hotel." Its most famous drink was the Singapore Sling, a concoction of pink gin adorned with a cherry and a slice of pineapple. In the middle of September, the Raffles featured an evening of music from the Argyll and Sutherland Highlanders in its outdoor Palm Court, where a favorite was Gin Pahits, a mixture of gin and bitters.[5] A large sign politely but firmly informed visitors that dancers had to wear formal evening attire. For the best wine and food, the place to go was Cyranos Restaurant, despite the fears of senior British officials that some of their officers were providing crucial information "into the ears of attractive women who hung around there."[6]

On Sunday mornings, the "thing to do," as Gallagher said, was to drive to the Seaview Hotel, which boasted that its covered ballroom was "perfectly air conditioned by sea breezes."[7] There, reporters and guests drank Pahits, beer, rum, and whiskey and sodas while a band played. At the end of the morning meal, the band struck up "There'll Always Be an England," and the crowd joined in to sing. For those unfamiliar with the lyrics, waiters discreetly placed cards on every table with the words. Then it was off to lunch.[8]

The reporters themselves were "big news," as one Singapore newspaper noted. "Their presence here has ensured for Singapore a world-wide reading public," the *Singapore Free Press* wrote. The paper pointed out that such well-known reporters as McDaniel, Steele, Carl Mydans of *Life*, and Harold Guard of United Press were in the city. But the paper appeared particularly enthusiastic about the pending arrival of Ernest Hemingway and Martha Gellhorn.[9]

There also were the sophisticated events to attend, such as a swimming party at the sultan of Johore's palace that Yates, Natalie, and other Westerners attended. Yates and Natalie were among a large group of the best of Singapore society invited to the Capitol Theatre by the Chinese general consul. First, they were treated to a showing in the ornamental auditorium of the Chinese film *The Light of Asia*, which described Japan's invasion of China. When the film ended, the guests made their way through the first-floor café to the restaurant, where they were served Pahits. Natalie dazzled the crowd of British army officers and Singapore civilian officials by wearing what was described as an "American flair"—a persimmon-red crepe dress "distinguished by its Fifth Avenue cut" and a wide-brimmed red straw hat.[10]

In the fall of 1941, Yates and Natalie, having lived like nomads in hotels since leaving Nanking, yearned for a real home. They bought furniture and rented their own place in the new Cathay Building, which at sixteen stories was Singapore's tallest building—the "jewel in the treasure chest of Singapore," as George Weller wrote. Yates asked for a room on the top floor, but hotel officials rejected his request because British soldiers used the top floor for communications and observation. It did not matter much, because from the balcony in their apartment on the fifteenth floor, Yates and Natalie had a stunning view of the harbor, the Straits of Johore, and the Sembawang Naval Base. The apartments offered the best in luxury, with hot and cold running water. There was a roof garden, indoor swimming pool, squash court, fifth-floor restaurant, and air-conditioned 1,321-seat film theater on the street level, which had opened two years earlier with the showing of Alexander Korda's *The Four Feathers*, an appropriate film for the British Empire. The theater, with its black marble pillars and green-tiled floors, offered comfortable armchairs and wide aisles between the rows of seats.[11]

The huge naval base included the world's largest floating drydock and a 1,000-foot-long dock on land, which Steele described as "the nearest thing to a man-made canyon I have seen."[12] It had taken more than six years to complete what the *Singapore Free Press* hailed as the piece de resistance of the base. It could accommodate the

48,000-ton battle cruiser *Hood*, the largest ship in the British navy. The British commemorated its opening in 1938 by inviting representatives of Australia, New Zealand, and Hong Kong, a signal the base would provide British dominions with absolute security. More than 11,000 people, including Malayan royalty, attended, and the British treated them to an impressive show. The aircraft carrier *Eagle* and forty-one other ships, including the American light cruisers *Trenton, Milwaukee,* and *Memphis,* sailed past the dock while more than sixty warplanes roared overhead. John Gunther wrote that the appearance of the three US cruisers "caused an outburst of speculation in Tokyo" that the Americans and British were allies in the Pacific. A single naval gun roared in celebration. Sir Shenton Thomas, the governor of the Straits Settlements, cut a ribbon at the base's entrance and hosted an elaborate dinner party for Adm. Julius Townsend, who commanded the US cruisers. As night fell, searchlights bathed the sky.[13]

To protect the sea approaches, the British installed five powerful 15-inch guns with armor-piercing shells that could strike enemy ships 21 miles away. "If you could take a 3,000-pound elephant and throw it . . . you could sense the power of the guns that defend Singapore," one official said.[14] During a demonstration, one reporter described the firing of one of the guns as "a huge belch of orange, doubly vivid against the green of palms and rubber trees." Using a stopwatch, the reporter discovered it took thirty-eight seconds for the shell to explode in the water 25,000 yards away. The British also added six 9.2-inch guns, normally used by World War I armored cruisers, and eighteen of the 6-inch guns used by light cruisers.[15]

The conventional wisdom was that the 15-inch guns made Singapore virtually impregnable. "No Japanese admiral is likely to risk his fleet in an attempt to prove otherwise," wrote David Waite of the *Singapore Free Press.* If war broke out, British naval units could swiftly steam to Singapore and take advantage of the most modern naval yard in the world.[16]

It was considered just as difficult for Japan to seize the island by an attack in Malaya. A sturdy causeway of concrete and stone linked Singapore to the 450-mile-long Malay Peninsula, whose British-operated plantations supplied much of the world's rubber. For years, military experts had believed that Malaya's heavy jungles made it unsuitable for tanks and masses of ground forces. But in fact, good roads and railways ran down the western side of Malaya, which allowed rubber to be exported through a key port near Penang on Malaya's western coast.[17]

Not long after his arrival in Singapore, McDaniel drove out to the base and was impressed. The base, he reported, had 10,000 British officers and engineers, along with Australian and New Zealand air force officers as well as Chinese, Malayan, and Indian workers. British Blenheim bombers roared overhead. McDaniel wrote that the British are "fast transforming Singapore from a potential defense base to a military powerhouse capable of supplying fighting energy to any part of the empire that might be threatened by the spread of the war to the southern Pacific." Sir Robert Brooke-Popham, commander of British air forces in the Far East, said, "We certainly could put up a good show against any enemy who might come against us."[18]

A few weeks later, McDaniel reported that the British had mined the east coast of Malaya to prevent any landing on the peninsula from the South China Sea.[19] The announcement was followed by the arrival of thousands of Australian troops, whom McDaniel described as "completely equipped" to guard the massive naval base. As they made their way off the ocean liners, the Australians sang "Waltzing Matilda" and flashed wide grins. They unloaded artillery and armored cars, and their arrival, McDaniel wrote, transformed the Malay Peninsula into "a veritable powerhouse of military energy." Maj. Gen. Gordon Bennett, commander of the Australians, said, "Your war is our war. Should any enemy come this way, Australia will be here."[20]

The following month, scores of British fighter pilots arrived to man planes at the RAF base adjacent to the naval yard and a grass airfield far up the east coast of Malaya at Kota Bharu, which theoretically gave the British the ability to strike Japanese units invading from Thailand or Japanese transport ships in the South China Sea. Brooke-Popham told McDaniel and other reporters that Britain's "greatly increased strength in the Far East is a threat to no one but is a great stabilizing force and influence for peace."[21]

The British troops and planes shipped into the Malay Peninsula reflected a change in British strategy. By June 1940, the British high command in London concluded that because of the development of long-range aircraft by the Japanese, they could no longer protect Singapore without defending Malaya as well. In a paper to the British War Cabinet, the British military chiefs predicted that Japan would avoid attacking Singapore by sea but instead would "attempt a landing up country in Malaya and then operate southwards under cover of shore-based aircraft" in Indochina. McDaniel almost certainly did not know about the top-secret report, but his own reporting made clear that the British intended to defend Singapore by holding Malaya. In an interview in April with Harold Guard of United Press, Gen. Bond, who was being replaced as commander of British forces in Singapore, warned that the threat of "invasion of Malaya definitely exists, and it would be foolish to think otherwise."[22]

During the first week of August, which was muggy and unbearably hot as usual, McDaniel was in the American consulate in the Union Building. Cecil Brown of CBS Radio had just arrived from the Middle East and introduced himself to McDaniel, who immediately took him upstairs to meet Cmdr. William Burrows, who dealt with the correspondents. The correspondents hated working with Burrows, who was notorious for using the dreaded blue pencil to censor even the most innocuous phrases. To make sure certain reporters did not change the copy after being read by the censor, British officials required them to place their stories in sealed envelopes before allowing them to head to the cable office.[23]

McDaniel usually worked his way around Burrows to cultivate good sources. One of his favorites was VAdm. Sir Geoffrey Layton, who commanded British naval forces in Southeast Asia. McDaniel had known Layton for years and often would stop by his office to "chew the fat."[24] Layton did not hold the Japanese military in contempt, as other senior British officers did. In a sober and realistic appraisal, Layton acknowledged, "I don't think we can defend Singapore indefinitely."[25] Another good source was Gen. Bennett, "a peppery type," McDaniel thought, who "looked like a field soldier" and "wanted the freedom to operate separately," which put him in conflict with Gen. Arthur Percival, the new commander of British, Australian, and Indian troops in Malaya. McDaniel thought Percival was a "scholarly, quiet type of soldier," a cultured and avid reader.[26] Others were more caustic. Alfred Duff Cooper, former First Lord of the Admiralty, described Percival as "a nice good man who began life as a schoolmaster. I am sometimes tempted to wish he had remained one." Megan Spooner, the wife of Adm. John Spooner, scathingly wrote in her diary that "Percival may have brains, but certainly is short of guts and decision."[27]

Bennett liked dealing with the press, which Brown discovered after he wasted time going through official channels seeking an interview with the Australian general. When they finally met, Bennett was astonished that Brown had any difficulty reaching him.

"You should call me direct," the general told the CBS Radio man. "I would see you any time."

Bennett showed Brown a map of Malaya with flags representing the position of Australian troops. "The English have a whole plan worked out with a series of points to retreat to. I won't train my men in retreating tactics. I won't let my men talk retreat. All we are going to do is attack." Brown sent the story to the British censors for clearance. Instead, Brown was summoned by Gen. Percival to his headquarters at Fort Canning.

"I cannot allow this story to go," Percival told Brown. "Gen. Bennett has no authority to comment on the conduct of the war. Moreover, you had no right to talk to Gen. Bennett."[28]

McDaniel had his own battles with censors. He was not as abrasive as Brown, who described Yates's style as "cool, dispassionate." But McDaniel was just as firm in his objections. Once a British censor killed a line in McDaniel's story that read "Wandering along the road today, I came upon a Shropshire lad." The soldier was from Shropshire, but the censor did not care. He focused on the mere fact there was a Shropshire regiment in the British army, and insisted the line had to go. "There's no Shropshire regiment here," McDaniel protested. In vain, he attempted to explain he was using a line from A. E. Housman's 1887 poem "A Shropshire Lad."[29]

In another incident of absurd censorship, Burrows refused to allow the correspondents to drive down to the dock and watch a second brigade of Australian troops arrive. Instead, Burrows issued a bland, twenty-five-word communique announcing more Australian troops had landed. McDaniel hunted Burrows down to seek more details.

"That's enough on it," Burrows replied. "The rest is all bilge."

McDaniel refused to back down. He protested that the AP "serves papers in Australia and the parents and friends of those men want to know additional detail." He argued with Burrows for an hour before the censor grudgingly provided McDaniel with "a few more details."[30] Given the paucity of information, McDaniel wrote a brief story that "slouch-hatted Australian fighting men marched singing and cheering from the piers of this Gibraltar of the East." He quoted a British spokesman saying the British had "an Army considered sufficiently numerous and powerful to make any potential invader think not twice, but ten times before attempting to strike at the empire's Far Eastern bulwark."[31]

One of the few British press officers who was helpful was Capt. Henry Steel, a slender young man described as "one of the most un-disillusioned press officers anywhere in the world." He and McDaniel became good friends. One reporter wrote that when Steel "could not smuggle the correspondents actually into the confidence of the general, he smuggled himself in, standing negligently by telephone conversations and putting in questions where he could."[32]

The rising anger of the reporters reached a crescendo in the middle of September, when Adm. Layton and Brooke-Popham agreed to meet with the reporters at the naval base. McDaniel and the other correspondents gathered about a long table. Brown pointed out that all the reporters were eager to cooperate "to help the British war effort." Nonetheless, Brown complained, "Burrows' office should be the funnel through which all our efforts flow. Instead it is a bottleneck."

McDaniel added his own criticism. "Burrows seems to have no conception of his work," he complained. When the meeting ended, Layton promised to call another meeting in the next few days. "We'll get to the bottom of this thing," he told Brown.[33]

With intelligence reports suggesting the Japanese were considering attacking Malaya and the Dutch East Indies, the British stepped up efforts to strengthen Singapore. On September 3, McDaniel went to the docks to watch what he described as a "fully motorized and equipped" contingent of Indian soldiers. They were assigned to the northern tip of Malaya, and their arrival gave the British 88,000 soldiers. That very day, Governor Shenton Thomas declared, "Japan's troops are in Indochina on the borders of Thailand. These are facts [that are] useless to ignore."[34]

On September 10, 1941, Duff Cooper, whom Prime Minister Winston Churchill named resident minister for Far Eastern affairs, and his wife, Lady Diana, arrived in Singapore on the flying boat *Anzac Clipper*. It had been a miserably bumpy, stomach-churning twelve-hour flight from Guam, with the plane hugging the sea at a height of less than 100 feet and flying through heavy rain. Their arrival was marked with fanfare. Six American-built Brewster Buffalo fighters escorted the clipper as it taxied up the channel, and then each fighter separately executed a salute. Brooke-Popham and Adm. Spooner greeted Duff Cooper and Lady Diana, who then were driven to Government House, where Governor Thomas met them on the steps. The couple and their staff were assigned a suite of rooms at the Sea View Hotel.[35]

But beneath the veneer of harmony, Duff Cooper's arrival fueled a widening gap among the senior British officials. In particular, Duff Cooper and Thomas clashed. Privately, Thomas referred to Duff Cooper as a "failure" and recalled that one senior British official in London described him as a "petulant little pipsqueak."

Duff Cooper held an equally low opinion of Thomas, describing him as "the mouth-piece of the last person he speaks to." Duff Cooper referred to Brooke-Popham as "Old Pop Off."[36]

As troops and guns flooded into Singapore, McDaniel and other Western reporters seemed optimistic the British could withstand any Japanese attack. Japan had "missed the bus in Southeast Asia," some British commentators were asserting. Edgar Mowrer, an extremely able reporter for the *Chicago Daily News*, expanded on that theme when he wrote the Japanese "have missed the boat," asserting that in the summer of 1940 the Japanese could have gobbled up Malaya and the East Indies because "they were virtually undefended."[37] Mowrer declared that "the war danger in the Far East is diminishing."[38] McDaniel did not go that far. But citing informed sources, he wrote that Singapore "has been so strengthened and reorganized that these observers believe it would require a Japanese force of nearly 500,000 men and more than 1,000 planes all in action at once to give Tokyo any hope of gaining an invasion foothold." McDaniel wrote that transport ships carrying Japanese troops to Malaya "would be subjected to constant submarine and air attack once [they] entered the China Sea."

He also hinted at one other development: the Singapore naval base was ready to receive a powerful British naval force.[39]

On the afternoon of December 2, McDaniel and the other Western correspondents were taken to the naval base. British officials escorted them up a signal tower, giving them a panoramic view of the Johore Straits. A mile away, they saw an imposing sight. The 32,000-ton battle cruiser *Repulse* steamed up the straits, followed by the new 35,000-ton battleship *Prince of Wales*, decked out in camouflage gray and looking "very fine against the green hills of Johore."[40] Four British destroyers, which the *Straits Times* wrote "looked like scooters beside the monster battleships," joined the two capital ships as they entered the base. The ships steamed past tiny villages, where enthusiastic Malays greeted them. When the base control tower flashed a message, a signal lamp from the *Prince of Wales* blinked in response.[41]

The next day, Adm. Tom Phillips, who would command the fleet, and his chief of staff, RAdm. Arthur Palliser, went to the docks to admire the powerful warships. Both officers were decked out in formal white naval dress, with Palliser towering over Phillips, who was so short he was nicknamed Tom Thumb, although it was carefully pointed out he was the same height as Lord Nelson. McDaniel thought Phillips was "very brainy" and a "good organizer" but worried he had "little [battle] line experience."[42]

McDaniel was suitably impressed. The *Prince of Wales*, McDaniel wrote, "was the first British capital ship ever to be sent out east prepared to fight." The *Malaya Tribune* said the arrival of the ships "has completely altered the balance of naval power in this part of the world." Euphoric Malayan cab drivers shouted, "*Kapal perang besar sudalh dating*," which meant "Big warships have arrived." Durdin wrote that the *Prince of Wales* and the *Repulse* created "a bulwark of sea power for Britain in the Orient at a time when the threat of war with Japan had reached its peak." Duff Cooper thought "they conferred a sense of complete security."[43]

Both capital ships anchored in plain sight, and within a day, a Japanese reconnaissance plane spotted them, but British censors were adamant about not mentioning the *Repulse* by name. To the correspondents, it made no sense. "The whole idea was to get tremendous publicity on the British Far East fleet and therefore scare" the Japanese, Cecil Brown of CBS thought. The correspondents were astonished at the clumsy censors. United Press referred to the *Repulse* as HMS *Blank*, even though the reporter noted "no attempt was made to conceal the arrival of the warships." Brown was so angry he opted not to broadcast a story, while McDaniel tartly wrote that the *Prince of Wales* was accompanied by "other heavy units and auxiliaries, which correspondents were not permitted to identify." He wrote his early story in such a hurry that he mistakenly referred to Phillips as Adm. Tom Collins, an error he corrected in an updated dispatch.[44]

As soon as the *Prince of Wales* entered the drydock, engineers went to work to clean all eight boilers, a demanding job made more miserable because Singapore's tropical weather roasted the engine rooms to 130 degrees. The intense heat and humidity of the long voyage in the Indian Ocean—temperatures reached 150 degrees in two of the machinery rooms—disabled her type 273 radar used to detect surface vessels, and no amount of work could repair it.[45]

The next evening, Adm. Phillips hosted an elegant reception aboard the *Prince of Wales*. Phillips personally greeted guests as they boarded the battleship to the sound of a bosun's whistle pipe. Guests were directed to comfortable chairs and a dance floor on the foredeck, which was covered by a red-and-white awning, a precaution not necessary on this sparkling evening without any chance of rain. Throughout the evening, a Royal Marine band played popular and upbeat tunes, including a boisterous rendition of "The Beer Barrel Polka." Among the guests were Gen. Percival; the sultan of Johore and his wife, rumored to be a teenager; Governor Thomas; and Duff Cooper and Lady Diana, who thoroughly enjoyed herself dancing on the "wide decks" and toasting future British victories. The British invited a Japanese diplomat from his country's consulate in Singapore, a none-too-subtle message that Great Britain was serious about defending its prized overseas possession.[46]

Phillips and Capt. John Leach then invited Western correspondents and editors of Malaya's newspapers for a tour of the *Prince of Wales*. "All the modern features of this great battleship were greatly admired by visitors," the *Times* of London noted. She carried ten 14-inch guns in three turrets, was protected by sturdy armor, was equipped with the latest radar and air-defense systems, and could steam at a brisk 28 knots. Leach showed the correspondents the visitors' book, which included the signatures of King George VI, Winston Churchill, and President Roosevelt. The ship's scrapbook featured a photograph taken of the *Hood* from the decks of the *Prince of Wales* as both raced to intercept the German battleship *Bismarck* a few months earlier in the North Atlantic. The *Hood* blew up during its engagement with the *Bismarck*, but one of the *Prince of Wales*' 14-inch shells struck the port side of the 42,000-ton German battleship, causing seawater to enter the lower fuel tanks. The hit ruined hundreds of tons of oil, a factor in the *Bismarck*'s destruction three days later by two British battleships.[47]

By contrast, the *Repulse* was from another era, having joined the British fleet during World War I. Like all British battle cruisers, the *Repulse* featured high speed at the expense of armor protection, a fatal flaw that led to three British battle cruisers exploding at Jutland in 1916 and the swift destruction of the *Hood* by the *Bismarck*. But the *Repulse* could land a punch with her six 15-inch guns. Not only was the combination of the two warships a match for any Japanese battleship in the area, but they could wreak havoc on Japanese transports attempting to land troops in Malaya.

Earlier, Churchill had ordered the *Prince of Wales* and the *Repulse* to Singapore over the objections of Sir Dudley Pound, the first sea lord, who had preferred to send three older and slower Resolution-class battleships to the Indian Ocean. Churchill was convinced modern warships would deter Japan, and when Foreign Secretary Anthony Eden backed Churchill, Pound capitulated. Field Marshal Jan Smuts, the South African prime minister, was appalled, and as usually was the case, Smuts was right. War with Japan was certain, Smuts thought, and sending the *Prince of Wales* and the *Repulse* to Singapore while keeping the US Pacific Fleet in Hawaii would divide the Allied fleet. In a cable to Churchill, Smuts warned that the two fleets would be "separately inferior to the Japanese Navy, which will thus have an opportunity to defeat them in turn," adding ominously that "there is here an opening for a first-class disaster." Churchill held Smuts in high regard but this time rejected his friend's advice. Adm. Layton was similarly worried. He told Harold Guard of United Press that without air cover, the two ships would be "left exposed and vulnerable to attack." Instead, he would have preferred smaller and faster ships.[48]

The day after the *Prince of Wales* and the *Repulse* docked in Singapore, British officials invited McDaniel, Brown, Tillman Durdin of the *New York Times*, O'Dowd Gallagher of the *London Daily Express*, and two dozen other reporters to the Royal Air Force headquarters near the Singapore Golf Club. There, Sir Robert Brooke-Popham would provide the reporters with an off-the-record briefing.

The reporters sat at small tables. British press officials had placed pads of paper on the tables. Reporters took copious notes, although they were warned they could not quote anything Brooke-Popham said. In the past, Brooke-Popham had been "reluctant" to talk to correspondents, although he had privately told a handful of reporters he trusted that he was upset about not having enough aircraft.[49]

On this day, Brooke-Popham was plainly worried that Japan might strike against the West, even though he said that "it is very difficult to see the logic of Japan going to war now." Even so, he warned that "it is very dangerous to look at Japan with what we call Western spectacles. We must look at them through Eastern eyes." With the *Prince of Wales* and *Repulse* in Singapore, Brooke-Popham did not believe the Japanese would attack Malaya, even though it was the key to seizing the oil, tin, and rubber of Malaya and the Dutch East Indies. Instead, he suggested they might dispatch troops and planes from Indochina into Thailand. He identified by name some of the Japanese army units in the area.

"All we can do is watch it the best we can," Brooke-Popham said.[50]

McDaniel asked whether a Japanese attack on Thailand would trigger a US and British response. Brooke-Popham acknowledged he had no idea whether the United States and Britain would enter the war over Thailand. But everyone in the room knew if Japan occupied Thailand, it would place Japanese troops on the Thai-Malaya border.

"There are clear indications that Japan does not know which way to turn," Brooke-Popham told the reporters. "Tojo is scratching his head," he said, adding "there is a reassuring state of uncertainty in Japan." Clark Kennard of the Malaya Broadcasting System asked how the American-built Brewster Buffalo fighter would match up against the best Japanese planes. "Oh, we are not worried about that," Brooke-Popham said. "We can get on all right with Buffaloes out here, but they haven't got the speed for England."[51]

Toward the end, Brooke-Popham passed on one other bit of news: the next day, Adm. Phillips would fly to Manila to meet with Adm. Thomas Hart, the commander of the US Asiatic Fleet. Phillips was hoping to persuade Hart to send him four of his four-stack destroyers left over from World War I.

McDaniel wanted to report what Brooke-Popham had said, but British officers resisted. Finally, by the end of the day they relented and said the reporters could quote what he said, without revealing his name.

Despite the confident talk, there were reasons to be skeptical. The British did not have any tanks in Malaya, which Brooke-Popham privately warned London "was a serious handicap to any offensive land operations."[52] Instead, the British relied on Rolls-Royce armored cars, which O'Dowd Gallagher considered obsolete weapons from the First World War. As far as he could tell, only one of every six armored cars even carried heavy machine guns.[53] The five 15-inch shore-based guns that the British boasted made Singapore invincible were designed to sink warships with armor-piercing shells. But their lack of high-explosive shells made them utterly useless against an invader marching down the Malay Peninsula. Only 182 aircraft were ready for use, even though the British had concluded that 566 modern aircraft should be the minimum.[54] They relied on sixty-four Buffaloes, which Gen. Archibald Wavell later wrote were "no match for the best Japanese fighter."[55] McDaniel himself thought they were a "primitive fighter." The British also had fifteen relatively modern Lockheed Hudson light bombers, thirty-four Blenheim light bombers, and twenty-seven Vildebeest torpedo bombers, which were obsolete biplanes with a top speed of only 100 miles per hour, prompting some British pilots to joke that the only danger they posed was to make Japanese pilots laugh themselves to death.[56]

By contrast, the Japanese had assembled more than 500 modern planes in Indochina and within easy reach of Malaya. They included seventy-two Nells and twenty-seven Betties, both twin-engine bombers that also could be armed with torpedoes. The Japanese torpedoes were faster and more destructive than anything in the American and British arsenals. Japanese troop transports heading toward Malaya were covered by the fast battleships *Kongō* and *Haruna*, seven heavy cruisers, and five light cruisers, as well as destroyers and submarines.

On December 1, Thomas declared a state of emergency. Thousands of British, Chinese, and Malayan soldiers exchanged their white tropical mufti for khaki-green uniforms, while the sultan of Johore mobilized his forces.[57] On December 6, British and Dutch airplanes sighted a large number of Japanese transports off the cost of Indochina, steaming toward the Malay Peninsula. The reconnaissance planes reported they were escorted by no fewer than nine Japanese cruisers. That same day, British officials in Singapore ordered all troops and sailors to report to their bases.[58]

But everything in Singapore seemed normal enough that Saturday, a beautiful cloudless evening with glistening stars. People lined up to see the film *Belle Star*, just released in September and starring Gene Tierney, Dana Andrews, and Randolph Scott. The Cathay Restaurant featured dinner and dancing, with the 7th Gordon Highlanders playing for much of the evening. Sir Earle Page, who briefly served as Australian prime minister in 1939, pronounced "enormous advances have been made, making Singapore not merely impregnable, but able, if necessary, to be a spearhead of a great offensive."[59]

On December 5, Adm. Phillips ordered the *Repulse* to sail to Darwin as a visible reminder to the Australians that the British intended to defend Singapore and Australia. But after talking to Adm. Hart in Manila and reading the reports of Japanese transports heading toward the Malay Peninsula, Phillips had a change of mind. Phillips flew back to Singapore a day early. The *Repulse* and her two escorting destroyers abruptly turned around and headed back toward Singapore.

Late on the evening of December 7, Singapore time, McDaniel and Natalie were trying to sleep in their room at the Cathay Building when they were awakened by the loud noise of a radio one floor above. Exhausted, Yates walked upstairs, knocked on the door, and said, "Chaps, would you knock it off? I'm trying to sleep."

"OK, chum," came the cheerful reply.

Yates returned to his room and tried to nod off. At 3:30 in the morning, the phone rang: a British press officer told Yates to get to the military press offices of the Union Building for a major announcement. Yates started to dress when Natalie shouted, "Here they are." They peered out their apartment window and saw a dozen Japanese planes caught in the glare of Singapore's powerful searchlights. Antiaircraft guns chattered, and bright flashes erupted from explosions near the naval base. Streetlights illuminated the city because nobody ordered a blackout.

Yates dashed down to the street to look for a taxi to take him to the Union Building. A car driven by a British air raid warden stopped. "Just another practice," the driver said as he drove off. McDaniel ran the three-quarters of a mile to the Union Building. He heard a loud shout: "Halt!" Yates dropped his typewriter and held up his hands. A policeman stuck his pistol into McDaniel's stomach. McDaniel told the policeman to check his shirt pocket for his press pass. The policeman allowed McDaniel to continue, but his typewriter was broken.[60]

By the time he reached the sixth floor of the Union Building, yawning correspondents were gathering: Tillman Durdin of the *New York Times*, Harold Guard of United Press, Cecil Brown of CBS, O'Dowd Gallagher of the *London Daily Express*, and a handful of others. A British press officer announced that Japanese troops had landed on Malaya's east coast 350 miles from Singapore, and that "the invaders are being engaged."[61]

Next stop for McDaniel was the cable office, which was in the same building as Reuters. The lights in the cable office didn't work, so he lit candles. He scrawled by hand a bulletin in large letters. He filed the brief paragraph, walked into the Reuters office, borrowed a typewriter, wrote a more detailed story, and filed.

Natalie called Yates at Reuters: the radio had just announced the Japanese had bombed the US Pacific Fleet at Pearl Harbor. For Americans such as Yates and Natalie, it was stunning news. It meant virtually the entire world was now at war.[62]

The Associated Press boasted that it was primed to cover every aspect of the Pacific war. In addition to McDaniel and photographer Frank Noel reporting from Singapore, the AP had R. P. Cronin, Clark Lee, and Russell Brines in Manila; Morris Harris and J. D. Harris in Shanghai; Spencer Moosa in Chungking; and Max Hill in Tokyo. Although the AP story suggested that Hill would continue to report from Japan, the day after the Pearl Harbor attack he was interned by the Japanese and held in solitary confinement in an unheated cell for six weeks.

McDaniel exchanged his civilian dress slacks and sports shirt for a British army khaki uniform complete with tin hat. The British released a communique that morning announcing the Japanese troop transports in the Gulf of Siam were landing soldiers on the east coast of the Malay Peninsula near Thailand. The Japanese goal was to seize the British air base at Kota Bharu and in one bold stroke eliminate British airpower at the Thai border. Those transports, however, made tempting targets, and if the British could destroy them, the Japanese invasion would be choked off.

Later that morning, McDaniel received a telephone call from Adm. Layton. "We're sending out two capital ships under Tom Thumb Phillips," Layton said. He asked McDaniel whether he would like to sail with the two ships for what would be a weeklong cruise.

"They'll get in range of a Jap convoy and shoot it to pieces," Layton said.

Two days earlier, British planes had spotted a Japanese troop convoy sailing toward the Gulf of Siam, a sign the Japanese planned to invade Malaya near the Thai border and push down the peninsula to attack Singapore. British intelligence reported the convoy was protected by the Japanese battleship *Kongō*. Although the *Kongō* was formidable, with 14-inch guns, she had been built in 1912 and was no match for the more modern *Prince of Wales*.

Yet, despite saying that Phillips hoped to destroy the convoy, Layton harbored doubts about the sorties. He candidly told McDaniel that plunging into the South

China Sea without air superiority was "not the thing to do." As Layton wrote less than a week later, "Operations in the South China Sea within range of enemy shore-based aircraft must be hazardous without fighter protection."[63]

As badly as McDaniel wanted to join the ships, he decided he could not chance leaving Singapore when the Japanese were attacking the Malay Peninsula. The British asked Durdin of the *Times*, but like McDaniel he was reluctant to leave Singapore when a big story was approaching. Next, they tried Cecil Brown and O'Dowd Gallagher, who were finishing lunch at the Raffles Hotel.

Brown and Gallagher agreed to go, and a Malayan driver whisked them out to the naval base, where they boarded the *Repulse* at 5:15 p.m. "It's a ready-made world scoop," Gallagher told Brown. "Laid on a plate for you and me. I shouldn't be surprised if we aren't going to keep a date with the American fleet."[64] Within a few minutes, the *Repulse* pulled away from the dock and made her way out of the naval base and into the Straits of Johore. Under a picturesque evening sunset that provided a beautiful silhouette of palm trees on shore, the *Prince of Wales*, the White Ensign waving majestically from her second mast, raced past the *Repulse*. Cheering sailors lined the decks of both great ships, and Adm. Phillips and Capt. Leach of the *Prince of Wales* waved their white hats to Capt. William Tennant of the *Repulse*. In his notebook, Gallagher jotted down the words "*Prince* slipped on past us to death or glory."

Even Brown, who rarely seemed impressed by anything, was overwhelmed. "Gosh, what a sight."[65]

# SINGAPORE, 1942

wo days after the *Prince of Wales* and *Repulse* sailed on December 8, air warnings screeched in Singapore, but to everyone's relief, Japanese planes did not appear. McDaniel mentioned the sirens in his daily story but focused on the Japanese seizing the British air base at Kota Bharu on the eastern Malayan shores of the Gulf of Siam. The Japanese relied on an amphibious assault to attack Kota Bharu—exactly the type of attack McDaniel had warned about a year earlier in his memo to British intelligence.

McDaniel had to rely on a thoroughly misleading British communique issued at 10:00 that night, declaring, "Our units have now reorganized themselves south of Kota Bharu. Elsewhere, our frontier remains unbroken." But no disingenuous communique could cloak the obvious: the Japanese had dealt the British a catastrophic setback. By taking Kota Bharu, the Japanese would control the air over most of Malaya. And rather than attack Singapore from the sea, they planned to cut their way through Malaya's thick jungle and rubber plantations or race down the roads on the west side toward the cement causeway that linked the peninsula to Singapore.[1]

Many American newspapers featured McDaniel's story on the front page, with the *Santa Ana Register* running a large headline above the paper's flag reading, "Japanese take English air base." But right below that headline was an even larger one: "British lose two warships to Japs!" In a bulletin from the AP's London bureau, the Admiralty announced the sinking of the *Prince of Wales* and *Repulse*. Alfred Duff Cooper, former First Lord of the Admiralty, privately called it the "worst single piece of news I have ever received." Before he broke the news to Lady Diana, he asked her, "How black can you take it?" After a brief discussion over dinner with a British official, Duff Cooper decided to immediately broadcast the news.[2] A car drove him to the Cathay Building, and he spoke on the radio from the Malaya Broadcasting Corporation studios: "This is not the first time in our long history of glory that we have met with disaster and have surmounted it. Indeed, there is something in our nature, as there was something in the nature of our fathers before us, that only disaster can produce."[3]

"Singapore heard in stunned silence of the sinking of the two powerful capital ships," McDaniel wrote.[4] Gen. Bennett wrote that the loss has "cast a heavy gloom over everybody."[5] Although a British torpedo bomber had disabled the *Bismarck* earlier that year with a hit in her steering compartment, and British torpedo planes in 1940 had sunk three Italian battleships anchored in Taranto harbor, planes had never destroyed a capital ship at sea. The *Singapore Free Press and Mercantile Advertiser* reported that "for a long time now it has been supposed that the battleship had little to fear from the bomber," but concluded the Japanese "have upset theories on the subject and for the time being it does look as if the bomber is winning."[6] In one stroke, Japan demonstrated that aircraft were now the key weapon in the war at sea, while simultaneously dealing a crippling blow to Great Britain's hopes of defending Singapore. During an informal dinner with McDaniel, Adm. Layton agreed with the view that the sinking of the two ships "was the beginning of the end." An equally discouraged Duff Cooper said, "This engagement makes me revise my belief in battleships. I don't have much confidence in them anymore."[7]

Having skipped a chance to sail with the *Repulse*, McDaniel played catch-up. He filed a fresh top to his story on Kota Bharu's capture:

> British destroyers and patrol planes swept over the South China Sea in search for survivors of the mighty battleship *Prince of Wales* and the battlecruiser *Repulse* while British troops consolidated their positions along strong new lines in Northern Malaya where the Japanese had driven a wedge across the frontier.

Later that evening as a heavy rain fell, McDaniel drove to the naval base. The British destroyers *Electra* and *Express* and Australian destroyer *Vampire* docked shortly before midnight, carrying more than 2,000 survivors. McDaniel saw Brown and Gallagher among the first brought to shore; Brown aboard the *Electra* and Gallagher on the *Vampire*. Each was determined to beat the other to Singapore and file his story first. It was a 14-mile trip along a paved highway that linked the base to the city. The rain was so heavy that the driver of Brown's car insisted on driving a plodding 10 miles per hour.

"Go faster," Brown insisted. Frightened, the driver replied, "I don't want to get killed."[8]

At the British press office in Singapore, the two correspondents—"worn and unshaven"—typed their dispatches.[9] Capt. Tennant had survived the sinking of the *Repulse*, but Adm. Phillips and Capt. Leach had died. Crew members told McDaniel about scores of twin-engine Japanese Betties and Nells attacking the two ships, with the first bomb smacking into the *Repulse*'s catapult deck. British sailors told him that they "clung to life aboard rafts, floats and lifeboats," and that they seemed surprised because Japanese planes didn't machine-gun them. McDaniel reported that British commentators speculated submarines may have finished the two ships with torpedoes. In fact, planes had scored every hit.[10]

The *Salt Lake Telegram* ran McDaniel's story on page 7 but, right above it, featured a photo of Cecil Brown along with a first-person story he cabled to CBS in New York: "Like hundreds of others, I jumped 20 feet into the water when the *Repulse* was already on its side[,] and swam as fast as possible to avoid the suction and the expected explosion." Brown reported that when he was "50 feet away from the *Repulse* and helped to safety, the battlecruiser's stern rose in the air like an ugly red wound and quickly slid below the surface."[11]

*Newsweek* sent Brown a telegram congratulating him on "coming through alive" and his "superb" CBS story, before asking whether Brown could file a 600-word article for the magazine. *Collier's* asked Brown for a 1,500-word story, while Random House offered him a book contract. CBS president William Paley dispatched a telegram saying, "All of us are overjoyed to learn of your rescue. Congratulations on wonderful story." Duff Cooper invited Brown to join him and Lady Diana for a drink.[12]

The *Malaya Morning Tribune* published a photo of Gallagher and other survivors. On December 15, Gallagher broadcast a detailed story, pointing out that the *Prince of Wales* and *Repulse* lacked air cover despite Phillips's requests for land-based fighter planes. In vivid detail, Gallagher described the Japanese torpedo planes flying "low and close," the "shattering barrage" of the *Prince of Wales'* antiaircraft guns, the torpedoes slamming into the two ships, and the *Repulse's* loudspeakers blaring "Everybody on the main deck" as the ship listed to starboard.

Brown won the prestigious Peabody Award, with the judges declaring that he "was frequently in hot spots and his eye-witness account of the sinking of the *Repulse* and the *Prince of Wales* was the most dramatic single story of the year. His news sense, his coolness under fire and his insistence—even under censorship—that the truth must get home sets an example for reporters everywhere." Within a year, Gallagher and Brown published books. McDaniel continued to second-guess his decision not to accept Layton's offer and seemed envious of Brown and Gallagher. Brown, McDaniel said, "came back a hero." McDaniel's decision not to sail on the *Repulse* had cost him the glory that Brown won. But McDaniel was doing what he was supposed to be doing as the only AP reporter in Singapore.[13]

The Japanese landed thousands of troops near the border separating Thailand from Malaya. They were trained for jungle warfare and often rode bicycles to strike deep into the British lines. They wore light cotton uniforms that were cool in the tropics, along with either khaki caps or steel helmets. Unlike the British, the Japanese believed that light tanks could poke their way through the jungle, which covered 70 percent of Malaya. By contrast, Ian Morrison of the *Times* of London thought British troops in Malaya were weighed down with boots, tin helmets, gas masks, and heavy packs.[14]

On December 11, Japanese planes bombed the harbor of Georgetown on Penang Island. Unable to reach the front lines, McDaniel was forced to rely on overly optimistic British communiques for his stories. On December 12, he reported that Japanese attacks had "dented" the British front lines.[15] To McDaniel, it was clear that the Japanese were trying to seize the key port of Penang, an island 15 miles long and 5 miles wide off the west coast of Malaya that had once served as a trading post for the British East India Tea Company. By December 18, McDaniel wrote, the imminent fall of Penang presented "the direst threat today on the road to Singapore." The next day, McDaniel reported the Japanese had pushed 100 miles down the peninsula, only 300 miles from Singapore itself. Even worse, he wrote, Singapore had lost radio contact with Penang.[16] On Christmas Day, Penang radio came alive again with a grim surprise. A Japanese announcer wished Singapore a Merry Christmas.[17]

On December 22, Sir Robert Brooke-Popham met with reporters and Singaporean civilian leaders and told them, "We may have lost a large part of northern Malaya, but it is for a time only. There must be no despondency over temporary setbacks." He pledged to vigorously defend Singapore.[18]

Although Tillman Durdin of the *New York Times* wrote that "the shock of the initial Japanese successes in Malaya . . . is resulting in a redoubling of the war effort" in Singapore,[19] McDaniel read between the lines of the British communiques and Brooke-Popham's talk. He reported that British, Australian, and Indian troops were in full retreat down the peninsula.[20] As early as December 13, the British and Dutch could muster only 106 mostly obsolete aircraft. Duff Cooper privately urged yielding northern Malaya, pointing out the impossibility of defending such a large mass with only three squadrons of aircraft and "without command of the sea."[21]

The official communiques were at complete odds with reality. Sir Gordon Whitteridge, the British consul stationed in Medan in Sumatra, caustically complained about the "unreliability" of the British military communiques, saying they often referred to "events at least 48 hours old." On December 24, McDaniel cited a communique that declared "some skirmishing on the northwestern Malaya front," while adding that the Japanese were still 300 miles away from Singapore. But that very same day, Richard Casey, the Australian ambassador to the United States, delivered a brutally frank assessment to Under Secretary of State Sumner Welles: "Without immediate air reinforcement, Singapore must fall." In stark terms, Casey warned the only thing that might save Singapore would "be the immediate dispatch from the Middle East by air of powerful reinforcements, large numbers of the latest fighter aircraft with ample operationally trained personnel. Reinforcements should be not in brigades but in divisions, and to be of use they must arrive urgently. Anything that is not powerfully modern and immediate is futile. As things stand at present, fall of Singapore is to my mind only matter of weeks." Casey asked Welles to show his memo to Roosevelt.

Everywhere the news was just as bleak. Hong Kong was under heavy Japanese attack and would fall by Christmas Day. Japanese forces had invaded the Philippines, forcing Gen. Douglas MacArthur to retreat to the Bataan Peninsula in the hope of holding out for six months. Japanese air attacks wiped out the American air force at Clark Air Base, and Adm. Thomas Hart ordered the heavy cruiser *Houston* and a handful of destroyers to sail south toward Dutch-held Java. Japanese amphibious forces were preparing their second—and successful—attempt to seize Wake Island with its 388 outnumbered Marines and twelve Wildcat fighter planes.

The British preparations were ineffective to the point of being comical. One general told Cecil Brown about a long-distance telephone call between Percival and Brooke-Popham in which an operator broke in to say, "Your three minutes have expired, sir." Because the British had neglected to take over the private phone company, the operator ended the call. The British arrested Tom Fairhall of the *Sydney Daily Telegraph* because he refused to reveal a source's name.[22]

By December 30, Japanese ground forces edged to within 290 miles of Singapore. That very evening under a dazzling moon, McDaniel watched from a rooftop as two formations of Japanese planes flew over Singapore. Bright searchlights illuminated the planes, and antiaircraft guns barked away. Although a British communique insisted that Singapore and the naval base were "raided severely," McDaniel counted only a handful of bombs falling, far fewer than the British claimed.[23] Later that evening, McDaniel updated his story. British authorities declared martial law, which meant military courts would handle cases of looting or sabotage.[24]

Privately, top British officials knew Singapore was doomed. Field Marshal Sir Alan Brooke, chief of the Imperial General Staff in London, said he did not "feel there is much hope in saving Singapore."[25] Japan controlled the air and the sea. The Japanese troops slicing their way down the peninsula were battle tested and well trained. Some British units, such as the Argylls, fought exceptionally well. But lacking armor and air support, the British forces had little chance of halting the Japanese advance.[26]

People already were leaving Singapore. On Christmas Eve, the US consulate publicly admitted it was preparing to evacuate Americans. Some correspondents were also departing. In late December, Gallagher flew to Rangoon to cover the Japanese invasion of Burma. Brown pleaded with him to stay; he was convinced Singapore would be a more important story. A month later, Brown would leave as well. British censors were so irritated with what he wanted to report that they pulled his credentials.

George Weller of the *Chicago Daily News* telephoned McDaniel and Harold Guard of United Press and urged them to write stories about Brown's plight. Both McDaniel and Guard decided not to, prompting Weller to tell Brown, "I think they both are afraid to touch it." Brown later hinted that McDaniel and Guard had motives that had more to do with competition than journalistic solidarity. Brown complained that "radio competes, in its swift, spot-news coverage, with the old-line agencies which service the newspapers in America." Brown boarded a British Airways plane on January 23 and flew to Batavia.[27]

McDaniel could have left. But after turning down a chance to sail on the *Repulse*, he decided to stick with the story. As in Nanking and Tientsin, he would stay.

Late on New Year's Eve, as twenty-seven Japanese planes appeared over Singapore, thousands of people celebrated at hotels and in their homes with what McDaniel described as a "calm and cheerful determination." A blackout imposed by Singapore officials did not dampen the celebration of people "removed by a half-a-world from home." As British antiaircraft guns chattered away, the Japanese dropped their bombs near the oil depot at the naval base, which did little physical damage and "even less to the spirits" of those who partied.[28]

Despite the outwardly festive mood, the British were increasingly aware of their precarious situation. The speed of the Japanese advance had taken the British by surprise, McDaniel thought. McDaniel quoted a British communique that said fighting continued at Kuantan off the South China Sea, another effort by the British to place a positive spin on what was turning into a disaster. But McDaniel pierced that optimistic report by pointing out the real story: the British were acknowledging that the fighting on Malaya's east coast was less than 200 miles from Singapore.[29] The news on Malaya's west coast was equally hopeless, with "waves of Japanese infantry and tanks" only 50 miles north of Kuala Lumpur, which McDaniel described as "the crude rubber capital of the world." Kuala Lumpur was 240 miles north of Singapore.[30]

The reporters were eager to get to the front. Ian Morrison of the *Times* of London summed up the feelings of most correspondents when he complained he was getting very poor material in Singapore, most of which was secondhand. To transport correspondents to the front, the British press officers relied on four staff cars and an army truck. After spending a day near the forward lines, the correspondents would return to temporary press headquarters about 40 miles away and write their stories, which would then be sent by rail or truck to be telegraphed to their news organizations.[31]

For the first couple of weeks of January, breaking news kept McDaniel in Singapore. Churchill and Roosevelt announced that Gen. Sir Archibald Wavell, whose troops had routed the Italian forces in Libya, would be supreme commander of British, American, Australian, and Dutch forces in Singapore, Burma, Sumatra, Borneo, and Java.[32] The fifty-eight-year-old Wavell was highly regarded for his tactical skills. McDaniel wrote that the combination of Wavell's appointment and the expected arrival of the British 18th Division was a signal that "confidence is mounting in the long-range possibilities of defense of Singapore."[33]

Despite McDaniel's optimistic report, some correspondents opted to leave. In the second week of January, photographer Frank Noel of the AP boarded a freighter sailing for India. On the evening of January 14, a Japanese submarine torpedoed the freighter about 270 miles off the west coast of Sumatra. Noel grabbed his cameras and hopped into one of four lifeboats. The submarine lurked nearby on the surface but chose not to attack the lifeboats. Instead, the submarine used her deck gun to fire five shells into the freighter, which sank by the stern. For the next five days, Noel and his companions floated about the ocean in brutal heat with little water. His photograph of an Indian man aboard another lifeboat pleading for water won him the Pulitzer Prize. When he reached the safety of the Dutch port of Padang in Sumatra, he filed the story.[34]

McDaniel noticed growing signs that Singapore was taking greater precautions. Every day, he reported there were more sandbags piled in front of buildings while shops were removing their glass windows.[35] He was alarmed enough that he asked Natalie to leave. On January 15, she boarded a Dutch steamer scheduled to sail to Java. For two days, the steamer remained in the harbor. From the decks, Natalie saw huge explosions from Japanese planes bombing Singapore. Large fires erupted in the center of the city, while a half mile away, she saw Japanese planes striking oil installations on an island. Finally, on January 17, the steamer left Singapore. Not a single Japanese plane flew over the ship, and it safely reached Batavia.[36]

Yates next filled a small trunk with what was left of his and Natalie's personal belongings, and arranged to have them shipped to the United States in the care of Elmer Stevens, a B. F. Goodrich representative in Singapore. Stevens was scheduled to leave on an American freighter on the same day Natalie was departing. Yates then wrote a letter to the Associated Press that had the eerie tone of a last will:

Mr. Stevens has very kindly consented to take a small trunk containing some of my personal possessions to the old country, as what with wars and disturbances of all kinds I am unlikely to get back to America for some time to come. The contents of this trunk are of little intrinsic value, but they represent the sum total of what I saved from our household the first time I was "captured" by the Japs; they have a sentimental value to the wife and myself. I have been following the wars out in this part of the world so long that I have no home in America. Consequently [there is] no address to which this trunk can be sent. So, I am casting this trunk on the mercy of the Associated Press until I can redeem it in person or find some other way out. I want to thank you in advance for this kindness, though I won't say that I hope I can do the same for you some time, as I do not wish you the same misfortune to be on the spot on which I am now sitting so precariously.

Stevens and the trunk made the 14,000-mile voyage from Singapore to New Orleans, where he turned the trunk over to Charles Nutter, the AP bureau chief there.[37]

With Natalie on her way to Java and the trunk off to America, Yates drove out of Singapore to do some reporting. Two formations of Japanese planes prowled above and dropped their bombs. McDaniel jumped from the car and dove into the doorway of a nearby building. After the explosions stopped, McDaniel cautiously took a look. To his dismay, the car was wrecked.[38] Undaunted, McDaniel commandeered a jeep, crossed the causeway, and drove 50 miles north of Singapore in search of Gen. Bennett and his Australians. McDaniel grabbed a bite to eat at Bennett's headquarters, which consisted of a simple tent with a cot. Japanese planes were a constant presence, but for some reason they ignored the headquarters. The lack of British planes in the sky was troubling. One British soldier grumbled, "When are we going to have planes to help us?"[39]

Bennett told McDaniel he was bitter about the British commanders. In particular, he thought that Maj. Gen. Louis Heath, who commanded the 3rd Indian Corps, had let him down. Bennett had pleaded in vain with Gen. Percival to launch a counterattack.

"We've got to make a counterattack," Bennett told McDaniel. "We can't worry about a few people being cut off in night operations."[40]

McDaniel's arrival coincided with a big story developing north of Bennett's headquarters. Two battalions of Australians and a brigade of Indian troops were cut off by the Japanese near the Muar River, 70 miles north of Singapore. During the evening of January 20, all radio contact with the Australians and Indians ceased.

The next morning, Bennett's headquarters received a cryptic and incomplete wireless message: "We now [sic] through roadblock with guns and transport." Bennett flashed a grim smile. Showing McDaniel a map, Bennett pointed out that the battalions had fought their way through 7 miles of Japanese machine guns. Bennett ordered fifteen commandos armed with Tommy guns to relieve the Australians, but they could not find their countrymen in the dense jungles. Bennett radioed the trapped battalions: "Regret there is little prospect [of] any success of attack to help you. You may at your discretion leave wounded with volunteers, destroy heavy equipment and escape. Sorry unable to help after your heroic effort. Good luck, Gordon Bennett."

By Thursday, about 400 Australians and 400 Indians, the shattered remnants of the original units, streamed toward Bennett's lines. McDaniel talked to a radio truck operator, who along with two other Australians manned the equipment until the radios died. They blew up the radio truck and sought a way out of the trap. Japanese snipers killed one of the soldiers, but the two others continued. They and thirty other Australians dashed through a swamp as Japanese machine gun bullets peppered the shallow water. The survivors reached safety, although Ian Morrison noticed their legs were bleeding from insect bites. The men were filthy and unshaven.[41] McDaniel filed his story and quoted Bennett as saying that "there has not been a more astounding effort in this war or the last." But for all the heroic talk, the Japanese had savaged the two Australian battalions. There literally was nothing between the Japanese and Singapore.[42]

McDaniel drove back toward Singapore. Before crossing the straits, he stopped to pay a final visit to the sultan of Johore. The sultan led McDaniel to a drawing room in his palace, where Yates had so often "enjoyed his hospitality." McDaniel noticed a silver plaque on the wall behind the sultan that displayed the mottos of the sultans of Johore: "Kepahad Allah," which means "Unto God, Resigned."

Antiaircraft guns raged at Japanese planes, but the sultan ignored the noise. The sultan told McDaniel he planned to stay with his people "no matter what happens to me or may be said against me by critics from away from this troubled land." The sultan's British advisers had left for Singapore, but his cabinet ministers, Indian policemen, and his wife were staying.

McDaniel urged the sultan to leave. McDaniel told him of how savage the Japanese had been in Nanking and Hankow. The sultan shook his head. As McDaniel stood to leave, the sultan said he would eventually visit America and Great Britain. "Tell Hollywood and Honolulu I am coming back someday" were his final words to McDaniel.[43]

McDaniel arrived in Singapore during yet another air raid. He counted twenty-seven Japanese planes over the city. They unloaded their bombs and vanished into the clouds. From London, Churchill issued a declaration that the "city of Singapore must be converted into a citadel and defended to the death. No surrender can be contemplated, and the commander, staffs and principal officers are expected to perish at their posts." Despite those bold words, McDaniel wrote, people in Singapore "could not help but recall that similar pledges of last-ditch fights preceded the loss of Norway, Greece, and Crete."[44]

Civilians and soldiers were trudging across the 1,153-yard causeway into Singapore from war-ravaged Malaya. Small trucks carried the household belongings of refugees. Civilians grasped their children in their arms, while United Press's Harold Guard saw a Malayan man and woman walking barefoot as they held hands.[45] On January 31, under what McDaniel described as a "brilliant moonlight," the last of the British, Australian, and Indian soldiers crossed the causeway. At dawn, the Argyll bagpipers, who as recently as September had entertained the elegantly dressed men and women at the Palm Court in the Raffles, crossed into Singapore, leaving Malaya to the Japanese. The pipes and drums blared out "A Hundred Pipers" and the Argyll march "Highland Laddie," both of which McDaniel described as stirring.[46] After everyone crossed to safety, an Argyll officer ordered the engineers to set off explosive charges, and 75 feet of the causeway's middle section crumpled into the strait, leaving what McDaniel called tangled masses of barbed wire and "granite rubble and concrete blocks." McDaniel looked through binoculars toward the Japanese side of the strait. Columns of smoke rose above Johore. He could not see any sign of Japanese troops. But a handful of Japanese planes ominously circled above.[47]

British officials imposed a curfew from nine in the evening until five in the morning. Gen. Percival issued what he hoped would be an inspiring call: "The battle of Malaya has come to an end, and the battle of Singapore has started." The appeal fell flat. As far as McDaniel could tell, the Japanese were ready to launch "a direct assault on this fortress once considered impregnable largely because of its [450] miles of protecting jungles to the north."[48]

The next day, McDaniel heard the thunder of Singapore's huge land guns as they fired for the first time toward Japanese positions across the Johore Strait. British officials told McDaniel that reconnaissance planes had spotted large formations of Japanese troops moving along the jungle roads just above the strait. Unlike many of the British, Indian, and Australian forces in Singapore, the Japanese were well trained. In his diary, Adm. Layton dejectedly wrote that "man-for-man, our men were inferior to the Japanese in training and in the moral qualities of audacity, tenacity, discipline, and devotion." Japan's navy controlled the South China Sea, and the only modern British planes the Japanese aircraft had to deal with were a few newly arrived Hurricane fighters, although McDaniel saw one Hurricane shoot down a Japanese bomber.[49]

Throughout the day of February 3, "the gloomy wail of air raid sirens filled the air" as Japanese bombers pummeled the city. As fires raged in the downtown area, McDaniel watched a civilian in shirt sleeves help Chinese workers as they laid down watering hoses for fire trucks. The man straightened up, and McDaniel recognized him: it was Governor Shenton Thomas. Not far away, Gen. Percival orchestrated the removal of valuable materials from a warehouse as the fires approached.[50]

The city was largely unprotected. In December 1941, Duff Cooper wrote Churchill that the civilian leadership in Singapore had completely failed, warning, "There are no air-raid shelters, no trenches even; no tin hats or gas masks for the civilian population." Now, nothing had changed, and people scrambled in vain for any place to hide from the bombs. In two days, sixty-three people were killed, although McDaniel sarcastically quoted officials as saying casualties were "comparatively light."

On the morning of February 4, Japanese planes carried out a raid. A pair of small bombs exploded about 100 yards from McDaniel's office, which did little more than scatter his papers about and cause plaster to tumble from the ceiling. When the raid ended, McDaniel drove to the Johore Straits. It was strangely quiet. He gazed through his binoculars. There was no sign of any Japanese forces on the other side of the straits. When McDaniel returned to Singapore, he read through a statement issued by Gen. Wavell. "Our part is to gain time for great reinforcements we and our American allies are sending to the eastern theater," Wavell said. That very same day, Wavell left Singapore for Java.

McDaniel that night monitored a broadcast by the senior air raid warden and was stunned at its frankness. "It's no use telling the people that Malta has had a thousand raids and they have stuck it out or that Chungking has had worse than we had," the warden bluntly said. "These places have ideal shelters, and we have nothing except drains and odd slit trenches." He quickly filed an update to his earlier story.[51]

On the evening of February 6, McDaniel attended a news conference that featured Percival. British press officers hastily found a room and dug up some chairs, although most reporters were forced to stand. Percival walked in and sat at a table. Percival acknowledged the obvious: RAF planes were not flying over Singapore. They had been removed from the airfields because of heavy Japanese bombing. But Percival said defiantly, "We will hold Singapore. There is no question about it." He laughed slightly, although it appeared a nervous laugh. "In any case, it's doubtful if we could withdraw from Singapore even if we wished to."[52]

As Percival spoke, McDaniel noticed smoke wafting in the air from burning oil tanks at the naval base, fires set by the British to keep the fuel out of the hands of the Japanese.

British officials prepared to evacuate women and children "regardless of race," to ships heading toward Java or Ceylon. Kenneth Patton, the US consul general, closed the American mission, asked the Swiss to handle US interests, and looked for passage out of Singapore. Admirals Layton and Palliser were sent to Java on January 5. Duff Cooper and his wife departed a week later, with Lady Diana sadly writing, "It was impossible not to look as though we were running for it."[53]

British public-information officers contacted the correspondents still in Singapore. "You better leave," one told McDaniel. "We have space for you on a small patrol boat heading for India or Java." Most reporters left. McDaniel opted to stay. Although he later explained he followed his old practice of staying "as long as my communications hold out," it was clear he did not want to repeat the mistake he made of not sailing with the *Repulse*.[54]

Japanese planes were destroying the homes of the wealthy and the poor, sending towering columns of smoke over the city. Hospitals were still operating while volunteers piled up bricks, metal, and earth to prevent Japanese planes from landing on racetracks, golf courses, cricket patches, and soccer grounds.

McDaniel's stories reflected the increasing despair of the city and its defenders and included a touch of history to show what was at stake. They also revealed his admiration for the British Empire:

> This day in Singapore 132 years ago: Sir Stamford Raffles hoisted the Union Jack over a struggling fishing village of straw huts set on stilts amid the ruins of the ancient City of Lions of a decayed Malayan empire. This was Singapore today at the end of one week of a siege that left little time for thought of history: The Union Jack still flies, but the guns behind the camouflaged ramparts are pounding the land forces and the planes of the first modern enemy to threaten this stronghold, containing a metropolis of 750,000 persons—a bastion of empire erected on the shrewd deal by Sir Stamford.

The Japanese, McDaniel wrote, "have twisted the tall tail of the British lion . . . but the guns which are pounding tonight from the ramparts are giving resounding proof that the king of beasts still roars defiance."[55]

The British were getting help from an unlikely source. Although they had treated Singapore's Chinese with disdain for years, about 1,000 Chinese residents volunteered to fight for the empire. McDaniel, Ian Morrison of the *Times* of London, and Henry Stokes of Reuters watched them train at an enclosed courtyard. They fumbled with Swiss target rifles, shotguns, and even axes and knives. As Col. John Dalley, the organizer of the volunteers, drove up, they stood at attention. One recruit saluted with his right hand, another with his left.[56]

On the afternoon of February 8, the Japanese unleashed what McDaniel characterized as a "withering" artillery and aerial bombardment west of the demolished causeway. The tempo of the Japanese gunfire sharply increased at night. The half moon did not rise until one in the morning on February 9, allowing specially designed Japanese invasion boats to cross the strait in complete darkness. British artillery shells exploded in the water, sending up huge geysers, but it was difficult in the dark to find the Japanese boats.

Gen. Bennett's Australians were defending the beach, and, as always, he exuded confidence. "The situation is well in hand," he told McDaniel. "We have taken a stand on a strong line and are organizing an attack which it is hoped will recover as much as possible of the lost terrain." Australian and Indian forces, bayonets attached to their rifles, launched a counterattack. To McDaniel, the invasion was "the test of tests. Alternatives were simple and unqualified: Death or victory."[57]

The burning oil tanks cast a bright orange glow over Singapore's night sky. By the next morning, a Tuesday, the orange had turned to a "pall of gray smoke," which hung above the northern part of the island. Sailors aboard one British ship could see the smoke from 50 miles away.[58]

McDaniel was furiously updating his stories. He reported that Japanese troops "were pouring onto this beleaguered island" and forcing battered Australian forces to retreat. A gloomy Governor Thomas said, "We are all in the hands of God from whom we can get comfort in our anxieties and strength to play the man and help one another in all the ordeals which are to come." Privately, Adm. Spooner predicted that Singapore "will probably be captured tonight or tomorrow."[59]

McDaniel returned to the Cathay Building and stood on the balcony of his room with its panoramic view of the madness and normalcy of Singapore's final hours. He looked north. Japanese dive-bombers were "darting in and out" of towering columns of black smoke. Light-gray smoke rose from rubber plants, pineapple canneries, and factories set on fire by the British. To the south, faraway "wisps" of smoke spiraled above fishing villages on small Dutch islands. Then he looked straight down. Streets were jammed with cars, trolleys, and rickshaws taking people home from their daily jobs. Cars dropped the fashionable set at the Raffles Hotel for the daily tea dance. On the street below his room, people lined up at the box office of the Cathay's air-conditioned theater, which was showing *Reaching for the Sun*, a new William Wellman film starring Joel McCrea and Ellen Drew.

At the afternoon press briefing, the British military spokesman addressed only three people—McDaniel and two reporters from Singapore's newspapers. Everyone else was gone. Just that day, Harold Guard of United Press found passage on a ship heading toward Java. A disconsolate Guard, one of the more courageous correspondents in Asia, wrote, "I regret leaving Singapore, leaving my home, and leaving my last story."[60] Durdin, too, had left a few days earlier and was reporting from Batavia in western Java. Athole Stewart, an Australian press officer, rooted about in vain for Ian Morrison of the *Times* of London, but all he could find was the correspondent's prized pipe on an empty table in the press room in the Cathay Building. He had no idea that Morrison had just boarded a Dutch cargo ship in Keppel Harbor on Singapore's south side.[61]

McDaniel filed his story at 7:30 in the evening. Not wanting to leave anything to the Japanese, McDaniel burned a pile of his papers and a thousand negatives of photographs he had taken years earlier in China. At the last moment, he decided to save his passport and British War Office credentials.

The next morning, his story was on the front pages of American and Canadian newspapers with an AP editor's note: "Terrible, yet bizarre, the following picture of Singapore—shellfire and the evening tea dance; dive bombers and placid movie-goers—comes from C. Yates McDaniel, the only American newspaperman to cover the nine-day siege and only foreign newspaperman to remain now in the battle of the island itself." Without Durdin in Singapore to provide copy, the *New York Times* ran McDaniel's story on its front page under a six-column headline: "Singapore tottering."[62]

Others were taking note of the daring American reporter staying with the story. DeWitt MacKenzie, the military reporter for AP Wide World News Service in the United States, wrote, "You probably have noted a steady stream of graphic, informative dispatches is coming out of Singapore" from McDaniel, whom he described as "a grand young fellow who now is risking his life to get the news. So next time you read McDaniel's byline in your paper as you drink your coffee, just wish him— and all his grand colleagues over there—a lot of luck."[63]

On Wednesday the eleventh, McDaniel typed away once more in his room at the Cathay Building. It was 10:30 in the morning, but the sky was so dark from smoke that McDaniel turned on the lights. Capt. O. K. Fearon, a British censor, sat next to him, eating a breakfast of biscuits and sipping brandy. McDaniel's hands were wet with perspiration. His heart was pounding.

> The sky over Singapore is black with the smoke of a dozen huge fires this morning as I write my last message from this once beautiful, prosperous and peaceful city. Over the low rise where the battle is raging, I can see relay after relay of Japanese planes circling, then going into murderous dives upon our soldiers, who are fighting back in a hell over which there is no protecting screen of fighter planes.

He watched two "antiquated" Vildebeest biplanes with their tiny .30-caliber machine guns tangle with much-faster Zeroes. He kept typing: "If ever brave men endured undying glory, those RAF pilots have on this tragic morning." Japanese bombs exploded near the hotel, and McDaniel and Fearon took cover behind a wall.

Capt. Henry Steel, a British press officer, told McDaniel, "You've got ten minutes to pack up and leave."

McDaniel pushed Steel's deadline, writing an extra paragraph. "I am leaving now in a car which I swear I will put into forward gear and head straight into the Straits of Malacca. I left one car for the Japanese in Nanking, but never again. Don't expect to hear from me for many days, but please inform Mrs. McDaniel, Hotel Preanger, Bandoeng, Java, that I have left this land of the living and the dying."

He continued to type: "When Henry says go, I go. First of the foreign correspondents to arrive and last to leave, I am taking my chance of getting clear of this beleaguered fortress. And so goodbye from Singapore." He added an unusual slug to the story that read "Definitely last." To his editors in New York, it was an ominous message.

They left the Cathay Building, with McDaniel stopping at the cable office to file his story. A beautiful young Chinese woman approached. She appeared to be about eighteen to twenty years old, and she gave him a note from Newsreel Wong, the legendary Chinese film photographer and a close friend. Yates read through it: "Doris can tell you what happened. Anything you can do to help Doris I'd appreciate."

Her name was Doris Lim, and the note explained she was Newsreel Wong's niece. Normally she had an infectious smile, but on this day she was "utterly forlorn."

She had tried to leave Singapore the previous evening with Newsreel Wong on a small tender bound for Java. Wong, Harold Guard, and Australian photographer Cliff Bottomley boarded, but Doris was denied passage because she could not prove she was a British citizen. She returned to her seventh-floor room in the Cathay. McDaniel clearly was not happy with this new responsibility, saying to himself, "So now I'm saddled with her."[64]

McDaniel, Doris, and Capt. Steel joined Australian press officers Athole Stewart and Sydney Downer to make their way to the wharfs. From there, ships had a clear path to sail through Keppel Harbor toward the safety of Dutch-held Java. Despite the repetitive explosions from Japanese bombs and the virtual collapse of British authority, there was no sign of panic or looting. British officials had gathered a motley collection of elderly steamers, yachts, and motorboats for those eager to leave before Gen. Percival surrendered, which was expected any day. McDaniel was assigned to the *Kung Wo*, a coal-burning relic from the Yangtze River.

The ship's captain, Lt. Cmdr. Thompson, was a stocky Royal Navy Reserve officer in his midthirties. The crew, in McDaniel's words, was a collection of "odds and ends." The captain agreed to take Doris, whom McDaniel explained was a British citizen born in Hong Kong. Thompson kept the *Kung Wo* at anchor for the rest of the day and through the night, waiting to see if stragglers would board.

The next morning, Thursday, February 12, Thompson ordered the *Kung Wo* to steam to a nearby dock next to the Singapore electrical power plant to pick up badly needed coal.

"All able-bodied hands to coal ship," an officer ordered. The men filled baskets with coal, dragged them across the wharf, and wheeled them into the bunkers. The work was brutal, and the men were soaked with sweat. By four in the afternoon, they had loaded 80 tons of coal onto the *Kung Wo*.[65]

McDaniel needed to make one last trip back to the Cathay Building. Accompanied by Doris, McDaniel drove to the city and went to his room for the final time. He collected two bottles of his favorite Liebfraumilch white wine, a pair of binoculars, two cameras—an Exakta and a Contax—a handful of biscuits, and four tins of Camel cigarettes, each tin holding fifty cigarettes.

Explosions rocked the city, and debris clogged the streets as McDaniel and Doris drove back to the dock where the *Kung Wo* waited. A thin stream of smoke wafted from her single funnel. "The game is up," McDaniel said. He had heard Japanese tanks were in Singapore. "It's only a matter of hours now."[66]

McDaniel snapped a photograph of six British soldiers pushing his car into the straits, and a second photo of thick plumes of smoke rising from the docks. At 3:45 p.m., he filed another paragraph:

> Lying offshore we were bombed incessantly until sundown yesterday and throughout today. We were dive bombed half-a-dozen times, but we are still afloat and may get away tonight.

Singapore was one day ahead of the United States because of the International Date Line, which allowed the *Boston Globe* to publish his first-person account on its February 11 front page. Inside, the paper ran a story recalling Natalie McDaniel's kidnapping from so long ago. The *Globe* included a photo of Yates and Natalie.

The *Detroit Free Press* spread his story on page 1 on February 12. Right next to McDaniel's story, the *Free Press* ran a companion piece from Java. It was written by Cecil Brown of CBS.

# SUMATRA AND JAVA

he vessel that was to carry McDaniel and more than 100 others from Singapore across 500 treacherous miles of sea to safety in Java was unimpressive. One British naval officer grumbled that the *Kung Wo* looked more like a Mississippi River boat than an oceangoing vessel.[1] Built in 1921, the 4,600-ton *Kung Wo* was designed to steam 15 knots but now was so worn out and battered that she could barely reach 10. After the Japanese invasion of China, she had escaped to Hong Kong and then Singapore, where the British utilized her as a minelayer, although they never took the trouble to arm her. With three dilapidated lifeboats and a handful of rifles, she "did not exactly instill confidence," one passenger thought, although everyone seemed somewhat reassured because she flew the White Ensign of the Royal Navy. She could float and was among a gaggle of aged vessels gathered by British officials in Singapore to give people some way to escape. For now, that was good enough.[2]

As the sun set on the twelfth, the *Kung Wo* gently moved away from the dock, but the captain was not ready to leave. Passengers gathered on the upper decks and leaned against the rails to see Singapore's powerful searchlights seeking Japanese planes. Their faces were illuminated by the glow of fires. Smoke covered the ship with a film of oily soot.[3]

Just past nine in the evening, a launch approached carrying the assistant harbor master. How many people aboard? The captain replied about 140, and the launch returned to the docks. By signal lamp, the captain asked naval headquarters for permission to leave. A handful of vessels sailed past the *Kung Wo*, but the captain wanted orders. Alerted by the flashing lamp, a British naval lieutenant steered a second motor launch toward the *Kung Wo*. He shouted that anyone who could give the captain an order had left, and he was only waiting to fetch Adm. Jack Spooner from Singapore.

"For God's sake, let's get cracking," Capt. Henry Steel pleaded.

A few minutes after midnight, the *Kung Wo* eased its way out of the flaming harbor in the forlorn hope of reaching Batavia. The passengers had no idea that directly in their path the Japanese aircraft carrier *Ryūjō*, seven cruisers, and a dozen destroyers were escorting troop transports set to occupy Dutch-held Sumatra, a prelude to the invasion of Java.[4]

The reflection of Singapore's fires created an eerie glow in the *Kung Wo*'s wake. "We haven't got a hope of getting away with this, Fergie," McDaniel said, using Stewart's nickname. Stewart ruefully realized it was Friday the thirteenth.[5]

The passengers and crew members were an unusual brew: Survivors from the *Prince of Wales* and *Repulse*, such as Lt. Cmdr. Anthony Terry and SLt. Geoffrey Brooke; about twenty pilots; a British censor named Welby; Capt. Steel; McDaniel; and Doris Lim, the only woman aboard. The men immediately took a liking to the Chinese woman dressed in a light-blue shirt and blue slacks, who Brooke thought "had apparently been left in the lurch by her MGM cameraman boss," a reference to Newsreel Wong.[6] McDaniel, Steel, and Stewart found an empty cabin for Doris. Nobody seemed to know much about her, which allowed the more creative minds to fill in the blanks. Some wove an unlikely tale that she had been a British agent in China as far back as 1933, although for that to be true she would have begun her espionage career at age eleven.[7]

She was raised by her mother in Hong Kong, although at some point she moved to Shanghai before returning to Hong Kong in 1941. With the threat of war looming, British officials evacuated civilians from Hong Kong to Singapore, the Philippines, or Java. Doris boarded a ship bound for Singapore, a voyage that included a layover in Manila. When she reached Singapore, Doris caught up with Newsreel Wong, worked as his assistant, and stayed with him at the Cathay. Those bits and pieces were all that anyone knew about Doris.[8]

The *Kung Wo* continued its perilous voyage. Some relaxed in cabin chairs while others tried to sleep. As the sun rose, McDaniel saw a handful of small islands in the distance. The *Kung Wo* had steamed 80 miles.

At 7:30 in the morning, McDaniel saw the menacing shapes of two Japanese bombers circle and dive on the little ship. The ship vibrated as its engines roared. Passengers fastened life belts, and someone from the bridge fired a rifle at the planes. The bombs exploded harmlessly astern of the ship. Two more planes buzzed the ship, and one bomb exploded with such force it seemed to lift the *Kung Wo* from the water, leaving a large hole in the forward hold near the riverboat-like superstructure.[9]

For the third time, Japanese planes returned, and this time McDaniel heard an ear-splitting crash as a bomb smacked into the deck above the engine room, killing a Chinese stoker. The *Kung Wo* veered into a half circle and began to list. The second engineer opened the valves to make certain the boilers would not explode. The ship would stay afloat for at least a few hours.

"All right, get the boats alongside," Lt. Cmdr. Terry shouted.

McDaniel saw a large island about 5 miles away. Crew members launched an empty lifeboat that sank in a matter of moments. A second was commandeered by Stewart and about twenty other passengers and slowly pulled away from the *Kung Wo*. Terry waved his arms and shouted for them to wait. Stewart wanted to row back, but the rest of the crew ignored him. They continued to row away from the stricken ship.[10]

That left just one lifeboat, which was not large enough for the roughly 100 people left on the ship. In what McDaniel called the British tradition of women first, Doris entered the boat. Others scrambled in and cast off. They promised to return as soon as they reached the island and unloaded their passengers. McDaniel, Steel, Brooke, and forty-two others waited on the *Kung Wo*. A Japanese seaplane flew by so close that they could see the Japanese observer examining the ship through his binoculars. The plane flew off without strafing the decks. Brooke was amused by McDaniel, who "would pop up at the most annoying moments, [camera] to eye and notebook ready. This was going to be the biggest scoop of his career." McDaniel snapped a photo of Terry eating his breakfast, and another of the damage caused by the Japanese bombs. When he wasn't snapping photos, McDaniel rested against a coil of rope and took notes, although twice he joined the others to form a bucket brigade and fight fires.[11]

At five in the evening, the lifeboat that had carried Doris to the island reappeared. McDaniel, Steel, Brooke, and another officer rustled up four crystal goblets and opened McDaniel's bottles of Liebfraumilch. They toasted one another, the British Empire, Singapore, and finally the "good ship *Kung Wo*." Then they smashed the glasses against the dining-saloon mantelpiece. Thirty-six men clambered into the boat, leaving six volunteers on the ship. McDaniel helped bail water from the leaky lifeboat as it clumsily made its way to the island. By the time they grounded on a coral reef near the beach, the sun was setting. An Australian officer told them he had found a stream of fresh water but could not scrounge up any coconuts to eat.

The lifeboat with Stewart approached. They had rowed to the wrong island and had spent the last three hours trying to reach the other survivors. To McDaniel, they were "a beat-up bunch." Believing those in Stewart's boat had deliberately abandoned the rest, nobody spoke to them until Stewart explained that he wanted to return to the *Kung Wo*.[12]

In addition to the six men left on the *Kung Wo*, a head count revealed there were 131 men and one woman on the island and the ship. They opened cans of bully beef with jackknives, added some biscuits seized from the *Kung Wo*, and ate dinner. Then they settled down for some sleep on the soggy beach infested with hermit crabs, ants, and mosquitoes. By midnight, the temperature plunged, making the evening more miserable.

Even though he was exhausted, McDaniel had trouble sleeping. He shared a ground sheet with Stewart, which offered some protection from the hermit crabs.

"Steady Fergie, I'm nearly off the sheet," McDaniel said.[13]

McDaniel heard someone moving about and quickly tapped Steel. A British official was trying to swipe extra food. At daybreak, the official tried again.

"If you try that again, I'll shoot you," Steel told him. The official then made a pass at Doris. Once again, McDaniel woke up Steel, who ordered the official to leave her alone.[14]

The sun rose to reveal a clear and beautiful turquoise sea. One officer was struck as "birds twittered, the sea lapped a few yards away, and the yellow sand of the very pleasant little bay was littered with stretching figures." They had breakfast of biscuits and muddy water that was as close as they could get to tea. McDaniel puffed away on his ever-present Camels. A lookout shouted. A gray-painted launch was snooping about the listing *Kung Wo*. If the launch was Japanese, the survivors thought they had little choice except to surrender. McDaniel and Steel decided they would hide in the jungle. "I don't propose to be taken prisoner," McDaniel told the others. "I could not endure any form of confinement, especially at their hands." But he decided he could not take Doris with him and told her to surrender.

"There's nothing I can do," McDaniel told her in Chinese. "You go along with the captain."[15]

The launch took the last six men off the *Kung Wo* and steered toward the island. To their relief, a bearded Dutch planter aboard the launch shouted he would arrange for a rescue ship to pluck them to safety. That left them with nothing to do but wait. They snapped photos of some of the survivors, including McDaniel, Doris, and Steel. Doris flashed a cheery smile. All were filthy and disheveled. McDaniel wore grimy short pants, torn tennis shoes, and a khaki military shirt he had borrowed in Singapore. Unable to shave, he had grown a thick beard. He perched a typewriter on a pair of fallen logs and typed notes. If he lived through the ordeal, at least he could write a story. McDaniel then took photos of Steel preparing a report on the same typewriter and Thompson checking his charts.

At noon, seven Japanese planes circled above the *Kung Wo* and dropped their bombs. When the smoke cleared away, the *Kung Wu's* stern rose high in the air. As the ship sank, the captain took off his cap and turned away.

A small rescue boat showed up as the sun was setting, and its light flashed the agreed-upon signal—two long and one short. Because of the low tide, the vessel had to anchor far offshore. A lifeboat from the rescue ship could not get any closer than a half mile from the island.

"You'll have to walk out to the lifeboats," Terry said. "For God's sake, wear your shoes."[16]

McDaniel hung his binoculars around his neck and held his cameras and notebooks above his head. Then McDaniel, Steel, Doris, and the others splashed through the shallow water. For the next forty-five minutes, they cursed and stumbled, cutting their feet on coral. About 20 yards from the lifeboat, McDaniel slipped off an underwater ledge and tumbled into a 10-foot hole, soaking his cameras and the exposed photos. He was so upset he could have cried. McDaniel, Doris, and Steel toppled into the lifeboat and, using its only oar and their hands, rowed toward the launch. Only fifty-five men and Doris reached it. The others waited on the island for another rescue boat. Stewart borrowed a cigarette and a light. The cigarette illuminated his watch: it was nearly 10:00 in the evening.

The launch veered toward nearby Sumatra. Mountainous waves splashed over the decks, and McDaniel and his companions hung on as best they could. He later would say that while the evening on the island was "miserable," the night on the launch was "indescribable" as they shivered from the frigid waves. By daybreak, they entered the mouth of a river. McDaniel knew they had reached the east coast of Sumatra, but had no idea exactly where. Given where the *Kung Wo* sank, they were at the mouth of the Indragiri River, which ran west into Sumatra's interior.

On the morning of February 16, the launch resumed its journey up the river to the Dutch settlement of Rengat, where the passengers disembarked. British and Dutch soldiers had hastily arranged supplies along a pathway from Rengat to Sumatra's west coast. The route included a gravel road through the mountains. It ended at Padang, a Dutch town just a few miles from the port of Emmahaven on the Indian Ocean. McDaniel and his group had little time because Japanese troops had already landed in northern Sumatra.

A Malay man with a truck offered to drive them the 235 miles to Padang. McDaniel handed him some cash. As darkness enveloped the winding gravel road, everyone fell asleep in the back of the truck. McDaniel occupied the passenger's seat and kept the driver awake by handing him one cigarette after another. At dawn, they had reached the top of a volcanic mountain, where they were serenaded by the sound of monkeys screeching in the trees. As they passed through small villages, chickens scattered away from the truck.[17]

A Dutch official warned them if the truck broke down, they would find themselves surrounded by ravenous tigers. But having gotten this far, they opted to continue, although everyone was alarmed when a black panther crossed the road in front of the truck. By midafternoon, McDaniel saw what he described as the beautiful sight of the Indian Ocean. They had reached the safety of Padang, whose Dutch architecture, wide avenues, and manicured gardens gave every appearance of a traditional town in the Netherlands. A Dutch woman operating a guesthouse took them in, fed them, and made tea. An exhausted McDaniel slept in a reception room.[18]

In Java, Natalie had no idea whether Yates was alive or dead. She told a British reporter that she had not heard anything about her husband since his last story from Singapore.[19] On February 18, the *New York Times* reported that McDaniel "was among those missing who had boarded boats at Singapore last week." The AP reported it had heard nothing from McDaniel since the thirteenth, when the *Kung Wo* was leaving Singapore. The *London Evening Standard*, which published McDaniel's final story from Singapore under the headline "Salute the Brave," ran a page 1 story declaring that McDaniel was missing. Natalie received a telegram from the US military declaring that Yates was lost and presumed dead. Alone and in shock, she wept. She had little choice but to figure out a way to get to the safety of Australia.[20]

As the AP editors in New York wondered where McDaniel might be, Yates—who had no way of contacting anyone outside Sumatra—was in a bar in the Oranje Hotel in Padang chatting with a British official he knew from Singapore.

"Do you believe in miracles?" the official asked McDaniel. After the past few days of barely surviving, Yates could only reply, "Yes."

"If you do, quietly without telling anyone, be at the north end of Emmahaven at two o'clock tomorrow afternoon," the official mysteriously said. McDaniel asked whether he could bring Steel, Welby, Doris, and another British officer. Fine, the official said.[21]

The next day they hunted about in vain for a taxi before hiring pony carts to carry them to the railway station and the short streetcar ride to Emmahaven. McDaniel found the harbor a "depressing sight" after numerous Japanese air attacks. He counted the sunken hulks of twenty ships in the harbor. McDaniel volunteered to find something to eat and bought some dried beans at a Chinese shop. The town seemed otherwise empty. Then they waited at the dock.

At two in the afternoon, the British destroyer *Encounter* steamed into the harbor and docked. The 1,400-ton destroyer was the most beautiful sight McDaniel had ever seen. British officials in Batavia had sent the destroyer to Emmahaven with orders to evacuate as many people as possible. As McDaniel and his companions walked up to the gangplank, a young British officer politely said, "Right on board, please." He didn't ask for names or inquire whether Doris was a British citizen. Minutes later, the destroyer glided out of the harbor and set a course for Java.[22]

The British sailors did their best to make their guests comfortable in cabins and on the decks. When McDaniel thanked one of the British officers, he laughed and said, "It's an old story for us. We have been rescuing the Army from Norway to Tobruk."[23] McDaniel collapsed on the steel deck, which seemed more comfortable than the deserted island's sandy beach. The *Encounter* raced along the Sumatra coast at more than 30 knots. Lightning erupted in the sky, followed by crashing thunder. Heavy rains pounded the deck. As night fell, the destroyer entered Sunda Strait, the deep and wide channel that separated Sumatra from Java. Clouds had cleared away and the moon shined brightly. The straits were as "calm as a lake." The destroyer docked the next morning, February 20, in Batavia.[24]

McDaniel was greeted by the familiar sound of air raid warnings. This time, Japanese planes did not appear. McDaniel walked to the AP headquarters at the Hotel des Indes, one of the most luxurious in all of Southeast Asia. Private rooms featured a veranda with screens and a view of the park, where deer strolled about. Every day at noon, the large dining room offered what was called *rijsttafel*, where waiters would stop by each table with bowls of rice, followed by an assortment of egg rolls, satay, fish, and scores of other dishes. Sitting in the lounge, sipping a beer, and smoking a new pipe was Ian Morrison of the *Times* of London, who had found passage on a ship out of Singapore a day before McDaniel left.[25]

McDaniel was desperate for sleep. But the AP in New York called and asked him to write a story of his escape as quickly as possible.

He rummaged through some of his photos that survived his swim. There was one of the battered *Kung Wo*, another of him typing on the island, and a third showing the survivors before they evacuated the island. His notebook had been transformed into "salt-water soaked pulp."

He began to type. Writing in the first person, he chronicled their improbable survival. First the escape from Singapore. The sinking of the *Kung Wo*. The island and its mosquitoes. The harrowing truck ride through Sumatra. The omnipresent threat from Japanese planes and Malayan tigers. The courage of Doris Lim, whom he described as "one plucky girl."

He typed: "I am glad to be alive and looking forward to sleeping in a bed for the first time in eleven days." Then he had the story cleared by censors and cabled it to New York.[26]

Reuters in Batavia flashed the word: Yates McDaniel was alive. The Reuters story described Doris Lim as a "Chinese girl from Shanghai who was an assistant to a Metro Goldwyn Mayer Movietone newsreel crew." Reuters quoted some survivors as saying Lim "never uttered a whimper, always was busy and bandaged the wounded, and made tea."[27]

McDaniel's gripping first-person account ran in scores of newspapers—the *Baltimore Evening Sun, Tampa Times, Santa Ana Register, Oakland Tribune, Elmira Gazette, Honolulu Star-Bulletin, Minneapolis Star-Journal,* and a host of smaller publications. The *New York Times* published the article under the headline "McDaniel travels 1,200 miles from city to safety at Batavia." In April, when the AP distributed McDaniel's photos, more than thirty newspapers across the United States published them. The *Minneapolis Star-Journal* featured one showing black smoke billowing above Singapore, the *Decatur Herald* opted for the photo of British soldiers pushing McDaniel's car into the harbor, and the *St. Louis Post-Dispatch* displayed the battered *Kung Wo* and the group photo with a beaming Doris Lim. The *Baltimore Sun* ran the iconic photo of McDaniel typing on the deserted island, with a cutline: "On the Job."

McDaniel instantly became one of the most famous reporters in the world, captivating American, Australian, and British audiences desperate for some good news. The AP ran a newspaper advertisement with a headshot of McDaniel under a large headline proclaiming, "Singapore—First to arrive. Last to leave." At the bottom, the AP general manager Kent Cooper declared, "AP men are the best in the world."

*Time* published a glowing profile: "C. Yates McDaniel is only 35, but his hair is almost white. It should be. As a Far Eastern correspondent for AP, he retreated up the Yangtze with the Chinese Army, had enough narrow escapes to earn many a thread of silver. His experiences of the past fortnight entitle him to a snow-white thatch for the rest of his life. For Yates McDaniel watched the collapse of Singapore at close hand, filed a dispatch that might well have been the last farewell of a crack reporter."[28]

The AP's Don Whitehead featured both McDaniel and the AP's Clark Lee—who covered the Japanese invasion of the Philippines—in a major story on the cover of the *St. Louis Post-Dispatch* Sunday Magazine. The two reporters "have added new chapters of bizarre adventure by their own daring to this unfinished saga of journalism," Whitehead wrote.[29] McDaniel became so well known that a few months later, a man wrote the *Philadelphia Inquirer* to ask, "What has happened to the newspaperman named McDaniel who writes of the evacuation of Singapore?"[30] In 1944 in Bougainville, Americans discovered on the body of a Japanese soldier a prewar photograph of McDaniel standing with Chiang Kai-shek, Madame Chiang, and J. B. Powell, editor of the *China Weekly Review*.[31]

Now living in California, Natalie's father, John Eills, was so delighted with the news of Yates's escape that he dashed off a letter to Yates and Natalie, writing that "few stories have won so much attention" as Yates's final story from Singapore. "Old Pops is as proud as a peacock. It's a great relief to know you are safe today and I hope for the duration." John sent the letter to Java, but to his chagrin it was returned unopened a few weeks later.

Geoff Hutton, a correspondent for the *Argus* in Melbourne, praised McDaniel, although he pointed out McDaniel was "one of the luckiest" correspondents who covered World War II. In fact, McDaniel *had* been incredibly lucky. Japanese planes and warships sank forty-six small ships fleeing Singapore during the week of February 12. Of the 3,000 people on those ships, more than 2,000 died—from shells, drowning, or disease on deserted islands. The dead included Adm. Spooner, Air Vice-Marshal C. W. H. Pulford, and Vivian Bowden, the Australian representative to Singapore, who was shot by the Japanese for no particular reason. Gen. Percival surrendered to the Japanese on February 15 and spent the rest of the war in a prison camp. Gen. Bennett managed to escape, although he ruined his reputation by leaving his troops on Singapore.

McDaniel expected to find Newsreel Wong in Java, but the photographer left the day before the *Encounter* arrived. Instead, Wong left a note: "Help Doris. On my way to Ceylon, then Calcutta."[32]

For an entire day, McDaniel rooted about for a way to get Doris out of Java. He found the British consul general and pleaded his case. Doris, he explained, was trying to reach India. Because he knew she was from Hong Kong, he signed a document "affirming" she was a British subject. McDaniel took Doris to the docks, where a "very modern" and fast passenger ship of 10,000 tons waited. The steamer headed toward Ceylon. McDaniel would never see or hear from Doris again.[33]

He had hoped to find Natalie, but she had left Java the day before the *Encounter* docked in Batavia. She left him a letter at the Hotel des Indes saying she was boarding a Dutch steamer for Australia. The ship was not completely filled, and most passengers were women who had left their husbands in either Singapore or Java. She roomed with a woman from New York whose husband could not sail with her because he lacked a visa. A couple of days later, Natalie telephoned Yates to say she had reached Melbourne, on Australia's south coast. She went ashore without either visa or permit. But Natalie was used to overcoming bureaucratic obstacles. She decided to wait for him there.[34]

McDaniel had a chance to sail on February 21 on the small steamer *Klang*, which would transport Stewart and a host of reporters and press officers to Australia. But as was customary, McDaniel told Stewart he would stay in Batavia. Red Knickerbocker of the *Chicago Sun* also remained, saying, "We're hopeful our consul here will get us on a cruiser a bit later on. Meanwhile we can be filing a few stories."[35]

Java, and its rich oil fields, was the next Japanese target for invasion. The Dutch fleet of obsolete light cruisers, destroyers, and submarines was eager to fight, but the Americans, British, and Australians believed Java was doomed. In a message to Churchill on the day after McDaniel reached Batavia, Gen. Archibald Wavell acknowledged that the "defense of Java cannot last long." Except for a handful of

Hurricanes, American P-40s, and B-17 bombers, the Allies lacked modern aircraft to control the sky, and, as Wavell wrote Churchill, the defense of Java "always hinged on the air battle."

Two convoys of Japanese troop transports were within days of reaching Java. One convoy of fifty-six transports would attack Java's west coast near Batavia, while the other, with forty-one transports, aimed for Surabaya on Java's east coast. The western convoy was covered by a small aircraft carrier, four modern heavy cruisers, two light cruisers, and sixteen destroyers, while the eastern convoy was protected by two heavy cruisers, two light cruisers, and fourteen destroyers.

The only senior officer who believed the Allies could still resist was VAdm. Conrad E. L. Helfrich, a Dutchman and commander of the Allied warships in Java. Tough and determined, he was convinced his ships could inflict serious damage on the Japanese. Opting to concentrate on the eastern convoy, he assembled the US heavy cruiser *Houston*, the Dutch light cruisers *De Ruyter* and *Java*, and six destroyers at Surabaya.

After a few days in Batavia, McDaniel—in contrast to Helfrich's optimism—concluded that Java would not last long. Getting out was another matter. Some correspondents such as Harold Guard of United Press found room on American B-17 bombers flying out of southern Java, but none of the giant four-engine planes were operating on Java's west coast. Freighters and smaller ships were rapidly fleeing Batavia, and on the evening of February 25, McDaniel decided it time to leave. McDaniel found a forty-year-old Dutch cattle boat preparing to sail. The ship weighed only 2,300 tons and could barely make 7 knots. He and ninety other Americans, Dutch, and British—many women and small babies—clambered aboard a ship packed with cattle, sheep, and fowl.

The cattle boat departed Batavia as the sun set, although nobody knew for sure where they were going. "Destination unknown," McDaniel joked. The cattle boat steered south through Sunda Strait, where at one point the British heavy cruiser *Exeter* steamed across its path toward Batavia. Later that night, the *Exeter* joined up with the *Encounter*, the Australian light cruiser *Perth*, and British destroyers *Jupiter* and *Electra*. The five warships sailed from Batavia to reinforce the Allied fleet assembled at Surabaya in the hope of destroying the forty-one Japanese transports now only 60 miles from Java's east coast.[36]

By dawn, the cattle boat passed the volcanic island of Krakatoa near Sumatra. The early-morning clouds settling on the volcano's tip provided passengers with a dazzling sight. The ship then entered the Indian Ocean, and the captain turned toward Fremantle, a major port on Australia's west coast near Perth. It would be a 2,000-mile journey aboard an unarmed ship. With Japanese submarines lurking about, few aboard held any realistic hope of surviving.

The ship rolled as ocean waves smacked against its hull. Passengers grew seasick. But they preferred to stay on deck because of the intolerable stench from the animals below. McDaniel and some of the men helped out by changing diapers, feeding the babies milk, and serving food on the rolling decks. When boredom set in, passengers passed the time by playing bridge, poker, and chess or reading. McDaniel borrowed a Bible and found exactly what he wanted: the book of Job.

A group of passengers frightened others by playing the game "Battleship," which was marked by loud cries of "direct hit by torpedo." To McDaniel, the game seemed "untimely."

On the morning of the eleventh day, McDaniel saw the west coast of Australia. Against all odds, they landed at the port of Bunbury, about 20 miles south of Fremantle.

The next afternoon, he boarded a train for the 100-mile ride north to Perth. When he arrived late in the evening, McDaniel was astonished to discover it had become a semi-American city. A quartet of soldiers greeted them by singing "Down by the Old Mill Stream." As he looked for a hotel, McDaniel saw scores of Americans milling about on the sidewalks or packing hotel bars and soda fountains.

Unable to find a room, McDaniel ran into a British officer he knew from Singapore. The officer had his own room with one bed, but McDaniel was welcome to sleep on the floor. He sent a relieved Natalie a telegram in Melbourne, saying he was safe.

Athole Stewart, who had arrived a few days earlier on the *Klang*, found McDaniel in the hotel typing a story about his voyage to Australia. McDaniel, Stewart marveled, was always "in the middle of a story." When McDaniel finished, he and Stewart rounded up a censor, cleared the story, and sent it to New York. Then they went to a nearby restaurant for dinner.[37]

The AP asked Natalie to write a separate story about her escape to Australia. On Sunday, March 8, newspapers in the United States paired Yates's and Natalie's stories, although in a sign of the times, the AP included an editor's note describing Natalie as "Pretty Natalie McDaniel."[38]

From New York, the AP's general manager, Kent Cooper, telephoned McDaniel. Congratulations, Cooper told McDaniel. He would be promoted to AP bureau chief in Melbourne. McDaniel hopped aboard a train for the three-day ride to Melbourne.

McDaniel's editors asked him whether the AP's Witt Hancock had escaped from Java. McDaniel had not heard anything about his colleague. On March 2, Hancock, still in Java, telephoned James Long, the AP's cable editor in New York. Long said Cooper was telling correspondents to use their best judgment on when to get out. Hancock said he was looking for a way to leave.

"Keep your fingers crossed," Hancock said.[39]

On March 6, Hancock and Bill McDougall of United Press boarded a Dutch liner leaving the southern coast of Java. The next morning, three Japanese dive-bombers attacked the liner. McDougall jumped clear of the battered ship, but machine gun bullets killed Hancock. The Japanese captured Bill McDougall and held him in a prison camp until the end of the war.

Other reporters suffered similar fates. Kenneth Selby-Walker of Reuters stayed too long in Java. On March 6, he cabled London: "I'm afraid it's too late to leave Java. I have only myself to blame. Good luck. I hope to see you all sooner than you expect." He was never heard from again.[40]

# MELBOURNE

cDaniel's extraordinary escape from Singapore catapulted him to celebrity status not only in the United States but across Australia as well. The *Argus* of Melbourne, *Daily News* of Perth, *Courier-Mail* of Brisbane, and *The Sun* of Sydney were among Australian newspapers to publish his "Farewell to Singapore" story. The *Melbourne Herald* ran the photo McDaniel took of British soldiers pushing his car off the dock in Singapore.[1] The *Argus* snapped a photo of Yates and Natalie as they arrived in Melbourne, with Yates looking more like a prosperous businessman in his dark-blue business suit than a rugged war correspondent.[2]

The *Sydney World's News* published a special story that McDaniel wrote about the graphic horrors he had seen in Nanking in 1937, when Japanese soldiers "were openly vying with each other to see how many Chinese they could slaughter."[3]

Everywhere McDaniel went, he was in demand. The day after he reached Perth, editors from the *West Australian* newspaper held an afternoon reception for McDaniel and other Western reporters at the Palace Hotel in the heart of the city. The guests included Tillman Durdin of the *New York Times*, Ian Morrison of the *Times* of London, and Red Knickerbocker of the *Chicago Sun*, who had reached Australia by a freighter out of Java. Naturally, McDaniel was interviewed, telling Australian reporters that "the time has come when we had better stop going backwards."[4] The next day, when he took the train from Perth to Melbourne, Australian reporters surrounded him during a stop in Adelaide. He warned that the chances of a Japanese attack on Australia were "50-50," adding "it looks like trouble in Australia."[5]

He also was busy as a speaker, something the AP expected its bureau chiefs to do. He told a gathering in Victoria in April that the Japanese regarded their military strategy in China as a "preparation for a major war." He spoke at a Constitutional Club luncheon in Melbourne and followed with an appearance before the Victoria League.[6]

In July, McDaniel bluntly warned a Rotary Club gathering in Melbourne: "If we are to win this war, we must recognize that we started off on the wrong foot. We cannot win by sitting down and talking and waiting to see which way the enemy is going to move. The occasional bombing of Tokyo will not end the war. We must get busy and retake every foot of land the Japanese have captured." For McDaniel, it was a major shift in his thinking. Before the attack on Pearl Harbor, McDaniel had warned against "the futile destruction of armed conflict." But after Pearl Harbor and the Japanese invasion of Malaya, he had changed his mind.[7]

A few days later, McDaniel delivered a talk at the University of Melbourne on the future of the free press. He spoke of the balancing act that reporters performed when dealing with military censorship while maintaining their freedom to report. His way of solving this dilemma was recognizing the war had "cut away or weakened some of the stoutest props of the free press." No responsible journalist, McDaniel said, "challenged the necessity for an intelligent censorship of military news." But something far worse awaited if the Western democracies lost the war: nothing would ever appear in print that did not win approval from the "overlords."[8]

Because friends joked that Japanese bombers followed McDaniel wherever he went, his presence in Melbourne was a "pretty accurate barometer" of how likely a Japanese invasion of Australia was. Java had surrendered, the thousands of American and Filipino troops on Bataan were short on food, and the nearby American garrison on Corregidor in Manila Bay had no hope of escape. Even before McDaniel reached Australia, four Japanese aircraft carriers launched 188 planes in an attack on Darwin, a northern Australian port. Joined by fifty-four land-based bombers, the Japanese attack wiped out an Australian airfield, sank a dozen ships—including the old US destroyer *Peary*—and killed 235 people. To Australians, the Japanese attack was an ominous sign that an invasion was imminent.[9]

To his dismay, McDaniel realized Australia was utterly unprepared to defend itself. Except for Australian troops returning from the Middle East, where they had been fighting the Germans and Italians, many Australian troops were poorly trained and so out of shape that Australian general Sir Thomas Blamey was plainly worried: "The first element in the making of a strong spirit is a strong body, so trained and hardened to physical endurance that we will force our way to victory or death." Australia's largest naval ships were two heavy cruisers, and its fleet was no match for the formidable Japanese navy. There were roughly 30,000 American soldiers in Australia, but they largely were engineers who barely could fire a rifle. When Gen. George Kenney was named Allied commander of all air units in Australia, he was told he had 517 airplanes, only to ruefully discover that most were in such a state of disrepair that only 80 of the 245 fighter planes could fly.[10]

McDaniel knew—but could not report because of censorship—that in early 1942, Australian officials had settled on a strategy that would yield the northern half of the country to the Japanese. Australians clearly were gloomy.[11] Blamey told correspondents that "the next year will decide whether Australia will live or die as a nation."[12] Another Australian officer told Clark Lee of the AP that "Australia, like the Philippines, is expendable in terms of global strategy."[13]

Yates and Natalie took a room at the relatively new Australia Hotel, a favorite of American reporters. Its twelve stories offered a dozen suites, ninety-four bedrooms, a fashionable ground-floor shopping arcade, and two movie theaters.

The AP assigned two reporters to McDaniel's bureau—Tom Yarbrough and Vern Haugland. All three were young—McDaniel just thirty-five, Haugland thirty-three, and Yarbrough thirty-two.

Yarbrough had covered the German bombing of London before the AP transferred him to Cairo. By chance, the Dutch ship he was taking to Cairo was approaching Honolulu on the morning of December 7. As he and three others were eating bacon and eggs, he heard a "rumbling in the direction of Diamond Head." Convinced it was a Navy maneuver, he sipped his coffee and then went below. A passenger shouted, "Come on up and see the show." Then he and others walked on deck and saw anti-aircraft guns firing at Japanese planes "in the bluest of blue skies." Clouds of black smoke "billowed and tilted" from the naval base, and "puffs" of smoke from anti-aircraft guns littered the sky. Yarbrough pitched in to help the AP bureau in Honolulu cover Pearl Harbor. He stayed in Hawaii until the AP shipped him to Australia, where McDaniel assigned him to Sydney.[14]

Haugland was a "writer of exceptional ability," but his background did not prepare him to be a war correspondent.[15] He flew in from Los Angeles, where his reporting job included taking Hollywood's most glamorous stars on dates and writing about the evening. He escorted Carmen Miranda to Ciro's, although to Haugland's consternation she insisted that her manager accompany them. The *Muncie Star Press* even ran a photo of Haugland dancing with the film star.[16] Over lunch with actress Ann Sheridan, she confided she hated her nickname, "the Ooomph Girl." This led to a discussion about whether her legs were more appealing than those of Vera Zorina, the sultry Norwegian ballerina. Sheridan insisted her legs did not compare, "despite assurances from one who has made a close study of both, or rather, of all four," Haugland wrote.[17] He bowled with Priscilla Lane, rode bicycles with Eleanor Powell, and sipped tea with Hedy Lamarr.[18] Just before flying to Australia, he interviewed actor Franchot Tone about his new marriage to actress Jean Wallace, whom MGM tried to sell as "another Jean Harlow."[19] He regarded Yates McDaniel as heroic and a man of "good judgment" and was eager to work for him.[20]

Melbourne was a magnet for correspondents. More than ninety-five reporters flocked to the city in what was described as a "journalistic invasion." They included twenty-nine American reporters, ten British reporters from London, and thirty-one from Australian newspapers. Another twenty-five reporters served radio stations and newsreels.[21]

Typical for the era, war reporting in Australia was largely by a male monopoly. A few years earlier, Freda Utley, Anna Louise Strong, Peggy Durdin, and Agnes Smedley covered the Japanese attack on Hankow, and Martha Gellhorn reported from Singapore and Hong Kong before the Pearl Harbor attack. Australia would be different. The only woman reporter to be accredited in Australia in 1942 was Annalee Whitmore, who had reported earlier from China.

The Australians and their reporters loved having the Americans in Melbourne and peppered them with requests for interviews, speeches, and even ideas on how to cook American-style food. Walter Murdoch, a professor of English at the University of Western Australia in Perth, decided Americans were "more courteous than we; I think we ought to admit it and mend our manners."[22] So many American pilots were stationed in Sydney that Australians nicknamed one section of the city

"Yanktown." Americans from Texas and Oklahoma found themselves right at home in the North, with its flat terrain and grasslands, prompting one soldier to joke, "Boy, I thought Texas was the only part of the world you'd find Texas."[23] The American servicemen described Australian beer as "OK" and Australian women as "grand."[24] Robert Sherrod of *Time* thought the Australian women "were an uncommonly handsome lot."[25] At one point, a major brawl erupted between Australian and American soldiers in Brisbane, in part because the Americans talked about their eagerness to sleep with Australian women.

Among those streaming into Melbourne were reporters such as McDaniel who escaped from the Japanese, including Annalee Whitmore and her husband, *Time* correspondent Mel Jacoby, who were already legendary figures throughout Asia. *Life* in 1941 published an iconic photo of Jacoby, puffing on a pipe and typing by candlelight after a Japanese air raid in Chungking knocked out electricity.[26] Whitmore had been a Hollywood screenwriter who cowrote *Andy Hardy Meets Debutante*, one of a series of films starring Mickey Rooney and Judy Garland. Whitmore was highly regarded with her own office and a secretary, but one day she told a colleague, "I'm giving up this whole career. I'm going to China."[27] She and Jacoby sailed to China before moving to Manila, where they were married two weeks before the Japanese attack on Pearl Harbor. With the Japanese troops pushing their way down Bataan, they joined the AP's Clark Lee on a small ship and survived a perilous voyage from Corregidor to Australia.

Dean Schedler of the Associated Press had an even more harrowing escape from Corregidor, a story he told to McDaniel from his hospital bed in Melbourne. McDaniel typed up the article, gave Schedler the byline, and underneath included the phrase "As told to C. Yates McDaniel."

Schedler's adventure began after Gen. Jonathan Wainwright, commanding U.S. forces on Corregidor, ordered Schedler to leave the island. On the evening of April 12, the reporter climbed into the back seat of a biplane trainer. Navigating in complete darkness, the Army Air Corps pilots flew over Japanese ships that opened fire. To gain altitude, the Americans threw out their guns, seat cushions, and other equipment. With gasoline running short, they were forced to land on a small island, where they slept under palm groves. Friendly Filipinos supplied them with enough gasoline to take off for a US base 200 miles away. Once again, gasoline ran out and they crash-landed in the surf near Panay Island, where US Army officers gave them "a hearty meal" before warning them to leave before the Japanese invaded the island.

> We went to the airfield and found an old monoplane which had been condemned as unflyable six years before, but had been lately reconditioned, Schedler told McDaniel. Six of us crowded into that old plane built for three and it got us in the air with Major W. R. Bradford of San Antonio, Texas, piloting. We flew over the city of Iloilo, where we saw Japanese boats tied up at the piers unloading tanks, automobiles and troops. The Japanese didn't open up with anti-aircraft fire, apparently believing the plane was Japanese.

Bradford landed the plane at another base on a small island. From that point, Schedler's journey remained a mystery, as McDaniel wrote: "How Schedler managed to reach Australia from this island is not disclosed and may remain a secret to protect others who may be taking this tortuous route."[28]

Two weeks after McDaniel reached Melbourne, Gen. MacArthur arrived in Australia. President Roosevelt had ordered him to leave the Philippines to command a new Allied army in Australia. In a daring three-part trip from Corregidor by PT boat to Mindanao, B-17 bomber to Batchelor Field near Darwin, and DC-3 civilian aircraft, MacArthur; his wife, Jean; their son, Arthur; and a handful of aides reached Alice Springs, a tiny settlement surrounded by desert. The MacArthurs boarded an antiquated train to Adelaide, where they were scheduled to transfer to a more comfortable train to take them to Melbourne. The train made a stop at two in the afternoon on March 20 at Terowie, about 137 miles north of Adelaide. Terowie looked like something out of the old American western frontier. MacArthur thought his arrival would be a secret, and was surprised to find cheering Australians complete with an honor guard commanded by an Australian major. After vigorously shaking the major's hand, MacArthur retrieved an envelope from his pocket on which he had scribbled some lines: "The president of the United States ordered me to break through the Japanese lines and proceed from Corregidor to Australia for the purpose, as I understand it, of organizing an American offensive against Japan. The primary purpose of this is the relief of the Philippines. I came through and I shall return."[29]

The locomotive lumbered to Adelaide, where MacArthur's party switched to a more luxurious train. Hoping for an interview with the general, Harold Guard of United Press boarded MacArthur's train in Ballarat for the final 60 miles of the journey to Melbourne. As Guard moved toward MacArthur's carriage, US officers blocked his way.[30] When MacArthur's train reached the Spencer Street Station in Melbourne on a sun-splashed Saturday morning, he received "probably the most fervent and spectacular reception Australia has given any man." He inspected a hastily assembled honor guard composed of US signalmen and engineers. As McDaniel, Vern Haugland, and other reporters scribbled in their notebooks, MacArthur promised the huge crowd he would launch a vigorous offensive against the Japanese, saying he was "glad indeed to be in immediate cooperation with the Australian soldier. I know him well from World War days and admire him greatly."[31]

Reporters were more interested in the pledge he made in Terowie to return to the Philippines. Because none of them had been in Terowie, they disagreed on the exact quote. Yates reported that MacArthur said he "will" return, which led the *Boston Globe* to print a huge headline, "I will return." Brydon Taves of United Press reported the general saying, "I shall return," which is what MacArthur actually said. To settle the dispute, the *Boston Globe* consulted a noted language expert at Boston University. The professor was certain MacArthur said "will," because it was the more emphatic promise he would go back to the Philippines.[32]

Australians were jubilant. In addition to those crammed inside the train station, 6,000 people outside burst into "ear-shattering cheers" as MacArthur emerged from the station. Many stood on cars, trucks, and even tree branches to get a glimpse of him. MacArthur climbed into a limousine. Police mounted on horses escorted him toward the Menzies Hotel, where a suite was reserved on the sixth floor. Children waved American flags, and scores gathered in the streets, at hotel windows, and on rooftops to cheer.[33]

That afternoon, Yates met MacArthur's wife, Jean. "You know, I've never been interviewed," she confessed. "I like to remain in the background and let the general do the talking." As she relaxed in the hotel suite, Jean told Yates that while on Corregidor, she and the general survived on canned foods and made as many as six trips a day to the bomb shelters. She relived the sixteen hours on fragile PT boats that whisked the general, her, and their four-year-old son from Corregidor. "Arthur's fine now," she said. "He was quite sick, but he seemed to recover on the train from Adelaide." McDaniel typed up his scoop and cabled it to New York.[34]

Two days later, US Army colonel LeGrand Diller called in McDaniel and other reporters to provide them with a detailed account of MacArthur's dramatic trip from the Philippines. Diller, who had accompanied MacArthur on the trip, clearly was trying to dispel reports that MacArthur abandoned his soldiers on Corregidor. Instead, Diller "emphasized MacArthur did not escape Bataan, but came through following a series of direct orders from Roosevelt."[35] In dramatic fashion, McDaniel took up that theme in an account that appeared in newspapers on March 24, 1942:

> The full story of Gen. Douglas MacArthur's hazardous voyage from the Philippines was told today. Col. LeGrand Diller told newspapermen that MacArthur's perilous race against time, darkness, and Japanese warplanes and warships was vindication of the general's long fight for recognition of motor torpedo boats. Some advisers, Diller said, urged MacArthur to use a submarine to make his way to Australia, but the general and Navy Lt. John D. Buckley, commander of six PT boats that reached the Philippines shortly before the war, pinned their faith on the speedy craft. Strong opposition was based on fear that the attempt was too dangerous.

Yates then quoted Diller's description of the trip, which began on the evening of March 11 when MacArthur and his staff could see three approaching PT boats. The boats collected their passengers and slid out of Manila Bay past Japanese signal lights on Bataan. The next evening, the boats reached a rendezvous point near a group of islands. A US submarine was anchored there, but MacArthur opted to continue with the PT boats. That evening they continued their voyage. In the darkness, they spotted Japanese destroyers but managed to evade them before reaching another island, where they expected to be flown to Australia. For the next three days, they waited. Finally, two B-17s landed. At midnight on March 16, MacArthur, his family, and staff climbed aboard one of the B-17s, which flew them directly to Australia. It was the most detailed and gripping account of the stories filed that day, and it accomplished what Diller wanted: MacArthur was a hero sent to Australia to command a new army. The story helped counter talk in America that MacArthur had fled his command in the Philippines.[36]

On the morning of March 26, MacArthur drove the 400 miles to the Australian capital of Canberra to meet Prime Minister John Curtin and his war cabinet. When MacArthur reached Canberra at 3:30 in the afternoon, thousands of Australians lined the streets to cheer and wave. After a two-hour meeting with Curtin and his war cabinet, MacArthur visited the Australian House and shook hands with every member.

That evening, MacArthur was the guest of honor at a dinner at Parliament House. Nelson Johnson, the former US ambassador to China and now ambassador to Australia, announced that MacArthur had been awarded the Medal of Honor. MacArthur, dressed in khaki shirt and slacks and eschewing a tie, rose to speak. His speech made such a vivid impression on Yates that years later he could recall the key line, delivered almost in a whisper. "Mr. Prime Minister," MacArthur said to Curtin, "We will not defend your country here. The battle for Australia shall be fought in New Guinea." An orchestra then burst into "For He's a Jolly Good Fellow."[37]

McDaniel returned to Melbourne the next morning and spoke on the NBC Blue Network, a broadcast sent by shortwave radio to San Francisco and heard throughout the United States. Yates said MacArthur's arrival was a major morale boost to Australians, but reported that "the Australian man in the street is asking" if American planes could reach Australia, what was to prevent "Japanese ships and planes" from doing the same. "Australia today knows the answer to that question. Australia also knows what should be done about it."

McDaniel explained why Australia was so important to the American war effort: "Look at the map of the southern Pacific, my Australian friends tell me, and you will see a very good reason why we cannot afford to be pushed out. If we are, what a job it will be to get back. Australia is not begging for help. Her leaders, the men and the women working in her arsenals and training to fight her battles firmly believe that Australia offers one of the best winning propositions Americans can hope to find."[38]

MacArthur tapped Diller to handle press operations, as he had done in Bataan. Known as "Pick" by everyone, Diller was well liked by reporters, although they grumbled that he wanted to simultaneously be press officer and censor. A press officer helped reporters get a story; a censor was regarded as the "natural enemy," using the blue pencil to hack some stories to pieces. Bill Dunn of CBS said trying to do both jobs was "something like the district attorney deciding also to head the defense.[39]

Clark Lee muttered that Diller's job was to "protect the general" instead of helping correspondents file accurate stories. If Diller decided a story would damage MacArthur's reputation, he would alter it or kill it. Whenever a reporter quoted a soldier swearing, Diller would strike the profanity, although as the war went on, correspondents were able to get some words past Diller's blue pencil. McDaniel was often embroiled in arguments with Diller.[40] Lewis Sebring of the *New York Herald Tribune* grumbled that the Army "does not always cooperate in furnishing us with as much news as can safely be released."[41]

To work around heavy censorship, reporters formed the Association of Overseas Correspondents in Australia and elected McDaniel as chairman. Although McDaniel was not as caustic as Cecil Brown of CBS had been in Singapore, he was widely respected for his toughness, which was badly needed.[42] Reporters were at the mercy of the military, which took its time in reporting setbacks. The Australian government did not announce the loss of the *Perth* until March 14, two weeks after the Japanese sank the light cruiser off Java. Not until April 3 did the US Navy acknowledge the loss of the *Peary* in Darwin and the old aircraft carrier *Langley* off Java—a month after they had been sunk.[43]

Diller recruited two Associated Press reporters to serve as his assistants, one of whom was Larry Lehrbas. The staff also included the wife of a British officer, who under the stage name Verna Gordon had been a dancer with the Ziegfeld Follies in New York. One AP story acknowledged the obvious: she "was popular with all the pressmen." Radio and newspaper reporters had to submit their scripts and stories for approval before they were sent out in one of two ways—either radio or cable. Sending a story took so long, one reporter considered it a major victory when it reached New York in only two hours. When stories arrived at New York's cable desk, any one of eighteen printers would punch the article out where editors would rework the copy and post it on the wire.[44]

For McDaniel, reporting from Australia was very different from his previous assignments in Tientsin, Nanking, and Singapore, where he could see the fighting at close range. It was dangerous, but he believed the best way to cover a war was to actually see it in person. Now he was dependent on American, Australian, Japanese, and British press releases and interviews with Allied pilots.

Unlike Singapore, Melbourne was "safe" and "unwarlike."[45] Well beyond the reach of Japanese bombers, correspondents settled into a comfortable routine in which they relied more on communiques released by MacArthur's staff than reporting from the front. On a typical day at the Australia Hotel, a correspondent would awaken around seven, read the three Melbourne newspapers left at the hotel door, and then go downstairs for a breakfast of poached eggs and toast. The food was excellent, and while Australians seemed to have little interest in serving vegetables to their guests, they provided correspondents with plenty of fresh milk, excellent tea, and mountains of butter for rolls. Americans could get coffee, but the best compliment to describe Australian coffee was "not bad." The only break in the routine was Sundays, when the dining room was closed and reporters had to make breakfast in their rooms. Correspondents often made their way to the room of Bill Dunn for a hearty breakfast of pancakes and sausage.[46]

In late March, the Australian Journalists Association invited the American and British reporters to what was described as an "informal dinner" at the Menzies Hotel in Melbourne. McDaniel was among those attending along with Pick Diller, Newsreel Wong, Vern Haugland, Lewis Sebring of the *New York Herald Tribune*, Brydon Taves of United Press, "Barney" Darnton of the *New York Times*, and Bill Dunn of CBS. The tone of news stories by American correspondents tended to be positive, a bit too positive for the *Times* of London, which complained that the coverage was too flattering to Australia. The *Times'* article irritated the American reporters, with McDaniel saying, "We are concerned only with getting out the news as we find it. If it's complimentary or the opposite, we can't help it."[47]

Every day, Diller and his staff released the morning communique just before the daily news conference at noon. Reporters gathered about Diller's desk and quizzed him on the latest news. When Prime Minister Curtin was in Melbourne, he held news conferences at one and six in the afternoon. His comments were scathing as he sharply criticized Allied policy on defeating Nazi Germany first before focusing on Japan. Curtin reserved particular venom for Sir Keith Murdoch, the publisher of the *Melbourne Herald*, once telling reporters, "I do not trust him. He is utterly unscrupulous in the way he conducts his newspapers."[48]

MacArthur, despite his well-deserved imperious reputation, had an easy rapport with reporters. "Don't get shot," MacArthur once said good-naturedly to *Life* photographer Carl Mydans. "Just as I tell my soldiers, a dead correspondent like a dead soldier is no use."[49] When MacArthur arrived in Melbourne he recognized Lehrbas, who as an AP reporter covered him when he was Army chief of staff in Washington. "Larry, you old rogue, how the hell are you?" MacArthur asked. After Clark Lee, Mel Jacoby, and Annalee Whitmore reached Melbourne, MacArthur invited them to his hotel office, shook hands, and said, "I knew you'd make it, Mel."[50]

In late March, MacArthur met with the reporters for what was described as an off-the-record briefing. Before the press conference, MacArthur shook hands with the reporters. When he saw Bill Dunn, who had left the Philippines just before war broke out, MacArthur told him, "You stay with me, Dunn, and I'll take you back to Manila." MacArthur did most of the talking: "My main purpose is not to suppress the news, but to get news for you." Pointing out that during the First World War he had briefly served as a press spokesman, MacArthur described himself as an "old censor myself. What I have said does not mean that what we give out here you have to take and use it or that you are limited to canned news and cannot use your brilliancy." He said he would always provide reporters "my full knowledge or opinion on any subject, but as background only." The reporters pleaded with him to let them attribute the remarks to him, and to their surprise, MacArthur agreed.[51]

The reporters wanted scoops and fought the censors. But the reporters did not have what could be called a truly adversarial relationship with MacArthur's staff. In key ways, they were like the soldiers they covered. Reporters wore the same khaki shirts and slacks that soldiers did, and they wanted the Allies to win the war. When Mel Jacoby and Annalee Whitmore left the Philippines, Diller managed to find a bottle of whiskey and toasted, "To our next drink." Upon their arrival in Melbourne, Diller threw a party in their honor at the Australia Hotel. Just about everyone showed up, including Yates, Natalie, Peg Durdin, Frank Hewlett of United Press, Theodore White of *Time*, and Carlos Romulo, a top official in the Filipino government in exile and known throughout America for his "Voice of Freedom" broadcasts.[52]

Later that night, Mel and Annalee joined Clark Lee in his room. Lee, who had been assigned to New Caledonia, was first making a quick stop in New Zealand. "When you get to New Zealand, Clark, don't forget to look around for a line of retreat," Jacoby joked. It was a none-too-subtle suggestion that Japan might soon conquer Australia and New Zealand.[53]

The next morning, Jacoby boarded a Lockheed C-40 transport plane for a flight to Darwin. The Lockheed made an unscheduled stop at Batchelor Field, only 30 miles from Darwin. A jeep was sent to fetch Jacoby and take him to the base headquarters. As Jacoby waited by the Lockheed's left wingtip, a P-40 fighter took off from one of the gravel runways about 100 yards away. The pilot lost control and veered toward the Lockheed, shearing off the cockpit and both engines. Jacoby, the jeep driver, and Gen. Hal George, a member of MacArthur's staff, were all killed.

The Army flew Jacoby's body to Melbourne, where a funeral service was held. An American flag covered his casket. McDaniel, Theodore White, Bill Dunn, and Pick Diller were among the pallbearers.[54]

On the afternoon of April 9, McDaniel interviewed Navy seaman Lawrence Farley, one of fifty-three survivors from the destroyer *Peary*. Farley told McDaniel the *Peary* had been slightly damaged during a Japanese air attack in Manila but steamed to Darwin. Just as the old four-stack destroyer entered the harbor, Japanese dive-bombers appeared overhead. "Hell was soon apopping," Farley said. Five bombs smashed into the *Peary*, one hitting the stern, another striking an engine room hatchway, and a third exploding in a passageway near the galley. One of the blasts badly burned Farley's face, but he and another seaman reached the upper deck and "plunged overboard," where they were plucked to safety by an Australian lifeboat. The *Peary* slowly sank by the stern.[55]

McDaniel filed his story. That afternoon, he picked up hints that the 78,000 Americans and Filipinos stranded on Bataan had surrendered. McDaniel and Clark Lee went to the Menzies Hotel and elbowed their way into an anteroom of MacArthur's suite. MacArthur's gloomy staff officers made clear the news from Bataan was bleak. "All our friends are there," one officer said. "We are all very much down in the dumps," another officer confessed. The Allied forces on Bataan fought without air cover, and most of the US and Filipino soldiers were on the point of starvation, with many suffering from dysentery and malaria.[56]

Yates was told MacArthur would speak to reporters. Instead, Larry Lehrbas appeared, grasping a single sheet of ruled paper. To Yates, it looked like it could "have been torn from a scribbling pad on which [MacArthur's] young son Arthur might have been trying to draw cows and cats." Yates could see pencil scribbling on the paper and assumed it was MacArthur's handwriting.

Lehrbas began reading: "The Bataan force went out as it would have wished, fighting to the end its flickering and forlorn hope. Nothing became it more than its last hour of trial and agony." The statement included a dig at Washington's unwillingness to supply Bataan: "No army has ever done so much with so little."[57]

Clark Lee followed with an incisive analysis, writing that the Philippines' fate "was sealed" just hours after the attack on Pearl Harbor, when Japanese bombers destroyed much of MacArthur's air force at Clark, Nichols, and Iba airfields near Manila. Lee wrote that "American officers did their best to fight the Japanese on the beaches, but the enemy's overwhelming numbers quickly overcame the opposition. Lacking effective air or sea support, MacArthur was forced to fall back on the strategy of a withdrawal into Bataan." Left unsaid by Lee or anyone else was the obvious—how could MacArthur and American commanders have been so surprised at a Japanese air attack on the Philippines after Pearl Harbor had been bombed?[58]

That same Friday at the Victoria Barracks, McDaniel interviewed Lt. Gen. George Brett, who commanded Allied air forces in the Pacific. MacArthur disliked Brett and derided his staff "as incompetent, bungling, nincompoop airmen" and was eager to replace them.[59] MacArthur himself told Clark Lee a month earlier he wanted to bomb the Philippines. Brett agreed to launch the raid, although it became clear to McDaniel that he was reluctant. "We've taken the offensive against the Japanese in the air and we'll continue to increase it," Brett vowed. But he acknowledged, "Our only limitation is equipment." Brett said he was short of aviation fuel and pointed out a typical plane burned 55 gallons of fuel every hour. He also lacked trained and experienced American and Australian pilots. The Australians were required to fly US-built planes, which they had never operated before.[60]

That evening, three B-17s and ten medium B-25 bombers flew from Darwin to a base in Mindanao, part of the Philippines still held by the Americans. It was a risky 1,500-mile trip, but the planes reached the airfield, where mechanics replaced long-range fuel tanks with bombs. The next day, the B-25s bombed the docks at Cebu Harbor and Davao while the B-17s attacked Nichols Field near Manila. Although one B-17 was destroyed by Japanese planes while on the ground at the airfield, the rest of the American bombers reached Batchelor Field on April 14. They brought back forty-four men who had been stranded in Mindanao. Most were US servicemen, but they also included Frank Hewlett of United Press and Nat Floyd of the *New York Times*. Hewlett had left besieged Corregidor on April 13 on "an old, patched-up Philippine training plane." As the plane took off at three in the morning, Japanese searchlights lit up the sky. When Hewlett finally reached the safety of Australia, he rejected an offer to write a book, saying, "The story I want to write and will write is an eyewitness account of American troops crossing Jones Bridge in Manila." He had a strong personal reason: in Manila, the Japanese had interned his wife, Virginia, an Army nurse.[61]

Relying in part on a communique released by MacArthur, Yates wrote that American planes "struck with destructive fury," demolishing five Japanese transports, smashing Japanese planes on the ground, and crippling the runways at Nichols. The

American communique did not disclose that the planes had used Del Monte Field in Mindanao to launch their attacks. But McDaniel also monitored a Japanese communique that declared the American planes "were compelled to flee from their base" in Mindanao. He wrote that the Japanese news dispatch "suggested the raiding parties may have flown from a base still held by the US forces in the Philippines." McDaniel reported that within minutes after returning to "their base somewhere in Australia," an American general awarded the Distinguished Service Cross to Gen. Ralph Royce, who commanded the mission.[62]

The next day in Melbourne, Royce and Australian officials briefed reporters. As McDaniel had guessed, the American planes flew into and out of a "base hidden in" the Philippines, prompting the *Lansing State Journal* to run the huge headline "Secret Island Base Used in Raid on Japs" above McDaniel's story. Prime Minister Curtin declared that the raid proved "the tide of war was turning against Japan." McDaniel wrote that it "was the first use of the B-25s on an extensive scale." Gen. Royce planned to tell the workers and executives at North American Aviation, which built the B-25, that they had produced a "helluva fine plane."[63]

Newspapers in Tampa, Miami, St. Louis, Oakland, and Salt Lake City published McDaniel's dispatch on their front pages. It was the first major attack by US planes on a Japanese installation, and Americans were thrilled. In reality, the planes caused little damage, but was a major boost to morale.

Two days later, Royce's attack was relegated to historical obscurity by a spectacularly daring mission. Sixteen B-25 bombers under the command of Lt. Col. James Doolittle took off from the aircraft carrier *Hornet*, flew 650 miles, and bombed Japan. The name Doolittle would be remembered. Not Royce.

For the most part, McDaniel and his colleagues were covering the war with secondhand information. It was difficult, putting them at a disadvantage in getting accurate stories. Just a few days earlier, McDaniel waded through a communique about an American air raid on the formidable Japanese naval base at Rabaul in New Britain. The Japanese had seized Rabaul from a poorly armed Australian force in January and sent dive-bombers and fighters to the base. From there, they could menace the key harbor of Port Moresby in New Guinea, the Solomon Islands, and Australia itself. American bombers had already attacked Rabaul with minimal results, but from April 9 through April 12, US B-26 medium bombers attacked Rabaul and Dutch East Timor. Relying on an Allied communique and interviews with the American pilots, McDaniel reported that the American bombers found heavy clouds over Rabaul. They dove to 500 feet and dropped their bombs, claiming one smacked a Japanese bomber as it attempted to take off. The Japanese on the ground were so startled that they didn't even run for cover but could be seen pointing toward the B-26 bombers. The flames from burning buildings were visible 50 miles away. The "savage weekend" of assaults destroyed twenty-seven Japanese planes, McDaniel wrote.[68] Records after the war suggest that not a single Japanese transport ship was sunk, and, except for the first attack, the damage to Rabaul was minimal. The *New*

*York Times* reported that pilots had damaged a Japanese aircraft carrier near Rabaul. The only carrier the Japanese had in the area was the *Taiyō*, an 18,000-ton vessel converted from a freighter and used to transport aircraft to Pacific bases. *Taiyō* was not hit in the attacks.

A couple of weeks later, McDaniel reported that Allied planes had launched a second round of attacks on Rabaul. B-26 bombers targeted the harbor and Lakunai Airfield. McDaniel wrote that the Americans were hampered by poor visibility from a tropical rainstorm. But they evaded fierce antiaircraft fire, dropped high-explosive bombs, and machine-gunned the field. This time, the Americans claimed forty Japanese planes were destroyed. Although two Japanese cargo ships were sunk in the harbor, the official Australian report concluded the airfield "received light damage."

It was the price that correspondents were forced to pay for covering a war so far away. McDaniel and many others wanted to get closer to the fighting. They would soon have their chance.

# BRISBANE

cDaniel and many of the war correspondents were with MacArthur in Melbourne on May 6 when devastating news arrived. Gen. Jonathan Wainwright had surrendered the besieged island of Corregidor, with its 11,574 US and Filipino combat soldiers and American female nurses. The garrison lacked air cover, water was running short, and the Japanese were mercilessly pounding the island with howitzers firing from nearby Bataan. Japanese landing craft dropped troops on the beaches. Casualties on both sides were horrifying. Faced with the certainty the Japanese would soon reach Corregidor's tunnel defenses, Wainwright sent word to the Japanese that he wanted a ceasefire.

McDaniel watched as MacArthur's "eyes darkened." He was furious with Wainwright. "They can't," MacArthur said. "They have no right to do that. I gave no order to surrender. I am still commanding in the Philippines."

The general's anger faded. He turned to look out a window. He knew better than anyone else that Corregidor could not hold out. In a soft voice, he said, "Corregidor needs no comment from me. It has sounded its own story at the mouth of its guns. It has scrolled its own epitaph on enemy tablets. I shall always seem to see a vision of grim, gaunt, ghastly men, still unafraid."[1]

McDaniel filed a story that one newspaper headlined "Radio at Corregidor Silent." The fall of Corregidor, he wrote, allowed Japan to use Manila Bay as a base for attacks in the Southwest Pacific and "released men and equipment for duty elsewhere." That "elsewhere" was a none-too-subtle hint that Australia might be Japan's next target.[2]

Corregidor's fall marked the beginning of what McDaniel called a week of "dread" for Australians.[3] After Australian antiaircraft guns opened fire on two Japanese reconnaissance planes over Townsville off the Coral Sea, McDaniel speculated that Townsville "might well be the first objective" of the Japanese. He pointed out that an 800-mile coastal rail line linked the village to Brisbane in the south. McDaniel quoted Gen. Blamey as saying that "increased enemy activity means [the Japanese have] some further plan," and Japanese transports and supply ships were landing troops on New Guinea and New Britain.[4]

Japanese warships were reported near the Solomon Islands, 2,000 miles from Australia. "Ominous" news, McDaniel wrote. He suspected the Japanese would invade either Australia or the "screen of islands" north of the continent—a reference to New Britain and New Guinea. McDaniel knew the 100-mile-wide waterway between New Britain and New Guinea "is the natural gateway through which a seaborne thrust against Australia's east coast would be launched." But neither McDaniel nor any other reporters could determine the size of the Japanese task force.[5]

The Japanese navy was eager to invade Australia. But the Japanese army, stretched to the breaking point with hundreds of thousands of troops scattered throughout China, Indochina, the Philippines, Java, Sumatra, and Malaya, wanted no part of such a daunting challenge. The Japanese army prevailed. As early as April, US intelligence, relying on intercepts from Japanese secret codes that had been broken, concluded the Japanese would not attack Australia but instead would occupy the island of Tulagi off the Florida Islands and invade the strategic port of Port Moresby on the southern tip of New Guinea. In March, the Japanese had seized Lae, a New Guinea port due north of Port Moresby. In 1937, aviator Amelia Earhart and navigator Fred Noonan took off from Lae for the long flight to Howland Island, a journey that ended in their deaths from a likely crash at sea. Combined with its base in Rabaul, taking Port Moresby would strengthen Japan's control over New Guinea.[6]

By the time McDaniel's story about a possible Japanese invasion of Australia was published, the fifty Australian soldiers garrisoned on Tulagi had evacuated, allowing the Japanese to seize the island without firing any shots. Tulagi's harbor was ideal for Japan to base seaplanes, the first step in its plan to build an airfield on Guadalcanal just across Savo Sound. The Japanese would then invade Port Moresby.

Once again, McDaniel would have to report from the safety of Melbourne as opposed to the front lines. To invade Port Moresby, the Japanese assembled a major fleet that included the 32,000-ton aircraft carriers *Shōkaku* and *Zuikaku*—which had taken part in the attack on Pearl Harbor. Together, the two carriers could launch more than 160 planes, many superior to the Allies' aircraft. The Japanese also formed a second task force around the light carrier *Shōhō* and a seaplane tender. Armed with intercepts of Japanese messages, Adm. Chester Nimitz, who commanded what was left of the US Pacific Fleet in the aftermath of Pearl Harbor, gambled and dispatched the carriers *Yorktown* and *Lexington*, nine cruisers, and thirteen destroyers into the Coral Sea. A separate Australian force headed by the heavy cruiser *Australia* and light cruiser *Hobart* undertook the hazardous job of covering the Jomard Passage off New Guinea—the vital link between the Coral and the Solomon Seas.

The battle of the Coral Sea would be the first in history in which neither fleet saw the other. All major operations were conducted in the air. During a five-day span in the first week of May, US carrier planes sank the 11,000-ton *Shōhō*, the first time in the war the Japanese lost a warship larger than a destroyer. By contrast, Japanese planes sank the *Lexington*, a 36,000-ton carrier with seventy-eight aircraft, a destroyer, and an oiler, while striking the *Yorktown* with two bombs. Japanese ships and planes had inflicted greater damage than the Americans had. The *Lexington* was a bigger loss than the *Shōhō*. Still, the Japanese canceled the attack on Port Moresby. It was Japan's first serious setback in the Pacific.

McDaniel scrambled to report the progress of a battle 2,000 miles away. He was dependent solely on American, Australian, and Japanese communiques. He wrote, "The greatest naval battle of the war is in progress in the seas directly east of Australia," declaring that the "immediate fate of this continent" depended on the outcome.[7]

McDaniel sorted through a maze of contradictory reports. Both sides made wild claims about their successes. The Japanese claimed they sank a California-class battleship even though not a single US battleship was anywhere near the Coral Sea. The Japanese also reported they sank an aircraft carrier, a clear reference to the *Lexington*, while damaging the old British battleship *Warspite*, which was operating off Ceylon 5,400 miles away. Japan also claimed to have hit the Australian heavy cruiser *Canberra*.[8] McDaniel reported that the Americans announced they had destroyed one Japanese aircraft carrier—which was true. The Americans incorrectly claimed to have destroyed a Japanese cruiser, along with sinking "destroyers, gunboats and other vessels." The US Navy delayed acknowledging the loss of the *Lexington*. Even though Stanley Johnston of the *Chicago Tribune* personally witnessed the sinking, he was not allowed to report it until a month later.[9]

McDaniel did his best to get the truth to the public. He clearly did not trust the claims from either the Americans or Japanese. He reported that eleven Japanese ships had been sunk, but warned that "because of the lack of news on the exact losses on either side and their original strength, observers were unable to assess the total battle results."[10] Others were not as cautious, and they printed wildly inaccurate stories. AP inserted into McDaniel's story a Reuters claim that the Americans and Australians sank eighteen Japanese warships, including two aircraft carriers.[11] The *New York Times* proclaimed in a bold headline that between seventeen and twenty-two Japanese ships had been destroyed.[12]

Many news organizations, trying to be accurate, resorted to printing the competing claims made by the Japanese and the Americans and letting the reader figure out what happened. The *Billings Gazette* published the Japanese communique right next to McDaniel's story, in which Japan said it sank the *Yorktown* and a Saratoga-class carrier.[13] *The Age* of Melbourne ran the Japanese and Allied claims under this headline: "Two Versions of the Battle."[14]

News organizations in Australia sharply criticized the willingness of the American press to print the most-exaggerated claims. *The Age* editorialized: "Here in Australia it is regarded as most unfortunate that in some quarters of the United States, including responsible and authoritative circles, an extravagant view of the Allied success in the Coral Sea was taken and presented to the public. There has as yet been no victory in the proper sense, but only a gratifying repulse of enemy sea and air forces."[15]

The inflated claims were a blend of wishful thinking and the confusion of war. Pilots under attack could not determine the actual battle damage. Japanese pilots scored hits on the *Lexington* and *Yorktown* and assumed both sank. Japanese planes dropped bombs near the *Australia*, and while near misses straddled the cruiser, not one bomb struck the ship. US dive-bombers hit the *Shōkaku* with three bombs, and an American flier snapped photographs of the carrier's bow ablaze. It did not take much imagination to conclude the giant carrier sank. But the *Shōkaku* slipped away to Japan for repairs.

On May 18, McDaniel traveled to Sydney to cover a major speech by Prime Minister Curtin. Curtin, who had feuded in January with Churchill about the lack of reinforcements for Singapore, delivered a grim warning. Despite the apparent victory in the Coral Sea, Australians might soon face "the shock of war upon their own soil." Curtin, like MacArthur, was seething over the decision by Great Britain and the United States to focus most of their resources against Nazi Germany, a policy that Australian foreign minister Herbert Evatt dismissed as "absurd."[16] Gen. George Kenney, who replaced Brett as commander of Allied air forces, grumbled that Australia was the "forgotten theater."[17]

In stark terms, Curtin told his audience he would "make no apology nor recant one word of the statements I made to the United States to regard this Pacific zone of war as being one of vital importance not only to us, but to the security of the United States." With Great Britain trying to defend itself against the Germans, Curtin said, only the United States could deliver the soldiers and supplies needed to save Australia.[18]

In his story, McDaniel wrote that Australian leaders believed their country faced "grave peril." He included scathing criticism of Roosevelt by Sir Keith Murdoch, the chairman of the *Herald* of Melbourne and father of modern media mogul Rupert Murdoch. When Roosevelt declared in a speech that "there is good reason to believe" the Japanese advance south had "been checked," Murdoch erupted, charging the speech "is only symptomatic of the optimism that has obstinately colored Washington thinking about the western Pacific." McDaniel's story made front pages across the United States.[19]

Murdoch had emerged as a persistent critic of the American strategy. In the aftermath of the battle of the Coral Sea, he warned, "It is sheer folly to say that we have smashed an invasion fleet. The naval and air engagement was against a comparatively light Japanese naval force, not against the main Japanese fleet. What must be realized is that a large Japanese expedition is beginning."[20]

Australians were genuinely frightened. "Our allies have got to realize the grim fact that we are still fighting a losing war and there is no possibility of an offensive from this country until real material aid is forthcoming," Norman Stockton wrote in the *Herald*. Stockton characterized MacArthur as an "offensive minded" general who did not have the equipment to launch an attack.[21]

While McDaniel was covering the war in Australia, his parents, interned by the Japanese in Soochow since the outbreak of war, were about to be released and returned to the United States. Following negotiations by neutral powers, the Japanese and Americans agreed to exchange diplomats and civilians who had been detained by both sides after the Pearl Harbor strike.

In the middle of 1942, Charles and Nannie boarded the *Gripsholm*, an 18,000-ton liner owned by the Swedish American Line and chartered by the State Department. Their fellow passengers included Joseph Grew, who had been the US ambassador to Japan before the war; thirty-three American newspaper reporters, including Max Hill, who had been the AP bureau chief in Tokyo; and scores of diplomats and missionaries. On August 25, the *Gripsholm* sailed into New York Harbor and docked on the New Jersey side of the Hudson River.[22]

Within a couple of weeks, Charles and Nannie were resting in upstate New York. Then they were off to Richmond. Charles was looking for a new assignment, writing that he had "two months of solid rest on our long voyage" and did not "feel the need of any further inactivity."[23] He told an Associated Press reporter that Japan would not be able to fight for much more than a year: "The average Japanese was very much discouraged and seemed to be about ready to stop fighting." If Charles said anything about his son Yates, now a famous correspondent who had escaped death many times, the reporter did not include it in the story.[24]

On June 4, US dive-bombers smashed the Japanese carriers *Akagi*, *Kaga*, *Sōryū*, and *Hiryū* near Midway. It was a decisive Allied victory but did not completely assuage Curtin. McDaniel covered a radio speech in which the prime minister warned that Midway was not the end of danger for Australia: "The combined effect of the Coral Sea, Midway and Aleutian battles, while frustrating from the Japanese viewpoint, was far from decisive in the struggle through which we must pass if we are to reach our men locked up in Singapore, free the Netherlands East Indies, re-enter the Philippines, release China, and strike at the very heart of Japan."[25]

MacArthur was eager to go on the offensive in New Guinea. To provide the manpower for an attack, two US divisions had been dispatched to Australia, and Australian troops were being recalled from Egypt. An Allied attack on New Guinea would be both brilliant and risky. By attacking New Guinea, MacArthur would force the Japanese to defend the huge island as opposed to invading Australia. Once the Allies controlled New Guinea, they could invade the Philippines, which lay less than 2,000 miles to the northeast. By doing so, they could avoid the Japanese strongholds in Java, Sumatra, and Borneo, all west of New Guinea.

On paper, the strategy was inspired. But New Guinea was a nightmare of steep mountains, thick jungles, leeches, pythons, and malaria. The trees were "tremendously tall" with creeper vines running down to the trunks. People lived in small villages in grass huts constructed on stilts.[26] Because New Guinea was near the equator, it offered virtually no twilight. One American general thought "you just paused to admire the truly wonderful color display of sunset when blackness and mosquitoes descended upon you."[27]

To get closer to New Guinea, MacArthur moved his headquarters in July from Melbourne to an office building in Brisbane. MacArthur and his wife occupied three of the flats in the year-old Lennon's Hotel. The hotel, constructed on the same site as the original Lennon's, a Victorian structure built in 1884, was less of an architectural masterpiece than its predecessor, but far more comfortable. In addition to sixteen flats, it included 140 air-conditioned rooms, many with a view of the Brisbane River, which wound through the center of the city.

Yates followed MacArthur to Brisbane, where he and Natalie took an apartment in Kangaroo Point, Brisbane's oldest suburb and one of its most fashionable.

Every day, US and Australian commanders conducted briefings on the fifth floor of the cable office building in Brisbane. Once the briefing concluded, reporters dashed toward two elevators to take them to the third floor, where tables were set up with typewriters. The reporters then cabled their stories to their home offices. There was so much pushing and shoving that the US military press office adopted a new system where everyone would have a chance to ride the elevator to the third floor and sit at their desks. Only after everyone was seated would they be allowed to start typing. [28]

MacArthur called in the reporters to explain his strategy. More than 100 reporters and editors showed up for what was billed as an off-the-record briefing. MacArthur sat in a chair in the conference room, but when McDaniel asked the first question, MacArthur stood and began to pace.[29] He explained that Australia could be saved only by taking Papua, the eastern province of New Guinea that includes Port Moresby on its southern coast and the village of Buna in the north. "We must attack, attack, attack, attack." Then he left. Reporters could not refer to MacArthur's strategy in their stories, but at least they understood his plan, which would help them write future stories.[30]

The day after MacArthur and Yates arrived in Brisbane, US planes spotted Japanese troop transports sailing near New Guinea's northern coast. McDaniel reported that Allied planes launched a "terrific bombing and strafing campaign," but the Japanese were still able to land as many as 2,000 troops in Buna. The Japanese invasion "was considered a greater threat to Port Moresby in that it put the invader closer to the Allied base," McDaniel wrote. But he pointed out that because Buna and Port Moresby were separated by the 13,000-foot-high Owen Stanley mountain range, it would be difficult for Japanese troops to reach their objective.[31]

The Buna landing set off fresh alarms among Australians, who told McDaniel it was a sign the Japanese were "planning something bigger than the storming of Port Moresby." Japanese planes had attacked Darwin, Townsville, and Port Hedland on the western coast of Australia.[32] The next day, McDaniel wrote, "A glance at the map was sufficient to demonstrate that each new link forged in the island chain gave the Japanese another potential starting point should Tokyo decide to order its war machine to resume rolling southward." There was mounting worry among the Allies that if the Japanese opted to attack Australia, "their recently acquired island-footholds would provide their forces with a considerably greater amount of land-based air support" than Japan had during the battle of the Coral Sea.[33]

On August 7, McDaniel's bureau colleague Vern Haugland hopped a ride on one of six B-26 medium bombers flying the 700 miles from Townsville to Port Moresby.

From there, they would take off to bomb Japanese positions in Lae on New Guinea's northern coast. As they approached, they were enveloped by thick clouds.

"We're completely lost," the pilot said. "We can't tell now whether we're over land or water. I think we almost hit a mountain back there." Then the pilot said, "Our gasoline is getting low. We're going to have to jump."

One after another, Haugland and the seven crew members tumbled into the black sky. The ground was 13,000 feet below. Haugland landed in a tree in a "dense forest or jungle." He ruefully remembered that the closest he had been to a jungle was on a Hollywood set, when director William Wyler filmed actress Bette Davis shooting her lover to death in the opening scene of *The Letter*.[34]

A week later, McDaniel told reporters that Haugland was missing.[35] Unknown to everyone, Haugland was still alive. After finding a crew member nicknamed Mike, Haugland and Mike followed a swollen river, since "frequently impassable cliffs forced us to the water's edge to detour around rocky jungle-clad hills." On August 13, Haugland scribbled in his black notebook: "Still no food, no sign of people." They survived on wild berries and nuts while sipping water from the river. He wrote about the endless rain. "I just lay in mud, soaked and stinking, all night." He became separated from Mike. Three days later he wrote, "Too deathly weak. Can't climb. I'm a goner, I fear."[36]

But he pushed himself to keep walking. Even though he rarely attended church as an adult, Haugland cited aloud the Lord's Prayer. He sang the Australian song "Waltzing Matilda." On September 9, he made his final entry in his journal: "Spent rainy a.m. in hut drying shoes. Where from here?"[37] Finally, he stumbled into a village and told an old man with a beard, "Hello. I'm lost." Two days later, natives carried him to missionaries, who took him to an Australian army unit. He was carried to a hospital bed in a brown tent in Port Moresby.[38] On September 24, the AP reported that Haugland and five crew members survived the ordeal. Mike was not among them.

Haugland was delirious. His weight had plummeted from 165 pounds to only 90. Haugland thought about how badly he wanted to recognize someone he "could trust, such as my immediate superior . . . Yates McDaniel."[39] He saw MacArthur's press aide Larry Lehrbas in the tent and said, "Hello, Larry. How's General MacArthur?"

MacArthur himself visited. "Hello, young man," MacArthur smiled. "How are you feeling?"

"Fine sir," Haugland replied.

To Haugland's astonishment, MacArthur pinned the Silver Star on his pajamas, as a movie camera and flashbulbs from still cameras illuminated the tent. Realizing Haugland was weak, MacArthur told the photographers, "One more, boys. Then let's be going."[40]

The Associated Press ran newspaper advertisements across the country that featured the photo of MacArthur pinning the Silver Star on Haugland. The advertisements concluded, "AP—The Byline of Dependability."[41]

Haugland felt guilty and unworthy of a medal. He had never thought of himself as heroic, remembering a woman who once called him timid and indecisive. What about reporters such as Yates McDaniel, Clark Lee, or Dean Schedler, who "had shown marked courage on the various warfronts without receiving medals?" he asked himself.[42]

Haugland's survival was just one of scores of stories about war correspondents that appeared in American newspapers. In an editorial, the *Honolulu Star-Bulletin* wrote, "In this war where the purpose and the actions of the democracies so greatly need interpretation to the world, the war correspondents are as valuable as the commanders." The editorial cited McDaniel, Cecil Brown of CBS, Clark Lee, and O'Dowd Gallagher.[43]

The invasion of Guadalcanal, which began on August 7, was largely a Navy and Marine effort, although the public would not have realized that from the descriptions in MacArthur's communiques. The general's press releases made it seem like MacArthur was directing the attack himself. In a misleading communique issued on August 10, MacArthur's headquarters announced, "Our naval forces are participating in an attack on the southeast Solomons." In reality, Adm. Nimitz was in charge of the operation. The Americans and Australians gathered seventy-five warships and transports and roughly 16,000 soldiers, mostly US Marines. The goal was to seize a nearly completed Japanese airfield on Guadalcanal.

Two correspondents landed with the Marines on the first day—Richard Tregaskis of International News Service, who less than six months later published the epic book *Guadalcanal Diary*, and Bob Miller of United Press. Not until September 1 did Tom Yarbrough of the AP and Tillman Durdin of the *New York Times* reach Guadalcanal, wearing "glamorous fresh uniforms" while Tregaskis and Miller looked more like "street urchins, for our hand-washed clothes are scarcely clean and our faces stand in need of a good scrubbing with hot water."[44]

McDaniel was 1,300 miles away but had the advantage of being in Brisbane, where information was pouring out of MacArthur's headquarters. Every day at noon, MacArthur's staff held a news conference, and during the Guadalcanal invasion they were jammed with reporters.[45] By assembling communiques from MacArthur's headquarters with sparse handouts from the Navy, McDaniel pieced together what he could about the initial landings, although he acknowledged that "only the scantiest details of the major engagement off the Solomons came from Allied sources."[46]

On August 11, McDaniel reported that Japanese "garrisons, planes, and warships were contesting the US attack with every means at their command." He acknowledged that the outcome of the naval battle "could not be guessed since fleet radio transmitters were sealed while the great naval rifles spoke." In fact, the US Navy was providing as little information as possible, in part because the Japanese inflicted grievous losses off Savo Island, with the American cruisers *Astoria*, *Quincy*, and *Vincennes* sunk with heavy loss of life.[47]

Guadalcanal vividly demonstrated the division of authority in the Pacific theater between MacArthur and Nimitz. In Washington, conservatives seized on the dispute to promote the idea of MacArthur challenging Roosevelt in 1944. The *Christian Science Monitor* reported that "political Washington was largely responsible for the establishment of two commands in the Pacific, partly because of the conservative opposition which launched the 'MacArthur for President' campaign."[48]

In late October, MacArthur issued a statement declaring, "I started as a soldier and I shall finish as one." McDaniel wrote that it was the first time MacArthur had ever publicly spoken about running for president. Referring to the *Christian Science Monitor* story, MacArthur said:

> I have no political ambitions whatsoever. Any suggestion to the contrary must be regarded as merely amiable gestures of good will dictated by friendship. The only hope and ambition I have in the world is for victory for our cause in the war. If I survive that campaign, I shall return to that retirement from which this great struggle called me.

MacArthur's statement was not completely sincere. He clearly had thoughts about the presidency. But he had more-pressing issues. He wanted to capture the Japanese bases of Buna, Gona, and Sanananda along New Guinea's northeastern coast. US intelligence estimated that fewer than 4,000 worn-out and malaria-ridden Japanese soldiers remained at the three bases. But the intelligence was dead wrong. The Japanese had fortified the three bases with roughly 10,000 troops. MacArthur's plan called for an Australian division to seize Gona and Sanananda, while the US 32nd Division would capture Buna. If they were successful, the Japanese would be forced out of eastern Papua.

His plans collided with reality. Neither Allied division was well trained. The two divisions would be forced to march through thick jungles and treacherous swamps during intense humidity and endless rain.

For McDaniel, it was a major story, and fortunately the AP sent him more reporters. Bill Boni arrived in November after finishing a series of articles on the booming US aircraft production in Long Beach, Seattle, and Los Angeles. Boni started his career as a sportswriter for the *New York Post* in 1935 before joining the Associated Press. Dean Schedler had recovered from his wounds during his escape from Corregidor and was available once again.

With Yarbrough on Guadalcanal and Haugland recovering in Port Moresby, McDaniel assigned Boni, Schedler, and Ed Widdis to cover New Guinea, where more than two dozen Western correspondents had gathered—including Barney Darnton of the *New York Times*, Lewis Sebring of the *New York Herald Tribune*, Harold Guard of United Press, Pat Robinson of International News Service, and Al Noderer of the *Chicago Tribune*. "Newspapermen are beginning to swarm in, so I guess they know where their bread is buttered," Gen. Robert Eichelberger wrote.[49] As a joke, one reporter sent a telegram to Army officials asking for a double room with bathroom and a view of the sea. Unfortunately, reporters slept on cots, and to take a bath they punched a few holes into an empty gasoline can and filled it with water. "It's tough on chaps who like to cover a war from a cocktail bar," wrote Bill Henry of the *Los Angeles Times*. The reporters woke up at dawn, ate breakfast, and then pored over the official military report at 10:00 in the morning. Most meals were eaten from a can, with bully beef a regular. The American reporters grumbled because they had to drink tea instead of coffee. There wasn't any hard liquor, and when they weren't working, reporters played baseball, poker, or chess. To get around the base, they had the use of a battered jeep, which Schedler drove so skillfully that his colleagues joked he missed his calling as an Indianapolis 500 race car driver.[50]

Henry particularly liked Barney Darnton. Late one evening in Port Moresby, they were sitting across from each other at a table in the press cottage when Darnton asked if Americans at home "know there is a war going on." American soldiers were dying in New Guinea, and Darnton wanted to tell their stories. As they chatted, a radio was broadcasting news from the BBC. When the BBC broadcaster announced the latest sports news, Darnton said, "Who cares," and switched off the radio. An American colonel walked in and offered the reporters a chance to sail on a trawler that could see action. Darnton immediately volunteered.[51]

The next morning, Darnton was aboard the wooden trawler when a bomber approached. "Japs or ours?" Darnton wrote in his notebook. It was an American B-25, but mistaking the trawler for Japanese, the plane dropped a bomb. Darnton was struck in the head by fragments and died in a small boat before reaching the beach. He was buried near the Port Moresby camp, with Schedler, Sebring, Noderer, and Robinson helping to carry the flag-draped casket. An honor guard fired three rounds in salute.[52]

With Boni, Schedler, and Widdis providing eyewitness reports on the Buna campaign, McDaniel remained in Brisbane, too far from the war to suit him. The daily Army communiques were wildly optimistic, and they often declared that MacArthur was personally commanding the offensive even though he spent most of his time in Brisbane rather than Port Moresby. On November 15, McDaniel wrote that "the jaws of an Allied pincers" closed on the Japanese as Australian troops crossed the Kumusi River and American forces pushed through jungles and swamps.[53]

MacArthur finally went to New Guinea himself, and McDaniel reported that Allied forces, now "directed in the field by Gen. MacArthur, were pushing on toward the coast." They were just 30 miles from Buna "without meeting serious opposition." On November 20, on the basis of communiques, McDaniel reported that American and Australian ground troops were forcing the Japanese into a "narrow corridor" along the coast while Allied airplanes sank a Japanese cruiser and destroyer trying to reinforce Buna.[54] In fact, the Allied offensive had bogged down to the point that on November 30, MacArthur summoned Gen. Eichelberger to Port Moresby and told him, "I want you to take Buna or do not come back alive."[55]

It took a month of brutal fighting before the last Japanese forces were destroyed. "At last, victory," Eichelberger wrote his wife on January 2, 1943.[56]

MacArthur's staff wanted reporters to write about one general, and that general was MacArthur. Correspondents were not permitted by censors to even mention Eichelberger's name, who joked that he was "the great mystery man of Australia."[57] So, McDaniel wrote during the first week of December that "MacArthur's air forces supporting ground troops closing in on the Buna-Gona area on the New Guinea coast have smashed new Japanese attempts to land reinforcements."[58]

Not until a week after Buna fell did MacArthur's headquarters acknowledge that Eichelberger commanded the Allied forces. Eichelberger wrote to his wife that when "my name appeared in headlines over the world and my photograph was seen in many prominent magazines," MacArthur appeared petulant. As far as MacArthur was concerned, he was the only star commander.[59]

McDaniel finished the most tumultuous year of his life by spending a few days with Natalie in Melbourne. Just before the year's beginning, he and Natalie had been in doomed Singapore as the British imposed martial law and Japanese planes flew above the city.

Since his arrival in Australia, however, he had been more of a manager and speaker than a frontline war correspondent, the job he loved and longed for. During the final months of 1942, he was overwhelmed with a "long siege of desk work" in Brisbane.[60] But he brought the same commitment to his desk job as he had to the front lines. He backed up his staff by "fighting their battles" both with Allied commanders and demanding editors. He badgered the New York office to raise his reporters' salaries. The responsibility and workload exhausted him and left him cranky.[61]

He had written analytical pieces throughout the year but had to sit back and watch as other reporters landed in Guadalcanal, tramped through the thick jungles of New Guinea, or flew risky bomber missions. He seemed eager to get back to what he did best—cover a war from the front lines.

In the days before Christmas, he and Natalie roamed about Melbourne. Just about every place they went they saw signs of government austerity regulations, which "provoked a chorus of grousing" by everyday Australians. Retail stores were prohibited from using the Lord's name to encourage people to buy gifts, and Santa Claus—known to Australians as Father Christmas—could not be used in newspaper advertisements. People could wish relatives a Merry Christmas only by mail as opposed to telegraph.

Australians could send packages of food to soldiers on New Guinea, provided they did not weigh more than 5.5 pounds. The twenty-five news correspondents on New Guinea had to find holiday food for themselves, although McDaniel discovered they rounded up a pair of "scrawny ducks." The government allowed Australians who were not in the military to take a four-day holiday from December 25 to December 28, and thousands of people took advantage of the warm weather to head to the beach resorts of South Australia and Queensland.[62]

McDaniel filed his story about Christmas in Australia. The *Richmond Palladium-Item* published it on December 16. Others waited. The *Jackson Clarion-Ledger* picked the right time—Christmas Day. By then, Yates and Natalie were back in Brisbane. But Yates would not be there for long. He was eager to return to the war.

# PORT MORESBY

n a transport plane far above one of the Allied airfields in eastern New Guinea, Yates McDaniel watched planes take off and fly over the Owen Stanley mountain range. The American and Australian planes headed north toward the Bismarck Sea, where a Japanese convoy of eight troop transports was trying to reinforce its garrison at Lae. The runways were so packed with Allied planes that Yates's lumbering transport had to wait before it could safely land.[1]

McDaniel's flight was just one leg of a 10,000-mile journey he had assigned himself to get back to the front lines. His plane had stopped in Darwin and the Gulf of Carpentaria east of Darwin before the long flight to Port Moresby.

It was his first trip to a combat zone since leaving Java and, not coincidentally, only six months since Vern Haugland nearly lost his life when his plane ran out of fuel. Because Japanese fighters roamed the skies, McDaniel's flight was dangerous, but he wanted to see the war up close. More important, as he once wrote to Natalie, he was determined to show "that I can do the difficult tasks that I sent the other boys out to do."[2] Risks went with the job. The *Honolulu Star-Bulletin* cited McDaniel, Clark Lee, Frank Hewlett, Cecil Brown, and O'Dowd Gallagher as "men who face the same hardships and the same dangers that the soldiers face and can die like soldiers, if death is written for them on that bullet or bomb or torpedo."[3]

The planes McDaniel watched taking off from air bases scattered near Port Moresby scored a major victory for the Allies. During a two-day span, Allied planes—American high-level B-17s, low-flying B-25 medium bombers, and Australian A-20 light bombers—sank all eight transports and four escorting destroyers.

At the height of the air attacks, McDaniel's transport readied for what would be a seven-hour flight over the Allied airfields in Papua. When the pilot of McDaniel's plane asked the air officer in Port Moresby for the best course to avoid the rugged mountains, the officer replied, "Oh, you don't have to know the way across the mountains. Just follow the traffic today." McDaniel's plane took off and followed a line of Douglas C-47 transports.[4]

When McDaniel returned to the Army base in Port Moresby, he scanned intelligence photos, with one taken by a plane as it skimmed above the funnels of a Japanese destroyer. McDaniel saw dead and wounded Japanese sailors scattered around one gun, while a nearby sailor swung his antiaircraft gun in search of a target. As each report about the carnage piled into Port Moresby, the Americans erupted with cheers. McDaniel thought the mood was more "like that found in a football bowl during a Thanksgiving Day game than would be expected around a war base."

As McDaniel interviewed a general, the phone at Army headquarters rang. "You say there are several hundred Japanese drifting in boats and rafts out there?" the general barked. "Then send a formation of Beaufighters out to kill some more." The general's order showed how savage the Pacific war had become.[5]

McDaniel wrote that Allied commanders had been dissatisfied in the past with high-level attacks on Japanese shipping. A year earlier at Midway, fifteen American B-17s failed to score a single hit after dropping bombs from 20,000 feet on the carriers *Hiryū* and *Sōryū*. This time, to prevent a replay, they adopted tactics used by the British in September 1939 when a squadron of Blenheim bombers flew at mast-height level and attacked the German pocket battleship *Scheer* in the port of Wilhelmshaven. Three bombs struck the *Scheer*, and while they failed to explode, the attack demonstrated that low-level flying could be effective against ships. The new tactics used by the American and Australian planes led to the "annihilation" of the convoy in the Bismarck Sea.

The US commanders showed McDaniel more ominous photos taken by Allied planes over the powerful Japanese base at Rabaul on the tip of New Britain, roughly 500 miles from Port Moresby. He counted more than sixty Japanese warships and merchant ships in Rabaul's harbor. The Japanese operated four airfields on the island, where roughly 100,000 Japanese troops were based.

The photographs reinforced what McDaniel already suspected: the war could last for years. In blunt terms, McDaniel wrote that "these facts lead informed observers to disagree with overseas commentators who have suggested that destruction of the Bismarck Sea convoy might force the Japanese to abandon some of their islands." He reported that American and Australian commanders lacked enough planes and soldiers, writing that the Allies were "husbanding" their forces. He pointedly noted the strength of the Allied forces "was not what might have been expected of a force which included two generals, a full admiral, and numbers of officers of flag or general rank." During a stop at the Gulf of Carpentaria, McDaniel wrote that the Australian bases simply did not "have enough planes to go around."

McDaniel's frontline reporting meant that he did not have to rely solely on the optimistic Army communiques. He could provide American readers with the truth about the war. The story of his daring 10,000-mile journey ran on the front pages not only of many American, Canadian, and Australian newspapers, but the *New York Times* as well. Once again, McDaniel was a "jump ahead of his colleagues."[6]

Yates flew to Brisbane to see Natalie and work on a news analysis about the one-year anniversary of MacArthur's arrival in Melbourne. MacArthur conducted an off-the-record news conference in Brisbane, his third since escaping the Philippines. American, Australian, British, and Dutch reporters gathered. He wore a black leather flight jacket with four stars and the name stripe "MacArthur." Except for the stars, any Army Air Corps officer could have worn the same jacket. He thanked the correspondents for their coverage and repeated what he told them a year earlier—he would not dictate coverage or criticize reporters unless their stories were based on false or incomplete information. The correspondents knew what MacArthur said about censorship was not true. His press officer, Pick Diller, was notorious for controlling coverage.

McDaniel's story, under the dateline "Somewhere in Australia," demonstrated his reporting skills and his firm grasp of Allied strategy. He revealed what he had known for the past year: a secret Australian plan that had called for yielding the northern half of the continent running west from Brisbane. MacArthur scrapped that plan in favor of attacking New Guinea. McDaniel was now free to report on the old plan without endangering any strategic secrets. He wrote that a year earlier, Australia "was unprepared to meet invasion. Practically all her fully trained and equipped troops were engaged on far-flung battlefronts." MacArthur wanted northern Australian bases for air attacks against New Guinea and New Britain. McDaniel wrote:

> The battle for Australia wouldn't be fought on Australian soil, but in the islands to the north. Borrowing a leaf from a bridge strategist's book, the order came to "lead through strength." Though many could not see it at the time, the Allies' strength was in the air.

In his story, McDaniel said the Japanese committed two blunders. When trying to occupy Port Moresby in May 1942, the Japanese sent naval ships into the Coral Sea without "first clearing the air" of Allied planes as they had done in Singapore and the Philippines. Japan's failure to seize Port Moresby, McDaniel wrote, allowed the Allies to transform "a weakly defended outpost" in eastern New Guinea "into a great offensive base for land and air forces."

Japan's second mistake was to attack Port Moresby with ground troops trying to cross the rugged and thick jungles of the Owen Stanley mountain range. "The sheer effort of conquering the natural obstacle left them too weak to press on to their real goal," which was Port Moresby, McDaniel wrote. The Japanese fell back on Buna on New Guinea's northern coast, where their forces were destroyed. In a sign that either MacArthur or Diller was a source for the story, McDaniel wrote:

> The success of MacArthur's Papuan campaign enabled the Allies to move their bomber line to the north. This move virtually doubled the Allied bombing power by halving the distance to Rabaul and other Japanese bases in the island littoral and made possible destruction of the convoy in the Bismarck Sea—a victory based not on Japanese mistakes but on Allied preparedness and meticulous planning.

McDaniel did not elaborate on why the Allies were so well prepared. But it appears he may have picked up hints of one of America's most important secrets. US intelligence had intercepted Japanese messages that the convoy planned to sail from Rabaul at the end of February to reinforce Lae. The intelligence gave the Allies time to refine their new tactic of low-level bombing. But McDaniel concluded his story with a clear warning that Japan's armed forces remained strong and controlled "the islands northwest of Australia."[7]

For the next two months, Yates was in Brisbane with Natalie. His work schedule was crammed. The AP sent him more reporters, including Murlin Spencer, a correspondent from San Francisco known by his friends as Spence. A 1929 graduate of the University of Colorado, Spencer joined the Associated Press in 1937, reporting from Salt Lake City and Sacramento before landing in San Francisco. Another arrival was Robert Eunson, a thirty-one-year-old graduate of Northern Arizona University who joined the AP in 1941. A few months later, Asahel Bush, a twenty-nine-year-old reporter whom everyone called "Ace," left San Francisco for Australia. The scion of an Oregon publishing family, Bush graduated from Amherst College in 1933 and, like Spencer, covered Sacramento and San Francisco for AP. He spoke fluent Spanish and French. McDaniel thought he had "some good men" working for him at "certain jobs." But he worried that his reporters seemed "temperamental." Some needed gentle coaxing, others a hard push.[8]

The extra reporters were needed because Gen. MacArthur was preparing to complete the conquest of New Guinea, the world's second-largest island and nearly the size of France. Japanese troops and airplanes were based on New Guinea's northern coast, which protected Rabaul's flank. The combination of seizing New Guinea, New Britain, and the Admiralty Islands north of New Guinea would allow MacArthur to neutralize Rabaul without directly attacking the base.

At the end of June, the Americans and Australians landed forces at Nassau Bay in eastern New Guinea and Viru Harbor in New Georgia. Both were weakly defended. The Allies wanted to develop a supply depot at Nassau Bay to intensify pressure on a Japanese airfield 12 miles north at Salamaua. The Viru landing was aimed at capturing the Japanese airfield 40 miles away at Munda.

McDaniel's colleague Bill Boni covered the landing at Nassau Bay. McDaniel took Boni's report and filed a dispatch that was folded into a larger main bar written in New York by AP war editor Roger Greene. "The shores of Nassau Bay were not strongly defended by the enemy," McDaniel wrote.[9] He made clear that "any push along the coast of Nassau Bay northward would be almost impossible because of the densely tangled jungle and swamps."[10]

A week after the July 9 landings, Boni joined eleven American soldiers on a barge leaving Nassau Bay. The sea was calm and the sky clear as the barge headed for deep water. Four Japanese Zeros chased a B-25, while a Japanese dive-bomber flew above the barge. Boni quickly put on his helmet. The dive-bomber fired, and Boni heard bullets smacking the barge. He didn't feel any pain but noticed blood on his left hip. A second Japanese dive-bomber joined the first and they dropped eight bombs, none of which hit. When they reached a first-aid station, Boni's wounds were cleaned and dressed.[11]

McDaniel sent a letter congratulating Boni for his "narrow escape. I am enclosing 60 pounds which you probably need." He asked Boni to give some of the money to Vern Haugland, who was scheduled to arrive in Port Moresby and pay a bill run up by Dean Schedler at the officer's mess.[12]

During the second week of July, McDaniel flew to Port Moresby. He and two dozen reporters jammed into a large hut near two press tents. Every day, the military held two press conferences. The briefings were held in the larger tent, and then reporters scrambled to the smaller tent, where typewriters were set up. This produced the predictable rush by correspondents to their typewriters until military officers instituted the same rule they'd adopted in Brisbane: Everyone would leave the larger tent for the filing tent and sit at their typewriters. An officer would announce, "Go." Reporters then frantically typed their stories and filed by radio or cable.[13]

As part of their coverage, AP reporters had to produce what was known as the "Joe Blo Yarn." In New York, AP general manager Kent Cooper demanded that AP get "stories with the names of boys in the frontline trenches."[14] Reporters had to interview soldiers in the field and get not only their names but also hometowns and street addresses. Murlin Spencer grumbled that "more risks" were taken to get those details "than in covering large-scale operations."

During one fight in New Guinea, Spencer took cover in a foxhole with two dead Japanese soldiers. A Japanese machine gun opened up from a pillbox, and a nearby American soldier grasped a grenade.

"What's your name and hometown?" Spencer shouted. The soldier looked at Spencer as if he were "crazy," but replied, "Robert Amans of Superior, Wisconsin." The soldier then tossed the grenade toward the pillbox. The AP sent out the story even though it might have been a bit embellished.[15]

McDaniel once asked a correspondent to fly a few thousand miles just to find the names and hometowns of pilots who carried out a bombing attack on Java. To McDaniel, it meant the soldier was not just another "serial number" but an actual person known in his hometown.[16]

The correspondents had one major advantage: MacArthur always made news. Because of Diller's demands, the news was favorable to MacArthur, which was not easy considering MacArthur's mismanagement of the Buna campaign. But MacArthur was adapting, and his strategy to wrest control of Lae from the Japanese was a stroke of brilliance. During the first week of September, the Australians were scheduled to land on beaches east of Lae while American paratroopers were to seize an airstrip northeast of Lae. The Japanese had not used the field for months, and it was covered by thick grass as high as 6 feet. Seizing the field would allow the Allies to avoid a direct attack on Lae and instead envelop the Japanese defenders.

McDaniel, Dean Schedler, photographer Ed Widdis, and Vern Haugland covered the operation. McDaniel reported from Port Moresby, while Haugland flew aboard a B-17 to watch the parachute drop. At seven in the morning, MacArthur arrived at the airfield and chatted with Gen. Richard Sutherland, his chief of staff. The engines of the transports roared. "I wouldn't trade this for a chance to stand on the corner of Times Square right now," a soldier told Schedler. Widdis snapped a photo of MacArthur and Gen. George Kenney, who commanded the Allied air forces, chatting with Lt. Col. J. J. Tolson, the leader of the paratroopers. When the photo was published, the caption naturally included Tolson's hometown of New Bern, North Carolina. As twin-engine P-38 fighters soared above, the transports took off. To everyone's surprise, MacArthur impulsively decided to watch the airborne operation from another B-17. Widdis snapped photos of MacArthur as the general stood outside the plane, then he scampered aboard ahead of MacArthur so he could shoot photos of the general boarding the aircraft.[17]

MacArthur saw Widdis and laughed: "You know I wouldn't be surprised to wake up some morning to find you in bed with me."[18]

Aboard one of the Allied planes, Haugland watched Australian A-20s pepper Lae with a protective blanket of smoke. Moments later, he saw MacArthur's B-17 leading a "breathtaking formation of transport planes with fighter escort." The transports flew so low that Haugland wasn't sure the paratroopers would have enough time to open their chutes. Then the sky filled with white parachutes blending with a handful of orange, red, and blue chutes. He could see the soldiers floating to the ground and landing in thick grass, with some falling into trees. He saw no sign of casualties.[19]

Aboard MacArthur's plane, Widdis took a stunning photo of the parachutes opening. Then he shot the iconic photo of MacArthur standing near a waist gunner and pointing out the bay window. "This is beautiful, truly wonderful," MacArthur shouted to the waist gunner. The photo ran on front pages across the country. "He saw the men seize strong positions without encountering any immediate resistance," McDaniel wrote. Every Allied plane returned. When MacArthur reached Port Moresby, he told reporters, "We have closed the ring at Lae and Salamaua." A communique proclaimed that 20,000 Japanese soldiers were now cut off from supplies.[20]

A few days later, McDaniel flew back to Brisbane. On September 19, MacArthur's headquarters issued a communique proclaiming the Allies had seized Lae. McDaniel's story began with the phrase "The hoisting of the Australian flag over Lae . . ."[21]

The photos of MacArthur in a combat zone only enhanced his heroic image in America. The theatrics helped him as he became embroiled in a major political battle with the British over the next phase of the war. Lord Louis Mountbatten, appointed on August 25 to command Allied forces in India, favored an attack against Burma or Malaya. By contrast, MacArthur wanted to utilize the Allied air and sea strength to bypass many of the remaining Japanese strongholds on New Guinea, avoid an attack on Rabaul, and then invade the Philippines. Although MacArthur was strategically correct, his ego demanded sole power to direct the Pacific theater, as opposed to sharing decisions with either Mountbatten or the US Navy.

MacArthur released a statement to reporters in New Guinea in which he said he would play a "subordinate role" if ordered. But the rest of his statement made clear he had no interest in being anyone's subordinate:

My strategic conception for the Pacific theater . . . contemplates massive strokes against only main strategic objectives, utilizing surprise, and air and ground striking power, supported and assisted by the fleet. This is the very opposite of what is termed "island hopping," which is gradually pushing back the enemy by direct frontal pressure with consequent heavy casualties, which will certainly be involved. Island-hopping with extravagant losses and slow progress—some press reports indicating victory might be postponed as long as 1949—is not my idea of how to end the war as soon and as cheaply as possible. Wars are never won in the past."

Bill Boni folded MacArthur's statement into a broader story. Boni pointed out that MacArthur had demonstrated his strategy with attacks east and west of Lae rather than directly confronting the well-fortified Japanese garrison in the town. Once New Guinea was essentially controlled by the Allies, MacArthur planned to bypass Java, Sumatra, and Borneo and aim directly for the Philippines.[22]

Three days later, McDaniel was given the task of explaining the controversy. His analysis was preceded by a note written by one of his editors:

Just what did General MacArthur have in mind when he issued his statement on September 22 commenting on press reports that his part in the war was to be curtailed and his command subordinated? While no official comment has been forthcoming from Washington, London or Canberra, there has been much professed bewilderment in official circles. C. Yates McDaniel, Associated Press Bureau Chief at MacArthur's headquarters . . . outlines the background for the statement that provoked the discussion and analyzes the reasons why MacArthur favors a full-scale assault on Japan from Australia instead of Burma, Hawaii, or Alaska.

McDaniel explained that the real issue was not who directed the Allied offensive but from "what base or basic area such an offensive is to be mounted." He pointed out there were four routes to invading Japan—originating from Dutch Harbor in the Aleutians, Midway in the Central Pacific, India, or Australia.

McDaniel noted the pitfalls of the first three possibilities. A fleet sailing from Dutch Harbor would have to navigate its way through a mass of fog. A task force from Midway needed to sail 2,250 miles past Japanese-held islands armed with bombers and torpedo planes. An attack from India into Burma might reopen the Burma Road into southern China. However, McDaniel wrote, "those of us who worked in Burma and China during the bitter pre–Pearl Harbor years know the Burma Road, far from being an end to itself, was the last and least efficient supply route resorted to by the Chinese," particularly after the fall of Hong Kong and Indochina.

By contrast, McDaniel wrote, Allied forces in Australia and New Guinea were composed of a "team of land, air, and amphibious experts who aggregate more practical experience with our enemy in the Pacific than probably all other commands together could muster." He even borrowed MacArthur's own phrase of massive strokes:

> The strategy of MacArthur envisions one of a series of massive strokes, which instead of involving the costly capture of island after island, would carry a powerful Allied force over and around numerous islands as far as the southern Philippines.[23]

The seizure of Lae led to a gruesome discovery. A captured Japanese soldier kept a diary, and an entry on March 29 described the beheading of an Allied aviator. Although MacArthur's headquarters claimed he was an American, he almost certainly was FLt. Bill Newton, an Australian whose A-20 twin-engine bomber crash-landed in the surf off the northern coast of New Guinea. A Japanese company of soldiers commanded by SLt. Uichi Komai captured Newton and another crew member. MacArthur's headquarters released a translation of the diary. McDaniel could have paraphrased the diary and spared readers the horrifying details. But reality was far starker than anything he could have written. So he wrote a short lead and let the diary tell the chilling story:

> We were assembled to witness the execution. The prisoner was given a drink of water outside the guard house. The chief surgeon, Lt. Komai, and a platoon commander bearing a sword comes from the officer's mess.
>
> The time has come. The prisoner of war totters forward with his arms tied. His hair is cut close. I feel he suspects what is afoot, but he is more composed than I thought he would be. At the execution ground, Lt. Komai faces the prisoner and says, "You are to die. I am going to kill you with this sword according to the Samurai code." The prisoner is made to sit on the edge of a water-filled bomb crater. The precaution is taken to surround him with guards. When I put myself in his place, the hate engendered by this daily bombing yields to ordinary human feelings. [Komai] draws his favorite sword, the famous "Osamune." The sight of the glittering blade sends cold shivers down the spine. First, he touches the prisoner's neck lightly with the sword. Then he raises it overhead. His arm muscles bulge. The prisoner closes his eyes for a second and at once the sword sweeps down.
>
> Swish—it sounds at first like noise of cutting but is actually made by blood spurting from arteries as the body falls forward. Everybody steps forward as the head rolls on the ground.

A Japanese seaman kicked Newton's lifeless body. Then the seaman buried the Australian.

McDaniel's story appeared on front pages across the country, from the *Atlanta Constitution* to the *Boston Globe*. The *Detroit Free Press* published the story above the paper's nameplate. McDaniel wrote that Komai's name "won't be forgotten by the men who fly for Gen. Douglas MacArthur." US officials vowed those responsible would be tried after the war. It turned out to be unnecessary. Komai died not long after in the Philippines.[24]

MacArthur next aimed at Japanese-held New Britain, which was due east of Lae. Many Allied officers believed an invasion of New Britain was unnecessary. MacArthur shrugged off their objections and ordered two landings—one at Arawe on the island's southern coast, and the second at Cape Gloucester on the northwest coast.

To cover the Arawe landing, McDaniel assigned Dean Schedler to fly above the combat zone in a B-24 Liberator while Robert Eunson would report from the old four-stack destroyer *Sands*, lying offshore. At the last moment, Eunson volunteered to go with the US 112th Cavalry Regiment. Going in with the first wave was risky because Eunson would head to the beach in a fragile rubber boat. At five in the morning on December 15, Eunson climbed down nets hanging on the side of the *Sands*. Except for a bright moon, it was still dark. The only noise came from soldiers paddling their boats. From the beaches, Japanese gunners fired. A corporal aimed his Tommy gun and fired until it was empty. Eunson and the soldiers took cover by leaping into the water. He grasped the arm of a young soldier who had been hit in the back. When the soldier stopped breathing a few moments later, Eunson let go of his arm. A Japanese machine gun bullet shattered his typewriter, which was still in the boat. The *Sands* approached, firing its guns. The Japanese machine guns went silent.[25]

The AP flashed the first word of the landing. New York cabled McDaniel to express its delight that AP had beaten United Press by four minutes. "With us, split seconds count," Yates wrote Natalie. But when Eunson returned to Port Moresby, he clearly was shaken at his narrow escape. He was haunted by the sight of US soldiers killed before his eyes. He spoke of being peppered by bullets in the water and thinking he would never see his wife and two daughters again. McDaniel was angry with Eunson for volunteering to land with the first wave in a flimsy rubber boat. Although McDaniel accepted more chances in combat than just about anyone, he constantly urged his reporters not to take unnecessary risks. "I hoped he has learned his lesson by now," McDaniel wrote.[26] Despite McDaniel's irritation, the AP published a newspaper advertisement boasting of Eunson's daring landing and declaring that he "wrote one of the most graphic stories to come out of the war."[27] After a few days of rest, Eunson was ready to "get back into it." But while Eunson had written a dramatic first-person piece, McDaniel thought Schedler "came through with probably the best of our stories on the whole show."[28]

In addition to bullets, reporters had to contend with New Guinea's brutal heat and humidity. One night, McDaniel sweated so much he could not sleep. Worried about contracting malaria, he slept under a mosquito net and took Atabrine, an antimalaria drug. He often worked until midnight and was so busy he found it difficult to leave the camp except for "a daily walk for exercise and sun," which tanned his skin a dark brown.[29]

During one of his walks, McDaniel found what he called a "secluded nook" and relaxed in the sun. It felt like a Turkish bath. The next day between news conferences he climbed a small mountain near the cottage. He liked being outdoors. The Army provided plenty of food, and he was "eating like a hog." A black kitten took a liking to him and often curled up next to him on his cot. He jokingly wrote Natalie there was no reason for their new dog Angus to be jealous.[30]

The next day, Yates wrote Natalie again, saying he hoped to return to Brisbane before the middle of January. "Until then, all my love and the very best of Christmases," he wrote.

He dropped a cryptic hint: "I will be elsewhere over Christmas."[31]

"Elsewhere" was Cape Gloucester in New Britain. The 1st Marine Division would land there and secure the beaches. Once the "bomber line" moved to Cape Gloucester, Allied planes from Cape Gloucester and Bougainville would have relatively short flights to bomb the Japanese naval and air bases in Rabaul. Bombers, not soldiers on the ground, would ravage Rabaul.

As the ships sailed from New Guinea, McDaniel, CBS's Bill Dunn, and four other correspondents gathered for a final briefing aboard the destroyer *Conyngham*. RAdm. Dan Barbey, who commanded the task force, was upbeat: "As you men know, it is customary to keep correspondents under wraps after their briefing on any given operation. Actually, you will have no opportunity to fall into enemy hands, at least not until the operation is well under way, but I'll tell you frankly, it wouldn't make any difference. This operation has been so well organized, and we are so well equipped both on the sea and in the air, that there's nothing the Japanese can do effectively, even if they knew our plans in detail."[32]

McDaniel's coverage plan for Cape Gloucester called for Murlin Spencer to land with the Marines. Bill Boni would be on a cruiser bombarding the Japanese positions, Dean Schedler aboard a B-24 Liberator circling above the landing, Ace Bush stationed at one of the Allied airfields, and Robert Eunson covering MacArthur's headquarters in Port Moresby.[33] McDaniel originally did not intend to go ashore with the Marines but instead planned to watch the progress from the decks of a destroyer offshore. But he soon had second thoughts. Marines would land on a wide swath of New Britain, and he worried that the only way Spencer could file an eyewitness account was to land and quickly return to the fleet to file. Unable to get in touch with Spencer to order him to change plans, McDaniel decided to go ashore with the Marines so he could file the first news of the invasion. But McDaniel had another reason. Even though he had chastised Eunson for landing with the first wave at Arawe, McDaniel felt he should accept the same risks.

On Christmas Eve, the sailors in the *Conyngham*'s boiler room invited McDaniel for an impromptu celebration. "We've got to have a little Christmas even though it is hot," one of the sailors laughed. It was 110 degrees in the boiler room, but the sailors set up a Christmas tree and wrapped gifts for their buddies.[34]

McDaniel spent Christmas Day on the *Conyngham*. The young Marines seemed thrilled to have the internationally famous McDaniel accompany them on the landing. But that night, despite Barbey's reassuring words, McDaniel developed "misgivings." He was not only much older than the Marines, he was even older than the destroyer's commander. For the first time in his life, McDaniel thought of himself as the "old gray-haired man." He told the Marines he might skip the landing. But seeing their disappointed expressions, McDaniel changed his mind and decided to join them.[35]

Shortly before seven the next morning, McDaniel eased himself over the side of the destroyer and into a small landing craft. The guns of US ships and bombs dropped by B-24 Liberators pounded the Japanese defenses. The landing craft chugged toward the shore. During the thirty-five-minute trip, McDaniel was nagged by the thought of the heavy casualties suffered by the Marines a month earlier when they landed at well-fortified Tarawa Island.

McDaniel reached the beach at Borgen Bay just five minutes behind the first wave. Except for the chattering of a few machine guns, there wasn't any sign of Japanese resistance. Not one landing boat had been hit, and McDaniel could not find a single Marine who had been wounded. He returned to the destroyer and radioed his story to AP. It was the first eyewitness account filed by any reporter.[36]

That very same day, Brydon Taves of United Press, Ian Morrison of the *Times* of London, Haydon Lennard of the Australian Broadcasting Commission, and Pendil Rayner of the *Brisbane Telegraph* climbed aboard a B-17 in New Guinea to get a good view of the Cape Gloucester landing. Shortly after takeoff, the B-17 crashed. The twenty-nine-year-old Taves died from a fractured skull and burns. Rayner and the two pilots also died, while Morrison and Lennard survived.

McDaniel served as a pallbearer for Taves's burial in the American cemetery in New Guinea. American planes flew overhead in a military salute, diving so low that the military chaplain had to raise his voice to be heard. Next, McDaniel took part in the burial service for Rayner, whom he described as "a very good friend of ours and one of the best in the game." As they stood before the cross on Rayner's grave, McDaniel and a reporter from *The Age* of Melbourne saluted.[37]

Natalie wrote a letter to Taves's widow, Diana Parnham, a well-known Australian film actress. The two had married only a few months earlier.

The deaths of Taves and Rayner "cast a pall over" the reporters. The fact that McDaniel beat United Press on the landings suddenly meant little. The combination of covering the landings, dealing with the deaths of colleagues, and working "literally night and day" had exhausted the reporters. During a four-day span, McDaniel had been to sleep for only two nights. He was so exhausted that he didn't think he "could hold up another minute." The strain was overwhelming, and he suspected it showed to his colleagues. But he wrote Natalie:

> For the sake of the rest of the staff and their morale it is very well that I went in on what we all thought was going to be a dangerous business. This all sounds

very grim and depressing, I know, probably because I am dead beat and all of us are feeling down in the dumps.

His mind clearly was on the dangers faced by reporters. He wrote to Natalie, "Taves was the ninth correspondent to be killed in this area and the fifth this month."[38]

For the reporters, the work level would only increase in the first few months of 1944. MacArthur planned a lightning offensive up the northern coast of New Guinea while simultaneously seizing the Admiralty Islands, with their deep anchorage, north of New Guinea and west of New Ireland. The attacks would allow the Americans and Australians to not only trap tens of thousands of Japanese in New Guinea but also permit the Allies to bypass New Ireland and Rabaul. Seizing the Admiralty Islands, McDaniel wrote, "very likely will play an early and decisive part in the elimination of" Rabaul "as pivotal point of the enemy's offensive and defensive operations." The Admiralty airfields would once again move the bomber line to allow Allied planes to cover American and Australian landings at Wakde, Hollandia, and Aitape on New Guinea's northern coast. Just off Humboldt Bay, Hollandia would provide the Allies with airfields and a deep harbor.

The landings on New Guinea's northern coast would be the most ambitious amphibious assaults so far in the Pacific war. AP increased McDaniel's staff to twelve reporters and photographers, boasting they formed the largest "team any press organization" had ever gathered in the Pacific theater.[39] In addition to Ace Bush and Murlin Spencer, McDaniel could call on Charles McMurtry. A graduate of the University of Missouri, the thirty-eight-year-old McMurtry joined the AP in Kansas City before being transferred to Los Angeles. McMurtry was a seasoned war correspondent. He was aboard the aircraft carrier *Hornet* when it was sunk by Japanese planes in October 1942. His hands and face were badly burned when a Japanese plane crashed into the signal bridge he was using for cover. McMurtry used his body to shield a sailor on the signal bridge, prompting the sailor to tell him, "Thanks, buddy, you sure saved me."[40] He later wrote a gripping first-person story about the Japanese attack.[41]

So many reporters and photographers moved into the journalists' hut in Port Moresby that McDaniel was unable to get much sleep. There was just too much noise. Yates and McMurtry would write the main story every day from Port Moresby. Spencer landed with American forces at Tanahmerah Bay north of Hollandia, while Bush went ashore at Humboldt Bay to the south. Spencer Davis landed at Aitape, while photographer Ernest King's job was to stick close to MacArthur at the landing. Eunson watched both landings and then flew to Port Moresby with reports from the correspondents, which Yates and McMurtry folded into larger stories.[42]

Relying on the firsthand accounts, McDaniel crafted a dramatic piece on the landing, writing, "Under cover of a tremendous naval and air blasting," thousands of Americans landed at Hollandia and Aitape. Using tractors and bulldozers, the US Army engineers quickly rebuilt the Japanese airfields. Allied bombers were now just 1,000 miles from the Philippines.[43]

On the second day of the landing, a Japanese plane dropped three bombs on an abandoned Japanese supply dump in Hollandia. The area erupted in flames. Bush, who was typing a story, jumped in a small foxhole and buried his face in the sand. The explosions destroyed his typewriter, the second typewriter he had lost in combat. Typewriters were in short supply; McDaniel lost a typewriter in Indochina in 1940. In a sheepish message to McDaniel, Bush described the attack before adding a paragraph: "I lost all my gear and when I say 'all' you know what that means. Just like some folks ought not to be trusted with firearms."[44]

Because McDaniel wrote so much, he found no time to relax in the sun or even take a brief walk. McMurtry was a real help, Yates thought, but "the more men, the more work for me." The press hut was so noisy from the crowd of reporters that every time McDaniel flopped down for a nap, he found it impossible to sleep. He hoped to get back to Brisbane for a few days to see Natalie. "I miss you very much and will be glad to get back to you," he wrote her. "I am very sorry for this miserable letter, but it takes with it all my love."[45]

On a spring evening in 1944, McDaniel had a private talk with MacArthur at his headquarters in New Guinea. Throughout the previous few months, MacArthur's name had been floated by Republicans as a challenger to Roosevelt, who was seeking his fourth term. Republican senator Arthur Vandenberg of Michigan spearheaded the nationwide effort to persuade MacArthur to run. But when Republican congressman Arthur Miller of Nebraska released private letters he had exchanged with MacArthur about the presidency, the general could no longer pretend he was only entertaining a draft. He would have to choose—invading the Philippines or launching an uphill campaign against Roosevelt. He chose the Philippines.

As he chatted with Yates, MacArthur was completely at ease, relaxing on the corner of a faded burgundy-colored sofa in his headquarters. Yates had first seen MacArthur in September 1930, when the general's ship made a stop in Shanghai during a voyage from the Philippines to the United States. MacArthur was leaving his post as commander of US forces in the Philippines to become Army chief of staff. There is no record that McDaniel spoke directly to the general in 1930. But years later, Yates vividly recalled that during his Shanghai stop, MacArthur warned that American officials needed to build its defenses in the Philippines as a "bulwark to withstand coming pressures the United States could not safely ignore."[46]

The discussion on this night in 1944 drifted toward Roosevelt's quest for a fourth term. The general opposed the president's bid for a third term in 1940 but now expected Roosevelt to win in November 1944. MacArthur had come to terms with Roosevelt, but except for Adm. William Leahy, Roosevelt's chief of staff, MacArthur had little use for the president's other advisers. MacArthur told Yates that most of Roosevelt's advisers had no understanding of how important it was to retake the Philippines. Controlling the Philippines would cut off Japan's supply lines from oil-rich Java and prove to Filipinos that America would keep its word. He did not name those advisers but clearly disliked Secretary of the Interior Harold Ickes, a longtime Roosevelt confidant.

"You know, Franklin and I have known each other a long time," MacArthur told Yates. "He understands the importance of making history, not waiting for it to happen."

The road to the Philippines was now open, but MacArthur told Yates that Washington had not settled on a strategy. The Navy wanted to attack Formosa, off the China coast, while MacArthur insisted on an assault on the Philippines. If the choice was the Philippines, McDaniel wanted to cover it in person. It would involve a major personal risk. But McDaniel was more comfortable witnessing history at the front than he was just writing about it from Australia.

# TACLOBAN

board a blacked-out ship off the Philippines during the early morning hours of October 20, 1944, Yates typed a brief note to Natalie. The moonless night in Leyte Gulf was so dark, it was difficult for McDaniel to see the hundreds of Allied ships gathered off Leyte Island. When McDaniel finished the letter, he handed it to a Navy pilot who was flying back to Australia.

In a few hours, scores of American and Australian warships would open fire on an 18-mile sector of beaches on Leyte Island. Then the first of 174,000 American soldiers would climb into their Higgins crafts and land on four beaches between the village of Dulag and the provincial capital, Tacloban City. McDaniel would be among those landing on the beaches in one of the largest amphibious assaults in history.

Leyte Island was ideal for an amphibious attack. In sharp contrast to nearby Samar, an island of thick forests and towering cliffs, Leyte was flatter and offered the Americans the chance to seize four Japanese airfields, all vital to an Allied success. MacArthur had opted to bypass Mindanao to the south, which meant that until Leyte's airfields were in the hands of the Army, the Americans had to rely on carrier planes for protection. Leyte is roughly 300 miles south of Manila, the Philippine capital, and capture of the island would clear the way for MacArthur to launch another amphibious attack on Luzon, the largest of the Philippine islands. The Bataan Peninsula and Manila were on Luzon, and Corregidor Island lay in Manila Bay.

The Americans and Allies assembled 700 ships, with eight fleet carriers, eight light carriers, twelve battleships, twenty-four cruisers, more than 160 destroyers, and roughly 1,500 carrier aircraft. The fleet featured the new fast battleships *Iowa* and *New Jersey*, but also six older prewar battleships, including five survivors of the Pearl Harbor attack. The *West Virginia* and *California*, sunk by Japanese torpedo planes, came "back from their Pearl Harbor graves" so completely rebuilt that they no longer resembled the dreadnoughts launched a quarter of a century earlier.[1]

For McDaniel, the past few months had been hectic. At the end of May, he flew to the United States aboard an Air Force plane for a three-month trip that included attending Vern Haugland's wedding in San Francisco and a visit with his parents in Richmond, a sign the split with his father had finally healed.[2] Yet, he worked throughout the trip. In June, when B-29 bombers—the new long-range Superfortresses—took off from bases in China to bomb the Japanese city of Yawata, McDaniel crafted an analysis that paired with a main bar written by AP correspondent Clyde Farnsworth. The B-29 raid, McDaniel wrote, sent a clear message to American allies and the Japanese that the United States had the means to regularly bomb Japan. "Doolittle's raid on Tokyo two years ago did little damage to anything but the Japanese pride," McDaniel wrote. "Yesterday's assault by American Superfortresses was no such hit-and-run affair." While Japan "still has enough warships and planes to put up a tough fight," the combination of US planes taking off from China and the American seizure of the islands of Saipan, Tinian, and Guam "mean the beginning . . . of a systematic aerial bombardment of the still formidable" Japanese military.[3]

McDaniel returned to Australia in August, making a quick stop in Hawaii, where the *Honolulu Star-Bulletin* noted his arrival as the author of "the famous news story, Goodbye to Singapore." After briefly seeing Natalie in Brisbane, Yates sailed to the Philippines for what would be the biggest story he had ever covered in the Pacific. AP supplied McDaniel with thirteen reporters and one photographer, the largest collection of correspondents by a single news organization in the Pacific theater. There were so many new arrivals that McDaniel joked half his staff were "virtually strangers."[4] Overall, there were forty-five American correspondents from wire services and newspapers, along with seven radio reporters and three newsreel photographers to cover the invasion. All newspaper and radio copy would have to be composed on the beaches and flown to New Guinea by a Navy courier plane.[5]

McDaniel devised an intricate coverage plan. On October 17, Richard Bergholz would land with a Ranger battalion on two islands at the entrance of Leyte Gulf. Three days later, the main assaults would take place on Leyte. Ace Bush, Jim Hutcheson, and Fred Hampson would land at the two northernmost beaches near Tacloban City, where MacArthur planned to establish his headquarters. Almost 20 miles south, near Dulag, Al Dopking, Elmont Waite, Leif Erickson, and Rembert James would go ashore with two other American divisions. McDaniel and Dean Schedler would watch the landings from a ship and then go ashore. Murlin Spencer would report from the amphibious command ship *Blue Ridge*—flagship of RAdm. Daniel Barbey—and land near Tacloban. Spencer Davis was assigned to the amphibious ship *Wasatch*, which served as flagship for Adm. Thomas Kinkaid, commander of the US 7th Fleet. Morrie Landsberg would report from an aircraft carrier.[6]

The morning when Yates finished his letter to Natalie, the US and Australian warships unleashed a "devastating" bombardment of Leyte. Thousands of American soldiers poured ashore on the four beaches. To Schedler, the landing craft carrying the Americans looked "like a parade of New York fireboats with great streams of saltwater sprouting in the air."[7] Before McDaniel went ashore, three Japanese shells struck his ship, prompting him to quip that he "had one of my narrow" escapes. "Completely all right. Not a scratch." McDaniel saw the Americans had landed on sandy beaches flanked by rows of coconut palms, not far from Tacloban. A good road ran along the beach's edge.[8]

McDaniel returned to the ship to write because "working conditions" on the beaches were in a "state of complete chaos." McDaniel was working harder than "even in the worst days of Singapore."[9] He wrote that unlike US landings in the thick jungles of New Guinea, the sandy beaches and roads of Leyte Island meant that "for the first time since Bataan, MacArthur's Army and artillery will have room" to maneuver.[10]

McDaniel and Schedler did not personally see the day's greatest drama. Four hours after the landing, MacArthur climbed down a ladder on the light cruiser *Nashville* into a small landing craft and headed for the beaches. Four correspondents jumped in the craft to file pool reports for their colleagues—Bill Dunn of CBS, Bill Dickinson of United Press, Frank Prist of Acme Newspictures, and Earle Crotchett of Paramount Newsreels.

Another landing craft glided near them. "Son, where is the hardest fighting going on?" MacArthur shouted to the sailor steering the second craft. The sailor pointed to a spot straight ahead.

"Head for that spot, son," MacArthur ordered the coxswain of his boat.

About 20 yards from shore, the landing craft ran aground, forcing MacArthur, his staff, reporters, and Philippine president Sergio Osmena to wade through the waves to the beach. For nearly an hour, MacArthur strolled about the beach waiting for the US Signal Corps to set up a microphone. Machine gun fire could be heard nearby. Curious soldiers gathered around MacArthur, who peppered them with questions about the operation.

It started to rain. Dunn took the microphone and said, "People of the Philippines. The next voice you hear will be that of Gen. MacArthur, speaking from a beach on the island of Leyte. The general will be followed by your own president, the honorable Sergio Osmena. Now, here he is, Gen. Douglas MacArthur."

MacArthur grasped the microphone with his left hand. "This is the voice of freedom, Gen. MacArthur speaking. People of the Philippines: I have returned." To some, it was MacArthur at his pompous worst. But the words "I have returned" appeared in headlines across the United States, electrifying anxious Americans.

McDaniel was infuriated by the lack of filing facilities. His temper was "flaring up again." The Domei News Agency, which was the mouthpiece of the Japanese government, beat the American newspapers on the Leyte invasion.[11] Despite that competitive setback, AP general manager Kent Cooper in New York cabled congratulations, although McDaniel grumbled that if Cooper "only knew what we have gone through to get them a single word of this blasted story." Night fell. Japanese planes roared above, leading to a complete blackout of the ship. Exhausted from work and stress, he nodded off on the ship's steel deck.[12]

The next day, McDaniel returned to the beach. He could see the Americans were close to capturing two key airfields near Tacloban. After another grueling day, it was back to the ship, where he wrote the main bar, folding in reports from Hampson, Bush, Spencer, and Dopking. "Every report from the invasion scene, while varying in the degree of opposition, placed the Yanks on the move," McDaniel wrote. The reports from the fighting were a major improvement over relying on communiques released by MacArthur and Nimitz.[13] Tacloban fell one day later, with McDaniel reporting that the largest airfield was captured within twenty-four hours of the invasion.[14]

When he went back to the ship that night, Yates found three letters from Natalie. Using a flashlight to illuminate the typewriter's keyboard, he typed a one-page reply:

> It was wonderful getting them when I was feeling thoroughly down on the world and in a vicious temper. Nothing calms me down more than to be told that you understand. I have had so little time to think, eat or sleep that I am in a fog. The only thing I know clearly is that I want to be with you.[15]

The clumsy censorship was maddening to the reporters. One morning in late October of 1944, McDaniel, Schedler, and Murlin Spencer watched three Japanese planes fly over the beaches. US antiaircraft guns barked. The planes caught fire, and while two crashed into the surf, the third smacked into an American warship. The AP reporters were puzzled. Did the Japanese deliberately crash the plane into an Allied ship? It would be days before they realized they had seen the first of what became known as kamikaze attacks. McDaniel wanted to write a story about the suicide attacks, but the Navy refused permission. A few days later, Tokyo Rose announced the new suicide attacks. McDaniel and other correspondents protested that because the Japanese had announced the kamikaze attacks, they should be permitted to write about them as well. The Navy refused to relent. The correspondents were astonished. Relying on reports from the Domei News Agency, the *Mason City Globe-Gazette* of Iowa wrote an editorial about the kamikazes, but reporters on the scene had been silenced.[16] Not for another six months were American correspondents allowed to write about the kamikaze attacks, which had taken such a toll on the Allies.[17] During the next year, Japanese kamikaze attacks sank thirty-four Navy ships, including three escort carriers and fourteen destroyers. The British fleet carrier *Formidable* and the American carrier *Intrepid* were struck by kamikazes, although both remained afloat.

The working conditions for the soldiers and reporters were made worse by the monsoon season: 18 inches of rain fell in one night, forcing soldiers to bail out their foxholes before getting some sleep. McDaniel described the "muck" as nearly impassable.[18]

Ace Bush reached Tacloban after it fell to the Americans in October 1944, and found the city "utterly poverty stricken." He described the homes as "ramshackle." People made clothes from old flour bags or burlap sacks, and only a few fortunate families had a handful of pigs and chickens. He filed his story on October 23, but because of delays it was not published until October 25.[19] That same day just before dawn, Japanese planes appeared overhead. One bomb exploded near Bush and a group of correspondents. Murlin Spencer found Bush lying about 15 feet from a bomb crater. At first, he assumed Bush was sleeping, but to be sure he called for a medic. The bomb's concussion had killed Bush instantly. Tex Gunn of the *Fort Worth Star-Telegram* and John Terry of the *Chicago Daily News* were badly wounded by the same bomb, and both died a few days later.[20]

McDaniel sent word of Bush's death to AP in San Francisco. Then he wrote the obituary. Bush was buried in the Army cemetery near Tacloban. Correspondents from the United States, Great Britain, and Australia gathered around the casket and bowed their heads. McDaniel stood to the left of the chaplain. As the chaplain finished speaking, US antiaircraft guns erupted at Japanese planes.[21]

A couple of weeks later, a Japanese sniper killed Acme photographer Frank Prist. He was buried in the same cemetery as Bush. A despondent Yates wrote Natalie, "Our death toll now stands at four."[22]

Aboard the *Wasatch*, Spencer Davis of the AP was in the right place for what would be the largest naval battle since Jutland in 1916. Japan desperately needed to repulse the US invasion. If the Americans controlled the Philippines and its airfields, it would no longer be possible to ship oil from Java to Japan. In effect, the still-formidable Japanese fleet would be confined to harbors.

Because they lacked enough planes for air cover, the Japanese devised a daring plan to attack the American transports anchored off Leyte Island. If those transports could be destroyed, the Americans on shore would have their supplies cut off. Four Japanese task forces would be formed. To the north off Luzon, four Japanese carriers—many without planes or pilots—would serve as decoys, hoping to lure Adm. William Halsey's fast battleships and large carriers away from the landing beaches. VAdm. Takeo Kurita, who commanded the Japanese forces that helped destroy the Allied fleet off Java in 1942, led a huge Japanese task force, which included the two largest battleships ever built—the 72,000-ton *Yamato* and *Musashi*. Kurita would steam through the narrow San Bernardino Strait south of Luzon, swerve right past Samar, and attack the US transports. To the south, two smaller Japanese task forces headed by the elderly and slow battleships *Yamashiro* and *Fusō* would navigate Surigao Strait, turn north, and envelop the US transports.

Adm. Kinkaid's ships guarded the southern approach where Kurita's attack would take place. Halsey's Task Force 34 fell for the trap. After delivering a series of punishing attacks on the Japanese in San Bernardino Strait—sinking the *Musashi*—Halsey steamed north to attack the Japanese carriers. Halsey's planes destroyed three Japanese carriers, but he had left San Bernardino Strait wide open except for a handful of small escort carriers and destroyers. The six old American battleships of the 7th Fleet along with torpedoes fired by US destroyers and PT boats destroyed the *Fusō* and *Yamashiro* in Surigao Strait, but only a desperate struggle by the US destroyers and escort carriers persuaded the cautious Kurita to turn away.

RAdm. Jesse Oldendorf, who commanded the six old battleships, provided Davis with a detailed account of the destruction of the *Fusō* and *Yamashiro* in a ferocious battle during the early morning hours of October 25. As the Japanese steamed through the strait, the old battleships waited. "It was the sort of naval battle you dream about," Oldendorf told Davis. "We completely crossed their T," a reference to a classic naval strategy in which one combatant forms a line perpendicular to an attacking force. All their guns can then fire on the approaching enemy, which can use only its forward guns. Jellicoe employed the tactics against Scheer at Jutland in 1916, and only a swift retreat saved the German High Seas Fleet.[23]

The next day, Spencer Davis interviewed a machinist's mate aboard one of the escort carriers. Davis wrote that the US destroyers *Johnston* and *Hoel* and destroyer escort *Samuel B. Roberts* launched a suicidal but effective series of attacks against Kurita's fleet. The machinist mate, Joseph Russell of Miami, told Davis the three small US ships laid a protective smoke screen around the vulnerable escort carriers and fired torpedoes at the oncoming Japanese ships. "This was one of the greatest performances I have ever seen," Russell said. It helped cement in history the epic charge of the three ships, all of which sank. Davis did not identify the names of the three ships, nor was he allowed to explain why a handful of vulnerable destroyers and escort carriers had been left by Halsey to cover the entrance of the strait.[24]

MacArthur established his new headquarters in a two-story mansion in Tacloban. McDaniel and his staff worked and slept in a nearby cottage, which was usually jammed with correspondents. McDaniel shared a room with Murlin Spencer. As always, McDaniel was plagued by insomnia. The heat and heavy rains made sleeping uncomfortable, and the bed bugs were "ferocious." The one saving grace was that McDaniel had his own desk. On the desk's left side, he placed a photo of himself, Natalie, and their new dog, Angus. On the right side was a photo of Natalie and him. As he wrote stories or letters, the photos meant that Natalie was as "close as possible" to him.[25]

Japanese artillery would "rumble" throughout the day and rattle the cottage windows. Japanese planes were a constant menace. One Japanese air attack was so unexpected that bombs fell near the cottage even as the air raid sirens still screeched. Lindesay Parrott of the *New York Times* rolled from his bed to the cottage floor, where he was wounded by bomb fragments. On another night, as McDaniel chatted with a member of MacArthur's staff at his headquarters, Japanese planes attacked. McDaniel peeked into the dining room, where an unperturbed MacArthur watched a Bob Hope film. Earlier that morning, a Japanese bullet had ripped through a wall near MacArthur's bed. MacArthur ignored the attack and finished sleeping.[26] The reporters were relieved when thick clouds swirled over their camp at night because it meant Japanese planes would not fly.

The logistics and equipment were poor, angering McDaniel. He complained about having "a good deal of typewriter trouble," being forced to type a letter to Natalie on a "wretched little baby portable."[27] He was constantly arguing with MacArthur's press officer, Pick Diller. Filing facilities were haphazard, and getting a truck filled with reporters to the front seemed beyond the Army's grasp. He wrote Natalie that "no one is trying or succeeding in frightening me at all, not for an instant, for I have been throwing my weight around more than ever and Diller now knows that he can't wrap me up."[28]

He hoped one of the senior officers might fly back to Brisbane, which would allow him to hitch a ride and see Natalie for a couple of days. But he quickly dismissed the idea. He tried to "reconcile" his "longing" to see Natalie with his duty. The responsibility weighed on him. He envied United Press's Bill Dickinson, who told his office in America that after the war he had no interest in a job as a newspaper executive or foreign-service chief. Instead, Dickinson wanted to finish the war, go back to America, and be a sportswriter. By contrast, McDaniel wanted to become the Pacific editor based in "Cronin's stomping ground," a reference to Ray Cronin, who was the AP's war editor in the San Francisco bureau. Natalie warned Yates that he set his "ambitions and objectives too high to be accomplished."[29]

Natalie urged Yates to adopt a more collaborative approach with his staff. For the first time, McDaniel asked his reporters for suggestions on how to cover the invasion. At times he planted ideas to allow the reporters to believe they thought of the stories themselves. He was quick to praise their work. They responded by unloading their own personal and professional problems to such a degree that he felt like "papa and mama."[30]

Because the base did not have hard liquor, there was no chance to relax with a drink after filing. McDaniel thought some bourbon around the cottage would help, and asked Natalie to send rye, gin, and bourbon. "Three or four bottles would suffice as I don't want to have so much on hand that it would encourage noisy drinking bouts," he wrote. Natalie quickly shipped him a few bottles.[31]

The weather remained miserable. A 100-mile-per-hour typhoon struck Tacloban on November 9 and "nearly blew us off the island." The storm was so severe that Japanese planes were grounded, sparing the Americans from air attacks.[32] "Muck and rain," a frustrated Carl Mydans of *Life* jotted in his notebook. Construction of new airfields halted, and the streets of Tacloban were "knee-deep in mud." To drive the 12 miles from Tacloban to the airfields in Dulag took as long as four hours.[33]

McDaniel developed a cold and deep cough, which he blamed on his feet being soaked from walking through the mud. He had three pairs of shoes that he changed throughout the day, but his feet were sopped. He developed a fever and grew so sick that his colleagues asked MacArthur's own physician to examine Yates. The doctor told McDaniel he had bronchial pneumonia, and prescribed a sulfa treatment. A few days later, a physician insisted on an x-ray so he could rule out tuberculosis.

McDaniel insisted that a "spell of dry weather" would clear up the infection in short order. He continued working, writing Natalie that he "cannot lay off altogether," although every day at noon he managed to take a thirty-minute nap. But the Japanese did not permit rest. On Thanksgiving night, two Japanese planes roared above and dropped their bombs. The correspondents took cover in slit trenches filled with 4 inches of water and 2 inches of mud. For the rest of the night, there was one alert after another, forcing reporters to sleep in the filthy trenches.[34]

As McDaniel recovered from his infection, he worked on a major story. The Japanese were sending convoys of troops and supplies to the port of Ormoc, on the western side of Leyte. Using the thick clouds and heavy rain for cover, six Japanese transports, two freighters, and six destroyers landed forces in Ormoc on November 14 and then vanished out to sea. It was only one of eleven convoys the Japanese sent to Ormoc, which allowed them to land 34,000 soldiers to reinforce the 20,000 troops they had on Leyte. MacArthur had long planned to seize Ormoc and cut off Japan's supply lines. In early December, an Allied task force steamed around Leyte's southern tip and then north up Leyte's west coast. It consisted of twelve destroyers escorting transports carrying the US 77th Division.[35]

McDaniel knew about the attack "well in advance." He "organized to cover it as a much bigger show than many people expected it to be," particularly his competitors. In modern newspaper terms, he flooded the zone with as many reporters as he could round up. McDaniel sailed on the destroyer *Hughes*, which served as RAdm. Arthur Struble's flagship. Four other correspondents would be scattered on four ships. Schedler would land with the first wave, but McDaniel added a special touch by having Al Dopking "perched on a hill" on Leyte's west coast.[36]

On the morning of December 7, six US destroyers opened fire on the beaches. Through binoculars, Dopking saw Japanese soldiers on a nearby hill watching the Americans land. From the beaches, Schedler reported light opposition.[37] McDaniel wrote the main story from the *Hughes*, asserting the "bold penetration of the Philippine inland seas to West Leyte" caught Japanese strategists by surprise:[38]

> Coming on the third anniversary of Pearl Harbor, the Ormoc attack was a bloody and grim reminder to the Japanese that American arms have grown powerful and lethal since that day which plunged the United States into the war.

On Christmas Eve, MacArthur invited Clark Lee, now with International News Service, who had just arrived on Leyte, for a private off-the-record chat at his headquarters in Tacloban. MacArthur had just won his fifth star, but on this particular evening he wore only four stars on the collar of his khaki shirt. To Lee, he looked "younger and fitter." Lighting his corncob pipe, he relaxed in a rocking chair on the porch. "You and Frank Hewlett are the last survivors of the original reporters who were with me on Corregidor and are here with me now," MacArthur said as his pipe went out.

Speaking with utter frankness, MacArthur said, "We've come a long way since Melbourne, despite the Navy cabal that hates me and the New Deal cabal. Since the last I saw you," referring to the spring of 1942, "our total casualties to date have been exactly 28,000 killed and wounded. On Leyte alone, we've killed 100,000 Japs," an exaggerated figure of actual Japanese losses. "We've done it by using our brains and artillery, not flesh. I have left behind, bypassed, and isolated more Japs than the 14 divisions I now have at my command. I had to bypass them, because if I had tried to wipe them out, they'd have wiped me out." He criticized Allied commanders in Europe, scornfully describing the American landing at Anzio in Italy as "a classic military mistake," a failure that killed 7,000 Americans. As for D-day, he complained that Gen. Dwight Eisenhower should have relied on Allied strength in the air and sea to land forces on northern Germany's Baltic coast as opposed to the Normandy beaches in France. With its air force dwindling and its surface fleet down to a handful of ships, Germany would have difficulty repelling an invasion in the Baltic, or so MacArthur thought. In 1914, British first sea lord Jacky Fisher, who was as daring as MacArthur, wanted to mount an amphibious landing on the Baltic coast. Fisher even designed special landing craft to carry troops to the shore. But most British officers considered such an operation reckless, and in 1944 US commanders regarded an attack on the Baltic coast just as foolhardy.

"In war, you have to fight with brains as well as muscles," MacArthur told Lee. "In war, you lead from strength, just as you do in bridge, in football or baseball. Where is our strength in Europe? On the sea and in the air. Where is the enemy's strength? On the ground."[39]

That same evening, McDaniel and the correspondents gathered in the press headquarters in Tacloban for a small party. The reporters had an improvised Christmas tree, a tropical bush they found by the roadside. They decorated it with bathroom tissue, which they attached to the tree with paper clips filched from MacArthur's headquarters.[40]

A group of Filipino children gathered under the balcony at MacArthur's head-quarters and started to sing "Silent Night." The air raid warning sounded, and a lone Japanese plane flew overhead. It turned out to be a "nuisance raider," designed to frighten, not cause damage. Red tracers from US antiaircraft guns illuminated the dark night before the plane vanished over a hill.

The children resumed singing. It was raining, and one reporter saw "a continuous stream of rain drops" falling from "the soggy palms." From Tacloban's muddy streets, soldiers and members of the Women's Army Corps joined the children to sing "I'm Dreaming of a White Christmas." . . . For one brief moment, everyone was trans-ported from the war zone.[41]

# MANILA

n Christmas Day, McDaniel and a dozen other correspondents gathered in front of their Christmas palm tree in Tacloban. As Carl Mydans of *Life* snapped pictures, they burst into smiles and hoisted bottles of beer to celebrate the holiday. The fighting on Leyte, as Spencer Davis wrote, "appeared fast reaching a conclusion, as Japanese resistance steadily weakened." MacArthur's headquarters announced the Leyte campaign was virtually over, and Gen. Eichelberger wrote, "We are all saying that we want to be home by next Christmas."[1]

MacArthur's staff had already told reporters privately that the Americans would soon invade Luzon. The 40,000 square miles of Luzon, which included Manila, was the largest of the more than 7,000 islands that made up the Philippines.[2]

As in Leyte, McDaniel had a large team of reporters to cover the landings, including Davis, Al Dopking, Dean Schedler, Richard Bergholz, Jim Hutcheson, and Fred Hampson. Murlin Spencer, one of McDaniel's favorites, was also scheduled to take part, but he became ill. US physicians operated on him in a tent in Leyte and sent him back to the United States to recover.[3]

A press officer briefed the reporters on plans to cover the attack. "MacArthur will go to the Luzon assault on the USS *Boise*," the officer said, referring to a cruiser. "Six of you will go in with him. You'll draw lots out of a helmet." McDaniel plucked one of the lucky six. It was exactly what he wanted.

On January 4, McDaniel, Mydans, and four other correspondents boarded the *Boise*, anchored in Leyte Gulf. The 10,000-ton *Boise* offered comforts that were unimaginable for correspondents who had lived at Tacloban. Laundry service was free and available twenty-four hours a day. A soda fountain offered ice cream, Coca-Cola, and malted milk.

At four in the afternoon, MacArthur boarded the cruiser, crisply saluted the captain, and was escorted to his quarters. A half hour later, a screen of destroyers led the *Boise* out of the gulf. That night, McDaniel and Mydans joined the correspondents and six officers for dinner of pork chops, boiled potatoes, ice cream, and cake.[4]

Minesweepers cleared a path through Surigao Strait, the narrow channel that led to the Sulu Sea, which washed up on Luzon's west coast. The destination was Lingayen Gulf on Luzon's northwestern tip. To Yates, MacArthur's voyage was the "last stretch of his long road back to Luzon and to the rendezvous with the destiny in Manila that he had set for himself nearly three years before."[5]

Back then—the end of 1941—Gen. Masaharu Homma landed thousands of well-trained Japanese troops in Lingayen Gulf, on Luzon's west coast, as well as an amphibious assault on Luzon's east coast. The pincers forced MacArthur to withdraw his ill-equipped Filipino-American army into the Bataan Peninsula.

Now, as Yates wrote, MacArthur was returning to "Luzon on a powerful warship," surrounded by more than 800 ships carrying 174,000 American soldiers. It was an enormous fleet even by World War II standards. Aboard Adm. Barbey's flagship *Blue Ridge*, Dopking estimated the convoy extended for 80 miles. To Davis, who reported from Adm. Kinkaid's flagship *Wasatch*, "there seemed no end to the parade of transports, freighters, landing ship docks, and amphibious craft."[6]

As the *Boise* crept into the Sulu Sea, a voice on the loudspeaker ordered sailors to battle stations. MacArthur stood at a gun deck rail, gazed to starboard, and puffed on his ever-present corncob pipe. He clearly was looking at something.[7] Covering his eyes against the "blinding tropic glare," McDaniel glanced at the sky. It was empty. Then he looked down and saw a Japanese torpedo—which had been fired by a submarine—heading directly for the cruiser. The *Boise* turned sharply to port, and the torpedo raced in front of the bow without exploding. MacArthur, Yates saw, did not "move a muscle or miss a pull on his corncob."[8]

Moments later, guns from a dozen US ships opened fire on what McDaniel called "two tiny flecks overhead." One Japanese plane shattered into pieces and plummeted into the sea less than a mile away. The second caught fire and smashed into the deck of the escort carrier *Ommaney Bay*. Destroyers scurried about the small carrier. Bright orange flames behind the carrier's island superstructure sent a towering column of thick gray smoke into the sky. MacArthur's pipe went out, but rather than lighting it, he kept his eyes on the mortally wounded ship. The convoy continued, steering so close to the shore that Bataan, Corregidor, and Manila were visible.[9]

On the evening of January 7, McDaniel and Larry Lehrbas of MacArthur's staff heard that *Time* correspondent Bill Chickering, a good friend of Mydans's, had been killed when a kamikaze smashed into the bridge of the old battleship *New Mexico* off Lingayen Gulf. McDaniel hunted about the *Boise* to tell Mydans but did not find him because he was holed up in the photo lab. The next morning, Lehrbas saw Mydans.

"I've got bad news for you: Bill Chickering has been killed in Lingayen on the *New Mexico*," Lehrbas told him. "I suppose they hit the bridge because the captain was killed and an Australian general was killed. Gen. MacArthur has sent a cable to Henry Luce."

MacArthur asked Mydans to join him on the ship's quarterdeck. For forty minutes, they paced. MacArthur told him that Chickering was "one of the finest correspondents I have known. And I've known Bill a long time." Then MacArthur steered the conversation toward his own disdain for *Time*. MacArthur said Chickering had been upset about "the way *Time* and *Life* used his stories. He told me about it several times."

MacArthur continued to pace. "I don't know what has happened to *Time* and *Life* in the last few years," the general said. "They have fallen into such disrepute that no one around here reads them anymore."[10]

The correspondents showered, shaved, and fell asleep just before midnight on January 8. The next morning at five, loudspeakers ordered crew and correspondents to breakfast. After they finished eating, they climbed up to the deck, where it was still so dark the nearest ships were mere shadows.[11] Just before dawn, the Allied warships opened fire. To Bill Dunn of CBS, the powerful guns of the older battleships erupted in a "deafening cacophony."[12]

At nine in the morning, as the guns of the American fleet continued to fire, soldiers scrambled into small landing crafts and steered toward shore. The barrage ceased, and the first four waves of American forces landed, encountering little opposition. Two hours later, Yates accompanied MacArthur to the beach. MacArthur relaxed on top of the landing craft's engine box. When the craft approached the shore, Mydans jumped on a pier constructed by American engineers. As he turned to photograph MacArthur, the landing craft's engines roared. The barge went into reverse for a few moments and then stopped. The ramp lowered, and MacArthur and his staff waded through the surf, just as they had done in Leyte. Mydans clicked away. Although word spread that MacArthur posed for the shot by exiting the landing craft several times, Mydans insisted the general walked from the craft only once.[13]

MacArthur climbed into a waiting jeep, which promptly broke down. Yates watched MacArthur walk to the command post, stopping to chat with privates and officers.

McDaniel wrote that there was "little evidence that the Japs ever intended to offer any" resistance. McDaniel could not find any Japanese pillboxes, underground dugouts, or land mines. Not a single American soldier died on McDaniel's beach. Except for eleven Japanese snipers killed by the Americans, the only people to meet the Americans on the beach were Filipino civilians. A young man told McDaniel, "Last night the Japanese heard the Americans are coming. This morning, they all ran away."[14]

After the Luzon landings, the AP transferred Dopking to cover the invasion of Iwo Jima. Leif Erickson, who had covered the Leyte landings, was sent to Hawaii to replace Charles McMurtry as the AP Honolulu bureau chief. Many news executives in the United States were convinced "the worst of the Philippines' fighting was ending."

In fact, McDaniel and his staff would have to cover a series of major stories breaking simultaneously. US divisions were racing south from Lingayen Gulf to Manila. In addition, US commanders hoped to free nearly 6,000 prisoners at three camps near Manila. They included not only American, British, Australian, and Dutch soldiers, but also sixty-nine American army nurses and scores of Allied civilians. One of the internees was Virginia Hewlett, the wife of United Press's Frank Hewlett, who was covering the Luzon invasion. Along with the others, Virginia had been in the prison since the fall of Bataan and Corregidor in 1942. MacArthur was obsessed with rescuing the prisoners, fearing that if he failed, the Japanese might execute them.

McDaniel deployed reporters to cover the rescue efforts at each camp. He and Richard Bergholz stayed near MacArthur's headquarters. He filed a main bar virtually every day, while the other correspondents wrote stories from the camps that could stand alone or be folded into McDaniel's stories. Fred Hampson was assigned to enter Manila with the first American troops. Jim Hutcheson would detail the invasion of Corregidor. Dean Schedler would report the efforts to rescue nearly 4,000 civilians held at Santo Tomas University outside Manila, and Russell Brines would report only ten blocks away at Bilibid prison, with its 1,300 prisoners. Brines had been captured by the Japanese in Manila in 1941 and sent to Santo Tomas, where he put his newspaper talents to work editing the *Camp Affairs*, a twice-weekly paper for the internees. In 1943, Brines was repatriated to the United States. He quickly signed up to return to the Pacific.[15]

The most hazardous assignment went to Clark Lee of International News Service, who, like Schedler, escaped from the Philippines before its surrender to the Japanese. On the evening of January 31, Lee and Mydans accompanied 121 US Army Rangers and 286 Filipino guerrillas on a 30-mile march behind enemy lines. They surprised the Japanese garrison guarding the Allied prisoners at Cabanatuan, a camp 70 miles north of Manila. They freed them all—486 Americans, twenty-three Britons from Singapore, three Dutchmen, and one Norwegian.[16]

Unlike Lee, McDaniel did not have a firsthand view of the rescue. But by piecing together interviews with eyewitnesses, McDaniel wrote that the prisoners "were snatched from under the flaming muzzles of Japanese guns" in an "exploit of un-matched daring." About 100 were so weak from disease and malnutrition that they could not walk and instead were taken back to Allied lines by carts or, in some cases, on the backs of the Rangers. Lee said some prisoners insisted on marching without help. Many looked old, with gray hair and "dazed sunken eyes."[17]

As the prisoners reached safety, an astonished Schedler found Capt. James Prippe of Los Angeles, whom he last saw in 1942 on Corregidor before Schedler's own escape to Australia. Bill Dunn met up with Earle Baumgartner, who had been in charge of sending his broadcasts from Manila before the war.

"Bill, if you don't think you are standing in the middle of the 500 happiest men in the world, you're crazy," Baumgartner joked.[18]

McDaniel interviewed Virgil Greenway, a twenty-six-year-old private from Tennessee who was wearing only a pair of white shorts and a bathrobe. When he first heard the shots fired by the Rangers, Greenway assumed they were Japanese and thought, "Well, they are going to wipe us out this time." But he quickly realized they were Americans. The Rangers ordered the prisoners to leave the camp, and Greenway was in such a hurry he didn't put on his shoes. He and the others marched 21 miles to the American lines. A Filipino woman gave the shivering Greenway a new bathrobe. By the time he reached safety, his feet were swollen and bloody.

He told McDaniel that he had been captured on Corregidor in 1942 and survived largely on rice, sweet potato wine, and greens. His normal weight of 140 had plummeted to 120 pounds, and like many prisoners he suffered from dysentery. He could not bring himself to talk about life in the camp, telling McDaniel, "Nobody would believe it if I could."[19]

The next camp to be liberated was Santo Tomas, on the north side of the Pasig River, which ran through the heart of Manila. The camp held sixty-nine Army nurses and 2,780 American, British, Australian, Canadian, and Dutch civilians. On February 3, one of the P-38 fighters flying over the camp dropped a small case. The internees opened it and read an enclosed note: "Roll out the barrel. There'll be a hot time in the old town tonight." The internees assumed the cryptic message meant the Americans were near. They were right. An American mechanized column of tanks, jeeps, and trucks was only a few miles away. It included a jeep with four reporters—Mydans, Hewlett, Dunn, and Schedler, who drove. By what Dunn described as "sheer chance," the reporters arrived at a main gate shortly before eight that night—the same time US Army tanks surrounded the camp.[20]

"Open up!" the commander of a tank shouted. Nobody answered. "Open the goddam thing or I'm coming through!" the commander snapped. Once again, no reply. The tank then plunged through the front gate. Its headlights illuminated the interior of the university.

Mydans and an Army officer peered through the opening in the wall. "Hello anyone. This is Carl Mydans. Are there any Americans there?" There was no answer, and for a moment the reporters feared the internees were dead. Then lights inside the camp flashed on, and they heard shrieks of joy. Hewlett and Mydans entered the lobby of the main building, where nurses kissed them and men hoisted them on their shoulders. A little girl directed Hewlett to the hospital. There he found his wife, Virginia, down to 80 pounds, but alive.[21]

In the education building, a Japanese colonel and a handful of his men barricaded themselves in a room on the top floor. They offered to surrender if granted safe passage. They held 213 internees, and the Americans feared they would use them as hostages. From MacArthur's headquarters, Yates reported the Japanese held out for thirty-four hours before the Americans allowed them to leave. US soldiers escorted them for about a mile and let them go.

In his story, Schedler quoted the tank commander swearing, a difficult decision because many American papers did not permit use of the word "goddam." Some papers deleted the word. But the *Decatur Review* kept it in the story.[22]

On the Sunday when American troops tried to persuade the last Japanese at Santo Tomas to surrender, US soldiers reached what Brines described as "musty, filthy, old" Bilibid prison in north Manila. The Japanese garrison had fled the day before, leaving 810 prisoners of war and 465 civilians unguarded.[23] One of those prisoners was US Army captain Theodore Winship. As he cooked a small amount of corn, he suddenly saw an American soldier.

"Hello, who are you?" the astonished Winship asked.

"I'm an American soldier of the 37th Division. We've come to free you."

"Where in the hell have you been? We've been waiting three years for you."[24]

H. D. Quigg of United Press made his way down a prison corridor. It was dark, but he sensed someone was near. He held out his hand: "I'm Quigg, United Press."

A man grasped his hand and replied, "Weissblatt, United Press." Franz Weissblatt had been captured by the Japanese in January 1942. Within days of being freed, he was put to work and assigned to the pool along with Carl Mydans to cover MacArthur.[25]

The dramatic rescues electrified readers in the United States, Great Britain, and Australia. Richard Bergholz crafted a chronology of the prisoners' ordeal at Santo Tomas, beginning with their capture in early 1942. They had not seen white bread since April 1942, and by early 1944 each internee was down to a paltry daily ration of 400 grams of cereal, which was cut even further by the end of the year. The Japanese jailed the camp physician, Dr. Todd Stevenson, a missionary from New York. When internees died, Stevenson refused Japanese demands to cite on the death certificates that the cause of death was heart failure. Instead, he insisted they died from starvation or malnutrition.[26]

The most-memorable photographs sent back to the United States were of the sixty-nine American nurses. They had slept on cots jammed together in classrooms. They had little to eat. Keeping clean was a challenge. They could not wash their hair in the showers because hair clogged the narrow drains. So, the women improvised. Enlisting the help of the men, the women scrounged up an old bathtub and placed a shower hose above it. There, out in the open and often wearing just bathrobes, three women at a time could wash their hair.[27]

Only one prison camp remained in the hands of the Japanese—Los Banos off Laguna Lake and south of Manila. The camp held 2,146 Allied prisoners, including Doris Rubens, the United Press reporter who stayed in Hankow in 1938 after McDaniel and the other correspondents left. There also was a prisoner at Los Banos whom McDaniel knew very well—Bill Donald, the Australian who had been a senior adviser to Chiang Kai-shek before the war. For three years, Donald had cleverly disguised his real identity from the Japanese.

After the prisoners at Santo Tomas had been liberated, AP editors peppered McDaniel with requests about whether Donald was among those now free. McDaniel, who knew from Army intelligence that Donald had been transferred to Los Banos, ignored the orders from New York. A radio report by McDaniel to New York would have "tipped off" the Japanese that they had Donald in their custody. Three weeks later, when Los Banos was liberated, McDaniel told the whole story of how Donald had fooled his Japanese interrogators.[28]

Before the war, Manila was "one of the most modern and beautiful cities of the Orient," known for "picturesque Spanish architecture and ancient walls."[29] Ray Cronin of AP once described it as a "strange mixture of modern and ancient," with down-town districts offering "air-conditioned buildings, fine apartment houses, hotels and clubs and residences" that compared with the best in America.[30] Doris Rubens thought it was a city of "graceful beauty." More than 800,000 people lived inside its 14 square miles. Manila Bay was one of Asia's largest ports, with exports that included hemp, rice, and tobacco.[31]

Back in December 1941, MacArthur chose to leave Manila undefended to save the city from destruction. He now assumed the Japanese would do the same. Gen. Eichelberger thought it "was generally accepted that the Japanese would declare Manila an open city or would evacuate."[32] Gen. Tomoyuki Yamashita had no desire to waste his forces in an urban setting and ordered Japanese army troops out of the city. Most obeyed, but RAdm. Sanji Iwabuchi refused. Instead, he instructed his 15,000 Japanese marines and 6,000 Army soldiers to set up strong defenses in Manila.

Two columns of US armor pushed southward from northern Luzon. Hundreds of Filipinos lined the roads leading into Manila, cheering MacArthur as he rode in a jeep. They handed hibiscus blossoms to US soldiers, many of whom wrapped them around their helmets. Church bells rang as MacArthur reached the outskirts of Manila.

"I believe we'll make it tomorrow," he confidently predicted.[33]

McDaniel could not detect any signs that the Japanese planned to defend the city. When Fred Hampson flew above Manila in a military plane, not a single Japanese gun fired at his aircraft.[34] Eichelberger dismissed reports by Filipino guerrillas that the Japanese would burn the city, saying he could "look right down into the town and see lights and one little fire."[35] Most of Manila "appears intact," the AP's San Francisco bureau reported, citing dispatches from Mutual Broadcasting and CBS.[36] But others were not as sanguine. NBC correspondent George Folster in Manila reported some Filipinos feared the Japanese would vigorously defend the city. He reported the Japanese had mined buildings and set up tank traps.[37]

MacArthur's staff advised the correspondents that the fall of Manila was imminent. Armed with the tip, McDaniel filed an advance on the morning of February 3. It was customary for reporters on deadline to file stories in advance, provided editors understood they could not be published until the reporter gave permission. The top of the story included the warning "Advance to be held for use when the fall of Manila is announced":

> The American flag flies once more over Manila, replacing the Japanese Sun banner raised over the city on January 2, 1942, and ending a marathon campaign unequalled in military history."[38]

McDaniel filed additional paragraphs throughout the day under the dateline "MacArthur's Headquarters," and with the understanding that the stories would not run until Manila had fallen. He provided a history of America's occupation of the Philippines, the construction of a modern city in Manila, and the promise by the United States to free the Philippines by 1946.

By the evening of February 5, MacArthur's headquarters had not announced Manila's capture. Instead, the Americans held only most of the sections of Manila north of the Pasig River, which bisected the city. McDaniel reworked his advance, writing that the "Stars and Stripes flew over half of Manila today, and thousands of American and British civilian prisoners were free as Yank columns . . . pressed against little more than sniper fire toward complete liberation of the Philippine capital." The story accurately noted that only the northern half of Manila had been occupied by the Americans. Now correspondents waited for word from MacArthur's headquarters that all of Manila had been conquered.[39]

That evening, reporters climbed up a tower at Santo Tomas University, on the north side of the Pasig. From there, they had a clear view of the Escolta Street district on the north side of the river. Before the war, the area had been home to the National City Bank of New York, Heacock's department store, and what McDaniel described as "many other imposing buildings." They could see the Jones, Quezon, Santa Cruz, and Ayala bridges, which linked the north shore to the south side. On the south side, the old Spanish enclave of Intramuros was visible to the reporters. Intramuros had cobbled streets and was surrounded by stone block walls reaching 25 feet high and 10 feet wide. Established by the Spanish in the sixteenth century, the walled city was home to tens of thousands of Filipinos and Chinese. Just beyond Intramuros were the docks that opened onto Manila Bay.

At sunset came the first dramatic signs that the Japanese would not retreat quietly. Japanese troops lit fires and set off explosive charges throughout Escolta Street. To McDaniel, it looked like a "flaming inferno" swept through the district. Strong winds blowing off Manila Bay "fanned" the fires. The Manila fire department was helpless because the Japanese had destroyed the water-pumping stations.[40] As civilians tried to flee toward American lines, Japanese machine guns fired on them.[41] Eichelberger now realized how wrong it was to ignore the guerrillas' warnings. "Smoke and flames were going way up in the air," he wrote.[42]

Fires continued to rage the next morning. The university area, although safe from the conflagration, shook from "explosions in the business district and by the thunder of American guns pounding the Japanese positions."[43] The large crystal arcade at Heacock's had been reduced to a "gigantic tangle of crooked, charred steel."[44]

Shortly after six in the morning on February 6, MacArthur's staff issued a communique announcing that "the fall of Manila marks the end of one great phase of the Pacific struggle and sets the stage for another. With Australia safe, the Philippines liberated, and the ultimate redemption of the East Indies and Malaya thereby made a certainty, our motto becomes 'On to Tokyo!'"[45]

McDaniel was "startled" when he read the communique. It simply was not true. Manila was in flames, and large sections were controlled by the Japanese. His first thought was MacArthur was making a "bid for continuing command in the campaign against Japan proper and a move to quiet rumors that the Philippines would be the end of the road for MacArthur." It was an opinion shared by Gen. Eichelberger. Others saw it as an example of MacArthur's obsession with publicity. Just two days before, MacArthur attempted to enter Manila accompanied by Gen. Robert Beightler, commander of the US 37th Division. Beightler thought MacArthur was "insane" for trying to reach the city in the middle of a fight. "Why we all didn't get killed I don't know," Beightler wrote in his diary, grumbling that MacArthur was "publicity crazy."[46]

Some newspapers relied on the release of the communique to publish McDaniel's advance story written on February 3, declaring Manila had been liberated. Leonard Milliman, the AP war editor in New York, wrote that "rifle and artillery fire are heard in the streets, but the Philippines' capital is free today after three years and a month of Japanese subjugation."[47] But near the battle, McDaniel and the other correspondents knew that American soldiers were engaged in "probably the most intensely bitter battle" of the Pacific theater. It was not some ordinary "mopping up" operation.[48]

McDaniel wrote a story describing the ongoing brutal fight. MacArthur's censors refused to send the dispatch, writing in blue pencil: "Publication prohibited." Word circulated that MacArthur's officers were planning a parade through the city, on the basis of a detailed plan drafted by MacArthur's staff. The plan called for MacArthur and President Osmena to travel by jeeps through Rizal Avenue, Taft Avenue, and Dewey Boulevard to the imposing building where the legislature met before the war. Troops would gather in front of the speaker's table before MacArthur's arrival. MacArthur and Osmena would speak, and a US Army band would play "The Star-Spangled Banner" and the Philippine national anthem. The ceremony would conclude with the raising of the Philippine flag. Diller selected areas offering the best views for reporters and photographers.[49]

McDaniel called for other correspondents to form a "united move to break through the censorship roadblock." He told them he would not include MacArthur's communique in any story "until and unless factual reporting of the grim happenings in Manila were permitted." McDaniel demanded that the Army send a message to the AP explaining the censorship.[50] An American officer refused, saying he needed MacArthur's personal approval. Other reporters were just as angry. During a news briefing conducted by Diller, Bill Dunn of CBS erupted, "There is no possibility physically of a parade."[51]

McDaniel and two other reporters grabbed a ride from Santo Tomas to MacArthur's headquarters, a sugar plantation 50 miles from Manila. They found MacArthur napping on a shaded veranda. Yates hesitated. When gravel "rattled" under Yates's shoes, MacArthur awoke. Yates retreated. Neither Yates nor MacArthur said a word to the other.

Half an hour later, MacArthur walked into a room where Yates and the two other correspondents waited. "Who said there is no fighting in Manila?" MacArthur demanded. The Japanese, MacArthur said, are "defeated. His position is hopeless, but he is putting up a magnificent fight. Report that."[52]

MacArthur's staff arrived from the front lines and sat down for dinner at the bungalow. To their astonishment, MacArthur invited Yates to join them. MacArthur then asked each officer to describe the latest developments in Manila. He listened as they talked about the "savage" fighting and the Japanese setting huge fires inside the city.

MacArthur stood and looked at each officer. "Who said there is no fighting?" he asked once again. Without waiting for an answer, the general told Yates, "Go back and tell your correspondents to see everything they can in Manila and write what they see as they see it."[53]

McDaniel returned to Manila. He wrote that "trapped Japanese soldiers put the torch to the Escolta district." Francis McCarthy of United Press reported that "whole areas of the city were engulfed in a roaring sea of fire." Thundering explosions erupted when fire reached munition dumps and gasoline supply centers. Gen. Beightler noted that the "skies burn red every night" as the Japanese "systematically sack the city."[54]

By Thursday, McDaniel reported that US troops had swept the Japanese from Escolta Street and the business district. But across the river, the Japanese were torching the center of the city, including the Manila Hotel, where MacArthur had lived before the war. The Japanese destroyed the four bridges crossing the river into Manila's southern sections.[55] The next day, Yates reported that amphibious vehicles ferried the US 37th Division across the river. On the basis of reports from Hampson inside the city and what he could see himself from Santo Tomas, McDaniel wrote:

> Filipino and Chinese residents of the explosion-shattered and fire-blackened city were reported dying from starvation at the rate of several hundred a day. The looters included the retreating garrison of destroy-and-die Japanese, who already had burned and blasted the business heart of the city into ruins. Artillery and mortar shells from enemy guns south of the Pasig River and the thundering crash of American artillery added to the city's horror.[56]

On Saturday the tenth, McDaniel reported that US soldiers attempted to navigate their way by jeep and truck through mined streets as Japanese soldiers fired away from pillboxes or the top floors of office buildings. The advance was slow, only 2,000 yards one day since "the trapped Japanese defenders would contest every yard of ground." Hampson saw one ambulance after another race through the center of Manila "with dismal regularity." Not far from the destroyed Santa Cruz Bridge, a Japanese shell exploded among a crowd of Filipino citizens. Hampson saw a Filipino woman in the debris, her dead baby burning at her feet. An elderly Filipino man carried his wife toward the badly damaged Jones Bridge and asked an American MP whether there was a doctor near. The MP realized the woman was dead.

"A burial detail is coming," the MP said to another American. "Let them tell him. I haven't got the heart."[57]

McDaniel wrote that the Japanese drilled holes through the stone walls of a churchyard and blazed away at the Americans with 20 mm guns. It took US mortars and flamethrowers to finally clear the churchyard of defenders. There were so many mines in the streets that one American officer was quoted as saying, "They were more densely planted than German minefields" he had seen in North Africa and Italy.[58] McDaniel angrily wrote that the Japanese

> never had any hope of escaping from the self-laid trap. Theirs is not a last-minute fight of desperation, but apparently a carefully calculated plan to set the price of the capture of Manila as high in lives and property as their destructive ingenuity can raise it.[59]

The Japanese had been forced back to Taft Avenue, which ran east and west about a mile from the docks. Before the war, Taft Avenue was the "home district of many leading Americans." Now it was the scene of brutal fighting.[60] McDaniel wrote that "fires blackened the skies" as Japanese demolition charges went off. Flames erupted from the port of Manila. Reports coming in from reporters close to the scene "increasingly predicted a story of horrors as enraged" Japanese soldiers "turned ruthlessly against unarmed Filipinos." McDaniel quoted NBC's George Folster as saying Japanese troops were murdering Filipinos of all ages, hacking some to death with bayonets or sabers or burning them alive in their homes. CBS correspondent John Adams declared that the Japanese atrocities in Manila "undoubtedly will go down in history as a darker chapter than the rape of Nanking." Hampson reported that Americans were engaged in a "dirty house-to-house fight," with US tanks firing into historic buildings and homes held by the Japanese. The stench from the dead in the street was so powerful that Filipinos used clothes to cover their noses.[61]

McDaniel had seen the same type of savagery eight years earlier when the Japanese sacked Nanking. After the war, Yamashita would be executed for what MacArthur concluded was his failure to control his troops, though there was never firm evidence that Yamashita wanted to destroy Manila. Instead, the 20,000 Japanese marines and soldiers defied his orders to leave, torched buildings, and killed civilians. The US heavy artillery fire turned architectural landmarks into rubble.

The AP correspondents filed one report after another, which McDaniel then folded into daily main bars. One Chinese merchant told Brines that Japanese soldiers machine-gunned Chinese civilians as they tried to escape from a burning building. Two American sergeants told Hampson they photographed more than twenty Chinese civilians—including six babies—who had been bayoneted and piled into a heap.[62]

Slowly, inexorably, the remaining Japanese were pushed inside the walled city of Intramuros. The Americans pleaded with the Japanese commanders to surrender and allow the 7,000 civilians inside the walled city to go free. In a radio message to the Japanese, Gen. Beightler appealed: "I exhort you that, true to the spirit of the Bushido and the Code of the Samurai, you permit all civilians to evacuate the [walled city] by the Victoria Gate." The Japanese did not reply. The Americans wheeled howitzers across new pontoon bridges spanning the Pasig. They opened fire at "a steady rate of a round per minute." The walls did not crumble. McDaniel knew the Americans could call on planes to "pulverize everything and everybody" inside the walled city. But MacArthur ruled out air attacks because he feared they would inflict even worse damage. US commanders were desperately trying to conserve American lives, save civilians from air attacks, and destroy the Japanese. It was an utter impossibility.[63]

US soldiers reached the Manila Hotel. Hampson scribbled down their reports as they searched for the Japanese defenders. At 10:15 in the morning, they entered. They found many of the hotel's hallways barricaded, and heard the cracking sound of Japanese rifles firing. The Americans reported at 11:00 that the Japanese set off mines in the lobby. By noon, the US soldiers said the hotel was secure. All the defenders had been killed.[64]

On the morning of February 23, US heavy guns erupted for ninety minutes in a siege of the walled city. The noise was so deafening that years later, Bill Dunn and other correspondents reported they suffered hearing loss. The shelling stopped at 8:30 in the morning, and US soldiers raced through a breach in one of the walls.[65] McDaniel gathered reports from correspondents and filed a grim story:

> At least 1,500 Japanese troops, mainly marines and naval corpsmen, are hopelessly penned up in the old Spanish citadel determined to fight and die. The Yanks who burst through the Intramuros eastern wall found another bloody scene of Japanese atrocities against civilians. George Thomas Folster of NBC termed the Intramuros a "wrecked place of murder" replete with "more mass murder of civilians." He said he saw dead civilians on all sides. He reported finding a large pile of dead Filipinos, their heads shaved and their hands tied behind their backs. The Japanese had tried to burn the pile of bodies, he said, but the fire failed to consume them.[66]

On February 25, McDaniel wrote that Manila was "completely liberated." The city, McDaniel wrote, was "strewn with the bodies of more than 12,000 Japanese." His story was one of despair, not of jubilation:

> The death grasp of the enemy's fanatical garrison was emitted within the centuries-old walls of the Intramuros where 3,000 frightened and tortured civilians were rescued. . . . Final victory crowned a battle so bitter that at times Americans were fighting on one floor of a building against Japanese above them or in the basement. Its last stages were marred by the Japanese practice of murder and raping against unarmed civilians.[67]

Like Nanking in 1937, Stalingrad in 1943, and Warsaw in 1944, Manila was virtually destroyed. There was no electricity. Water and sewage systems could not function. As many as 100,000 civilians were dead. Roughly 1,000 American soldiers died, while more than 16,000 Japanese sailors and marines were killed. Only a handful of Japanese soldiers surrendered. RAdm. Sanji Iwabuchi, who defied orders to leave Manila, killed himself with a hand grenade. "I have never seen a place so battered up," Lt. Col. Nathan Deutsch wrote in a letter. "The Japs really made a mess of it, and we didn't do it any good when we took it away from them."[68] "So much for Manila," Beightler wrote. "It is a ruined city—unhealthy, depressing, poverty stricken."[69] Just released from Los Banos, a horrified Doris Rubens thought the destruction staggered "the imagination; it was like a phantasmagoria conjured up by some surrealist or Dadaist artist—huge buildings tottering drunkenly, pillars of stone suspended crazily in midair, mountains of crumbling stone."[70]

There was no doubt that American heavy guns killed thousands of civilians. But the Japanese killings had been premeditated. Hampson reported that captured Japanese documents revealed military orders to kill with chilling efficiency. He quoted from one document dated February 8:

> When Filipinos are to be killed, they must be gathered into one place and be disposed of with the consideration that ammunition and manpower must not be used to excess. Because the disposal of dead bodies is a troublesome task, they should be gathered into houses which are scheduled to be burned or demolished. They should also be thrown into the river.[71]

McDaniel was both exhausted from the ceaseless work and sickened by the carnage. For five consecutive months since landing at Leyte, there had been "no relief from the sounds and rigors of warfare and for the most part without spending a single night in a normal bed," Bill Dunn would later write. The reporters were older than the soldiers and not in the same peak physical condition. The "strain," Dunn wrote, "was beginning to show."[72]

As the fighting ebbed, the AP was moving some of its reporters out of the Philippines. In late February, Spencer Davis boarded a B-25 bomber on Luzon and flew to Tacloban. It was the beginning of an 8,300-mile trip to San Francisco, passing over the "islands which Americans have fought and bled over these past 39 or 40 months." Someday those memories would fade. But "right now," Davis wrote, "it is impossible to forget. The scars are too fresh."[73]

Hampson and Bergholz assumed more of the writing duties as McDaniel prepared to return to the United States and a home he barely knew. He and Natalie would be stationed in San Francisco, where he would serve as AP's Pacific foreign editor.

But he had one more major assignment—the official transfer of civilian authority from MacArthur to the Philippine government headed by President Sergio Osmena. The ceremony, broadcast by radio to the United States and Australia, took place in the Reception Hall of Malacañang Palace, which had served before the war as the residence for the Spanish and American governors of the Philippines and later housed the pro-Japanese government. The Army instructed McDaniel and the other correspondents to wear suntan-colored uniforms with casual garrison caps. "Wear no side arms," an officer told the reporters.[74]

Scars from the brutal Manila campaign were evident in the palace. The room was devoid of furniture, forcing everyone to stand. Sunlight filtered through windows cracked by artillery explosions. Gunfire could be heard in the distance.

MacArthur stood at the center of the hall, with generals and surviving soldiers of Bataan and Corregidor behind him. Filipino officials gathered on one side of the hall and cheered throughout the ceremony. They knew this was the first step toward America's pledge of complete independence, a promise kept the following year.

MacArthur spoke first. His speech was brief, particularly for a historic moment that was the culmination of the general's vow in 1942 to return to the Philippines. Coincidentally, it marked the end of a chapter of Yates's life covering the most devastating war in history. At times, MacArthur's voice broke from emotion. The destruction of Manila hit him particularly hard. He held his speech in his right hand, which Yates noticed trembled. MacArthur's eyes appeared "misty":[75]

> My country has kept the faith. These soldiers have come here as an army of free men dedicated, with your people, to the cause of human liberty and committed to the task of destroying those evil forces that have sought to suppress it by brutality of the sword. An army of free men has brought your people once again under democracy's banner, to rededicate their churches, long desecrated, to the glory of God and public worship; to reopen their schools to liberal education; to till the soil and reap its harvest without fear of confiscation; to re-establish their industries that they may again enjoy the profit from the sweat of their own toil; and to restore the sanctity and happiness of their homes unafraid of violent intrusion. Your country thus is again at liberty to pursue its destiny to an honored position in the family of free nations. Your capital city, cruelly punished though it be, has regained its rightful place—Citadel of Democracy in the East.

Osmena then spoke, far longer than the general. "The present victory of American arms is not a victory for power, control, or domination, but a victory for freedom, democracy, and independence," an emotional Osmena said. "To Gen. MacArthur, this campaign has been a crusade. Friend and defender of our race, he never lost faith in the spiritual strength of our people."

When Osmena finished, a band broke into "The Star-Spangled Banner."[76]

Yates left by a side door to watch MacArthur exit the palace. Flanked by a Filipino honor guard, MacArthur's car slowly rolled down the driveway where Yates was standing. MacArthur leaned forward in the back seat and waved. Yates responded with "something that was a cross between a wave and salute." MacArthur ordered his car to stop, and an aide motioned Yates over. MacArthur opened the car door and vigorously shook Yates's hand.

"We did it," MacArthur said emotionally. "I told you we would do it."[77]

# SAN FRANCISCO AND DETROIT

cDaniel reached California in May 1945 aboard an Air Force plane, landing at Hamilton Field near San Francisco. Natalie joined him a month later, sailing from Australia on the steamer *Kanangoora*, which docked in Portland on June 8. They leased an apartment in the Keystone Apartments on Hyde Street, not far from the AP bureau in the offices of the *San Francisco Chronicle* on Mission Street. Before the war, the San Francisco bureau had been little more than a "modest . . . relay point." Now, it was "the clearing center for a rising flood of news" generated by the war.[1]

For McDaniel, San Francisco was a major adjustment. While the bureau chief's job was a promotion, now he would focus on management, not the part of the job he loved so much. McDaniel directed more than forty reporters and editors, many of them transferred from Washington, New York, and Europe. Though he would still write analyses, his days on the front were over. The reporter who thrived on being close to the fighting and producing vivid descriptions of the brutal reality of war was now at a desk.[2]

Adolf Hitler was dead, Berlin was in the hands of the Soviets, and Germany had surrendered. But the Pacific War raged on, and McDaniel did not see a rapid end:

> We just read a few days ago of the ferocity of the fighting in Berlin. We have no reason to doubt it. But at the end of 12 days' battle, there were still 70,000 Germans in the city to surrender alive. In Manila, a mixed Japanese garrison of only a fraction of that strength held out for three weeks of bitter fighting against vastly superior and overwhelming power. During that time we succeeded in taking only 18 prisoners. These were men who had exhausted their food and ammunition, probably several days before they surrendered, and who gave up only after we had turned everything we had on them, including flame throwers. There are still some 35,000 to 50,000 Japs on northern Luzon. Australians are still fighting Japs down in Bougainville.[3]

McDaniel almost certainly did not know the United States would soon test an atomic bomb, a weapon that would quickly end the Pacific War while simultaneously raising the specter of nuclear annihilation. Years later, McDaniel would write that the bomb "still clouds the future of mankind." Like most everyone else, McDaniel assumed the US would invade Japan in the fall of 1945. He helped devise a coverage plan for what was expected to be "the biggest event of the Pacific War."[4]

Those plans were "discarded and remade" in two horrifying moments during the week of August 6, when American B-29 bombers dropped atomic bombs on Hiroshima and Nagasaki, destroying both cities in a flash of intense light and killing nearly a quarter of a million people, many of whom died in the following weeks from radiation.

Five days after Nagasaki, Emperor Hirohito announced Japan would surrender on US terms. With an invasion no longer necessary, McDaniel scrambled to redeploy his army of reporters and photographers. From Manila, Spencer Davis messaged McDaniel that MacArthur would fly to Japan and that there was room for one AP reporter on the plane. McDaniel tapped Russell Brines, who had covered Japan before the war, to take the seat, while Davis and photographer Frank Filan reached Okinawa from Manila—"Don't ask me how exactly they did it," McDaniel wrote as he approved their ingenuity to travel about the Pacific. Dean Schedler, Jim Hutcheson, and James Halsema stayed in the Philippines to cover the surrender of the last Japanese forces there.

Murlin Spencer sailed from Guam to Japan along with reporters Hal Boyle and Duane Hennessy. Vern Haugland boarded an American plane for Japan. Murlin Spencer and Spencer Davis—"the firm of Spence and Spence" as McDaniel called them—would cover the official Japanese surrender on September 2 aboard the battleship *Missouri* in Tokyo Bay.

Spence and Spence not only obtained an advance copy of MacArthur's planned speech to the Japanese delegates aboard the *Missouri*, they also sent McDaniel the text of a communique issued by Emperor Hirohito, who ordered "all my people forthwith to cease hostilities" and "lay down their arms."

The ceremony on the decks of the 45,000-ton *Missouri* was the climax to a story McDaniel began covering thirteen years earlier in Shanghai, when he was in his twenties. He had written about Japanese troops swarming throughout China in the 1930s, leaving a path of unspeakable carnage. He watched Singapore crumble before the Japanese army. He tramped through the jungles of New Guinea and landed in the Philippines with MacArthur.

Now, however, McDaniel was nowhere near the action. Instead, he handled reports filed by AP correspondents and helped weave them into a broader story of the surrender. McDaniel wrote that in the "crowded 'press gallery' ringing the ceremonial table" aboard the *Missouri*, "four AP war correspondents and three AP photographers caught every word, every dramatic picture of this great climax . . . of bloody conflict."[5] The AP filed a main story from Tokyo that included the names and ranks of all the Allied commanders attending the ceremony, and identified the eleven members of the Japanese delegation. The AP reporters dispatched the official text of surrender, a map showing the *Missouri*'s exact location in Tokyo Bay, and scores of photographs. One showed a jubilant MacArthur hugging an emaciated Gen. Jonathan Wainwright, who had just been released from a Japanese prisoner-of-war camp, where he had been held since the surrender of Corregidor. They also sent the iconic photo of MacArthur signing the surrender document on the battleship's deck.[6]

But the day's euphoria was a "fleeting experience." The AP reporters were about to enter a devastated Japan, where cities had been ravaged by conventional and atomic weapons. Two days after the surrender on the *Missouri*, Vern Haugland hopped aboard a B-17 bomber to Hiroshima, scene of unimaginable devastation. He wandered about the shattered city, writing that "street cars rattle along the streets where not a single building stands." A week later, Haugland was in Nagasaki, writing that "smoke rises from fires" by the bomb, adding "the smell of death is heavy over the city."[7]

The AP in New York seemed happy with McDaniel's performance. "From this corner, the news report from the Pacific area looks excellent these days, from the standpoint of reporting and writing, as well as balance and brevity," Alan Gould, the AP's assistant general manager, wrote McDaniel in January 1946.[8]

With the war in the Pacific over, the appetite for Asian news quickly declined. News organizations focused on stories about men and women returning to their prewar lives in offices, factories, and homes. Although Hollywood still churned out some war films, the industry and the public had moved on. Darryl F. Zanuck's *Leave Her to Heaven*, with Gene Tierney as the femme fatale, and Tay Garnett's steamy murder thriller *The Postman Always Rings Twice* were the major hits during the first year of peace. William Wyler's *The Best Years of Our Lives*, the powerful story of three American servicemen returning to their prewar lives, would be released near the end of 1946.

The AP wanted to scale back its Pacific coverage and, with it, McDaniel's role. After one editor complained in February 1946 that the "Pacific file is being over-written," Gould replied that "the Pacific report must, of course, be kept in reasonable and proportionate bounds. But I would like to toss in my two cents worth that it is, on the whole, being well-written, even if at times over-done."[9]

Later that spring, however, Gould joined in the carping about McDaniel and San Francisco. Because the AP was charged by the number of words that were sent over the wire, Gould demanded "sharper action and more effective measures in our combined efforts to cut down operational costs—in the Pacific and elsewhere." In a tartly worded memo, Gould wondered why McDaniel had not reduced the weekly number of stories from Asia at a time when the dominant story was a massive tsunami striking the Hawaiian Islands.[10]

In reviewing the week's report, we find increases in the wordage from Shanghai, Tokyo, Manila and Seoul, with only a slight decrease from Chungking. Obviously, with only so much space on the wires and in newspaper columns, one of our prime "musts" is to keep the report in bounds. This means when transcendent news breaks in any area, that prompt and effective steps must be taken to cut the report elsewhere. This is the responsibility which control points, such as the foreign desk here and in San Francisco, must constantly exercise if we are to avoid waste words and tolls.

In July 1946, the AP transferred McDaniel to Detroit as bureau chief. It was a puzzling assignment, because before the transfer there is no record of McDaniel spending any time in Michigan. Nor is there any sign in his stories that he had the slightest interest in or knowledge about the automotive industry. The *Detroit Free Press* reported Yates and Natalie were "looking forward to the 'romance' of a domestic assignment after 30 years in the much-publicized 'mystic fascination of the Orient.'" There is a hint from Natalie that Detroit was a place for her and Yates to recover from the exhausting pace during the past decade. Natalie described herself as "more than content to be quietly settled in the United States." As far as she was concerned, they were "home for keeps." Yet, home for Yates and Natalie had always been Asia, not America.[11]

They lived on the second floor of the Palms, a six-story apartment building that offered a sweeping view both of Belle Isle in the Detroit River and the Canadian province of Ontario. Built in 1903, the apartment building was one of the right addresses, featuring octagonal towers at the corners. It was just a short drive to the AP's bureau in the downtown offices of the *Detroit News*.

They had a real chance to enjoy the holidays they had so often missed in Asia. The *Free Press* took note that Natalie and Yates celebrated New Year's Eve in 1947 with champagne as they listened to a radio broadcast. For the first time, they had the opportunity to travel for relaxation. They made their way through Michigan's Upper Peninsula to get a look at Iron Mountain, Indian Lake, and Big Spring, which Native Americans had called the "Mirror of Heaven."

Following one dinner party as they sipped coffee, their host told Natalie, "It certainly must be interesting to be the wife of a foreign correspondent and be able to see the world."

"I wouldn't have for the world missed the fireworks," she replied. But she explained she could do "without" postwar Asia with their "greatly inflated rates of exchanges and deflated ideas of even the simplest comforts."

Natalie had once joked that if she ever wrote her memoirs, she would title them "Proceed Immediately," which was the first line of scores of AP telegrams sent to Yates ordering him to get on a plane or board a train to cover a major story. But the more she thought about her host's question, the more she was convinced she had a fascinating story to write for a magazine.

So she went to work. She wrote about the ambulance ride from Shanghai to Nanking in 1937 and dug out a photograph of her standing next to its front wheel. She found another photo of her sitting atop a captured Japanese tank. She described the thrill of being invited to swimming parties at the sultan of Johore's palace in Singapore, and contrasted that with her unhappiness on Christmas Eve in 1937, when the AP ordered Yates to "proceed immediately" to Hong Kong, leaving her alone in Shanghai:

> It's true a correspondent has one thing in common with other newspapermen the world over. When a story breaks, off he goes like the proverbial bat out of hell, no matter what he's doing or what the hour. Woe betides anyone—including

the little women—who stands in his way or offers any argument about "Waiting until morning" or "It's Joe's turn, have him to do it."

She titled the story "Some of my best friends are correspondents, but . . ." Then she sent the piece to major magazines in New York. But as the AP and Hollywood had discovered, war news no longer was in style; Natalie received one rejection after another. Sylvia Wright, an associate editor of *Harper's Bazaar*, wrote that Natalie's story "isn't quite right for us, partly because it is a good deal longer than most of the things of this kind we publish."[12]

The city where Yates and Natalie made their home was the prosperous center of the automotive industry and the nation's fifth-largest city, with a population of 1.8 million. Its bustling downtown featured some of the finest art deco skyscrapers in the United States, including the thirty-story Fisher Building on West Grand Boulevard and the forty-seven-story Penobscot, which had been the country's fourth tallest when it opened in 1928.

The city thrived economically, and its population grew during the first half of the century. Factories in Detroit and other cities in Michigan churned out tanks and planes for the war effort. But the city seethed with racial tensions, which exploded in a brutal riot in 1943 when whites and blacks clashed near the city's main street, Woodward Avenue. More than 6,000 federal troops were called in. Before order was restored, twenty-five African Americans and nine whites had been killed.

During the war, organized labor had agreed not to press for wage increases. But with the war over and factories once again producing cars, refrigerators, and other consumer goods, unions argued it was time for pay raises. In late 1945, more than 320,000 workers at General Motors went on strike for 113 days before winning a 17.5 percent pay increase.

Labor talks and strikes would dominate McDaniel's time in Detroit. At the end of 1947, one of McDaniel's reporters—F. Glenn Engle—wrote that the emergence of Walter Reuther as president of the United Auto Workers was a sign that he would "gain for its members substantial wage increases to meet the spiraling cost of living."[13]

At a news conference in January 1948, Reuther called for a twenty-five-cent-per-hour wage boost from GM and Chrysler at a time when the average hourly salary for auto workers was $1.50. He also insisted on an additional five cents an hour for health insurance. Reuther said the union "will not hesitate" to strike if the automakers refused its demands.[14]

A month later, the union increased its demands to thirty cents an hour for wages, five cents for health insurance, "an adequate" pension plan, and additional vacation time.[15] By contrast, Chrysler, the nation's third-largest automotive company, was willing to offer its 75,000 workers a paltry raise of only six cents an hour.[16]

On May 12, Chrysler workers went on strike at its sixteen plants. Violence erupted at a picket line surrounding Chrysler's headquarters in the Detroit enclave of Highland Park. Governor Kim Sigler dispatched state police to the picket lines to restore order. Federal and state officials worried the work stoppage could spread to GM.[17]

On May 24, McDaniel's bureau beat United Press by twenty minutes with a bulletin that Sigler had "stepped into the thirteen-day Chrysler strike" and succeeded in getting management and labor to resume negotiations. It was the first sign not only that the Chrysler strike would soon end, but also that a potential strike of GM would be avoided.[18]

A settlement was near. McDaniel assigned Engle to "stay with the negotiations until the payoff." Engle began his watch at noon on May 24 and remained throughout the day. In the early-morning hours of May 25, Engle telephoned Margaret Hyde, the bureau's early editor, and told her a settlement was near. In meticulous fashion, AP's coverage plan unfolded. News editor Ken Gregory headed toward the office while reporter Felix Wold joined Engle.

"We scored" a major scoop, McDaniel wrote, because the "team acted smoothly and speedily on accurate information received as the result of planning."[19]

On May 29, Chrysler's workers "began trickling back to their plants" after the company agreed to a thirteen-cent-per-hour wage increase. It was twice as much as the company had been offering, and provided labor peace until the summer of 1950, when the contract would expire.[20]

In what should have seemed obvious to everyone, McDaniel was not a comfortable fit in Detroit. His passion remained the Pacific and international affairs as opposed to labor relations, cars, and trucks. "He was strictly a square peg in a round hole," one AP reporter said years later.[21] When he spoke publicly, it was always about international affairs, not the auto industry. Unlike his stories, where he rarely offered his personal views, McDaniel's speeches were heavily opinionated. McDaniel thought American newspapers were making a mistake by scaling back foreign coverage, telling a group of high school and college journalism students at Michigan State University that foreign news coverage was even more important now than it was during the war. He also asserted, "Today, we've got to tell the truth, the whole truth."[22]

He was handed an opportunity to get involved with Asian affairs thanks to a book—*One Last Look Around*—published in the spring of 1947 and written by Clark Lee, McDaniel's former AP colleague in Australia. Like McDaniel, Lee had been a peripatetic traveler during the war—from the Philippines in 1941 to Italy in 1943 to Normandy in 1944, and back to the Philippines in 1945. He was called "an Ernest Hemingway hero in the flesh," a "tall, dark, husky, handsome experienced newspaperman." Lee seemed to be at the right place for every major postwar story. He and another reporter interviewed Tokyo Rose in Japan, and he was on the scene when former Japanese prime minister Hideki Tojo attempted to commit suicide.[23]

Both McDaniel and Lee had lived in China before the war. But they were "far different in background and temperament."[24] McDaniel was a stickler for accuracy. By contrast, Lee on occasion "seemed to trade facts for color." In his new book, Lee wrote that because of MacArthur in February 1945, correspondents "were not allowed to write the truth about Manila. There could be no fighting, no rape, no shooting down of Filipinos with hands tied behind their backs . . . no burning of the city." Lee's assertion was not true; McDaniel and other correspondents wrote extensively about the destruction of Manila.[25]

Like many war correspondents, Lee "found it hard to gear down to peacetime routine."[26] And he emerged from the war hopelessly disillusioned. One reviewer said Lee's book "slams, bangs, analyzes, criticizes, condones and condemns nearly every factor in our war" against Japan.[27] Lee assailed MacArthur's supervision of postwar Japan and wrote that "as long as we coddle Hirohito and protect the Emperor system instead of destroying it, the danger will exist of a new, rebuilt, re-militarized Japan—this time with all the modern weapons it needs—going on the warpath again in the holy name of the Emperor."[28]

Lee saw the Chinese Nationalists as "notoriously corrupt" with "no visible public backing." By contrast, he wrote that Mao's Communists "brought education and enlightenment to many regions of the remote hinterlands" of China and "cracked the landlord system and distributed lands to the needy." Lee wrote that Mao's troops "fight for a cause, not for money." He blamed the United States for the growing hostility between America and the Soviet Union. Pointing to American support for the Chinese Nationalists and a democratic Japan, Lee asked, "How would we feel if as the result of a series of wars we found Red forces holding Mexico and Cuba and Canada and the governments of those countries being bolshevized?"[29]

He directed even more intense anger at "the entrenched powers of the imperialists in London and Wall Street and Washington and Rotterdam." The imperialists, he charged, "with their superior weapons and their disregard for human lives, are a hardy breed." Why, Lee asked, could not Great Britain "grant the Malayans" some independence and still sell them British goods? "The answer is that unless they were forced to buy British, the people of Malaya would purchase the same items cheaper, and sometimes, better" from Japan, the United States, India, or China.[30]

"Most Americans are anti-imperialists," Lee wrote. "But the average American makes neither foreign policy nor wars. He merely fights the wars. If the average American does not want his son to go to war again, he must be vigilant against our imperialists."[31]

The book was released in May 1947. It is unclear when—or even whether—McDaniel read the book. But McDaniel could not have more sharply disagreed with Lee's conclusions. McDaniel took a far more benevolent view of British colonial policy in Singapore, Malaya, and Burma. When McDaniel first returned to China in 1929, he wrote that he was carrying "the white man's burden by teaching English," a clear hint that he endorsed Rudyard Kipling's views on British imperialism. Years later, in a March 1947 speech in the Canadian city of Windsor, McDaniel said Kipling's "The White Man's Burden" was one of the "truest ideas he ever expressed."[32]

In that same speech, McDaniel told the audience that he deplored "any move Britain herself may take—or which any outside power forces her to take—which will suddenly break down the stabilizing force she has exercised so successfully not only for the British Empire but for the people she is governing." In a none-too-subtle warning about the rise of communism in Asia, McDaniel said "something has got to take the place" of British rule, "and whose ideas are these people going to adopt—ours or someone else's?"

McDaniel called China a "country that has been in turmoil—politically, militarily and economically for a century." The Chinese were a likable people, McDaniel said. If China could ever unite, McDaniel said, it would become a potent force for peace in Asia. Since 1850, China had never attacked its neighbors, McDaniel said, but instead suffered through endless civil wars or invasions by foreign powers. Before the war with Japan in the 1930s, McDaniel said, China under the Nationalists had made dramatic gains economically. But the Japanese invasion "completely uprooted" their economy, adding "it will take years for China to get over the psychological effects of war."[33]

In a stance sharply at odds with Clark Lee and many Allied officials, McDaniel sided with Gen. MacArthur on rebuilding Japan. The mood in America after the war was to get rid of Emperor Hirohito. Senator Richard Russell, a prominent Georgia Democrat, introduced a resolution in 1945 demanding that Hirohito be tried as a war criminal. "Failure to put the emperor on trial would be a tragic mistake," Russell said. "If we fail to try Hirohito, we will surely sow the seed of a future war."[34] A Gallup Poll showed that 70 percent of Americans wanted Hirohito tried, with 33 percent saying he should be executed, 17 percent saying the courts should decide his fate, and 11 percent saying he should be in prison for the rest of his life.[35]

It would have been easy for McDaniel to join the anti-Hirohito crowd. McDaniel had personally witnessed more deaths at the hands of the Japanese than any other reporter in the world. Instead, he had a more farsighted view. He enthusiastically endorsed MacArthur's efforts to democratize Japan, which included voting rights for women and permission to form labor unions. McDaniel made clear it would have been foolish for the Americans to depose Hirohito, and predicted Japan would emerge from the turmoil as a reliable American ally.

"Would it not be better for us to mold the Japanese today while we have the chance so that in the future, they will be started off on a track parallel to our own?" McDaniel asked.[36]

It was not a new theme for him. Punishing Japan further was idiocy, he believed. A year earlier, in 1946, during a panel discussion in San Francisco, he warned, "Japan can't be held down indefinitely. It is stupidity to think of Japan without thinking of her in relation to the rest of Asia. We must not allow some other nation to take over control in Japan," a clear reference to the Soviet Union. "If we do, it will mean another war."[37]

While Clark Lee saw Western imperialism as the chief cause of Asian misery, McDaniel believed that imperialism produced stability. Today, McDaniel's support of imperialism seems anachronistic. But he made his views clear in the summer of 1947 in a speech in Michigan's Upper Peninsula. At that time, the Dutch, who were the colonial rulers in Java, were engaged in a bloody struggle with Indonesian Republican soldiers. Australia and India refused to help the Dutch, even though the

Netherlands had pledged full independence to Java by January 1, 1949. McDaniel said, "There is something to be said in favor of the Dutch in this latest dispute. They have done an outstanding job of ruling their colonies, and their people have settled in the Netherland Indies permanently. Some families have lived there for generations, and there even has been some intermarrying with the natives. The Dutch have not been like others who have gone to the colonies to make some money and return home after several years."[38]

McDaniel believed that the decline in Western imperialism in Asia would leave a vacuum and embolden the Soviet Union to extend its power to the east. During his Windsor speech, McDaniel said that the Korean Peninsula was a "natural" for a potential clash between the West and the Soviet Union. Korea had been divided in half after the Pacific war ended. Soviet troops occupied Pyongyang in August 1945 and supported the creation of a pro-Moscow regime headed by Kim Il-sung, while Syngman Rhee pushed for a separate pro-Western government in South Korea. Like Chiang Kai-shek, Rhee was an autocrat. But to McDaniel there was no real alternative to Rhee.[39]

McDaniel was prescient about Korea. Speaking before newspaper executives in Grand Rapids in May 1947, he warned that the prospects for peace in Korea were "very poor," and he said the Soviet Union "has the advantage" if war breaks out between South and North Korea.[40]

He implored Americans to see the broader picture. Speaking to a Kiwanis Club in Battle Creek in the summer of 1947, McDaniel said that all too often the press ignored relatively small events that eventually mushroomed into cataclysmic conflicts. He harkened back to the exchange of gunfire between Japanese and Chinese troops at the Marco Polo Bridge in 1937, telling the audience that this seemingly insignificant clash received little attention in the American press. Yet, McDaniel said, the correspondents who covered the conflict at the bridge regarded it as the real beginning of the Second World War, as opposed to the German invasion of Poland in 1939.[41]

At the end of 1948, the AP transferred McDaniel to Washington, the "news capital of the Free World." Although working in Washington was a dream for many reporters, the move marked the end of McDaniel's managerial career. From now on, he would be a reporter, not a bureau chief.

Bill Beale had just been promoted to the prestigious job of Washington bureau chief and presumably wanted McDaniel as one of his reporters. A graduate of Princeton, Beale joined the Associated Press in 1930 and became news editor in 1934. He was serious and shy and rarely smiled, although he displayed a dry sense of humor. He was famous throughout the bureau for typing notes to his staff on small sheets of yellow paper. When one reporter wrote that a House committee passed a bill, Beale sent the reporter a terse note: "House committees do not pass bills. Only the full House or Senate can pass a bill."

While most reporters thrived under his direction, Beale clashed with a young, ambitious Robert Novak, who pleaded to get off the regional staff and cover national news. In 1958, Novak asked Beale to add a beat on atomic energy. Beale not only declined to create the new beat but also made clear to Novak he would never be promoted to the national staff, prompting Novak to take a political reporting job with the *Wall Street Journal*. Novak became a famous syndicated columnist. Later, when both Beale and Novak were members of the prestigious Gridiron Club in Washington, Novak avoided speaking to his former boss.[42]

The AP offices were in the *Washington Star* building at the corner of Pennsylvania Avenue and 11th Street NW, an ideal location for covering the White House, federal agencies, and Capitol Hill. At its peak, the AP's switchboard had fourteen incoming lines; on a single business day, 1,125 calls went through the switchboard. AP was vital to the nation's newspapers. The AP supplied copy not only to major newspapers, but also smaller ones that lacked the finances to staff a Washington bureau of their own.[43]

McDaniel spent his first year in Washington covering the Indiana and Michigan congressional delegations. Although he churned out the routine regional stories on lawmakers from both states, as always his interest remained Asia. In March 1949, McDaniel spoke about foreign affairs before graduates of the University of Richmond—his alma mater—at a gathering in Baltimore.

As McDaniel was speaking, the China he knew so well continued its descent into chaos. In 1946, war once again broke out between Chiang and Mao. President Harry Truman sent Gen. George C. Marshall to China to negotiate a settlement, but by January 1947 a discouraged Marshall gave up and returned to the United States. While there was little sympathy for the Communists, there was no sentiment in the United States to send combat troops to China to defend the Nationalists. Mao's Communists seized Manchuria, and in early 1949 they swept south to drive the Nationalists from Nanking, Hankow, and Shanghai. In April 1949, the Communists conquered Soochow, where Sophie Lanneau, whom McDaniel knew when he was a young man, was desperately trying to keep open the Wei Ling girls school. In October 1949, Mao assumed complete control of China. Chiang and his loyalists fled to Taiwan. By August 1950, Lanneau was forced to leave Soochow and return to the United States.

Chiang's defeat exacerbated a searing dispute between Republicans and Democrats in Washington over what caused the Nationalists to fall. Republicans blamed the Truman administration for failing to support Chiang. In an effort to defuse Republican criticism, the Truman administration issued a special "White Paper" in August 1949, which had been drafted by the State Department just before Chiang fell. The paper contended that "the predicament in which the National Government finds itself today is due to its failure to provide China with enough to eat. A large part of the Chinese Communists' propaganda consists of promises that they will solve the land problem."

The State Department pointed out that during World War II, the Nationalists "had apparently lost the crusading spirit that won them the people's loyalty during the early years of the war. In the opinion of many observers they had sunk into corruption, into a scramble for place and power, and into reliance on the United States to win the war for them and to preserve their own domestic supremacy."[44]

There are hints that McDaniel was unhappy with Chiang's collapse. In a 1950 speech, Republican congressman Ralph Harvey of Indiana told a small gathering of Republican women in Indiana that McDaniel warned him a year earlier "that the determination was made within our own State Department more than ten years ago to turn China and the Far East over to the Communists. He not only made this statement to me, but later made the same on my weekly radio broadcast for my Indiana stations."[45]

McDaniel was soon named the number 2 reporter at the Pentagon behind Elton Fay, a military correspondent who reported on the atomic bomb tests at Bikini. Arriving at the Pentagon in January 1950, McDaniel quickly produced a major story. Secretary of Defense Louis Johnson asserted that military readiness was "greater today than in any previous peacetime period in our nation's history. The threat of war has been diminished as our strength has increased." Johnson's rosy assessment would quickly be proved wrong.[46]

As McDaniel had long feared, war erupted in Korea. On the morning of June 25, 1950, more than 90,000 North Korean troops and 200 Soviet-built T-34 tanks punched across the thirty-eighth parallel separating North from South Korea. Within days, the North Korean army had gobbled up Seoul and pushed south down the peninsula.

The US was hopelessly unprepared to counter the North Korean offensive. Since the end of World War II, the Army had been slashed from eight million soldiers to only 591,000. They were organized in ten divisions, four of which were stationed in Japan under Gen. MacArthur's command. Even that strength proved illusory. Tanks were in short supply, and of those that existed, fewer than 400 were modern M-46 tanks. Because Secretary Johnson placed a higher priority on Air Force bombers, he declined to spend all the money authorized by Congress for the Army.[47]

Russell Brines, the AP bureau chief in Tokyo, took charge of war coverage and flooded South Korea with reporters. In Washington, Fay wrote dailies three times a week for afternoon papers and often added a major Sunday piece that offered a broader look at the war. McDaniel and Max Boyd, former AP bureau chief in Egypt, wrote analytical stories for morning newspapers.[48]

This time, McDaniel was nowhere near the conflict he was writing about. Instead of following ground troops into battle, he drove safely from home to his Pentagon office every day. He relied on sources and his vast knowledge of China, Manchuria, and Korea to produce explanatory stories. When the US and British proposed a sea blockade of Korea, McDaniel wrote that it would not prevent the Soviets from re-supplying the North Korean forces. His analysis was correct:

In the days when Japan controlled both Manchuria and Korea, she tied the road and rail systems of the two countries together and angled both in a northernly direction toward Russian borders. Thus, a fairly good land route exists for shipments of supplies into North Korea from Russian territory."[49]

In the middle of July, McDaniel wrote that North Korea may have "committed a military sin" when its forces "plunged recklessly" into South Korea without "even minimal air support." He pointed out that North Korea was relying on the Soviet-built Yak-9 fighter—a match for German fighters in World War II, but unable to contend with more-advanced US planes. McDaniel warned that "while American military men are convinced that the lack of Red airpower will cost the invaders dearly, Allied airpower alone is not expected to turn the tide in Korea."[50]

McDaniel's analysis appeared one day after the AP in New York sent out another major story: in Korea, MacArthur announced that Marguerite Higgins of the *New York Herald Tribune* would become the first woman reporter to cover the war. In September, she landed with the Marines at Inchon, vividly writing that "the bullets were whining persistently, spattering the water around us. We clambered over the high steel sides of the boat, dropping into the water and, taking shelter beside the boat as we could, snaked onto our stomachs into a rock-strewn dip in the sea wall." Higgins, not McDaniel, covered MacArthur's bold landing, which trapped the North Korean army. A year later, Higgins and five male reporters were awarded Pulitzer Prizes for their coverage.[51]

As a new generation of reporters made its mark in Korea, McDaniel focused on the turmoil inside the Pentagon. Although Secretary Johnson had largely slashed the Pentagon budget on Truman's orders, the shortages in Korea provoked howls of protests against Johnson from both political parties. Democrats seeking reelection in November were busy defending themselves against accusations that they were to blame for Mao's seizure of power in China. McDaniel reported that Johnson charged that his critics had been "misled by misinformation."[52]

On September 13, Truman fired Johnson and replaced him with retired general George C. Marshall, the former Army chief of staff and secretary of state. Johnson said in a letter to Truman that he was leaving because of the "enemies I have acquired during the eighteen months I have served" in the cabinet. Elton Fay, not McDaniel, wrote the main story. A week later, McDaniel reported that Johnson refused a ceremonial departure and left the Pentagon before most of the "30,000 people in the building knew their chief was gone." Johnson rode down the private elevator from his office, climbed into his own car, and drove off. No limousine, no chauffeur, no official send-off.[53]

Following MacArthur's dramatic landing at Inchon, the North Korean army quickly collapsed. With the support of the White House and Pentagon, MacArthur ordered his troops to cross the thirty-eighth parallel. Although Communist China warned it would intervene if the Americans approached the Yalu River, separating Manchuria from North Korea, the threats were dismissed by MacArthur and officials in Washington.

On October 15, as US and South Korean troops occupied Pyongyang, Truman flew to Wake Island in the mid-Pacific to meet personally with MacArthur. Although Truman ostensibly wanted MacArthur's views on whether China would intervene, the president clearly hoped for a political boost by being photographed with the general, whose popularity had reached its zenith. Truman engaged in a grueling 14,000-mile round trip for what amounted to a two-hour meeting with MacArthur.

McDaniel stayed in Washington as the White House correspondents for the AP, United Press, and International News Service transmitted pool reports from Wake to Honolulu. Pentagon officials in Washington provided McDaniel and other reporters with a background briefing about the Wake Island meeting. In an upbeat assessment, the officials said MacArthur assured Truman "that neither Communist China nor Russia will intervene."[54]

It was a wildly optimistic briefing and a fundamental misreading of China's intentions. While Gen. MacArthur knew that more than 300,000 Chinese troops had assembled in Manchuria, he was confident that US airpower would make it impossible for more than a fraction of them to cross the Yalu River into North Korea.

In late October, McDaniel and other reporters pestered Pentagon officials about reports that US forces encountered an estimated 20,000 Chinese troops near the North Korean town of Chosin, on the Yalu River. Officials remained confident, saying they "still do not expect any open, large-scale intervention" against Allied forces. McDaniel reported that the Pentagon was convinced that China simply wanted to protect the dams on the Yalu River that provided electric power to parts of Manchuria and the Soviet naval base at Port Arthur.[55]

But on November 30, the same day that China launched a full-scale invasion of Korea, McDaniel relied on his deep knowledge of Chinese history to quickly write an analysis. China's attack, he wrote, had less to do with Soviet pressure and more to do with 350 years of Chinese history. McDaniel pointed out that more than a "half-a-dozen times," Chinese emperors had sent forces into Korea to battle the Japanese. The Chinese Communists were behaving much like their predecessors in fearing foreign troops in Korea.

In the last decade of the 16th century, a Japanese warlord, Hideyoshi, sent an army of 300,000 men into Korea. This force quickly overran South Korea and captured the capital at Seoul. Then his powerful war machine, like that of Gen. Douglas MacArthur's this week, bogged down in the mountains north of the 38th Parallel. Hordes of Chinese poured across the Yalu River and drove Hideyoshi back to the sea.[56]

As the AP sent out McDaniel's story, Chinese troops were already flooding into North Korea. "We face an entirely new war," MacArthur said in Tokyo. From Seoul, AP reported that two US divisions had escaped across the icy Chongchon River in northwest Korea. But the same story warned that Chinese troops "swarming through a wide gap threatened to trap a big Allied force." As heavy snow fell and temperatures plunged, Allied forces were forced to retreat to safety.

In Washington, Pentagon officials briefed reporters. McDaniel quoted an Army spokesman as calling the Chinese attacks "serious, but not catastrophic." The same spokesman admonished reporters about "over-pessimism," insisting that the Allied forces "have not lost their organizations and are not destroyed. The fact that they are regrouping and have their organizations would indicate that their losses were not as heavy as initially reported."[57]

But in private, the joint chiefs were increasingly fearful that MacArthur was on the verge of a calamitous defeat. Army chief of staff Gen. J. Lawton Collins flew to Tokyo to meet with MacArthur on December 4. Then Collins was off to Korea to talk with other senior US military commanders. On December 6, Collins again met with MacArthur before flying back to Washington. As he emerged from his plane, Collins was surrounded by McDaniel and other reporters. Collins expressed confidence that MacArthur had enough forces to withstand the Chinese attack.[58]

For McDaniel, it was his last major story of the year about Korea. A few days later, he and Natalie flew to Florida for a vacation with friends in Tampa.[59]

The AP had a golden resource—a reporter who had covered MacArthur for years at the front lines and knew him well. For whatever reason, the AP did not use McDaniel to cover the deepening split between Truman and MacArthur in early 1951. MacArthur wanted to attack Chinese bases in Manchuria, a move rejected by the White House because it might provoke World War III. MacArthur's challenge to Truman could end one way, and on April 11, 1951, the president fired the five-star general. It was the year's biggest and most explosive story, and it fueled a bitter dispute between Republicans and Democrats. Republicans demanded Truman's impeachment. While John Hightower, Jack Bell, and Elton Fay wrote the lead stories for the AP, McDaniel produced an insignificant sidebar about how, as a member of a military court in 1925, MacArthur voted against convicting Gen. Billy Mitchell of insubordination.[60]

A couple of weeks later, after his return to the United States, MacArthur spoke to a gathering in Washington of the American Society of Newspaper Editors. The general spotted McDaniel in the receiving line. It was the first time they had seen each other since MacArthur officially handed over control of Manila to Philippine president Sergio Osmena.

"Of course, I remember you," MacArthur said as he shook McDaniel's hand. "It was outside of Malacañang Palace in 1945 and I called you to my car and said, 'We did it. I knew we could do it.'"[61]

It was a symbolic moment. Both MacArthur and McDaniel were home for good. MacArthur was part of the past. And so was McDaniel.

# WASHINGTON, DC

O
n one of those sunny, invigorating autumn mornings that the nation's capital does so well, Yates McDaniel arrived at Arlington National Cemetery for the 1953 Armistice Day ceremonies and saw a face from his past. An elderly Japanese man had shown up without an invitation for the observance at the Tomb of the Unknown Soldier.[1]

The old gentleman "stood unrecognized by American leaders" as he used a cane to hobble up the steps of the Memorial Amphitheater. When he reached the top, he removed his hat and leaned against a portico. Because all the seats were reserved for American officials and members of patriotic organizations, an usher waved for him to leave.

McDaniel quickly stepped in. He explained to the usher that the man was retired admiral Kichisaburo Nomura, once one of the more recognized people in Washington. Twenty years earlier in China, Nomura had been one of McDaniel's sources. As a reporter for the *Shanghai Evening Post*, McDaniel had covered the 1932 bombing attack that cost the admiral one of his eyes. And in December 1941, Nomura served as Japanese ambassador to the United States, engaging in a strenuous and ultimately futile effort to prevent what he knew would be a catastrophic war for Japan. The chastened usher then showed Nomura to a seat.

After President Dwight Eisenhower placed a wreath of yellow chrysanthemums at the tomb's base and the ceremony concluded with a twenty-one-cannon salute, McDaniel and the admiral walked down the Virginia hillside. McDaniel reminded Nomura about their first encounter in 1932 aboard the old Japanese armored cruiser *Izumo*, anchored off Shanghai.

Finally, McDaniel asked the obvious question: "Why did you come here today?" Nomura brushed at an autumn leaf on his heavy outer coat and answered, "I came because it is right, because I wanted to be here."[2]

In his story, McDaniel noted Nomura's presence at the ceremony and arranged for an AP photographer to shoot a photo of the admiral, giving the AP a nice scoop. But much like the usher who didn't know what to do with Nomura, nobody could find a comfortable fit for McDaniel in postwar America.

The 1950s were heady times for most national reporters. The United States and Soviet Union were locked in the Cold War. Both sides possessed enough nuclear weapons to wreak unspeakable carnage. The United States was developing nuclear submarines and long-range missiles and could deliver nuclear weapons throughout the world with the new B-47 and B-52 jet bombers. The Soviets were sending Sputnik into orbit.

In theory, McDaniel had a prestigious post. The Associated Press described his job as "one of the top reportorial spots in all Washington."[3] He was among the reporters the AP showcased. He wrote about the Soviets detonating their own hydrogen bomb. He speculated that the Soviets were developing their own nuclear-powered submarines.[4] In January 1954, he was among a panel of reporters on NBC's *Meet the Press* who questioned the outgoing Army chief of staff, Gen. J. Lawton Collins. Later that year, McDaniel spoke to a gathering of broadcasters in Columbia, South Carolina.[5] A year later, he was the featured speaker at the Maryland Press Association.[6]

In 1956, he was one of a dozen reporters and photographers to sail on the *Nautilus*, the world's first nuclear-powered submarine. Five years earlier, McDaniel had written that the Navy had signed a contract with Electric Boat of Connecticut to build a nuclear submarine that would reach a top speed of 60 knots, far faster than conventional diesel-powered submarines.[7] Now that that submarine was a reality, it instantly rendered obsolete every other submarine in the world. The correspondents boarded the *Nautilus* in New London, Connecticut, for the short twenty-four-hour voyage to New York City. McDaniel shared a cabin with Adm. Hyman Rickover, father of the US nuclear submarine fleet, who told reporters that "this is not an air-breathing machine, so we can operate in enemy-controlled waters without having to come up to breathe."

McDaniel stood in the control room as the submarine "dove deeper than he ever expected to go, and then climbed up again with a speed and zoom that recalled a ride on a carnival roller coaster." The Navy would say only that the *Nautilus* could dive "more than" 300 feet and reach 20 knots submerged. The cooks grilled rib-eye steaks and served them with a green salad, and pineapple upside-down cake. When the *Nautilus* sailed under the George Washington Bridge, the submarine received a festive welcome as police helicopters whirled overhead and fireboats "spurted jets of water." It was the type of descriptive journalism that McDaniel excelled at.[8]

There were a few other gems for McDaniel. In 1958, he wrote a profile of Army general James Gavin, who was retiring at the youthful age of fifty. Gavin had infuriated Pentagon officials throughout his career. In 1957, he told a Senate committee that to speed up military decisions, the Joint Chiefs of Staff should be broken up.[9] McDaniel wrote that military officials were also livid in 1956 when Gavin told a Senate subcommittee that a US nuclear attack on the Soviet Union would kill "several hundred million" through the explosions and radioactive fallout, and that the fallout could reach US allies in western Europe, Japan, and the Philippines, "depending on which way the wind blew."[10] In his story, McDaniel described Gavin—perhaps unintentionally—in a way that might well have been a description of himself:

Known as a studious man who is generally grave in manner, Gavin rarely raises his voice. His most effective tone is something close to a stage whisper. But it is a whisper that often echoes far beyond his office, frequently jolting the Pentagon. Gavin is not only a nonconformist in words but in deeds as well. During World

War II, he frequently roamed the front lines with forward patrols, carrying a carbine."[11]

These assignments suited McDaniel's skills, honed over years roaming Asia, staying at the center of the action, and writing narratives about his amazing adventures. But now, most days, McDaniel was assigned to a desk at the Pentagon. Rather than climbing into his car and driving around battlefields near Nanking or watching Japanese planes dive near his Singapore apartment, he was attending news conferences and reading press handouts. Unlike his time in Singapore, when he flopped about in sport shirts and casual slacks, he now wore business suits, a white shirt, and either a necktie or bow tie.

The AP wanted institutions covered—the White House, Congress, Pentagon, Supreme Court, and Treasury Department, and the horde of agencies that made up the federal government. It was what the AP did best. Colorful stories that depended on getting out of the office were fine for war correspondents. But the AP sold itself as thorough and reliable, not flashy. If the president or secretary of defense said something, the AP promised newspapers that it would be there to cover the event.

To some in the AP bureau, McDaniel did not seem very enthusiastic. "My recollection was the AP wasn't happy with him at that job, and he wasn't happy in that job," said Fred Hoffman, a reporter in the AP's Washington bureau. "I really felt sorry for him. I was in my 20s and he was an old China hand. I remember him sitting at his desk, white hair, looking very unhappy. He was a man born in Asia, didn't know anything about the United States, and they had trouble fitting him in."[12]

McDaniel may have been burned out, much like other foreign correspondents who returned home after the shooting stopped. McDaniel's onetime AP colleague Clark Lee "missed the robust hardships and excitement of war, the thrill of gambling his life to get" a major story. Lee "never was meant for the humdrum life."[13] After the war, Natalie said that she could "do with some peace and quiet now," a hint perhaps that McDaniel needed a rest as well. In fact, McDaniel *looked* burned out. His thinning hair was completely white even though he would not turn fifty until 1956. His hands shook from an old bout of malaria.

Yet, there were aspects of his job he loved. He would chase down Gavin in a Pentagon corridor as the general raced to a meeting. He enjoyed chatting with Pentagon officials, such as Adm. Rickover, Adm. John Sides, who championed the development of the Navy's guided-missile program, and RAdm. Charles Kirkpatrick, the chief of information for the Navy. Because he knew so much about the military and diplomacy, those in power did not hesitate to speak with him.

In Richmond, Yates's parents—Charles and Nannie—were fading fast. By the spring of 1954, Yates and his sisters moved them into a nursing home in Richmond. Yates estimated it would cost as much as $325 a month to keep both parents in the home. In a May 26 letter, Yates asked the Foreign Mission Board to provide $150 a month to pay for those costs "in addition to their regular emeritus payments."[14]

Less than two weeks later, Nannie died at age eighty-two. In the spring of 1956, Charles was moved to a Baptist nursing home in Culpeper, in northern Virginia. The home's superintendent wrote Yates in April 1956 that Charles was receiving care twenty-four hours a day: "He is perfectly happy and comfortable with the present arrangement and eats heartily three times a day." The superintendent added that Charles wanted Yates to send him a small desk he had used in the past, "where he can continue to engage his thoughts and mind in writing."[15]

Two weeks later, Yates received a telegram from the Foreign Mission Board: Charles had died at age eighty-four. "Thanking God for the wonderful life of your father and remembering all of you in prayer at this time," the telegram read.[16]

At the time of Nannie's death, Yates and Natalie were living in a 1,000-square-foot one-story house in the Foxhall-Palisades section of Washington, not far from the Potomac River. By 1956, they had moved to an apartment in Virginia near Fort Myer and just a short drive to McDaniel's Pentagon office. A few years later, they moved to McLean, a tony suburb in northern Virginia, where they bought a house on a bluff above the Potomac River. It was one of the right addresses; their neighbor was Robert Kennedy. Natalie was selling real estate, and with her outgoing personality she was a natural fit as an agent. Yates developed an interest in gardening, something that never quite appealed to Natalie.

Yates did not belong to the prestigious journalism organizations in Washington such as the Gridiron Club. But he and Natalie enjoyed entertaining at their McLean home. He was "a master host," and to his relatives he appeared happy. He and Natalie would often be invited to dinner at the home of his boss, Bill Beale. Beale's son, David, thought of McDaniel as an intellectual, often wondering why he did not write a book about his stunning adventures. But McDaniel shrugged when anyone suggested it.

By the summer of 1960, McDaniel was looking for ways to get out of the daily Pentagon grind. Adm. Sides was named to command the US 7th Fleet in the Pacific and talked to McDaniel about joining him for a patrol through the Formosa Strait. Adm. Kirkpatrick helped craft a plan that would allow McDaniel to also visit the US Marines on Okinawa, as well as US military bases in Japan and the Philippines. In a memo to Beale, McDaniel wrote that he would make the trip as part of his own vacation:

> Needless to say, I will pay all my own food and lodging expenses and any others that are permitted to be paid while traveling with a strictly military organization. I will be able to cover the distances and see and talk to the key people involved, particularly in the more distant areas, only because my old friend, and the new commander-in-chief of the Pacific Fleet, Adm. John H. Sides, will be making an inspection trip at the time.[17]

McDaniel promised he would write any "spot news" that developed, but told Beale he primarily wanted to renew contacts with his sources. Beale and Alan Gould in New York approved the trip. McDaniel's timing was perfect. He was in Formosa as Democratic presidential nominee John F. Kennedy was arguing that the United States should not defend the islands of Quemoy and Matsu, which provoked a sharp debate with Vice President Richard Nixon. McDaniel filed a story from Taipei that Nationalist Chinese defense minister Yu Ta-Wei vowed to "fight like hell" for the two small islands near the coast of China.[18] By October 17, he had reached Tokyo, where he wrote a dispatch about whether the Soviets had developed their first nuclear-powered submarine. He reported that the US carrier *Kearsarge* had been tracking a Soviet submarine 850 miles off the West Coast of the United States and that VAdm. John Thatch said it "was a long way from known submarine bases" and that he was determined to discover "what it is."[19]

McDaniel's time covering the Pentagon was coming to an end. On a Saturday in March 1961, Elton Fay stopped by the AP offices to pick up his mail. He saw Fred Hoffman and told him McDaniel was "being taken off the Pentagon" beat, and asked whether he was interested in the job. "Elton being a very kind man, I doubt whether he submarined" McDaniel, Hoffman said. "It was clear the bureau chief and the New York bureau didn't know what to do with him."[20]

Instead, Beale shipped McDaniel to Capitol Hill as part of a five-man staff covering the US House of Representatives. It is hard to imagine why the AP assigned McDaniel to a beat he knew so little about. Young and energetic reporters thrive on Capitol Hill, where they develop scores of sources who will help them for decades. But McDaniel was neither young nor energetic. When the AP circulated a photo of its Capitol Hill staff, McDaniel looked completely out of place.

As McDaniel was moving to the Hill, Random House released John Toland's epic book *But Not in Shame*, which cataloged the Allied failures during the first six months after the attack on Pearl Harbor. As part of his research, Toland conducted six interviews in 1959 with McDaniel, both at the Pentagon and at his McLean home. McDaniel spoke for the first time since 1942 about the sinking of the *Prince of Wales* and *Repulse*, covering Generals Percival and Bennett, and helping Doris Lim escape from Singapore.

McDaniel's colleagues were astonished after the book came out. Many had no idea that the frail, white-haired man in the AP office had been at the epicenter of the Pacific war in those tumultuous days, because "he didn't talk about them." Even his nieces rarely heard him talk of the fall of Singapore or the destruction of Manila.[21]

Because he no longer covered the Pentagon, McDaniel had only a peripheral role in the Cuban Missile Crisis in October 1962. He wrote a sidebar to President John F. Kennedy's news conference on September 14, quoting Navy sources as saying, "There had been a step-up in aerial surveillance of Cuba" during the previous three weeks.[22] A couple of weeks later, he wrote that the House of Representatives expected to pass a resolution warning Moscow against any major arms buildup in Cuba.[23] He kept up with the latest developments, telling one relative that "reporters gave a lot more deference to the government" during the early 1960s than they would have a decade later. "We knew a lot of what was going on, but we didn't report it," McDaniel said.[24]

In March 1963, McDaniel's reputation as a defense expert remained such that NBC's *Meet the Press* invited him to take part on a panel that questioned Adm. George Anderson, chief of US naval operations. McDaniel zeroed in on a sharp dispute between Anderson and Secretary of Defense Robert McNamara on the size of the US fleet, after a House committee had approved money to construct only forty-three new ships.

"Obviously, the Navy wanted more than that number, and you were turned down by your civilian superiors," McDaniel noted in questioning Anderson. McDaniel pointed out that McNamara had rejected Anderson's request for more ships, complaining that "he had not received from the Navy an acceptable analysis as he had from the ground and air forces. Why didn't the Navy come up with something that [McNamara] could buy?"

Anderson defended himself: "Of course we have to make a presentation which is fully acceptable to the secretary of defense. This we will try to do and will continue to do so in the future."

McDaniel bored in. He reminded Anderson that McNamara had not approved construction of a new destroyer: "You get a number of escorts and various types of support, auxiliary and what the British call 'odds and sods.' Do you . . . consider that the future of the Navy seems to be going the way of the B-70 . . . if the secretary of defense is questioning the cost and capability of the fleet?"

Anderson replied, "We are doing the best we can with the funds that are available."

The split between McNamara and Anderson was on full display during the interview. President Kennedy sent Anderson a "very short, extremely complimentary" note about his performance. But that did not stop McNamara from firing Anderson a few months later.[25]

Except for the *Meet the Press* appearance, McDaniel seemed to be consigned to the "history beat." In April 1963, when the advanced nuclear submarine *Thresher* sank 200 miles off Cape Cod during a test dive, Fred Hoffman wrote the lead story. It was a major story—all 129 men on board the submarine died in the first nuclear submarine disaster in the nation's history. The *Thresher*'s commanding officer was John W. Harvey, who had served as an officer on the *Nautilus* in 1956, when McDaniel sailed aboard the nuclear submarine. McDaniel contributed a piece describing the sinking off New Hampshire in 1939 of the USS *Squalus*, a diesel-powered submarine. Because the ocean depth was only 240 feet, a Navy diving bell was able to rescue thirty-three of the submarine's fifty-nine crew members.[26] The day after the story appeared, McDaniel wrote a short piece about President Kennedy having to skip the White House annual egg roll celebrating Easter.[27]

When Gen. MacArthur died in April 1964, McDaniel wrote a first-person piece recalling meeting MacArthur in Shanghai in 1930 and recounting in riveting detail the time in 1945 when he pressed the general to allow coverage of the destruction in Manila.[28] One month later, he reminisced over the death of Adm. Nomura. And in August, he authored a piece recounting the 150th anniversary of the British burning of the White House. "A peace cross rises among the beer parlors, used car lots and lumber yards cluttering the place where British redcoats and rockets launched the assault that ended in the burning of Washington," he wrote.[29]

In the turbulent November 1963, a month that would shake America for decades, McDaniel played a marginal role. When South Vietnamese generals overthrew the government of President Ngo Dinh Diem, the AP's Forrest Edwards from Tokyo wrote the lead, while McDaniel had to be content with a sidebar on whether the former South Vietnamese ambassador to the United States would be part of a new government in Saigon.[30]

Three weeks later, President Kennedy was assassinated in Dallas. McDaniel wrote a piece about "the staggering job" US security officials faced trying to protect newly sworn-in president Lyndon Johnson and the scores of heads of state who planned to attend the funeral.[31]

Within a year, McDaniel was off the Capitol Hill beat and relegated to general assignment reporting. In March 1965, he wrote that "foodstuffs held in cooler and frozen storage at the start of this month remained at high levels."[32] He produced stories about new ZIP codes, food stamps for low-income Americans, and a campaign by Washington officials to attract tourists to the nation's capital.

Every now and again, there would be a brief reminder of his extraordinary past. Newspapers such as the *Fort Lauderdale News* and *Baltimore Sun* ran a major piece on the great war correspondents of the twentieth century, featuring Richard Harding Davis of the *New York Herald*, Edward R. Murrow of CBS, Ernie Pyle of Scripps Howard, Leland Stowe of the *Chicago Daily News*, Dean Schedler of the AP, Frank Hewlett of United Press, and, of course, Yates McDaniel and his daring escape from Singapore.[33]

In 1971, McDaniel's old colleague Tillman Durdin obtained a visa from Communist China to report about a British ping-pong team traveling in China. Along with Seymour Topping and James Reston, the three *New York Times* reporters made a series of trips to China from April through August. They reported on a China that few Westerners knew anything about. Only a handful of reporters had been there since the collapse of the Nationalists in 1949.

What the three reporters did not know was that at the same time they were in China, President Nixon and White House national security adviser Henry Kissinger were concluding nearly three years of secret diplomacy with Mao Tse-tung and Premier Chou En-lai, who had been a helpful source for Western reporters in Hankow in 1938. Reston himself was in Canton at the precise time Kissinger was in Peking for his secret talks with Chou from July 9 through 11. The *Times'* columnist learned of Kissinger's trip too late for the huge scoop he might have had because Nixon on

July 16 announced in a nationally televised address from California that he would visit China in 1972.

The AP produced a main story by Frank Cormier that was datelined San Clemente and an analysis by Lewis Gulick, one of AP's State Department reporters. There was a story describing Kissinger's trip to Peking as "one of the most closely guarded secrets in US diplomacy," a sidebar with reactions from members of Congress, and a story crafted by the Tokyo bureau in which Chiang Kai-shek made clear he opposed the trip.[34] John Bausman from Moscow reported that the proposed trip to China "is bound to raise the Kremlin's suspicions that anti-Soviet motives lie behind the new Washington-Peking overtures."[35]

While Durdin was in China and younger AP correspondents were writing the news that astonished the nation, McDaniel—who along with Theodore White and Durdin knew more about China than any other correspondent—was writing about labor negotiations between coal companies and their unions. If McDaniel had anything to do with the AP's coverage of Nixon's announcement, there is no record of it.[36]

On August 21, 1971, McDaniel wrote his final story: the US Commerce Department reported that the gross domestic product of the United States had shown a "modest improvement."

It was time. He retired shortly after, and he and Natalie moved south, first to an island in the Caribbean. A year later, they bought a two-bedroom condo in Florida with a stunning view of the bay in St. Petersburg. They decorated it with Asian art, much of it they bought after they left the Pacific.[37] When Yates's sister Nancy visited, he would talk to her in Chinese as opposed to English. His nieces Betty and Nancy would visit and play bridge with Natalie. They noticed that when neighbors died, Yates often delivered the eulogy.

Betty and Nancy loved being around him. He liked to cook, insisting on fixing everything himself. "He doesn't let anyone in the kitchen," Natalie told Betty. "He doesn't let me in the kitchen." Yates relented once and allowed Betty to help roast the potatoes.[38]

In late February 1983, McDaniel was diagnosed with lung cancer, the result of his three-pack-a-day cigarette habit. Three weeks later, on March 14 at age seventy-six, he died at Bayfront Medical Center in St. Petersburg.

His death received little attention outside his family. McDaniel seemed like just another retiree whose final years passed with no notice. The family held a memorial service at the John S. Rhodes West Chapel in St. Petersburg. The family asked that friends skip the flowers and instead contribute to the American Cancer Society.[39]

The only hint that he was anyone famous came in a short obituary sent out by the AP. But even that obituary was buried on the inside pages of the *New York Times*, the *Daily News*, and the *Philadelphia Inquirer*, although the *Inquirer* ran a photo of Yates when he was much younger. The obituary mentioned he had been the last correspondent to leave Singapore in 1942.

For the most part, though, McDaniel's name faded into obscurity, unlike those of Edward R. Murrow, William Shirer, or Ernie Pyle. His decision not to write his memoirs was certainly one reason. He had a powerful story to tell but chose not to. By contrast, Shirer's 1960 epic, *The Rise and Fall of the Third Reich*, became a major bestseller. In his 1959 autobiography of his years running the Associated Press, Kent Cooper, who had congratulated Yates for his escape from Singapore and his coverage of the invasion of Leyte, never mentioned McDaniel in his chapter about the best correspondents in World War II.

For the next decade, Natalie lived by herself in St. Petersburg. But she remained the same effervescent personality. Unlike Yates, who spoke of his past in Asia only when prompted, Natalie loved to reminisce about their years in China, Singapore, Java, and Australia. Once when her niece Amity and a friend visited, Natalie recounted the story of Yates's escape from Singapore. As she waited in Batavia, Natalie told Amity and her friend that she had received word that Yates was missing and presumed dead. Even though four decades had passed, "the raw emotion was so obvious." Natalie began to cry. It was such a poignant moment that Amity began to cry as well.[40]

When Natalie died in 1992 at age eighty-six, the *Tampa Bay Times* printed a brief death notice that did not even mention Yates. Every now and again, McDaniel's name would appear in a story, particularly in the mid-1990s, when newspapers were writing about the fiftieth anniversary of World War II. In a 1991 story about the visit to Nanking by Japanese prime minister Toshiki Kaifu, a Scripps Howard correspondent wrote that McDaniel and Durdin had covered the 1937 massacre in the city.[41]

Six years later, McDaniel's name resurfaced when Penguin Books published Iris Chang's *The Rape of Nanking*, a meticulous reconstruction of the Japanese massacre. She wrote of Durdin, Steele, and McDaniel providing the most-vivid descriptions of the beginning of the massacre, saying "an adventurous streak ran through all three men . . . McDaniel was perhaps the most daring of the three; before the massacre he had driven through battle lines in the countryside."[42] McDaniel makes an appearance in Robert Weintraub's 2016 book, *No Better Friend*, the gripping story of a soldier and his dog trying to escape the horrors of Singapore. Weintraub even reprinted McDaniel's "Goodbye to Singapore" story that had made McDaniel so famous in the 1940s.

Yet, McDaniel always seemed more a man of Asia than the United States, and his years covering the Japanese attacks in Shanghai, Tientsin, Nanking, and Hankow. And those in China knew that as well. On the walls of the Nanking Massacre Memorial Hall, which honors the memory of the 300,000 Chinese people murdered by the Japanese, the Chinese reproduced his dramatic 1937 diary of his final days in Nanking. Even as right-wing Japanese scholars and officials have expressed doubts about the massacre, McDaniel's story proves them wrong, particularly the haunting final line—"My last remembrance of Nanking: Dead Chinese, dead Chinese, dead Chinese."

Others in China remembered as well. An eighty-four-year-old Chinese man who knew Yates when both were boys seven decades earlier in Soochow wrote Natalie when he heard of Yates's death:

It's a great shock to me when I received the news that Mr. C. Yates McDaniel, my dear old boyhood friend, had passed away. What a pity and how sad. Words are inadequate to express my deepest feelings under such an affliction. For decades and decades, I had known him as a correspondent of great renown, a gentleman of noble character, a scholar of great attainment and virtue, and a man of integrity. His sudden departure will surely give me a bitter grief in the rest of my remaining life.

# THE SEARCH FOR DORIS LIM

A tantalizing mystery remains about one chapter in Yates McDaniel's life: Whatever happened to Doris Lim, the "plucky girl" who along with McDaniel survived the sinking of the *Kung Wo*, endured a perilous trip across Sumatra, and reached Batavia in Java in February of 1942? Within days, McDaniel booked her on a passenger ship bound for Ceylon. That was the last time McDaniel ever saw her, and the last time we can be certain that she was alive.

That March, when Yates and Natalie were living in the Australia Hotel in Melbourne, there was a knock at their door. It was Newsreel Wong, who had flown from Ceylon to find Doris, Wong's onetime assistant at Hearst/MGM Metrotone News. McDaniel and Wong checked shipping records to determine whether Doris's ship had arrived in Ceylon. But they discovered no trace of her or the ship.[1]

For years, Doris Lim's fate has been shrouded in mystery. "I had from time to time wondered what happened to the pretty little Chinese girl, who captivated all of us by her combination of *sangfroid* and high spirits in unpromising situations," Geoffrey Brooke, one of the *Kung Wo*'s survivors, wrote years later.[2]

What little is known about her comes from snippets written by friends and acquaintances. Paul Dietz, a representative for B. F. Goodrich in China who knew Doris before the war, wrote in a 1988 private memoir that Doris grew up in Hong Kong, attended convent schools, and learned to speak English without any Asian accent. She and her mother were comfortable fits in British and American society. When Dietz and his wife, Hannalene, first met Doris in 1940, he thought she was seventeen years old. She worked for a British trading firm in Shanghai, Dietz wrote, adding that "no one appeared to know about the nature of her employment." Paul and Hannalene "observed Doris in the company of our American and Chinese friends, among whom she moved with easy grace and apparent frankness."

Hannalene met Doris again a year later, in the fall of 1941 in Manila, and brought her as a guest to an elegant wedding dinner for a young British couple. The men looked resplendent in white dinner jackets, while Doris and the women wore glamorous evening gowns. Not long after, Doris sailed to Singapore, where in February 1942 she once again caught up with Newsreel Wong and first met McDaniel. Within a couple of days, Singapore was evacuated, and Doris and McDaniel escaped to Java.[3]

In trying to unravel the mystery of Doris's disappearance we are left with four stories—one that McDaniel told historian John Toland, a second by Scottish corporal Walter Gibson, a third by Chinese nurse Janet Lim, and a fourth by two Malayan sailors.

Two versions revolve around the small Dutch passenger ship *Rooseboom*, which left Batavia on February 22, 1942, stopped in Padang to pick up more passengers, and was torpedoed and sunk in the Indian Ocean on February 28 by the Japanese submarine *I-59*.

In his 1959 interviews with Toland, McDaniel said that two days after he and Doris arrived in Batavia following their close encounter with death, he put her aboard a British passenger ship bound for Ceylon. McDaniel told Toland the ship was fast and "very modern" and weighed about 8,000 to 10,000 tons. To get Doris aboard, McDaniel signed a document affirming that Doris was a British subject. According to Toland's notes, McDaniel told him the ship "took off. Ship torpedoed. No survivors." Unfortunately, Toland's notes did not identify the ship by name.

The second version emerged in 1949 and 1950, when *Reader's Digest* and newspapers in the United States, Great Britain, Canada, and Australia published a series of articles written by Gibson, a corporal in the Argyll and Sutherland Highlanders who escaped from Malaya before its fall to the Japanese. Gibson claimed that he and Doris survived in a lifeboat after the Japanese torpedoed the *Rooseboom*, which was crammed with British and Dutch evacuees. They were among roughly 135 survivors who swarmed about the only undamaged lifeboat, according to Gibson. Because they could not all fit in the boat, Gibson claimed some hung by ropes over the side. One by one, most died from the intense sun, excessive heat, exhaustion, lack of water, and drinking seawater, and at least one instance of cannibalism. After twenty-six days in the boat, Gibson wrote that he, Doris, and three sailors from Java reached an island off Sumatra. Gibson and Doris were handed over to the Japanese, questioned, and placed in separate cells in Padang. Gibson said he never saw her again.[4]

In 1952, Gibson expanded the *Reader's Digest* story into a book, *The Boat*, published by W. H. Allen & Company Limited. The *Philadelphia Inquirer, Minneapolis Star-Tribune*, and other newspapers printed excerpts in 1953.

It is a spellbinding story, one that weaves tragedy and courage into a struggle for survival. But Gibson's tale is littered with enough discrepancies—and facts that changed between the newspaper stories and the book—to make it seem improbable.

The third version also involves the *Rooseboom*. Two Malay stokers said that shortly before midnight on February 28, the *Rooseboom* was rocked by a huge explosion. The two sailors jumped into the ocean. They saw others in the water who had escaped the rapidly sinking ship, but the next morning the sea was empty. They constructed a makeshift raft and survived because of the "continual showers" of heavy rain, allowing them to drink water by cupping their hands. The Dutch freighter *Palopo* rescued the two stokers and took them to Ceylon, where they told their story to a British diplomat. The stokers did not mention Doris Lim being aboard the *Rooseboom*, and they did not see a lifeboat or any other survivors. Their version is backed up by the log kept by the captain of the *Palopo*, which rescued them:

Saw floating in the afternoon a few life jackets and wreckage. At 15:45 we sighted a large floating object and steam to it. It appeared to be a small raft composed of 2 air tanks of a lifeboat and a few deck parts tied together with strips of sarong. On it were found 2 natives in exhausted condition. Searched the surroundings for further survivors, but nothing else in sight. The persons saved appeared to be Firemen Jattemo and Trimmer Dai of the S.S. *Rooseboom*. They stated that the S.S. *Rooseboom* sailed from Padang about the 26th of February with about 200 passengers on board. Amongst them were 3 women and children who had embarked already at [Batavia]. The starboard lifeboats were immediately destroyed. Of the port boats, one became out of order whereas the second capsized through overloading. They [Jattemo and Dai] kept themselves floating till daylight, and they composed the raft mentioned above. They have not seen any other survivors.[5]

This version, documented by the *Palopo*'s captain and the British diplomat, undermines Gibson's story. The two sailors said they did not see any other survivors. They survived by drinking water from the heavy rains, while Gibson reported that it rained only "three times," and those on board the lifeboat survived on the limited rain, six jars of fresh water, and a case of bully beef. The two seamen reported all the lifeboats were destroyed; Gibson claimed one floated clear of the ship.[6]

His story about Doris Lim also changed in significant ways from the time he first told a British intelligence officer in London about the *Rooseboom* in 1946 to the publication of his book in 1952. In 1946, Gibson described Doris as a "Chinese girl." In the *Reader's Digest* piece, Gibson wrote that Lim "had been working with British intelligence."[7] In the 1950 newspaper articles, Gibson wrote that Doris "had worked for our intelligence in northern China."[8] In the 1952 book, Gibson claimed that "as far back as 1933, in the early days of Japanese aggression in China, she had been engaged in work for Chinese and British intelligence."[9] But if she were no more than twenty, as McDaniel thought when he met her in 1942, she would have started her espionage career in 1933 at the absurd age of eleven. It is telling that in his book *Let's Get Cracking*, Athole Stewart, who escaped with McDaniel and Doris on the *Kung Wo*, never suggested Doris was a British agent, writing that "in Singapore we had known Doris as an assistant to Newsreel Wong."

In addition, Gibson's description of Doris was contradicted by others who knew her. Gibson said Doris spoke English with an American accent, which he claimed was a "relic of the American convent in Shanghai whose sisters had brought her up" because her parents were dead.[10] By contrast, Dietz wrote that she had been educated by English nuns in Hong Kong, and that "her English was almost flawless with no hint of an Asian accent."[11] Dietz said she was raised in Hong Kong by her mother. McDaniel told John Toland that he heard that Doris was born in Hong Kong. Stewart wrote that Doris "had come to Singapore when the Japanese had invaded Shanghai. Her parents, I think she said, were prisoners in Hong Kong. She had no intention of sharing their fate nor the fate of unprotected Asiatic women at the hands of the Japanese."[12]

Gibson wrote that after he and Doris reached the safety of an island off Sumatra, the natives fed them and for some curious reason handed him a mirror. He wrote that when he looked in the mirror, he saw a "wild, black, high cheek-boned face, like the face of an Indian *fakir*, and that his body was "completely without flesh, the skin stretched black and burned over the ribs."[13] Yet, a British officer who saw Gibson not long after at a Japanese prison camp said he appeared "no more emaciated than the other prisoners."[14]

In his 1946 statement, Gibson declared that he and Doris were handed over to the Japanese.[15] In his 1950 articles, Gibson wrote that after the Japanese captured him and Doris, they were taken to Padang, questioned by Japanese officials, and placed in separate cells, and that he never saw her again.[16] In the book, Gibson said that on the eve of his transfer to the prisoner-of-war camp in Padang, a Japanese officer told him Doris had been shot as a spy.[17]

Gibson's own Argyll colleagues had doubts about many stories he told. During his interview in 1946, Gibson called himself a lieutenant, although the War Office official wrote down in parenthesis that Gibson was a corporal. Argyll sergeant Rab Kerr, who was in the same Japanese prison camp with Gibson, later said this:

Arriving in the afternoon as a lieutenant, by evening he was a sergeant, and the next day he was down to corporal, which was his true rank. Needless to say the people in the camp who didn't know him were absolutely astounded that anyone could be so brazen as to even try such a trick, but nothing was beyond the possibilities where [Gibson] was concerned. To relate all the stories about him would take weeks of writing and even then, something would be missed out.[18]

Gibson's strongest defense is that he knew of Doris Lim by name and that the *Rooseboom* actually was torpedoed on February 28. The escape by McDaniel and Doris was widely reported in the United States, Canada, and Australia in 1942, so it is possible Gibson was familiar with her name. But there is no explanation of how he would have learned about the details and the date of the sinking of the *Rooseboom*.

Then in 1958, a fourth version of Doris Lim's fate emerged in *Sold for Silver*, an autobiography written by Chinese nurse Janet Lim. Janet was born in Hong Kong in 1923 with the name Chiu Mei and was not related to Doris. As a young girl of eight in China, Janet was sold for $250 to a Chinese landowner in Singapore as a *mui tsai*, which in Cantonese literally means "younger sister." She worked as a domestic servant until British authorities removed her from the home and sent her to a missionary school. When she was baptized in 1935, she was given the name "Janet" and became a nurse in Singapore. In one of those coincidences of history, Janet left Singapore on the small steamer *Kuala* the same day that Doris Lim left on the *Kung Wo*. Both ships were sunk by the Japanese within sight of each other, a fact that Janet duly noted in her book. Janet reached Padang in March 1942, although she and Doris had not yet met. In early 1943—a full year after the *Kung Wo* and *Rooseboom* sank—Janet wrote that Doris Lim showed up in the Sumatran village of Indareong.

Janet first spoke of Doris when she was interviewed after the war on February 22, 1946, by a British official in Singapore. The single-page document refers to part of the story Gibson told British intelligence in London one month earlier. According to the document:

Gibson and [Doris] Lim then returned to Padang[,] where they gave themselves up to the Japs. Gibson was interned, but Miss Lim's story was dis-believed and she was charged with being an American spy. After numerous rigorous interrogations, she was allowed to go free and worked in the Local Hospital. It was here where she met the informant, Janet Lim, who was also working there. On March 7, 1945, Doris Lim was murdered by a Chinese boy Chong Teck Lim whose offer of love she had refused.[19]

It appears the officer who drafted the memo combined Gibson's story with Janet's claim she met Doris at a hospital in Sumatra. In the book, Janet never wrote of either Gibson or the *Rooseboom*. She did not say Doris was a spy, although Janet wrote that Doris "lived in terror of being taken for a spy, because she had seen what happened to spies in China."

In the book, Janet wrote that Doris "was a survivor of a shipwreck during the evacuation of Singapore." It is inconceivable that Janet would not have written about Doris and Gibson surviving the *Rooseboom*'s sinking and her journey in a lifeboat. Nor did Janet even mention the *Kung Wo* and Doris's subsequent escape with McDaniel to Batavia. In the book, Janet wrote that Doris married a Chinese man who murdered her in late 1944 or early 1945 after a "violent quarrel." Janet did not provide a name for the husband.[20]

In the book, she included a photo of Doris taken in 1944, but it is difficult to tell for certain if the woman in the photo is Doris. Janet failed to mention obvious and dramatic details about Doris, such as surviving the *Kung Wo*. The fact that the *Kuala* and *Kung Wo* sank near each other would have been a ready topic of conversation for the two women. But there was not a word in Janet Lim's book about this coincidence.

The key may be in the book's acknowledgments, where Janet wrote this curious paragraph:

The names of some of the people mentioned in this book are fictitious, and if there should be any resemblance to persons, living or dead, bearing these names, this would be purely coincidental. But the story is true and alterations have only been made where it is desirable to hide the identity of some of the people involved.

Is that a hint that the Doris Lim of her book was a fictional character? There is no way to know for certain. Janet Lim was a meticulous observer, but the book's acknowledgments raise doubts about whether she was writing about the Doris Lim that McDaniel knew.

So, what are the possible explanations for Doris's disappearance? The *Rooseboom* left Batavia's harbor of Tanjong Priok on February 22, roughly close to the time that McDaniel said Doris's ship sailed. But McDaniel's description of the ship that Doris boarded does not in any way match the *Rooseboom*. The *Rooseboom* was Dutch, not British. She was neither modern nor fast. She was built in 1926, was a plodding 1,000-tonner, and had a top speed of 10 knots.

There is no reason to doubt McDaniel's version. He was a trained observer and would have known the difference between a 10,000-ton modern British passenger ship and the much-smaller Dutch steamer *Rooseboom*.

McDaniel's version was confirmed by Athole Stewart, who wrote, "When at last we reached Batavia, Doris elected to go to India. Yates McDaniel made certain that everything was in order for her. He booked her passage, securing priority in the next ship to India," before adding the curious phrase that McDaniel "was not in Batavia when she was expected to sail." Because McDaniel left Batavia on either February 24 or 25, that would suggest that Doris Lim did not sail on the *Rooseboom*, which departed on February 22.[21]

Gibson's story could be true, although a preponderance of evidence suggests it was not. There is every reason to believe that he was in Padang, near the harbor of Emmahaven, when the *Rooseboom* departed, but no proof he ever actually boarded the ship.

A more likely explanation? Gibson never boarded the *Rooseboom*. There were large crowds of people at Padang's port of Emmahaven trying to push their way aboard the ship, and Gibson would have known the names of many of those who sailed. If he did not board the ship, he would have been taken prisoner by the Japanese in Padang. Because he did not know about the two surviving Malay sailors, he could have assumed that everyone who boarded the *Rooseboom* died, and nobody could contradict his story. The fact that he inflated his own rank demonstrates that he was more than willing to embellish a story.

As for Doris Lim? She could have been aboard the *Rooseboom* and died when the ship was torpedoed. She could have boarded one of a number of ships that left Batavia in late February, and died when they were sunk by the Japanese. Or she could have reached Sumatra a year later, where Janet Lim claimed she met her. On the basis of the available information, the unfortunate answer is that nobody knows for sure what ultimately happened to the "plucky girl" who escaped close calls with death along with Yates McDaniel.

"Brave Doris," Stewart wrote. "When we said good-bye to her in Batavia, we all believed that henceforward her way was the safe one; that ours was the dangerous venture. Her future ought to have been one of ever-lasting happiness in that she made men marvel at the courage and bravery of women."[22]

# ACKNOWLEDGMENTS

This book took more than three years to research and write, but the idea has been in my mind for decades since first reading John Toland's *But Not in Shame*, the chronicle of the first six months of the Pacific War after the Japanese attack on Pearl Harbor. That is when I first read about Yates McDaniel. I always wanted to know more about this largely forgotten reporter. How does someone so critical to our understanding of the events of the Pacific war—then and now—escape notoriety so completely?

One reason was that McDaniel did not write his own memoirs. When relatives suggested his life would make an exciting book, he dismissed the idea. Unlike his contemporaries, such as Tillman Durdin, Randall Gould, Arch Steele, and Jack Belden, McDaniel did not seem to save documents about his life. If his personal papers exist, they have defied every effort to locate them.

Fortunately, there is a rich trove of documents that allowed me to weave together a portrait of the lives of Yates and Natalie. In particular, this book could not have been written without the assistance of the Associated Press archives in New York. I am indebted to the help from Kathleen Carroll, former executive editor and senior vice president of the AP, and the AP archivists Francesca Pitaro and Valerie Komor, who helped dig out memos and other documents about McDaniel.

Because McDaniel often wrote first-person accounts, especially from Nanking and Singapore, his own published articles provide a deep insight into the way he approached journalism. The stories McDaniel wrote for the Associated Press from 1935 to 1971 are available through Newspapers.com. The files of the *New York Times* contain the articles he wrote for that newspaper. And thanks to the efforts of Yuhan Xu, who has worked for National Public Radio in Shanghai, I obtained copies of some of the stories McDaniel wrote for the *Shanghai Evening Post and Mercury*. The National Library of Australia provides access to newspaper articles from Australian newspapers, helping me piece together his years as the AP bureau chief in Australia. The National Library Board of Singapore has files of the *Straits Times*, *Malaya Tribune*, and other Singapore newspapers to help describe the Japanese invasion of Malaya.

The Library of Congress in Washington, as always, offered a wealth of information, including Toland's handwritten notes of his six interviews in 1959 with McDaniel, only a fraction of which Toland used in *But Not in Shame*. Toland's interviews appear to be the only time McDaniel spoke in detail about his time in Singapore, Sumatra, and Java. By comparing Toland's notes with the first-person stories McDaniel wrote in 1942, I was able to put together an hour-by-hour account of McDaniel's thrilling escape from Singapore.

I was fortunate that McDaniel's relatives kept records of this remarkable reporter. Nancy Eills, Natalie's niece, gave me access to letters that Yates wrote to Natalie while he was in Bangkok, Nanking, Tientsin, New Guinea, and the Philippines. She also made available Natalie's unpublished magazine story about their lives during the Japanese invasion of China. I am in debt to Andrew Eills of New Hampshire, who made it possible for me to contact Nancy Eills and visit her in New York City.

McDaniel's nieces, Betty Barber of Portland, Oregon, and Nancy Beecher of Wisconsin, offered recollections of their uncle. The Foreign Mission Board of Richmond kindly provided hundreds of letters written by Yates's father, Charles McDaniel, and his mother, Nannie. Those letters feature rich details about the lives of their children growing up in Soochow.

Patricia Startzman of College Station, Texas, was an immeasurable help in tracking down the details of Doris Lim's tragic life. She provided me with her father's three-page remembrances of Doris and included the photo taken of Doris during an elegant wedding party in Manila.

Mary Gladstone and Jonathan Moffatt, both in Scotland, provided documents dealing with Walter Gibson and his entertaining tale about the sinking of the *Rooseboom*. Gladstone read the chapter on the search for Doris Lim and offered excellent suggestions.

The University of Richmond sent me the essay McDaniel wrote as an undergraduate, while the University of North Carolina provided McDaniel's graduate thesis.

Michael Pether of New Zealand is the gold standard for trying to track down the movement of ships fleeing Singapore, Sumatra, and Java in 1942. Ahyaan Raghuvanshi obtained portions of Carl Mydans's journal at Yale. Researcher Gregory T. Smith dug out records of Lewis Sebring of the *New York Herald Tribune* held at the University of Wisconsin.

I have been fortunate to have superb journalists and professors read through parts or all of the manuscript to check for accuracy. They begin with my wife, Saundra Torry, a retired editorial writer at *USA Today* and former reporter for the *Washington Post*. She read through two drafts of the manuscript and dramatically improved the content. Thuan Elston of *USA Today*—who could be the world's best copy editor—proofread the final version and caught numerous typos and fact errors. Tom Bendycki, a superb retired copy editor at the *Columbus Dispatch*, a *Jeopardy!* champion, and a friend of mine since undergraduate school at Ohio State University, went through the manuscript and caught errors.

Rick Dunham, codirector of the Global Business Journalism Program at Tsinghua University in Beijing, and Marilyn Geewax, a former visiting professor at Tsinghua University and onetime reporter for Cox News in Washington, kindly read through portions of the manuscript dealing with McDaniel's years in China.

Because nobody would ever accuse me of being a military expert, retired Army colonel Pete Mansoor, the Gen. Raymond E. Mason Jr. Chair in Military History at my alma mater, Ohio State University, read through the chapters on the Allied campaigns in New Guinea and the Philippines and offered important suggestions. Stephen MacKinnon, a professor of history at Arizona State University and one of the great China experts, read through the chapter on Hankow, while Jim Ross, a professor of journalism at Northeastern University in Boston, read the Nanking chapter.

Tom Diemer, a former Washington reporter for the *Cleveland Plain Dealer*, read through the manuscript and offered excellent suggestions. Carl Leubsdorf, who worked at the Associated Press in Washington during McDaniel's final years at the bureau, read through much of the manuscript and provided invaluable insights. George Hager, a retired editorial writer at *USA Today*, and Chuck Raasch, a former reporter for Gannett News Service, read portions of the manuscript. George Condon, a reporter at the *National Journal* in Washington, provided major help on sections of the manuscript.

# ENDNOTES

**Chapter 1**

1. Yates McDaniel's autobiography sketch for the Associated Press. See also *Wilkes-Barre Semi-Weekly Record*, June 22, 1909.

2. Charles McDaniel's letter, June 19, 1909, document 9, p. 5.

3. Yates's interview with author John Toland, 1959.

4. Charles McDaniel's letter, August 7, 1923, document 3, p. 49.

5. Yates's interview with Toland.

6. Letter from Yates's boyhood friend Big Voong to McDaniel's niece Betty Barber, 1983.

7. Interview with Yates's niece, Nancy Beecher.

8. Charles McDaniel's personnel record, Foreign Mission Board, document 1, p. 4.

9. Rana Mitter, *Forgotten Ally: China's World War II, 1937–1945* (Boston: Houghton Mifflin Harcourt, 2013), 51–52.

10. Charles McDaniel's letter, April 21, 1922, document 14, pp. 26–28.

11. Mitter, *Forgotten Ally*, 52.

12. Yates's letter to his wife, Natalie, November 25, 1944.

13. Nannie McDaniel's diary, August 28, 1907, and August 28, 1908, in *Escanaba Daily Press*, July 26, 1947.

14. Unpublished biography of Helen McDaniel Craven, written by her grandson Eric Barber, courtesy of Betty Barber.

15. Carl Crow, *The Travelers' Handbook for China (including Hong-Kong)*, 4th ed. (New York: Dodd, Mead, 1925), 112–13.

16. Charles McDaniel's letter, September 28, 1912, document 10, p. 33.

17. Nannie McDaniel's letter, September 26, 1912, document 10, pp. 31–32.

18. Yates's letter to Natalie, December 9, 1944.

19. Charles McDaniel's letter, September 8, 1921, document 13, p. 39.

20. Charles McDaniel's letter, September 16, 1921, document 13, p. 33.

21. *North China Herald* and *Supreme Court & Consular Gazette*, August 18, 1923.

22. *Richmond Times-Dispatch*, November 6, 1924.

23. *Richmond Times-Dispatch*, January 17, 1925, and June 5, 1926.

24. AP dispatch, *St. Louis Post-Dispatch*, February 22, 1942.

25. Yates's autobiography sketch for the AP.

26. Yates's essay published in *Richmond College Messenger*, June 1925.

27. Unpublished biography of Helen McDaniel Craven; and Athole Stewart, *Let's Get Cracking: The Malayan Campaign* (Sydney, Australia: Frank Johnson, 1943), 149.

28. Charles McDaniel's letter, April 18, 1927, document 20, pp. 9–10.

29. Yates's autobiography for the AP. See also the *Tampa Times* for a brief profile of McDaniel on December 12, 1937.

30. *Daily Tar Heel*, December 8, 1928.

31. Editorial, *Des Moines Register*, May 16, 1945.

32. Interview with Amity Eills in 2020; and article by Professor John Eills, March 1942.

33. Yates's graduate thesis, University of North Carolina, 5.

34. Ibid., 49.

35. *Richmond Times-Dispatch*, August 14, 1929, gives the travel plans of Yates, Charles, and Nannie.

**Chapter 2**

1. Charles McDaniel's letter, November 27, 1929, document 1, p. 33.

2. Yates's interview with Toland.

3. Hannah Pakula, *The Last Empress: Madame Chiang Kai-Shek and the Birth of Modern China* (New York: Simon & Schuster Paperbacks, 2009), 222; and Lloyd E. Eastman, *The Nationalist Era in China, 1927–1949* (Cambridge, UK: Cambridge University Press, 1991), 36.

4. Eastman, *Nationalist Era*, 36.

5. Ibid., 40.

6. Hans van de Ven, *China at War: Triumph and Tragedy in the Emergence of the New China* (Cambridge, MA: Harvard University Press, 2018), 38.

7. Paul French, *Carl Crow—a Tough Old China Hand: The Life, Times, and Adventures of an American in Shanghai* (Hong Kong: Hong Kong University Press, 2006), 18.

8. Stephen R. MacKinnon and Oris Friesen, *China Reporting: An Oral History of American Journalism in the 1930s and 1940s* (Berkeley: University of California Press, 1987), 32–34.

9. Diary of Gen. Joseph Stilwell, May 17, 1923.

10. Courtesy of Taras Grescoe, author of *Shanghai Grand*.

11. John A. Glusman, *Conduct under Fire: Four American Doctors and Their Fight for Life as Prisoners of the Japanese, 1941–1945* (New York: Penguin Books, 2006), 9.

12. Bill Dunn, *Pacific Microphone* (College Station: Texas A&M University Press, 1988), 43.

13. *China Press* newspaper, October 7, 1931.

14. Hallett Abend, *My Life in China: 1926 to 1941* (New York: Harcourt, Brace, 1943), 152.

15. "Memo of conversation," Nelson Johnson, June 10, 1932.

16. Cable from Edwin Cunningham, US consul general in Shanghai, to Secretary of State Henry Stimson, January 21, 1932.

17. Abend, *My Life in China*, 187–89; Earl Albert Selle, *Donald of China* (New York: Harper, 1948), 275; and cable from Edwin Cunningham, the US consul general in Shanghai to Secretary of State Henry Stimson, January 21, 1932.

18. Edgar Snow, *Far Eastern Front* (New York: H. Smith & R. Haas, 1933), 212. See also "A Month of Reign of Terror," published by the *China Weekly Herald*, which included articles reproduced from the *Shanghai Evening Post* and *North China Daily News*.

19. United Press dispatch, the *Missoulian of Montana*, February 2, 1932.

20. AP dispatch, *Boston Globe*, February 22, 1932.

21. *Philadelphia Inquirer*, February 24, 1932.

22. AP dispatch, *Boston Globe*, February 23, 1932.

23. *Paducah Sun-Democrat*, February 23, 1932.

24. Transcript of telephone call between Secretary Stimson and British foreign secretary John Simon, February 2, 1932.

25. Yates's interview with John Toland. See also *Shanghai Evening Post*, April 29, 1932, University of Southern California digital library.

26. AP dispatch, *Baltimore Sun*, April 30, 1942.

27. Lytton Report, 69 and 125.

28. *Shanghai Evening Post*, May 11, 1933.

29. MacKinnon and Friesen, *China Reporting*, 31.

30. Yates's interview with Toland.

31. *New York Times*, November 19, 1937.

32. Wen-hsin Yeh, *Becoming Chinese: Passages to Modernity and Beyond* (Berkeley: University of California Press, 2000), 140.

33. *New York Times*, July 15, 1935.

34. *Shanghai Evening Post*, October 29, 1933.

35. *Shanghai Evening Post*, November 6, 1933.

36. *Shanghai Evening Post*, November 24, 1933.

37. Charles described his eye difficulties in three letters to the Foreign Mission Board in August and September 1933, document 22, pp. 15–19.

38. Charles McDaniel letter, April 29, 1934, document 23, p. 12.

39. Nannie McDaniel letters, August 8, 1936, and November 7, 1936; and a letter dictated by Charles to Nannie, December 11, 1936, document 24, pp. 20, 36, and 45.

40. Natalie's personality was described in interviews with Natalie's niece, Nancy Eills, Nancy's daughter Amity, and Nancy Beecher. See also AP dispatch, *St. Louis Post-Dispatch*, February 2, 1942, and *Detroit Free Press*, August 19, 1946.

41. *San Francisco Call*, June 29, 1913.

42. *Detroit Free Press*, May 13, 1913.

43. *Oakland Tribune*, May 13, 1913.

44. *Boston Globe*, October 14, 1913.

45. *Fitchburg Sentinel*, June 20, 1917.

46. John Eills news story, March 1942.

47. Interview with Betty Barber.

48. *Japan Advertiser* (Tokyo), April 8, 1934.

## Chapter 3

1. AP dispatch, February 22, 1942.

2. Natalie McDaniel's unpublished magazine story.

3. AP dispatch, *Reno Gazette*, July 12, 1945.

4. United Press dispatch, June 14, 1934.

5. *Asia* magazine, September 1935.

6. *New York Times*, October 6, 1935.

7. AP dispatch, December 23, 1934; and *New York Times*, December 23, 1934.

8. *New York Times*, March 31, 1935.

9. *New York Times*, April 28, 1935.

10. Natalie's magazine story.

11. Cables from US consul general Willys Peck in Nanking to Secretary of State Cordell Hull, October 25 and October 29, 1935.

12. Cable from Nanking Embassy Second Secretary George Atcheson to Hull, November 1, 1935; AP dispatch, *Johnson City Press*, November 1, 1935; and AP dispatch *Tampa Bay Times*, November 2, 1935.

13. AP dispatch, November 1, 1935. The story was published in the *New York Times*, November 1, 1935.

14. AP dispatch, *Richmond Times Dispatch*, December 7, 1935.

15. Cables from Nelson Johnson in Nanking to Hull, December 9 and 12; and cable from Monnett Bain Davis, US consul general in Shanghai, to Hull on December 24, 1935.

16. Cable from Peck to Hull, January 17, 1936. Peck wrote that the press was under "strict orders" not to publish Chiang's comments.

17. AP dispatch, *Rapid City Journal*, January 27, 1936.

18. AP dispatch, *Valley Morning Star*, July 2, 1936.

19. Cable from Peck to Hull, January 17, 1936.

20. Cable from Peck to Hull, February 6, 1936; and cable from Johnson to Hull, March 7, 1936.

21. Cable from Peck to Hull, April 6, 1936.

22. AP dispatch, *Florence Morning News*, March 30, 1936.

23. AP dispatch, *Valley Morning Star*, October 9, 1936.

24. Abend, *My Life in China*, 224.

25. Theodore White, *In Search of History: A Personal Adventure* (New York: Harper & Row, 1978), 134.

26. Alfred Emile Cornebise, *Soldier Extraordinaire: The Life and Career of Brigadier General Frank "Pinkie" Dorn* (Fort Leavenworth, KS: Combat Studies Institute Press, 2019), 62.

27. Abend, *My Life in China*, 227 and 235; and Craig Collie, *The Reporter and the Warlords: An Australian at Large in China's Republican Revolution* (St. Leonards, Australia: Allen & Unwin, 2014), 232.

28. AP dispatch, *Baltimore Sun*, December 26, 1936.

29. AP dispatch, *Piqua Daily*, December 26, 1936.

30. Natalie's unpublished magazine story.

31. The party is described in an AP dispatch published by the *New York Daily News*, March 12, 1937, and the *China Herald* on March 17, 1937.

32. AP dispatch, *McComb Enterprise-Journal*, May 26, 1937.

33. Nannie McDaniel's letter, August 8, 1936, document 24, p. 20.

34. Charles McDaniel's letter, December 11, 1936, document 24, p. 44.

35. Charles McDaniel's letter, December 17, 1936, document 25, p. 10.

36. Charles McDaniel's letter, July 27, 1937, document 25, p. 24.

37. Natalie's unpublished magazine story, p. 8.

38. Barbara Tuchman, *Stilwell and the American Experience in China, 1911–45* (New York: Macmillan, 1970), 164.

39. Abend, *My Life in China*, 173.

40. Selle, *Donald of China*, 338.

41. *Asia* magazine, October 1935.

42. Abend, *My Life in China*, 243.

43. Yates's letter to Natalie, July 22, 1937.

44. Jo Barnes St. John, *China Times Guide to Tientsin and Neighbourhood* (Tientsin, China: China Times, 1908), 7 and 50.

45. Ibid., 9 and 14.

46. Yates's letter to Natalie, July 22, 1937.

47. AP stories published by the *Washington Court House Herald* on July 31, 1937, the *Valley Morning Star* on August 1, 1937, and *Jackson Sun* on August 25, 1937.

48. Johnson cable to State Department, July 16, 1937.

49. Tientsin general consul John Caldwell, cable to Hull, July 18, 1937; and Johnson cable to Hull, July 19, 1937.

50. Trove, *Philippines Tribune*, August 5, 1937.

51. AP dispatch, *Baltimore Sun*, August 28, 1937.

52. AP dispatch, *Corvallis Gazette*, July 21, 1937.

53. United Press dispatch, *Pittsburgh Press*, July 28, 1937.

54. AP dispatches *Moberly Monitor*, September 29, 1937; and *Staunton News Leader*, July 30, 1937; and Caldwell cable to Hull, July 29, 1937.

55. Caldwell cable to Hull, July 31, 1937; and AP dispatch, *Escanaba Daily Press*, July 30, 1937.

56. AP dispatch, *Hartford Daily Courant*, August 20, 1937.

57. AP dispatches, *Oshkosh Northwestern* on August 9, 1937; and *Oakland Tribune*, August 10, 1937.

58. AP dispatch, August 30, 1937.

59. Natalie's magazine story.

60. AP dispatch, *Owensboro Messenger*, August 24, 1937.

61. AP dispatch, Trove, *Philippines Tribune*, August 30, 1937.

62. Natalie's magazine story.

**Chapter 4**

1. In an August 15, 1937, letter, Robert O. Wilson, a surgeon at the University of Nanking Hospital, wrote that the first Japanese air raid was on that very day, and the target was the city's commercial airport. Courtesy of the Nanking Massacre Archival Project, Yale University. See also

cable from Nelson Johnson to Secretary Hull on August 15, 1937, in which he says the bombing took place at two in the afternoon.

2. AP dispatch, *Gettysburg Times*, September 21, 1937.

3. Natalie McDaniel's unpublished magazine story, p. 15

4. Russell D. Buhite, *Nelson T. Johnson and American Policy toward China* (East Lansing: Michigan State University Press, 1969), 132.

5. AP dispatch, *Ironwood Daily Globe*, September 21, 1937; and Dr. Wilson's letter of September 24, 1937. Clark Lee's criticism of Johnson was in a letter he wrote to the editor of the *Honolulu Star-Bulletin*, September 24, 1937.

6. Buhite, *Nelson T. Johnson and American Policy*, 77.

7. Johnson cable to Secretary Hull, September 22, 1937, 6:00 p.m.

8. AP dispatch, *Ironwood Daily Globe*, September 21, 1937.

9. AP dispatch, *Iola Register*, September 22, 1937.

10. Cable from Hull to Johnson, September 21, 1937.

11. AP dispatch, *Ironwood Daily Globe*, September 25, 1937; and letters from Dr. Wilson, September 25 and 26, 1937. The Nanking radio broadcast is from a letter written by Charles McDaniel, October 12, 1937, document 25, p. 33.

12. Nannie McDaniel's letter, September 5, 1937, document 25, p. 49.

13. Charles McDaniel's letter, October 17, 1937, document 25, p. 36.

14. Charles McDaniel's letter, October 12, 1937, document 25, p. 32.

15. Ibid.

16. Ibid.

17. Charles McDaniel's letter, October 17, 1937, document 25, p. 36.

18. Ibid.

19. Ibid.

20. Ibid.

21. Ibid.

22. Johnson's cables to State Department, November 12 and 16, 1937.

23. Cable from Secretary Hull to Baptist Mission Board, December 2, 1937, included in Charles McDaniel's document file 26, p. 2.

24. Natalie's unpublished magazine article, pp. 13 and 19.

25. *Detroit Free Press*, August 19, 1946. On November 10, 1937, Adm. Yarnell cabled Washington that 2,083 Americans were evacuated to Shanghai on November 6, although it is unclear whether they all came from Nanking.

26. Natalie's unpublished article, pp. 12–14.

27. *New York Times*, November 19, 1937.

28. Ibid.

29. AP dispatch, *St. Louis Post-Dispatch*, November 16, 1937. Although the story does not have McDaniel's byline, it is datelined Nanking, which means he almost certainly wrote it.

30. J. Hall Paxton papers, Yale University, document 1, p. 2.

31. Dr. Wilson letter, December 9, 1937, Yale Archives, p. 35.

32. Yates's letter to Natalie, December 2, 1937.

33. Ibid.

34. AP dispatch, *Reno Gazette-Journal*, December 6, 1937.

35. McDaniel's diary of Nanking's final days, AP dispatch, December 18, 1937.

36. Ibid. In his story, McDaniel does not mention being accompanied by Arch Steele at the wall. But in a letter dated December 9, 1937, Dr. Wilson wrote that "Steele, the *Daily News* reporter, got a baptism of fire when he went with Yates McDaniel at the Kwanghua Gate." Wilson's description of the bombing matches McDaniel's, adding that the bombs fell within 200 yards of the reporters. In a cable to the State Department on December 9, George Atcheson of the US embassy in Nanking wrote that just after noon "there was considerable bombing in the Kwanghua Gate area, some bombs falling inside the city."

37. AP dispatch, *Ogden Standard-Examiner*, December 12, 1937.

38. J. Hall Paxton papers, vol. 1, pp. 22–26.

39. Dr. Wilson letter, December 15, 1937, Yale Archives.

40. McDaniel's diary, AP dispatch, December 18, 1937.

41. Iris Chang, *The Rape of Nanking: The Forgotten Holocaust of World War II* (New York: Basic Books, 1997), 245.

42. *World's News*, April 11, 1942.

43. AP dispatch, *Wisconsin Rapids Daily Tribune*, December 16, 1937.

44. Dr. Wilson letter, December 15, 1937, Yale Archives.

45. AP dispatch, *Wisconsin Rapids Daily Tribune*, December 16, 1937.

46. George Fitch's letter from Nanking, December 24, 1937.

47. AP dispatch, July 12, 1945.

48. Chang, *Rape of Nanking*, 265n144. Durdin is quoted as joking about Steele slipping the operator $50. It is unclear whether Durdin was joking or serious.

49. *New York Times*, December 18, 1937.

50. AP dispatch, *Oakland Tribune*, December 17, 1937.

51. Natalie McDaniel's unpublished article, p. 16.

52. McDaniel's diary, December 18, 1937.

## Chapter 5

1. Natalie McDaniel's unpublished magazine story.

2. Freda Utley, *China at War* (London: Faber and Faber, 1939), 27.

3. United Press dispatch, *Salem Capital Journal*, January 1, 1938.

4. International News Service (INS) dispatch, *Corpus Christi Caller Times*, January 19, 1938.

5. AP dispatch, *Ottawa Citizen*, January 25, 1938.

6. AP dispatch, *Richmond Palladium-Item*, February 4, 1938.

7. United Press dispatch, *Orlando Evening Star*, February 5, 1938.

8. AP dispatch, *Honolulu Star-Bulletin*, January 14, 1938.

9. Utley, *China at War*, 40.

10. Ibid., 39.

11. W. H. Auden and Christopher Isherwood, *Journey to a War: W. H. Auden and Christopher Isherwood* (London: Faber and Faber, 1939), 42.

12. Utley, *China at War*, 42.

13. Auden and Isherwood, *Journey to a War*, 44.

14. Utley, *China at War*, 43 and 196.

15. Ibid., 188.

16. White, *In Search of History*, 78.

17. Auden and Isherwood, *Journey to a War*, 43.

18. Martha Gellhorn, *Travels with Myself and Another* (New York: Jeremy P. Tarcher / Putnam, 1978), 35.

19. Utley, *China at War*, 172.

20. *New York Times*, July 15, 1938.

21. Utley, *China at War*, p. 156.

22. Johnson cable to Hull, February 3, 1938.

23. Hollington Tong, *Dateline China* (New York: Rockport, 1950), 51.

24. AP dispatch, *Carroll Daily Herald*, June 11, 1938; and *North China Herald*, May 11, 1938.

25. AP dispatch, *Mason City Globe-Gazette*, August 29, 1938.

26. Johnson cable to Hull, April 19, 1938.

27. AP dispatch, *Bloomington Pantagraph*, May 27, 1938.

28. AP dispatch, *Lubbock Morning Avalanche*, August 6, 1938.

29. Feature story about Seaman Charles Murphy by the *Billings Gazette*, November 27, 1938.

30. Adm. Yarnell cable to chief of US naval operations, June 16, 1938.

31. AP dispatch, December 18, 1937.

32. Cable from Laurence Salisbury, first secretary of the US embassy in Nanking, to Secretary Hull, July 13, 1938.

33. Charles McDaniel's letter, February 25, 1938, document 26, p. 11.

34. Nannie McDaniel's letter, June 13, 1938, document 26, p. 24.

35. Nannie McDaniel's letter published in *Newport News Daily Press*, July 12, 1938.

36. *New York Times*, April 28, 1935.

37. AP dispatch, *Binghamton Press* and *Sun-Bulletin*, August 24, 1938.

38. Feature story on Seaman Murphy, *Billings Gazette*, November 27, 1938.

39. Cable from Johnson to Hull, July 27, 1938.

40. Utley, *China at War*, 193.

41. Cornell Capa and Richard Whelan, eds., *Robert Capa, Photographs* (New York: Alfred A. Knopf, 1985), 145.

42. Utley, *China at War*, 213.

43. The party and mock trial are described in Utley, *China at War*, 213 and 217; MacKinnon and Oris Friesen, *China Reporting*, 46–47; and Michael Blankfort, *The Big Yankee: The Life of Carlson of the Raiders* (Boston: Little, Brown, 1947), 256. There is some confusion on the exact date of the party, but a story in the *Honolulu Star-Bulletin* on October 27, 1938, said Utley left Hankow on October 1. By contrast, Gen. Stilwell's diary note for September 20, 1938, reads: "Carlson's dinner at Rosie's."

44. AP dispatch, *Honolulu Star-Bulletin*, October 19, 1938.

45. AP dispatch, *Hawaii Tribune-Herald*, October 20, 1938.

46. AP dispatch, *Lincoln Star*, October 24, 1938.

47. Tong, *Dateline China*, 64.

48. AP dispatch, *Eau Claire Leader*, October 26, 1938; and AP dispatch, *Reno Gazette-Journal*, October 26, 1938.

49. AP dispatch, *Oshkosh Northwestern*, October 26, 1938.

50. *New York Times*, October 28, 1938.

51. AP dispatch, *Staunton News Leader*, October 27, 1938. That same day, Paul Josselyn, the general consul at Hankow, cabled Hull that there were more than thirty-five Japanese naval ships in the harbor.

52. AP dispatch, *Sandusky Register*, October 28, 1938; and *New York Times*, November 1, 1938.

53. AP dispatch, *Honolulu Star-Bulletin*, November 2, 1938.

54. *China Press*, November 5, 1938; and Doris Rubens, *Bread and Rice: An American Woman's Fight to Survive in the Jungles and Prison Camps of the WWII Philippines* (New York: Thurston Macauley, 1947), 59.

55. Natalie McDaniel's unpublished magazine article.

**Chapter 6**

1. AP dispatch, Trove, *Philippines Tribune*, January 4, 1939.

2. AP dispatch, *St. Louis Post-Dispatch*, July 27, 1939.

3. George S. MacDonell, *One Soldier's Story, 1939–1945: From the Fall of Hong Kong to the Defeat of Japan* (Toronto: Dundurn, 2002), 68.

4. Newspaper Enterprise Association (NEA) dispatch, *Billings Gazette*, October 27, 1940.

5. Pakula, *Last Empress*, 324.

6. *National Geographic Society Bulletin*; and *Decatur Herald*, December 6, 1937.

7. *Arizona Republic*, August 22, 1939.

8. *Decatur Review*, January 7, 1938.

9. Article by Catherine Haggerty, *Central New Jersey Home News*, March 6, 1938.

10. Stewart Alsop column, *Newark Advocate*, May 30, 1939.

11. Advertisement in *Honolulu Advertiser*, October 4, 1937.

12. Gellhorn, *Travels with Myself and Another*, 22.

13. Martha Gellhorn, "Time Bomb in Hong Kong," *Collier's*, June 7, 1941.

14. Stewart Alsop column, *Newark Advocate*, May 30, 1939.

15. AP dispatch, *Saskatoon Star-Phoenix*, September 2, 1937.

16. AP dispatch, *Staunton News Leader*, July 1, 1937.

17. Cable from Ambassador Joseph Grew in Japan to Secretary Hull, February 10, 1939.

18. AP dispatch, *Boston Globe*, February 14, 1939. See also Freda Utley, *Japan's Feet of Clay* (New York: W. W. Norton, 1937), 28.

19. AP dispatch, *Tampa Bay Times*, February 18, 1939.

20. Letter written by Yates's mother, Nannie, January 21, 1939, document 26, p. 40.

21. AP dispatch, *Rochester Democrat and Chronicle*, February 1, 1940; and Taras Grescoe, *Shanghai Grand: Forbidden Love, Intrigue, and Decadence in Old China* (New York: St. Martin's, 2016), 280. The newspaper published photos of Yates, Natalie, and Sir Victor Sassoon.

22. AP dispatch, *Sioux Falls Argus Leader*, February 1, 1940.

23. Staff report, *Des Moines Register*, February 10, 1940.

24. AP dispatch, *Freeport Journal*, April 22, 1940.

25. AP dispatch, *Decatur Herald*, April 23, 1940; and *New York Times*, April 23, 1940.

26. *Ironwood Daily Globe*, February 9, 1942.

27. *Honolulu Advertiser*, June 14, 1940; and *San Francisco Examiner*, June 8, 1940.

28. Gellhorn, *Travels with Myself and Another*, 55.

29. AP dispatch, *Monroe News*, July 1, 1940.

30. Cable from Grew to Hull, July 7, 1940.

31. O'Dowd Gallagher, *Action in the East* (London: Viking, 1942), 164.

32. Cable from Nelson Johnson to Hull, July 18, 1940.

33. AP dispatch, *Tampa Bay Times*, September 6, 1940.

34. Bill Lascher, *Eve of a Hundred Midnights: The Star-Crossed Love Story of Two WWII Correspondents and Their Epic Escape across the Pacific* (New York: HarperCollins, 2016), 109.

35. Ibid., 105; and letter from Mel Jacoby to Shanghai, October 9, 1940.

36. AP dispatch, *Danville Bee*, September 16, 1940; and Yates's 1959 interview with Toland.

37. *Los Angeles Times*, May 19, 1940.

38. Cable from Adm. Thomas Hart to Adm. Harold Stark, November 13, 1940. Hart's cable makes clear that he was under no illusions about Japan's ultimate goals. It was a plea for the United States to make a firm stand against Japan.

39. Cable from RAdm. Walter Anderson to Stark, October 16, 1940.

40. AP dispatch, *Honolulu Star-Bulletin*, September 20, 1940; and cable from Charles Reed, the US consul in Hanoi, to Secretary Hull, September 22, 1940.

41. Cable from Reed to Hull, September 22, 1940.

42. AP dispatch, *Bristol Herald Courier*, September 24, 1940.

43. AP dispatch, *Burlington Free Press*, September 27, 1940.

44. AP dispatch, *Baltimore Evening Sun*, October 1, 1940.

45. AP dispatch, *Rochester Democrat and Chronicle*, October 6, 1940.

46. Cable from Reed to Hull, October 4, 1940. Reed reports that an unnamed newspaper correspondent provided him with the details of the number of Japanese troops in Hanoi. Because it matches McDaniel's story sent to New York, the assumption is that Reed was referring to McDaniel.

47. *Battle Creek Enquirer*, January 24, 1947.

48. AP dispatch, *Paris News*, September 26, 1940; and AP dispatch, *Ogden Standard Examiner*, September 29, 1940.

49. AP dispatch, *Corsicana Daily Sun*, October 16, 1940.

50. Letter from Yates to Natalie. Although it is undated, it appears to have been written on November 17, 1940.

51. Abend, *My Life in China*, 291.

52. French, *Carl Crow—a Tough Old China Hand*, 229.

53. AP dispatch, *Rapid City Journal*, November 21, 1940; and AP dispatch, *Baltimore Evening Sun*, November 22, 1940.

54. Lascher, *Eve of a Hundred Midnights*, 113–17.

55. *Escanaba Daily Press*, July 26, 1947.

**Chapter 7**

1. Yates's interview in 1959 with Toland.

2. Arch Steele's dispatch for *Chicago Daily News*, published in *St. Louis Post-Dispatch*, March 5, 1941; and George Weller, *Weller's War: A Legendary Foreign Correspondent's Saga of World War II on Five Continents*, ed. Anthony Weller (New York: Crown, 2009), 174.

3. Yates's interview with Toland, *Malaya Tribune*, March 19, 1936, and *Singapore Free Press and Mercantile Advertiser*, March 20, 1936.

4. Advertisement for the Adelphi in the *Malaya Tribune*, January 13, 1941.

5. *Straits Times*, September 8, 1941; and Cecil Brown, *Suez to Singapore* (New York: Random House, 1942), 127.

6. Brown, *Suez to Singapore*, 200.

7. Gallagher, *Action in the East*, 13; and advertisement in the *Singapore Free Press*, June 10, 1941.

8. Gallagher, *Action in the East*, 13.

9. *Singapore Free Press*, March 13, 1941.

10. *Malaya Morning Tribune*, October 17, 1941.

11. Natalie's magazine story; Weller, *Weller's War*, 223; and Yates's interview with Toland.

12. Arch Steele's story, published in *St. Louis Post-Dispatch*, March 6, 1941.

13. *New York Times*, February 14, 1938; and John Gunther, *Inside Asia* (New York: Harper & Brothers, 1939), 43.

14. Howard Norton dispatch, *Baltimore Evening Sun*, November 13, 1941.

15. Brown, *Suez to Singapore*, 159.

16. Dispatch by David Waite of the *Singapore Free Press*, distributed by NEA and published in the *Abilene Reporter-News*, February 17, 1941.

17. Ronald McCrum, *The Men Who Lost Singapore, 1938–1942* (Singapore: NUS Press, 2017), 74.

18. AP dispatch, *Minneapolis Star Journal*, Sunday edition, February 2, 1941.

19. AP dispatch, *Burlington Free Press*, February 17, 1941.

20. AP dispatch, *Oakland Tribune*, February 19, 1941.

21. AP dispatch, *Ottawa Citizen*, March 31, 1941.

22. McCrum, *The Men Who Lost Singapore*, 87; and United Press dispatch, *Honolulu Advertiser*, April 29, 1941.

23. Brown, *Suez to Singapore*, 371.

24. Yates's interview with Toland.

25. Brown, *Suez to Singapore*, 148.

26. Yates's interview with Toland.

27. McCrum, *The Men Who Lost Singapore*, 69; and Megan Spooner diary entry, November 29, 1941, reprinted in Jonathan Parkinson, *The Royal Navy, China Station: A History as Seen through the Commanders in Chief, 1864–1941* (Kibworth, UK: Matador, 2018), 489.

28. Brown, *Suez to Singapore*, 211–14.

29. Ibid., 188; and Yates's interview with Toland.

30. Brown, *Suez to Singapore*, 188.

31. AP dispatch, *Windsor Star*, August 15, 1941.

32. Weller, *Weller's War*, 181.

33. Brown, *Suez to Singapore*, 187–90.

34. AP dispatch, *San Francisco Examiner*, September 4, 1941.

35. Lady Diana Cooper, *Trumpets from the Steep* (Boston: Houghton Mifflin, 1960), 101.

36. McCrum, *The Men Who Lost Singapore*, 66 and 69; and Christopher Bayly and Tim Harper, *Forgotten Armies: The Fall of British Asia, 1941–1945* (Cambridge, MA: Harvard University Press, 2005), 112.

37. Edgar Mowrer article, *Boston Globe*, December 4, 1941.

38. Ibid.

39. AP dispatch, *Tampa Bay Times*, November 12, 1941.

40. Megan Spooner diary, December 2, 1941, reprinted in Parkinson, *The Royal Navy, China Station*, 490.

41. *Times* of London, December 3, 1941.

42. AP dispatch, December 3, 1941; *Straits Times* in an article looking back, December 3, 1961; and *New York Times*, December 3, 1941. Although it is unclear whether Adm. Phillips was on the dock when the *Prince of Wales* arrived, Tillman Durdin of the *New York Times* reported that "he was not present when the squadron arrived." By contrast, Matthew Wills in his biography of Capt. John Leach—Matthew B. Wills, *In the Highest Traditions of the Royal Navy: The Life of Captain John Leach MVO DSO* (New York: History Press, 2011)—said Phillips and Palliser were at the base to greet the *Prince of Wales*. In Martin Middlebrook and Patrick Mahoney, *The Sinking of the* Prince of Wales *&* Repulse*: The End of the Battleship Era* (Barnsley, UK: Pen & Sword Maritime, 1977), the authors wrote that Phillips watched the *Prince of Wales* arrive at her berth and was "the first of the large welcoming party up the gangplank." Yates McDaniel's description of Phillips is from his interview with John Toland.

43. AP dispatch, December 3, 1941. Further descriptions of the arrival of the *Prince of Wales* can be found in the *Malaya Tribune*, December 3, 1941; *Times* of London, December 2, 1941; *New York Times*, December 3, 1941; and Nicholas Best, *Seven Days of Infamy: Pearl Harbor across the World* (New York: Thomas Dunne, 2016), 24. See also "The Last Weekend at Cabaret," *Straits Times*, December 3, 1961.

44. The British censorship is described by McDaniel in his daily story on December 3, 1941; Brown in *Suez to Singapore*, 276–77; and United Press in the *Arizona Republic*, December 3, 1941. McDaniel referred to Phillips as Adm. Sir Tom Collins in an early edition that appeared in the *Altoona Tribune*, December 3, 1941. In a classic mistake that every newspaper person could understand and laugh about, McDaniel then refers to Phillips without his title and first name in the next paragraph. The copy editors failed to ask who this man Phillips was.

45. *Service Histories of Royal Navy Warships in World War II*, notation on December 2, 1941.

46. The reception is described by Lady Diana Cooper in *Trumpets from the Steep*, 128; Best, *Seven Days of Infamy*, 25; and Colin Smith, *Singapore Burning: Heroism and Surrender in World War II* (London: Penguin Books, 2005), 95.

47. *Times* of London, December 6, 1941; and the *New York Times*, December 7, 1941.

48. Naval Staff, Historical Section, *Loss of the H.M. Ships* Prince of Wales *and* Repulse*, 10th December 1941*, Battle Summary 14 (London: Historical Section Admiralty, 1955), 3; and Harold Guard, *The Pacific War Uncensored: A War Correspondent's Unvarnished Account of the Fight against Japan*, ed. John Tring (Philadelphia: Casemate, 2011), 55.

49. John Grehan and Martin Mace, *Disaster in the Far East, 1940–1942: The Defence of Malaya, Japanese Capture of Hong Kong, and the Fall of Singapore* (Barnsley, UK: Pen & Sword Military, 2015), 40.

50. Brown, *Suez to Singapore*, 277–82; and Yates's interview with Toland.

51. Gallagher, *Action in the East*, 94–95.

52. Grehan and Mace, *Disaster in the Far East*, 52.

53. Gallagher, *Action in the East*, 93.

54. Naval Staff, Historical Section, *Loss of the H.M. Ships* Prince of Wales *and* Repulse, 23.

55. Gen. Archibald Wavell's report to Australian prime minister John Curtin, June 1, 1942, p. 7.

56. Naval Staff, Historical Section, *Loss of the H.M. Ships* Prince of Wales *and* Repulse, 23.

57. *Baltimore Sun*, December 3, 1941.

58. Parkinson, *The Royal Navy, China Station*, December 6, 1941.

59. "Last Weekend at Cabaret," *Straits Times*, December 3, 1961.

60. McDaniel described the evening in his interview with Toland and in a 1942 story in the *Brisbane Sunday Mail Magazine* dated December 6, 1942. Also see Ian Morrison, *Malayan Postscript* (Sydney, Australia: Angus and Robertson, 1943), 40. Because of the International Date Line, it was already December 8 in Singapore, which made it December 7 in Hawaii.

61. AP dispatch, *Detroit Free Press*, December 8, 1941.

62. The sequence of events of the first night of the war is confusing. In his interview with Toland, Yates indicates he went to the cable office, scribbled a lead, and went to the Union Building for the official announcement. By contrast, in his Brisbane magazine story, he indicates he went directly to the Union Building for the announcement. It makes more sense that he went to the Union Building first, but it is possible the version he told Toland was the correct one. In their accounts, Cecil Brown, O'Dowd Gallagher, and Harold Guard wrote they went to the Union Building before filing.

63. Yates described the conversation with Sir Geoffrey Layton in his interview with John Toland. See also Layton's diary reviewing the first week of the war, available through Parkinson, *The Royal Navy, China Station*, December 1941 through March 1942.

64. Gallagher, *Action in the East*, 37.

65. Ibid., 39.

## Chapter 8

1. AP dispatches, *Santa Ana Register*, December 10 and 11, 1941.

2. Lady Diana Cooper's diary, December 11, 1941, in Cooper, *Trumpets from the Steep*, 130.

3. Duff Cooper's speech published in the *Singapore Free Press*, December 11, 1941.

4. AP dispatch, *Uniontown Morning Herald*, December 11, 1941.

5. A. B. Lodge, *The Fall of Gordon Bennett* (Boston: Allen & Unwin, 1986), 70.

6. *Singapore Free Press*, December 12, 1941.

7. Brown, *Suez to Singapore*, 343; and Toland's interview with Yates. For further reading, check the accounts of the sinking by Cecil Brown in *Suez to Singapore* and O'Dowd Gallagher's *Action in the East*. They remain the best descriptions of the sinking of the *Prince of Wales* and *Repulse*. See also Gallagher's first-person account published in the *Singapore Free Press*, December 15, 1941.

8. Brown, *Suez to Singapore*, 338.

9. Morrison, *Malayan Postscript*, 52.

10. Sir Geoffrey Layton's war diary said the destroyers arrived in Singapore with survivors between 11:00 in the evening and 1:30 in the morning.

11. *Salt Lake Tribune*, December 11, 1941.

12. Brown, *Suez to Singapore*, 342 and 343.

13. Yates's interview with Toland.

14. Morrison, *Malayan Postscript*, 70.

15. AP dispatch, *Philadelphia Inquirer*, December 13, 1941.

16. AP dispatch, *Lansing State Journal*, December 18, 1941; and AP dispatch, *Wilkes-Barre Record*, December 19, 1941.

17. Brown, *Suez to Singapore*, 370.

18. Ibid., 359 and 360. By contrast, Sir Geoffrey Layton as early as December 11 warned the Admiralty he needed "all possible reinforcements" of submarines, minesweepers, destroyers, and "whatever air reinforcements can be provided." He added ominously, "If Singapore is to be held, we must have the necessary forces with which to do it."

19. *New York Times*, December 23, 1941.

20. AP dispatch, *Bloomington Pantagraph*, December 22, 1941.

21. Layton diaries, December 13, 1941.

22. Brown, *Suez to Singapore*, 370; and Weller, *Weller's War*, 195.

23. AP dispatch, *East Liverpool Evening Review*, December 30, 1941.

24. AP dispatch, *Burlington Free Press*, December 31, 1941.

25. Smith, *Singapore Burning*, 265.

26. McCrum, *The Men Who Lost Singapore*, 150.

27. Brown, *Suez to Singapore*, 349, 351, 402, and 436. On page 197 of his book *Weller's War*, George Weller of the *Chicago Daily News* wrote that "not all the correspondents, not even all the Americans, rallied to his defense." There is no record that McDaniel wrote anything about Brown in January 1942.

28. AP dispatch, *Klamath Falls Evening Herald*, January 1, 1942.

29. AP dispatch, *Rapid City Journal*, January 2, 1942.

30. AP dispatch, *Tampa Times*, January 9, 1942.

31. Morrison, *Malayan Postscript*, 65 and 67.

32. *London Observer*, January 4, 1942.

33. AP dispatch, *Corsicana Semi-Weekly Light*, January 6, 1942.

34. AP dispatch, Frank Noel's first-person account, *Montpelier Evening Argus*, January 20, 1942.

35. AP dispatch, *Hampshire Telegraph of Great Britain*, January 16, 1942.

36. Natalie McDaniel's first-person piece, AP dispatch, *Atlanta Constitution*, March 8, 1942.

37. Yates's letter was printed in full by *Alexandria Town Talk* of Louisiana on March 24, 1942. *The Akron Beacon Journal* published stories about the trunk on April 9, 1942, and July 11, 1948.

38. AP dispatch, *Richmond Palladium-Item*, January 20, 1942.

39. *New York Times*, January 15, 1942.

40. Yates's interview with Toland.

41. Morrison, *Malayan Postscript*, 120.

42. AP dispatch, *St. Louis Post-Dispatch*, January 26, 1942.

43. AP dispatch, *Waterloo Courier*, February 1, 1942. See also *San Bernardino County Sun*, February 1, 1942. Although the story was published in the United States and Canada on February 1 and 2, McDaniel's visit had to take place on his return to Singapore, before British soldiers blew up the causeway.

44. AP dispatch, *Jackson Sun*, January 28, 1942.

45. United Press dispatch, *Philadelphia Inquirer*, February 1, 1942.

46. Jonathan Moffatt and Audrey Holmes McCormick, *Moon over Malaya: A Tale of Argylls and Marines* (Stroud, UK: Tempus, 2003), 196.

47. AP dispatch, *Billings Gazette*, February 1, 1942.

48. AP dispatch, *St. Louis Post-Dispatch*, February 1, 1942.

49. Layton's diary was quoted in a story published by the *Independent*, January 26, 1993.

50. AP dispatch, *Appleton Post-Crescent*, February 3, 1942.

51. AP dispatch, *Salt Lake Tribune*, February 5, 1942; and AP dispatch, *Sacramento Bee*, February 5, 1942.

52. Morrison describes Percival's press conference on p. 156 of *Malayan Postscript*. See also McDaniel's story in an AP dispatch, *Philadelphia Inquirer*, February 7, 1942.

53. Cooper, *Trumpets from the Steep*, 140.

54. Yates's interview with Toland.

55. AP dispatch, *Amarillo Daily News*, February 7, 1942.

56. AP dispatch, *Kane Republican*, February 9, 1942.

57. AP dispatches, *Marion News Star* and *Mason City Globe-Gazette*, February 9, 1942.

58. Parkinson, *The Royal Navy, China Station*, 496; and AP dispatch, *Jackson Sun*, February 10, 1942.

59. AP dispatch, *Burlington Free Press*, February 10, 1942; AP dispatch, *Jackson Sun*, February 10, 1942; and Spooner letter to Capt. Peter Grenville Cazalet, commanding officer of the British cruiser *Durban*, February 10, 1942.

60. United Press dispatch, February 17, 1942.

61. The search for Morrison is part of a newspaper article published on March 19, 1942, by Athole Stewart in the *Perth Western Mail*, titled "Let's Get Cracking." The article was a condensed version of Stewart's 1943 book with the same title. The reference to Morrison is on p. 11 and is confirmed by Morrison in *Malayan Postscript*, 179.

62. *New York Times*, February 11, 1942; and AP dispatch, *The Tennessean*, February 11, 1942.

63. AP dispatch, *Charlotte Observer*, February 9, 1942.

64. Yates's interview with Toland. Stewart described Doris as "utterly forlorn" in *Let's Get Cracking*, 11.

65. Stewart, *Let's Get Cracking*, 20 and 21.

66. Ibid., 51.

**Chapter 9**

1. Geoffrey Brooke, *Alarm Starboard: A Remarkable True Story of the War at Sea* (Barnsley, UK: Pen & Sword Books, 2004), 135.

2. Geoffrey Brooke, *Singapore's Dunkirk: The Aftermath of the Fall* (Barnsley, UK: Pen & Sword Military, 2014). 26.

3. Brooke, *Alarm Starboard*, 136.

4. Brooke, *Singapore's Dunkirk*, 136.

5. Stewart, *Let's Get Cracking*, 24.

6. Brooke, *Singapore's Dunkirk*, 136.

7. Stewart, *Let's Get Cracking*, 24.

8. Personal recollections of Paul Dietz, a B. F. Goodrich executive in China.

9. AP dispatch, *Richmond Palladium-Item*, February 22, 1942; and Brooke, *Alarm Starboard*, 144.

10. Stewart, *Let's Get Cracking*, 27. Stewart claimed that those in the lifeboat could not hear Terry's order to return. But in Toland's *But Not in Shame*, the men in the first boat deliberately ignored the orders and shouted, "The hell with you, sonny boy."

11. Brooke, *Alarm Starboard*, 144. The photo McDaniel took of Terry eating breakfast is included in Stewart *Let's Get Cracking*, 93.

12. Yates's interview with Toland.

13. Stewart, *Let's Get Cracking*, 56.

14. Yates's interview with Toland.

15. Ibid.; and Brooke, *Alarm Starboard*, 145. See also Stewart, *Let's Get Cracking*, 58. In his interview with Toland, McDaniel said he spoke to Doris in Chinese, a puzzling comment because everyone said she spoke flawless English.

16. Stewart, *Let's Get Cracking*, 67–68.

17. AP dispatch, *Richmond Palladium-Item*, February 22, 1942; Richard Gough, *The Escape from Singapore* (London: William Kimber, 1988), 126, 146–47; Robert Weintraub, *No Better Friend: One Man, One Dog, and Their Extraordinary Story of Courage and Survival in World War II* (New York: Back Bay Books, 2015), 136–39; and Stewart, *Let's Get Cracking*, 102–03. Stewart wrote that he and McDaniel sat in the front seat. Although McDaniel called the vehicle a truck, Stewart said it was a bus.

18. Yates's interview with Toland; and AP dispatch, *Richmond Palladium-Item*, February 22, 1942.

19. *Sutherland Daily Echo*, February 14, 1942.

20. Interview with Amity Eills; and AP dispatch, *Oakland Tribune*, February 18, 1942. *The Arizona Republic* on April 5, 1942, referred to the *Evening Standard* story. See also Natalie McDaniel's first-person story in an AP dispatch, *Atlanta Constitution*, March 8, 1942.

21. Yates's interview with Toland. McDaniel did not identify the hotel's name, but on p. 112 of *Let's Get Cracking*, Stewart said it was the Oranje.

22. Yates's interview with Toland; and *Time* article, March 2, 1942. British naval records confirm the *Encounter* was sent from Batavia to Emmahaven on February 18. On p. 175 of *Malayan*

*Spymaster: Memoirs of a Rubber Planter, Bandit Fighter, and Spy* (Singapore: Monsoon Books, 2011), author Boris Hembry writes that the *Encounter* left Emmahaven in the evening. But McDaniel told Toland the destroyer sailed from Emmahaven in the afternoon.

23. AP dispatch, *Richmond Palladium-Item*, February 22, 1942.

24. Hembry, *Malayan Spymaster*, 175; and Stewart, *Let's Get Cracking*, 121.

25. Stewart, *Let's Get Cracking*, 11.

26. AP dispatch, *Richmond Palladium-Item*, February 22, 1942.

27. AP picked up Reuters' story, *Lancaster New Era*, February 20, 1942.

28. *Time* magazine, March 2, 1942.

29. AP dispatch, *St. Louis Post-Dispatch*, February 22, 1942.

30. *Philadelphia Inquirer*, October 29, 1942.

31. AP World, June and July 1944.

32. Yates's interview with Toland.

33. Ibid.

34. AP dispatch, *Atlanta Constitution*, March 8, 1942.

35. Stewart, *Let's Get Cracking*, 128–129. On p. 211 of *The Escape from Singapore*, Richard Gough said the *Klang* sailed from Batavia on February 21. According to British naval records, the *Klang* safely reached Fremantle in Australia on March 4. Among those who sailed on the ship was Al Noderer of the *Chicago Tribune*, who described the voyage in a *Tribune* story dated March 5, 1942. Other passengers included Allen Raymond of the *New York Herald Tribune* and Joe Harsch of the *Christian Science Monitor*. Joseph C. Harsch provided an excellent description of the *Klang*'s voyage in his book *At the Hinge of History: A Reporter's Story* (Athens: University of Georgia Press, 2010).

36. AP dispatch, *Atlanta Constitution*, March 8, 1942.

37. Stewart, *Let's Get Cracking*, 149.

38. AP dispatches by Yates and Natalie, *Atlanta Constitution*, March 8, 1942. See also *Queensland Times*, March 10, 1942.

39. Oliver Gramling, *Free Men Are Fighting* (New York: Farrar and Rinehart, 1942), 334.

40. Ibid., 335.

**Chapter 10**

1. *Melbourne Herald*, March 23, 1942.

2. *The Argus* (Melbourne), March 14, 1942.

3. *Sydney World's News*, April 11, 1942.

4. *West Australian*, March 9, 1942, and March 10, 1942.

5. *The Argus* (Melbourne), March 13, 1942.

6. *The Age* (Melbourne), April 16, 1942; *The Argus* (Melbourne), April 27, 1942; and *The Argus* (Melbourne), May 30, 1942.

7. *Charleville Times*, Friday, July 17, 1942; and *Western Star and Roma Advertiser*, March 10, 1942.

8. *The Argus* (Melbourne), July 14, 1942.

9. AP dispatch, *Lansing State Journal*, March 29, 1942.

10. George Kenney, *General Kenney Reports: A Personal History of the Pacific War* (Washington, DC: Office of Air Force History, 1987; originally published in 1949), 61.

11. AP dispatch, *St. Louis Dispatch*, March 18, 1943.

12. AP dispatch, *High Point Enterprise*, March 31, 1942.

13. Clark Lee, *They Call It Pacific: An Eye-Witness Story of Our War against Japan from Bataan to the Solomons* (New York: Viking, 1943), 286.

14. AP dispatch by Don Whitehead, *Tampa Tribune*, January 4, 1942; Yarbrough's first-person account, AP dispatch, *Staunton News Leader*, December 8, 1943; and Associated Press, *World War II: Unforgettable Stories and Photographs by Correspondents of the Associated Press* (New York: RosettaBooks, 2015).

15. *Montana Standard*, March 3, 1942.

16. *Muncie Star Press*, October 5, 1941.

17. AP dispatch, *Salem Statesman Journal*, December 10, 1939.

18. Vern Haugland, *Letter from New Guinea* (New York: Farrar & Rinehart, 1943), 42.

19. AP Wide World dispatch, *The Tennessean*, April 19, 1942.

20. Haugland, *Letter from New Guinea*, 132.

21. AP Wide World dispatch, *Palm Beach Post*, May 17, 1942.

22. AP dispatch, *Boston Globe*, August 25, 1942.

23. *Australian News Letter* and *Montreal Gazette*, August 18, 1942.

24. AP dispatch, *Tampa Times*, March 19, 1942.

25. Letter from Robert Sherrod to John Darnton and reprinted in Darnton's book *Almost a Family: A Memoir* (New York: Anchor Books, 2012). 295.

26. Lascher, *Eve of a Hundred Midnights*, 185.

27. Sidney Skolsky's Hollywood, *Cincinnati Enquirer*, April 28, 1942.

28. AP Wide World dispatch, *Salem Statesman-Journal*, May 12, 1942.

29. *Melbourne Age*, March 21, 1942; Douglas MacArthur, *Reminiscences* (New York: McGraw-Hill, 1964), 145; and *Adelaide Advertiser*, March 21, 1942. There has always been some confusion about where MacArthur made his dramatic announcement that he would return to the Philippines. In his memoirs, MacArthur wrote that he delivered the statement after his B-17 landed at Batchelor Field. But Australian newspapers reported he spoke the words "I shall return" at Terowie after he reviewed the Australian honor guard.

30. United Press dispatch, *Philadelphia Inquirer*, March 21, 1942; and Guard, *The Pacific War Uncensored*, 108.

31. The scene at the railroad station is re-created by Vern Haugland's dispatches in the *East Liverpool Review* and *Oakland Tribune*, March 21, 1942; a United Press dispatch by Harold Guard in the *Philadelphia Inquirer*, March 21, 1942; the *Melbourne Herald*, March 21, 1942; and MacArthur, *Reminiscences*, 151.

32. AP dispatch, *Boston Globe*, March 20, 1942 and AP dispatch, *Atlanta Constitution*, March 21, 1942. McDaniel's byline is on the *Constitution* story, which uses the word "will," making it one of McDaniel's rare mistakes.

33. United Press dispatch, *Santa Maria Times*, March 21, 1942.

34. AP dispatch, *Cincinnati Enquirer*, March 22, 1942.

35. AP dispatch, *Decatur Daily Review*, March 26, 1942.

36. Gramling, *Free Men Are Fighting*, 344–45.

37. AP dispatch that McDaniel wrote after MacArthur's death, April 6, 1964. See also an article in the *Louisville Courier-Journal*, March 27, 1942. Story was compiled from cable dispatches.

38. AP dispatch, *Richmond Times-Dispatch*, March 28, 1942.

39. Dunn, *Pacific Microphone*, 152.

40. Clark Lee, *One Last Look Around* (New York: Duell, Sloan and Pearce, 1947), 138, 140, and 143.

41. Letter by Lewis Sebring, June 21, 1942, courtesy of the Wisconsin Historical Society.

42. AP WideWorld dispatch, *West Palm Beach Post*, May 17, 1942.

43. United Press dispatch, *El Paso Times*, April 4, 1942.

44. AP Wide World dispatch, *Palm Beach Post*, May 17, 1942.

45. Haugland, *Letter from New Guinea*, 6.

46. Sebring letters, April 7, 1942, June 21, 1942, and July 5, 1942.

47. *Melbourne Herald*, March 30, 1942; and *Evening Advocate*, April 27, 1942.

48. John Edwards, *John Curtin's War* (Melbourne, Australia: Viking, 2017), 100.

49. Carl Mydans, notebook 9, p. 4, Yale University.

50. Lascher, *Eve of a Hundred Midnights*, 330; and Lee, *They Call It Pacific*, 284.

51. MacArthur's news conference was described by Bill Dunn in *Pacific Microphone*, 146–47; and AP dispatch in the *Tampa Times*, March 24, 1942.

52. Lascher, *Eve of a Hundred Midnights*, 284–85.

53. Lee, *They Call It Pacific*, 212.

54. Lascher, *Eve of a Hundred Midnights*, 351–52; and United Press dispatch, *Dayton Herald*, May 1, 1942. *The Argus* of Melbourne published a photo of McDaniel and other correspondents serving as pallbearers at the funeral service, May 2, 1942.

55. AP dispatch, *Hackensack Record*, April 9, 1942.

56. AP dispatch by Clark Lee, *Minneapolis Star Tribune*, April 10, 1942; and United Press dispatch, *Brooklyn Eagle*, April 9, 1942.

57. Larry Lehrbas's statement and the mood at MacArthur's headquarters is from United Press dispatches, April 9 and 10, and the *Montgomery Advertiser*, April 11, 1942. See also Chekel, *They Couldn't Pay Me Enough Money* (Martin Chekel, 2014), 91; and a story by McDaniel on April 6, 1964, after MacArthur died.

58. AP dispatch, *Shreveport Journal*, April 10, 1942.

59. Lee, *One Last Look Around*, 31.

60. AP dispatch, *Staunton News Leader*, April 11, 1942.

61. AP dispatch, *Park City Daily News*, April 16, 1942. See also AP dispatch of William Hipple's interview with Frank Hewlett, *Honolulu Star-Bulletin*, May 28, 1942.

62. AP dispatch, *Tucson Daily Citizen*, April 15, 1942.

63. AP dispatch, *Lansing State Journal*, April 16, 1942. For Royce's description of the B-25, see AP dispatch, *Clovis News-Journal*.

**Chapter 11**

1. AP dispatch by McDaniel following MacArthur's death, *Philadelphia Inquirer*, April 6, 1964.

2. AP dispatch, *Rapid City Journal*, May 7, 1942.

3. AP dispatch, *Des Moines Register*, May 10, 1942.

4. AP dispatch, *Philadelphia Inquirer*, May 3, 1942.

5. AP dispatch, *Lansing State Journal*, May 7, 1942.

6. Craig Symonds, *The Battle of Midway* (New York: Oxford University Press, 2011), 148.

7. AP dispatch, *Mason City Globe-Gazette*, May 8, 1942.

8. Ibid.

9. *Boston Globe*, June 13, 1942; and *Chicago Tribune* story distributed by AP.

10. AP dispatch, *Richmond Palladium-Item*, May 9, 1942.

11. Ibid.

12. *New York Times*, May 9, 1942.

13. AP dispatch of Tokyo's communique, *Billings Gazette*, May 9, 1942.

14. *Melbourne Age*, May 12, 1942.

15. Editorial, *Melbourne Age*, May 12, 1942.

16. Editorial in *San Francisco Examiner*, May 26, 1942.

17. Kenney, *General Kenney Reports*, 67.

18. AP dispatch, *Charlotte Observer*, May 19, 1942.

19. AP dispatch, *Richmond Palladium*, May 19, 1942.

20. *Sydney Morning Herald*, May 14, 1942.

21. AP dispatch from Washington, *Mansfield News Journal*, August 8, 1942.

22. AP dispatch, *Cincinnati Enquirer*, August 26, 1942.

23. Charles McDaniel's letter, September 5, 1942. document 27, p. 10.

24. AP dispatch from Richmond, *Baltimore Evening Sun*, October 14, 1942.

25. AP dispatch, *Altoona Tribune*, June 18, 1942.

26. Sebring's letter, October 4, 1942, courtesy of the Wisconsin Historical Society.

27. Kenney, *General Kenney Reports*, 40.

28. William F. Boni, *Want to Be a War Correspondent? Here's How* (Highland City, FL: Rainbow Books, 1995), 8.

29. *Sydney Daily Telegraph*, July 20, 1942.

30. William Manchester, *American Caesar: Douglas MacArthur, 1880–1964* (Boston: Little, Brown, 1978), 298.

31. AP dispatch, *Ironwood Daily Globe*, July 23, 1942.

32. AP dispatch, *St. Louis Post-Dispatch*, August 2, 1942.

33. AP dispatch, *Windsor Star*, August 4, 1942.

34. Haugland, *Letter from New Guinea*, 14.

35. *Melbourne Herald*, August 13, 1942.

36. Haugland, *Letter from New Guinea*, 19 and 45.

37. AP dispatch, *Kansas City Star*, September 29, 1942.

38. Ibid.

39. Haugland, *Letter from New Guinea*, 49, 61, 93, 122, 123, 126, and 136.

40. AP dispatch, *Casper Star-Tribune*, October 7, 1942.

41. AP advertisement, *Tampa Bay Times*, October 21, 1942.

42. Haugland, *Letter from New Guinea*, 129–30.

43. *Honolulu Star-Bulletin* editorial, Sept. 17, 1942.

44. Richard Tregaskis, *Guadalcanal Diary* (New York: Random House, 2000), diary entry, September 1, 1942.

45. Sebring's letter, August 16, 1942.

46. AP dispatch, *Greenville News*, August 10, 1942.

47. AP dispatch, *Fort Worth Star-Telegram*, August 11, 1942.

48. AP dispatch, *Tampa Bay Times*, October 29, 1942.

49. Robert Eichelberger, *Dear Miss Em: General Eichelberger's War in the Pacific, 1942–1945* (Westport, CT: Greenwood, 1981), 41, letter of December 7, 1942.

50. Bill Henry column, "By the Way," *Los Angeles Times*, November 3, 1942.

51. Bill Henry column, "By the Way," *Los Angeles Times*, November 2, 1942.

52. Darnton, *Almost a Family*, 52; and AP dispatch, *Baltimore Evening Sun*, October 22, 1942.

53. AP dispatch, *Salem Statesman Journal*, November 15, 1942.

54. AP dispatch, *Cumberland Evening Times*, November 18, 1942; and AP dispatch, *Gettysburg Times*, November 20, 1942.

55. Eichelberger, *Dear Miss Em*, 32.

56. Ibid., 50.

57. Ibid., 47.

58. AP dispatch, *Newark Advocate*, December 3, 1942.

59. Eichelberger, *Dear Miss Em*, 65.

60. AP dispatch, *Indianapolis Star*, December 28, 1943.

61. Yates's letter to Natalie, November 9, 1944.

62. AP dispatch, *Chillicothe Gazette*, December 24, 1942.

**Chapter 12**

1. AP dispatch, *Danville Bee*, March 6, 1943.

2. Yates's letter to Natalie, December 28, 1943.

3. *Honolulu Star-Bulletin* editorial, September 17, 1942.

4. AP dispatch, *St. Louis Post-Dispatch*, March 6, 1943.

5. AP dispatch, *Des Moines Tribune*, March 6, 1943. The fact that Army censors cleared McDaniel's story with the order to destroy the Japanese lifeboats is surprising. But it was a sign of how savage the Pacific war had become.

6. AP dispatch, *New York Times*, March 9, 1943; and AP dispatch, *Kansas City Star*, March 8, 1943.

7. AP dispatch, *St. Louis Post-Dispatch*, March 18, 1943.

8. Yates's letter to Natalie, November 25, 1944.

9. AP dispatch by Roger Greene, *Tallahassee Democrat*, July 1, 1943.

10. AP dispatch, *Marshfield News Herald*, July 3, 1943.

11. AP dispatch, *Fort Worth Star-Telegram*, July 14, 1943.

12. Boni, *Want to Be a War Correspondent?*, 44–45.

13. Ibid., 9.

14. Kent Cooper, *Kent Cooper and the Associated Press* (New York: Random House, 1959), 241.

15. AP dispatch, *Vernon Daily Record*, January 16, 1945.

16. AP dispatch by Trudy McCullough, *Arizona Republic*, October 1, 1944.

17. AP photos, *Oakland Tribune*, September 7, 1943.

18. *Chicago Tribune* News Service, published in the *Los Angeles Times*, September 7, 1943.

19. AP dispatch by Vern Haugland, *Chicago Tribune*, September 7, 1943.

20. AP dispatch, *Lubbock Morning Avalanche*, September 7, 1943.

21. AP dispatch, *Atlanta Constitution*, September 20, 1943.

22. AP dispatch by Bill Boni, *Oakland Tribune*, September 22, 1943.

23. AP dispatch, *Tampa Times*, September 25, 1943.

24. AP dispatch, *Atlanta Constitution*, October 5, 1943.

25. Eunson's first-person account, AP dispatch, *St. Louis Globe-Democrat*, December 17, 1943.

26. Yates's letter to Natalie. It is undated, but Yates probably wrote it December 19, 1943.

27. AP advertisement, *Oakland Tribune*, December 17, 1943, p. 36.

28. Yates's letter to Natalie, probably December 19, 1943.

29. Yates's letter to Natalie, December 21, 1943.

30. Yates's letter to Natalie, probably December 1943.

31. Yates's letter to Natalie, December 21, 1943.

32. Dunn, *Pacific Microphone*, 199.

33. AP dispatch, *Indianapolis Star*, December 28, 1943.

34. AP dispatch, December 25, 1943, available through Ancestry.com.

35. Yates's letter to Natalie, December 28, 1943.

36. AP dispatch, *Paris News*, December 27, 1943.

37. Yates's letter to Natalie, December 28, 1943. A photo of McDaniel saluting was published in the *Australian War Memorial*, December 29, 1943.

38. Yates's letter to Natalie, December 28, 1943.

39. AP dispatch, *Richmond Palladium-Item*, April 25, 1944.

40. AP dispatch, *Baltimore Evening Sun*, November 21, 1942.

41. AP dispatch, *Tampa Bay Times*, December 3, 1942.

42. AP dispatch, *Richmond Palladium*, April 25, 1944.

43. AP dispatch, *Oakland Tribune*, April 24, 1944.

44. AP dispatch, *Salem Capital Journal*, April 28, 1944. Nancy Eills said McDaniel told her he lost a typewriter in Indochina.

45. Yates's letter to Natalie, April 25, 1944.

46. AP dispatch written by McDaniel after MacArthur's death, April 6, 1964.

## Chapter 13

1. AP dispatch by Spencer Davis, *Harrisburg Telegraph*, October 21, 1944.

2. US Air Force, Ancestry.com, June 1, 1944.

3. AP dispatch, *Hazleton Plain Speaker*, June 16, 1944. McDaniel's piece flatly contradicted the belief by many Americans that the Doolittle raid in 1942 caused major damage to Japan. The film *Thirty Seconds over Tokyo*, which was released in November 1944, suggested that the American bombers caused major damage to Tokyo. In fact, McDaniel was right.

4. Yates's letter to Natalie, December 9, 1944.

5. *New York Times*, October 21, 1944.

6. AP dispatch, *Oakland Tribune*, October 20, 1944.

7. AP dispatch, *St. Louis Post-Dispatch*, October 20, 1944.

8. Yates's letter to Natalie, October 22, 1944.

9. Ibid.

10. AP dispatch, *St. Louis Post-Dispatch*, October 20, 1944.

11. AP dispatch, *Sioux Falls Argus Leader*, October 19, 1944. The paper's headline reads "Japanese report, Americans invade Philippines."

12. Yates's letter to Natalie, October 22, 1944.

13. AP dispatch, *Birmingham News*, October 21, 1944.

14. AP dispatch, *Jackson Sun*, October 22, 1944.

15. Yates's letter to Natalie, October 22, 1944.

16. Editorial, *Mason City Globe Gazette*, January 16, 1945.

17. AP dispatch, *Reno Gazette*, April 20, 1945.

18. AP dispatch, *Vancouver Sun*, October 24, 1944.

19. AP dispatch, *Tucson Daily Citizen*, October 25, 1944.

20. Staff story by *Fort Worth Star-Telegram*, October 31, 1944. See also McDaniel's AP dispatch in *Salem Statesman Journal*, October 31, 1944.

21. McDaniel's AP dispatch, *Salem Statesman Journal*, October 31, 1944. The *Salem Statesman Journal* on November 15, 1944, published the photo of the funeral. McDaniel, Dean Schedler, and Jim Hutcheson were among the AP reporters in the photo.

22. Yates's letter to Natalie, November 15, 1944; and *Honolulu Star-Bulletin*, November 14, 1944.

23. AP dispatch, *St. Louis Post-Dispatch*, October 28, 1944. From New York, Russell Brines wrote a sidebar explaining Oldendorf's strategy, which also appeared in the *St. Louis Post-Dispatch* the same day.

24. AP dispatch, *Fresno Bee*, October 29, 1944.

25. Yates's letters to Natalie, November 9 and November 13, 1944.

26. Chekel, *They Couldn't Pay Me Enough*, 91. See also Murlin Spencer's story on Lindesay Parrott, *Wilkes-Barre Record*, November 28, 1944.

27. Yates's letter to Natalie, December 9, 1944.

28. Yates's letter to Natalie, November 25, 1944.

29. Yates's letter to Natalie, November 9, 1944. Dickinson returned to the United States and eventually became editor of the *Philadelphia Bulletin*.

30. Yates's letter to Natalie, December 9, 1944.

31. Yates's letter to Natalie, November 9, 1944. In his December 9 letter, Yates wrote that the liquor had arrived.

32. Yates's letter to Natalie, November 9, 1944; and AP dispatch, *Iola Register*, November 9, 1944.

33. Carl Mydans, notebook 9, p. 17; and Kenney, *General Kenney Reports*, 478.

34. Yates's letters to Natalie, November 9 and November 25, 1944; and Mydans, notebook 9, p. 31.

35. Kenney, *General Kenney Reports*, 479–93.

36. Yates's letter to Natalie, December 9, 1944; and AP dispatch, *Arizona Republic*, December 11, 1944.

37. Yates's letter to Natalie, December 9, 1944; and AP dispatch, *Salt Lake Tribune*, December 11, 1944.

38. AP dispatch, *Ithaca Journal*, December 8, 1944.

39. Lee, *One Last Look Around*, 30–34. See also Clark Lee's INS dispatch, *St. Louis Star and Times*, December 26, 1944.

40. The Christmas tree can be seen in a photograph on p. 269 of Dunn, *Pacific Microphone*.

McDaniel is among the correspondents in the photo hoisting beers to celebrate Christmas.

41. Lee, *One Last Look Around*, 3. McDaniel wrote about that Christmas a year later, on December 24, 1945, in an AP dispatch in the *Muncie Evening Press*. See also AP dispatch by Spencer Davis in the *Muncie Evening Press*, December 25, 1944.

## Chapter 14

1. Carl Mydans, notebook 9, p. 120; AP dispatch, *Bloomington Pantagraph*, December 25, 1944; Dunn, *Pacific Microphone*, 269; and Eichelberger, *Dear Miss Em*, 180, Eichelberger letter, December 25, 1944.

2. Lee, *One Last Look Around*, 29. MacArthur told Clark Lee in their meeting in Tacloban that he would land at Lingayen Gulf. MacArthur told Lee that "the press doesn't know about it yet," but Lee wrote that correspondents had already "been briefed."

3. AP dispatch, *Salem Capital Journal*, January 16, 1945.

4. Mydans, notebook 10, January 4, 1945.

5. Chekel, *They Couldn't Pay Me Enough*, 89.

6. AP dispatch by Davis and Dopking, *Alexandria Weekly Town Talk*, January 13, 1945.

7. Chekel, *They Couldn't Pay Me Enough*, 89.

8. AP dispatch, *St. Louis Post-Dispatch*, January 10, 1945; and AP dispatch written by McDaniel after MacArthur's death, April 6, 1964.

9. MacArthur, *Reminiscences*, 240; AP dispatch by McDaniel after MacArthur's death, April 6, 1964; and Chekel, *They Couldn't Pay Me Enough*, 89.

10. Mydans, notebook 10, January 9, 1945.

11. Ibid.

12. Dunn, *Pacific Microphone*, 274.

13. John Loengard, *Life Photographers: What They Saw* (Boston: Bulfinch, 1999).

14. AP dispatch, *St. Louis Post-Dispatch*, January 10, 1945.

15. Gramling, *Free Men Are Fighting*, 415–16.

16. INS dispatch by Clark Lee, *Albuquerque Journal*, February 2, 1945.

17. AP dispatch, *Argus Leader*, February 1, 1945.

18. Dunn, *Pacific Microphone*, 287–88.

19. AP dispatch, *Decatur Daily*, February 4, 1945.

20. Richard Connaughton, *Battle for Manila* (Novato, CA: Presidio, 1995), 93.

21. The scene at the prison gate is from Dunn, *Pacific Microphone*, 299 and 301; AP dispatch by Schedler and Hampson in *Decatur Review*, February 5, 1945; and United Press dispatch by Hewlett, *Hayward Daily Review*, February 5, 1945.

22. AP dispatch, *Decatur Review*, February 5, 1945.

23. Carl Mydans provided the number of prisoners in his notebook 10, p. 100.

24. AP dispatch, *Baltimore Evening Sun*, February 6, 1945.

25. United Press dispatch by H. D. Quigg, *Pittsburgh Press*, February 6, 1945. In his notebook on February 16, Mydans wrote that "Weissblatt, just released . . . with wasted body and twisted leg, covering the pool with me." Weissblatt's first byline appeared in the *Honolulu Advertiser* on February 19, 1945.

26. AP dispatch, *Danville Bee*, February 8, 1945.

27. AP photo, *Detroit Free Press*, February 6, 1945. See also United Press dispatch by Frank Hewlett, *Detroit Free Press*, December 6, 1945. He reported the nurses went right back to work to take care of the wounded. For the first time in three years, they had clean bandages and up-to-date drugs.

28. AP dispatch by McDaniel and Schedler, *Kansas City Star*, February 23, 1945. In the story, McDaniel recounted the time in 1936 that Donald helped win the freedom of Chiang Kai-shek after he was kidnapped by a Chinese marshal.

29. United Press dispatch, *Miami News*, February 4, 1945.

30. AP dispatch, *San Bernardino County Sun*, February 5, 1945.

31. Rubens, *Bread and Rice*, 234.

32. Eichelberger, *Dear Miss Em*, 218.

33. United Press dispatch by Bill Dickinson, *Oakland Tribune*, February 4, 1945.

34. AP dispatch, *Lancaster Eagle-Gazette*, February 3, 1945.

35. Eichelberger, *Dear Miss Em*, 209.

36. AP dispatch datelined San Francisco, *New York Daily News*, February 4, 1945.

37. Folster's report was published in the *Reno Gazette-Journal*, February 3, 1945.

38. AP files, moved on February 3, 1945, and scheduled for publication on February 5, 1945, if Manila fell to the Americans.

39. McDaniel's rewritten story about half of Manila under control of the Americans was part of an AP dispatch, *Hanover Evening Sun*, February 5, 1945.

40. McDaniel's AP dispatch, *Iola Register*, February 6, 1945.

41. *Melbourne Age*, February 8, 1945.

42. Eichelberger, *Dear Miss Em*, 212.

43. AP dispatch, *St. Louis Post-Dispatch*, February 6, 1945.

44. AP dispatch, *Fresno Bee*, February 8, 1945.

45. AP dispatch, *St. Louis Post-Dispatch*, February 6, 1945.

46. Diary of Gen. Robert Beightler, February 4, 1945, and March 3, 1945. See also McDaniel's story on February 6 in the *St. Louis Post-Dispatch*, in which he raises the possibility that MacArthur issued the statement so he would retain command of the Allied forces. On p. 218 of *Dear Miss Em*, Eichelberger wrote that the "On to Tokyo" release was a bid for further high command beyond the Philippines."

47. AP dispatch by Leonard Milliman, *Decatur Daily*, February 6, 1945.

48. Chekel, *They Couldn't Pay Me Enough*, 92.

49. The orders for entry into Manila were published in Connaughton, *Battle for Manila*, 209.

50. Chekel, *They Couldn't Pay Me Enough*, 92–93.

51. Dunn, *Pacific Microphone*, 306–08.

52. McDaniel's AP dispatch written after MacArthur's death, April 6, 1964.

53. Chekel, *They Couldn't Pay Me Enough*, 93.

54. United Press dispatch, *Tucson Daily Citizen*, February 7, 1945; and Beightler's diary, February 7, 1945.

55. AP dispatch, *Arizona Republic*, February 8, 1945.

56. AP dispatch, *Lubbock, Texas*, February 9, 1945.

57. AP dispatch by Fred Hampson, *Marshall News Messenger*, February 12, 1945.

58. AP dispatch, *Big Spring Daily Herald*, February 11, 1945.

59. AP dispatch, *Sheboygan Press*, February 13, 1945.

60. AP dispatch, *Oakland Tribune*, February 14, 1945.

61. AP dispatch, which included Adams's reference to Nanking, was published by the *Detroit Free Press* on February 15, 1945. See also McDaniel's updated story, which includes Hampson's dispatch, *Santa Rosa Democrat*, February 15, 1945. See also Mydans, notebook 10, February 15, 1945.

62. AP dispatch written by McDaniel and including Hampson's report, *St. Cloud Times*, February 17, 1945.

63. AP dispatch, *Arizona Republic*, February 21, 1945. Beightler's diary entries of February 18–22 include his radio message to the Japanese. After the battle, the handful of Japanese prisoners acknowledged that they received the message, but that their commander refused to reply.

64. AP dispatch by Hampson, *Fort Worth Star-Telegram*, February 23, 1945.

65. Dunn, *Pacific Microphone*, 313.

66. AP dispatch, *Pottstown Mercury*, February 24, 1945.

67. AP dispatch, *Owensboro Messenger*, February 25, 1945.

68. AP dispatch, *Davenport Daily Times*, April 9, 1945.

69. Beightler's report on the activities of the 37th Infantry Division, 1940–1945.

70. Rubens, *Bread and Rice*, 234.

71. AP dispatch by Hampson, *Marshfield News Herald*, April 2, 1945.

72. Dunn, *Pacific Microphone*, 315.

73. AP dispatch by Spencer Davis, *Greenville News*, February 27, 1945.

74. Mydans's notebook, 159.

75. McDaniel's AP dispatch written after MacArthur's death, April 6, 1964; and Chekel, *They Couldn't Pay Me Enough*, 95.

76. AP dispatch, *Chicago Tribune*, February 27, 1945. MacArthur's speech was published by the Tribune.

77. Chekel, *They Couldn't Pay Me Enough*, 95.

**Chapter 15**

1. *AP World*, June 1945. Yates's and Natalie's trips to the United States are documented on Ancestry.com.

2. *AP World*, June 1945.

3. AP dispatch, *Des Moines Register*, May 16, 1945.

4. *AP World*, September and October 1945.

5. Ibid.

6. AP dispatch, *Minneapolis Star Tribune*, September 2, 1945.

7. AP dispatches by Vern Haugland, *Hawaii Tribune-Herald*, September 4, 1945, and September 10, 1945.

8. Memo from Gould to McDaniel, January 23, 1946, courtesy of AP archives.

9. Memo written by Gould, February 25, 1946, courtesy of AP archives.

10. Memo from Gould to McDaniel, April 12, 1946, courtesy of AP archives.

11. Natalie's memoirs, pp. 1 and 19.

12. Natalie's memoirs.

13. AP dispatch, *Lansing State Journal*, January 1, 1948.

14. AP dispatch, *Sioux City Journal*, January 17, 1948.

15. AP dispatch, *Charlotte Observer*, February 14, 1948.

16. AP dispatch, *Idaho Falls Post-Register*, April 23, 1948.

17. AP dispatch, *New York Daily News*, May 18, 1948.

18. AP dispatch, *Janesville Daily Gazette*, May 24, 1948.

19. AP Weekly Log, May 1948, courtesy of AP archives.

20. AP dispatch, *St. Louis Post-Dispatch*, May 29, 1948.

21. Interview with Fred Hoffman, 2018.

22. *Lansing State Journal*, October 18, 1947.

23. Clark Lee's obituary by Hal Boyle, AP dispatch, *Sacramento Bee*, February 17, 1953; and Lascher, *Eve of a Hundred Midnights*, 217.

24. AP dispatch written by Don Whitehead, February 22, 1942.

25. Lascher, *Eve of a Hundred Midnights*, 217; and Lee, *One Last Look Around*, 145.

26. Clark Lee's obituary, by Hal Boyle.

27. *Hartford Courant*, May 27, 1947.

28. Lee, *One Last Look Around*, 45.

29. Ibid., 258–60.

30. Ibid., 222 and 254–55.

31. Ibid., foreword.

32. McDaniel's autobiography sketch for the AP.

33. *Windsor Star*, March 20, 1947.

34. AP dispatch, *Cincinnati Enquirer*, September 19, 1945.

35. AP dispatch, *Palm Beach Post*, January 8, 1989.

36. *Windsor Star*, March 20, 1947.

37. *San Francisco Examiner*, February 26, 1946.

38. *Escanaba Daily Press*, July 26, 1947.

39. *Windsor Star*, March 20, 1947.

40. AP dispatch, *Lansing State Journal*, May 14, 1947.

41. *Battle Creek Enquirer*, January 24, 1947.

42. Robert D. Novak, *The Prince of Darkness: 50 Years Reporting in Washington* (New York: Crown Forum, 2007), 45.

43. *AP World*, September 1961.

44. Letter of transmittal to Congress by Secretary of State Dean Acheson as part of the White Paper, August 1949.

45. *Richmond Palladium-Item*, July 7, 1950. See also *Muncie Evening Press*, May 31, 1951. I have been unable to locate a copy of the radio broadcast. Nor is there any record that McDaniel ever wrote a story about the claim that Washington had decided to dump Chiang. But McDaniel tended to be more opinionated on radio and in speeches than in his news stories.

46. AP dispatch, *Shreveport Journal*, January 31, 1950.

47. Institute of Land Warfare, March 1992.

48. AP dispatch, *Hornell Evening Tribune*, July 15, 1950.

49. AP dispatch, *Logan Daily News*, July 1, 1950.

50. AP dispatch, *Tampa Tribune*, July 19, 1950.

51. *New York Herald Tribune*, September 15, 1950; and AP dispatch, *Tampa Tribune*, July 19, 1950.

52. AP dispatch, *Ithaca Journal*, August 31, 1950.

53. AP dispatch, *Rocky Mountain Telegram*, September 19, 1950.

54. AP dispatch, *Sedalia Democrat*, October 19, 1950.

55. AP dispatch, *Rocky Mountain Telegram*, October 31, 1950.

56. AP dispatch, *Argus Leader*, November 30, 1950.

57. AP dispatch, *Oakland Tribune*, November 29, 1950

58. McDaniel's photo appears in the *Muscatine Journal*, December 8, 1950.

59. AP dispatch, *Tampa Tribune*, December 13, 1950.

60. AP dispatch, *Battle Creek Enquirer*, April 12, 1951.

61. AP dispatch, *Philadelphia Inquirer*, April 20, 1951.

**Chapter 16**

1. AP dispatch, *Richmond Times-Dispatch*, November 12, 1953.

2. AP dispatch by McDaniel, *Lansing State Journal*, May 12, 1964, two days after Nomura died at age eighty-six; and AP dispatch, *Chicago Tribune*, November 12, 1953.

3. AP dispatch, *Greenwood Index-Journal*, September 15, 1954.

4. AP dispatch, *Massillon Evening Independent*, August 25, 1954.

5. AP dispatch, *Greenwood Index-Journal*, September 15, 1954.

6. AP dispatch, *Salisbury Daily Times*, February 4, 1955.

7. AP dispatch, *Owensboro Messenger*, August 22, 1951.

8. AP dispatch, *Newport News Daily Press*, May 14, 1956; and AP dispatch, *St. Louis Post-Dispatch*, May 14, 1956.

9. AP dispatch, *Honolulu Star-Bulletin*, December 14, 1957.

10. AP dispatch by Elton Fay, *St. Louis Globe-Democrat*, June 29, 1956.

11. AP dispatch, *Birmingham News*, January 7, 1958.

12. Interview with former AP correspondent Fred Hoffman.

13. AP dispatch by Hal Boyle, February 18, 1953.

14. Yates's letter to the Foreign Mission Board, May 26, 1954; document 27, p. 25.

15. Letter to Yates from the superintendent of the Baptist Nursing Home, April 3, 1956, document 27, p. 33.

16. Telegram to Yates from the Foreign Mission Board, April 23, 1956; document 27, p. 34.

17. Memorandum written by McDaniel to Alan Gould, August 3, 1960, courtesy of AP archives.

18. AP dispatch by McDaniel, datelined Taipei, *Sacramento Bee*, October 11, 1960.

19. AP dispatch by McDaniel, datelined Tokyo, *Philadelphia Inquirer*, October 17, 1960.

20. Interview in 2018 with former AP correspondent Fred Hoffman.

21. Interview in 2018 with former AP correspondent Walter Mears.

22. AP dispatch, *St. Louis Post-Dispatch*, September 14, 1962.

23. AP dispatch, *Fort Worth Star-Telegram,* September 26, 1962.

24. Interview in 2019 with Andrew Eills.

25. Adm. Anderson's oral history at the John F. Kennedy Library.

26. AP dispatch, *Lansing State Journal*, April 14, 1963.

27. AP dispatch, *Mansfield News-Herald*, April 15, 1963.

28. AP dispatch, *Asheville Citizen*, April 7, 1964.

29. AP dispatch, *Tampa Tribune*, August 24, 1964.

30. AP dispatch, *Decatur Daily*, November 2, 1963.

31. AP dispatch, *Spokane Chronicle*, November 25, 1963.

32. AP dispatch, *Greenfield Daily Reporter*, March 17, 1965.

33. *Baltimore Sun*, June 2, 1968.

34. AP dispatches, *Sacramento Bee, San Mateo Times*, and *Baltimore Evening Sun*, July 16, 1971.

35. AP dispatch from Moscow, *Santa Cruz Sentinel*, July 16, 1971.

36. AP dispatch, *Paducah Sun*, July 16, 1971.

37. Natalie's obituary, *Tampa Bay Times*, December 19, 1992.

38. Interview with Betty Barber.

39. McDaniel's death notice, *Tampa Bay Times*, March 16, 1983.

40. Interview in 2020 with Amity Eills.

41. Scripps Howard dispatch, *Honolulu Star-Bulletin*, August 16, 1991.

42. Chang, *The Rape of Nanking*, 144.

## Epilogue

1. Yates's interview with Toland. There are multiple reports that Doris worked for Newsreel Wong. On p. 136 of *Alarm Starboard*, Geoffrey Brooke wrote that Lim was an assistant to Wong at MGM. In 1942, Reuters reported that Lim was a "Chinese girl from Shanghai who was an assistant to a Metro Goldwyn Mayer Movietone Crew." AP picked up the Reuters story in a dispatch, *Ottawa Citizen*, February 20, 1942. In *Let's Get Cracking*, on p. 10, Athole Stewart wrote that he and other press officers in Singapore "had known Doris as an assistant" to Wong.

2. Brooke, *Singapore's Dunkirk*, 216.

3. Paul Dietz's memoirs, written in 1988, kindly made available by his daughter, Patricia Startzman.

4. *Sydney Morning Herald*, January 22, 1950; and "Death in the Lifeboat," *Reader's Digest*, condensed from the *Sunday Express*, July 1950.

5. The *Palopo*'s log is included in the unpublished memoirs of Sir Gordon Whitteridge, whose wife, daughter, and baby son died on the *Rooseboom*. Whitteridge was the British diplomat who interviewed the two Malay sailors. His memoirs are in the Imperial War Museum in London and were kindly made available by Michael Pether, a researcher in New Zealand who has written extensively about the *Rooseboom*.

6. Walter Gibson's 1946 interview with the British War Office at Curzon Street in London, January 3, 1946. There is some confusion about the date of the interview. Whitteridge said the interview took place on January 3, 1946, while the document signed by the British intelligence officer uses the date March 1, 1946. The only possible explanation is that next to the date, the officer included the phrase "Certified true copy of original statement," a suggestion that the interview took place earlier than March 1.

7. "Death in the Lifeboat," *Reader's Digest.*

8. *Vancouver Sun*, April 22, 1950.

9. Walter Gibson, *The Boat: Singapore Escape* (Singapore: Monsoon Books, 1952), 74.

10. Ibid., 30.

11. Dietz's memoirs.

12. Yates's interview with Toland; Stewart, *Let's Get Cracking*, 49; and Dietz's memoirs provide strong evidence that Doris was born and raised in Hong Kong. Curiously, Gibson mentioned the *Kung Wo* only in his 1952 book. In the *Reader's Digest* story and newspaper articles in 1950, he wrote that Doris escaped from Singapore. But in the book on pp. 73–75, Gibson wrote for the first time that Doris told him that she had left Singapore on the *Kung Wo*. But there is an explanation for that addition to the book. On p. 75, Gibson acknowledged that Athole Stewart contacted Gibson after the 1950 newspaper stories were published. It is safe to assume that Gibson learned of the *Kung Wo* from Stewart.

13. Gibson, *The Boat*, 72.

14. Moffatt and McCormick, *Moon over Malaya*, 272.

15. Gibson's statement to the British War Office in 1946. In the statement, Gibson claimed to be a lieutenant, but the officer who conducted the interview correctly noted that Gibson was a corporal.

16. *Sydney Morning Herald*, January 22, 1950.

17. Gibson, *The Boat*, 87.

18. Moffatt and McCormick, *Moon over Malaya*, 271–72.

19. One-page memorandum of Janet Lim's interview by British officials in Singapore, February 22, 1946.

20. Janet Lim, *Sold for Silver: An Autobiography of a Girl Sold into Slavery in Southeast Asia* (Singapore: Monsoon Books, 1958), 219 and 223–33.

21. Stewart, *Let's Get Cracking*, 151.

22. Ibid., 151.

# BIBLIOGRAPHY

Abend, Hallett. *My Life in China: 1926 to 1941*. New York: Harcourt, Brace, 1943.

Associated Press. *World War II: Unforgettable Stories and Photographs by Correspondents of the Associated Press*. New York: RosettaBooks, 2015.

Auden, W. H., and Christopher Isherwood. *Journey to a War: W. H. Auden and Christopher Isherwood*. London: Faber and Faber, 1939.

Bayly, Christopher, and Tim Harper. *Forgotten Armies: The Fall of British Asia, 1941–1945*. Cambridge, MA: Harvard University Press, 2005.

Best, Nicholas. *Seven Days of Infamy: Pearl Harbor across the World*. New York: Thomas Dunne, 2016.

Blankfort, Michael. *The Big Yankee: The Life of Carlson of the Raiders*. Boston: Little, Brown, 1947.

Boni, William F. *Want to Be a War Correspondent? Here's How*. Highland City, FL: Rainbow Books, 1995.

Brooke, Geoffrey. *Alarm Starboard: A Remarkable True Story of the War at Sea*. Barnsley, UK: Pen & Sword Books, 2004.

Brooke, Geoffrey. *Singapore's Dunkirk: The Aftermath of the Fall*. Barnsley, UK: Pen & Sword Military, 2014.

Brown, Cecil. *Suez to Singapore*. New York: Random House, 1942.

Buhite, Russell D. *Nelson T. Johnson and American Policy toward China*. East Lansing: Michigan State University Press, 1969.

Capa, Cornell, and Richard Whelan, eds. *Robert Capa, Photographs*. New York: Alfred A. Knopf, 1985.

Chang, Iris. *The Rape of Nanking: The Forgotten Holocaust of World War II*. New York: Basic Books, 1997.

Chekel, Martin. *They Couldn't Pay Me Enough Money*. Martin Chekel, 2014.

Collie, Craig. *The Reporter and the Warlords: An Australian at Large in China's Republican Revolution*. St. Leonards, Australia: Allen & Unwin, 2014.

Connaughton, Richard. *The Battle for Manila*. Novato, CA: Presidio, 1995.

Cooper, Lady Diana. *Trumpets from the Steep*. Boston: Houghton Mifflin, 1960.

Cooper, Kent. *Kent Cooper and the Associated Press*. New York: Random House, 1959.

Cornebise, Alfred Emile. *Soldier Extraordinaire: The Life and Career of Brigadier General Frank "Pinkie" Dorn*. Fort Leavenworth, KS: Combat Studies Institute Press, 2019.

Crow, Carl. *The Travelers' Handbook for China (including Hong-Kong)*. 4th ed. New York: Dodd, Mead, 1925.

Darnton, John. *Almost a Family*. New York: Anchor Books, 2012.

Dunn, William. *Pacific Microphone*. College Station: Texas A&M University Press, 1988.

Eastman, Lloyd E. *The Nationalist Era in China, 1927–1949*. Cambridge, UK: Cambridge University Press, 1991.

Edwards, John. *John Curtin's War*. Melbourne, Australia: Viking, 2017.

Eichelberger, Robert. *Dear Miss Em: General Eichelberger's War in the Pacific, 1942–1945*. Westport, CT: Greenwood, 1981.

French, Paul. *Carl Crow—a Tough Old China Hand: The Life, Times, and Adventures of an American in Shanghai*. Hong Kong: Hong Kong University Press, 2006.

French, Paul. *Through the Looking Glass: China's Foreign Journalists from Opium Wars to Mao*. Hong Kong: Hong Kong University Press, 2009.

Gallagher, O'Dowd. *Action in The East*. London: Viking, 1942.

Gellhorn, Martha. *Travels with Myself and Another: A Memoir*. New York: Jeremy P. Tarcher / Putnam, 1978.

Gibson, Walter. *The Boat: Singapore Escape*. Singapore: Monsoon Books, 1952.

Glusman, John A. *Conduct under Fire: Four American Doctors and Their Fight for Life as Prisoners of the Japanese, 1941–1945*. New York: Penguin Books, 2006.

Gough, Richard. *The Escape from Singapore*. London: William Kimber, 1988.

Gould, Randall. *China in The Sun*. Garden City, NY: Doubleday, 1946.

Gramling, Oliver. *Free Men Are Fighting*. New York: Farrar and Rinehart, 1942.

Grehan, John, and Martin Mace. *Disaster in the Far East, 1940–1942: The Defence of Malaya, Japanese Capture of Hong Kong, and the Fall of Singapore*. Barnsley, UK: Pen & Sword Military, 2015.

Grescoe, Taras. *Shanghai Grand: Forbidden Love, Intrigue, and Decadence in Old China*. New York: St. Martin's, 2016.

Guard, Harold. *The Pacific War Uncensored: A War Correspondent's Unvarnished Account of the Fight against Japan*. Edited by John Tring. Philadelphia: Casemate, 2011.

Gunther, John. *Inside Asia*. New York: Harper & Brothers, 1939.

Harmsen, Peter. *Nanjing: Battle for a Doomed City*. Philadelphia: Casemate, 2015.

Harsch, Joseph C. *At the Hinge of History: A Reporter's Story*. Athens: University of Georgia Press, 2010.

Haugland, Vern. *Letter from New Guinea*. New York: Farrar & Rinehart, 1943.

Hembry, Boris. *Malayan Spymaster: Memoirs of a Rubber Planter, Bandit Fighter, and Spy*. Singapore: Monsoon Books, 2011.

Hohenberg, John. *Foreign Correspondence: The Great Reporters and Their Times*. 2nd ed. Syracuse, NY: Syracuse University Press, 1995.

Hunt, Frazier. *The Untold Story of Douglas MacArthur*. New York: Manor Books, 1977.

Jordan, Donald Allan. *China's Trial by Fire: The Shanghai War of 1932*. Ann Arbor: University of Michigan Press, 2001.

Kenney, George. *General Kenney Reports: A Personal History of the Pacific War*. Washington, DC: Office of Air Force History, 1987. Originally published in 1949.

Lascher, Bill. *Eve of a Hundred Midnights: The Star-Crossed Love Story of Two WWII Correspondents and Their Epic Escape across the Pacific*. New York: HarperCollins, 2016.

Lee, Clark. *One Last Look Around*. New York: Duell, Sloan and Pearce, 1947.

Lee, Clark. *They Call It Pacific: An Eye-Witness Story of Our War against Japan from Bataan to the Solomons*. New York: Viking, 1943.

Lim, Janet. *Sold for Silver: An Autobiography of a Girl Sold into Slavery in Southeast Asia*. Singapore: Monsoon Books, 1958.

Lindstrom, Russell. *The Associated Press News Annual, 1945*. New York: Rinehart, 1946.

Lodge, A. B. *The Fall of Gordon Bennett*. Boston: Allen & Unwin, 1986.

Loengard, John. *Life Photographers: What They Saw*. Boston: Bulfinch, 1999.

MacArthur, Douglas. *Reminiscences*. New York: McGraw-Hill, 1964.

MacDonell, George S. *One Soldier's Story, 1939–1945: From the Fall of Hong Kong to the Defeat of Japan*. Toronto: Dundurn, 2002.

MacKinnon, Stephen R. *Wuhan, 1938: War, Refugees, and the Making of Modern China*. Berkeley: University of California Press, 2008.

MacKinnon, Stephen R., and Oris Friesen. *China Reporting: An Oral History of American Journalism in the 1930s and 1940s*. Berkeley: University of California Press, 1987.

Manchester, William. *American Caesar: Douglas MacArthur, 1880–1964*. Boston: Little, Brown, 1978.

McCrum, Ronald. *The Men Who Lost Singapore, 1938–1942*. Singapore: NUS Press, 2017.

Middlebrook, Martin, and Patrick Mahoney. *The Sinking of the* Prince of Wales *&* Repulse*: The End of the Battleship Era*. Barnsley, UK: Pen & Sword Maritime, 1977.

Mitter, Rana. *Forgotten Ally: China's World War II, 1937–1945*. Boston: Houghton Mifflin Harcourt, 2013.

Moffatt, Jonathan, and Audrey Holmes McCormick. *Moon over Malaya: A Tale of Argylls and Marines*. Stroud, UK: Tempus, 2003.

Morrison, Ian. *Malayan Postscript*. Sydney, Australia: Angus and Robertson, 1943.

Naval Staff, Historical Section. *Loss of H.M. Ships* Prince of Wales *and* Repulse*, 10th December 1941*. Battle Summary 14. London: Historical Section Admiralty, 1955.

Novak, Robert D. *The Prince of Darkness: 50 Years Reporting in Washington*. New York: Crown Forum, 2007.

Pakula, Hannah. *The Last Empress: Madame Chiang Kai-shek and the Birth of Modern China*. New York: Simon & Schuster Paperbacks, 2009.

Parkinson, Jonathan. *The Royal Navy, China Station: A History as Seen through the Commanders in Chief, 1864–1941*. Kibworth, UK: Matador, 2018.

Reporters of the Associated Press. *Breaking News: How the Associated Press Has Covered War, Peace, and Everything Else*. New York: Princeton Architectural Press, 2007.

Rubens, Doris. *Bread and Rice: An American Woman's Fight to Survive in the Jungles and Prison Camps of the WWII Philippines*. New York: Thurston Macauley, 1947.

Scott, James M. *Rampage: MacArthur, Yamashita, and the Battle of Manila*. New York: W. W. Norton, 2018.

Selle, Earl Albert. *Donald of China*. New York: Harper, 1948.

Smith, Colin. *Singapore Burning: Heroism and Surrender in World War II*. London: Penguin Books, 2005.

Snow, Edgar. *Far Eastern Front*. New York: H. Smith & R. Haas, 1933.

Stewart, Athole. *Let's Get Cracking: The Malayan Campaign*. Sydney, Australia: Frank Johnson, 1943.

St. John, Jo Barnes. *China Times Guide to Tientsin and Neighbourhood*. Tientsin, China: China Times, 1908.

Suping Lu. *They Were in Nanjing: The Nanjing Massacre Witnessed by American and British Nationals*. Hong Kong: Hong Kong University Press, 2004.

Symonds, Craig. *The Battle of Midway*. New York: Oxford University Press, 2011.

Toland, John. *But Not in Shame: The Six Months After Pearl Harbor*. New York: Random House, 1961.

Tong, Hollington. *Dateline China*. New York: Rockport, 1950.

Tregaskis, Richard. *Guadalcanal Diary*. New York: Random House, 2000.

Tuchman, Barbara. *Stilwell and the American Experience in China, 1911–45*. New York: Macmillan, 1970.

Tunny, Noel. *Winning from Downunder*. Moorooka, Australia: Boolarong, 2010.

Utley, Freda. *China at War*. London: Faber and Faber, 1939.

Utley, Freda. *Japan's Feet of Clay*. New York: W. W. Norton, 1937.

van de Ven, Hans. *China at War: Triumph and Tragedy in the Emergence of the New China*. Cambridge, MA: Harvard University Press, 2018.

Weintraub, Robert. *No Better Friend: One Man, One Dog, and Their Extraordinary Story of Courage and Survival in World War II*. New York: Back Bay Books, 2015.

Weller, George. *Weller's War: A Legendary Foreign Correspondent's Saga of World War II on Five Continents*. Edited by Anthony Weller. New York: Crown, 2009.

White, Theodore. *In Search of History: A Personal Adventure*. New York: Harper & Row, 1978.

Wills, Matthew B. *In the Highest Traditions of the Royal Navy: The Life of Captain John Leach MVO DSO*. New York: History Press, 2011.

Womack, Tom. *The Allied Defense of the Malay Barrier, 1941–1942*. Jefferson, NC: McFarland, 2016.

Yeh, Wen-hsin. ed. *Becoming Chinese: Passages to Modernity and Beyond*. Berkeley: University of California Press, 2000. http://ark.cdlib.org/ark:/13030/kt5j49q621/.

# INDEX

Some of the 132 survivors from the sunken *Kung Wo* gather on a deserted island as they await the arrival of a Malay rescue ship. McDaniel stands at far right in the back row, while Doris Lim, whom McDaniel tried to save, is at far left in the first row. *AP photo*

The famous photo of Gen. Douglas MacArthur by Ed Widdis of the Associated Press during a US parachute attack in New Guinea in 1943. MacArthur watched the attack from a B-17 bomber. *AP photo*

The iconic photo of McDaniel typing his notes on the deserted island. The *Baltimore Sun* published the photo in April 1942 with the caption "On the Job." *AP photo*

McDaniel took this photograph of British soldiers pushing a civilian car into the harbor at Singapore to keep it out of the hands of the Japanese; it was believed to be McDaniel's personal car. He had lost his first car to the Japanese in Nanking in 1937. *AP photo*